HOW SEX CHANGED

DBS Arts Library

£19.55stg
DIB

Harvard University Press
Cambridge, Massachusetts
London, England

2002

Library of Congress Cataloging-in-Publication Data

Meyerowitz, Joanne J. (Joanne Jay)
How sex changed : a history of transsexuality / Joanne Meyerowitz.
p. cm.
Includes bibliographical references and index.
ISBN 0-674-00925-8 (alk. paper)
1. Transsexualism—Europe—History.
2. Transsexualism—United States—History.
3. Sex change—Europe—History.
4. Sex change—United States—History.   I. Title.

HQ77.95.E85 M48 2002
306.77—dc21
2002020536

FOR PAT SWOPE

and

IN MEMORY OF IRVING MEYEROWITZ

CONTENTS

Illustrations follow page 140

HOW SEX CHANGED

INTRODUCTION

*O*n December 1, 1952, the *New York Daily News* announced the "sex change" surgery of Christine Jorgensen. The front-page headline read: "Ex-GI Becomes Blonde Beauty: Operations Transform Bronx Youth," and the story told how Jorgensen had traveled to Denmark for "a rare and complicated treatment." For years, Jorgensen, born and reared as a boy, had struggled with what she later described as an ineffable, inexorable, and increasingly unbearable yearning to live her life as a woman. In 1950 she sailed to Europe in search of a doctor who would alter her bodily sex. Within months she found an endocrinologist who agreed to administer hormones if she would in return cooperate with his research. Over the next two years she took massive doses of estrogen and underwent two major surgeries to transform her genitals. At the end of 1952 the *New York Daily News* transformed her obscure personal triumph into mass media sensation.

The initial scoop immediately escalated to a frenzy. In the first two weeks of coverage, according to *Newsweek,* the three major wire services sent out 50,000 words on the Christine Jorgensen story. Reporters cast Jorgensen, who was young and conventionally beautiful, as the personification of glamour, akin to a Hollywood starlet on the rise. They followed her every move in Copenhagen and hounded her parents at their home in the Bronx. In the winter of 1953 Jorgensen returned to the United States and surrendered to her celebrity. In the summer she launched a successful nightclub act that kept her name on marquees and her body in spotlights for the rest of the decade.[1]

Jorgensen was more than a media sensation, a stage act, or a cult figure. Her story opened debate on the visibility and mutability of sex. It raised questions that resonated with force in the 1950s and engage us still today. How do we determine who is male and who is female, and why do we care? Can humans actually change sex? Is sex less apparent than it seems? As a narrative of boundary transgression, the Jorgensen story fascinated readers and elicited their surprise, and as an unusual variant on a familiar tale of striving and success, it inspired them. It opened possibilities for those who questioned their own sex and offered an exoticized travelogue for armchair tourists who had never imagined that one could take a journey across the sex divide. In the post–World War II era, with heightened concerns about science and sex, the Jorgensen story compelled some readers to spell out their own versions of the boundaries of sex, and it convinced others to reconsider the categories they thought they already knew. In response, American doctors and scientists began to explore the process of defining sex.

$\mathscr{I}$n the mid-twentieth century, sex was already high on the American cultural agenda. For decades Americans of all sorts had found themselves inundated with news, research, stories, opinions, and imperatives about the multiple meanings of "sex." The study of sex hormones and sex chromosomes had removed the biology of sex from the visible realm of genitals to the microscopic gaze, and the uncertainty of it all eventually set the International Olympic Committee, among others, on an elusive quest to decide who counts as a woman and who counts as a man. The growing numbers of women in the labor force and the early twentieth-century women's movement had put issues of sex equality and sex difference at the forefront of political life, and the emergence of gay and lesbian subcultures had created visible spots of sexual variation within the urban landscape. Meanwhile the mass media had made sex a mainstay of the visual culture, and popular versions of Freud and other sexologists had given sex a recognized role in the modern discourse of psychology. The new ideal of "consenting adults" had positioned sex as a key component of liberal freedom, while older ideals still made moving targets of anyone who strayed from expectations that sex belonged in marriage. In broad outline and narrow, American society had "sexualized" in the first half of the century.[2]

And the vocabulary of sex had begun to change. At the dawn of the century the word *sex* covered a range of phenomena. In popular and scientific formulations, sex signified not only female and male but also traits, attitudes, and behaviors associated with women and men and with erotic acts. In various attempts to delineate the components of sex, some observers tried to sort the sex "characteristics." They separated "primary sexual features," found in the genitals and gonads, from "secondary" features, seen in breasts, beards, and other physical differences that usually appeared after puberty, from "tertiary" features, as evidenced in erotic drives, from "fourth-order" features, manifest in traits, mannerisms, and even occupations and clothes. Or they distinguished "anatomical" sex, the sex of the body, from "functional" sex, the ways men and women thought and behaved.[3] Despite a few dissenters, most observers adhered to a biological determinism. The desires and practices known as masculine and feminine seemed to spring from the same biological processes that divided female and male. All came bundled together within the broad-ranging concept of "sex."

By midcentury this concept had begun to break down. Various experts used different terms to distinguish one meaning of sex from another. Anthropologist Margaret Mead chose *sex roles* to describe the culturally constructed behaviors expected of women and men. Sex researcher Alfred C. Kinsey adopted the term *sexual behavior* to outline a range of erotic practices.[4] And the "sex" of the body no longer provided adequate explanation of either "sex roles" or "sexual behavior." By the end of the century the earlier understanding of sex had given way to three categories of inquiry and analysis: "biological sex" referred to chromosomes, genes, genitals, hormones, and other physical markers, some of which could be modified and some of which could not; "gender" represented masculinity, femininity, and the behaviors commonly associated with them; and "sexuality" connoted the erotic, now sorted into a range of urges, fantasies, and behaviors. Once seen as outgrowths of a primary sex division, "gender" and "sexuality" no longer seemed to spring directly from the biological categories of female and male. In fact some scholars envisioned sex, gender, and sexuality as constructed categories constantly defined and redefined in social, cultural, and intellectual processes and performances.[5] They thus directly rejected the older belief in a universal, unchanging biological sex that dictated both the behavior of women and men and their sexual desires.

Jorgensen's story and the history of transsexuality are central parts of this reconceptualization of sex in the twentieth century. The notion that biological sex is mutable, that we define and redefine it, that we can divide it into constituent parts, such as chromosomes, hormones, and genitals, and modify some of those parts, that male and female are not opposites, that masculinity and femininity do not spring automatically from biological sex, that neither biological sex nor gender determines the contours of sexual desire—these were significant shifts in American social and scientific thought. As we will see, they occurred piecemeal through vociferous conflict and debate, and because not everyone accepted them, they laid the groundwork for ongoing contests over the meanings of biological sex, the sources of gender, and the categories of sexuality.

At the start of the twenty-first century, we routinely distinguish sex, gender, and sexuality, but we cannot, it seems, seal off the borders. Scientists, their popularizers, and their critics still debate whether sex-linked genes or prenatal sex hormones or specific sites of the brain determine the behaviors associated with masculinity and femininity and with hetero- and homosexuality. In much of the popular culture, sex still seems to dictate particular forms of gender, which in turn dictates particular forms of sexuality. In this default logic, a female is naturally and normally a feminine person who desires men; a male is naturally and normally a masculine person who desires women. All other permutations of sex, gender, and sexuality still appear, if they appear at all, as pathologically anomalous or socially strange. As this book will show, the categories of sex, gender, and sexuality—now analytically distinct—remain insistently intertwined in American science and culture.

*J*orgensen was not the first transsexual, nor was the publicity accorded her the first media coverage of sex-change surgery. Cross-gender identification, the sense of being the other sex, and the desire to live as the other sex all existed in various forms in earlier centuries and other cultures. The historical record includes countless examples of males who dressed or lived as women and females who dressed or lived as men.[6] Transsexuality, the quest to transform the bodily characteristics of sex via hormones and surgery, originated in the early twentieth century. By the 1910s European scientists had begun to publicize their attempts to transform the sex of animals, and by the 1920s a few doctors, mostly in Germany, had agreed to alter the bodies of a few patients who longed to change their sex.

In Europe the medical practice of sex change arose less as a result of new technology than as a result of new understandings of sex. In the early twentieth century the scientists and doctors who endorsed sex-change surgery posited a universal mixed-sex condition, in which all males had female features and all females male features. This theory of universal bisexuality directly challenged a nineteenth-century vision of binary sex that saw female and male as distinct, immutable, and opposite. With this novel conception of sex, a few doctors began to use hormones and surgery to enable a few people who pleaded for bodily change to move toward the female or male ends of a perceived continuum.

The sex-change experiments in Europe reached the United States through the popular culture. From the 1930s on, American newspapers and magazines—and later radio, television, and film—broadcast stories on sex change. The stories in the press allowed a few American readers to imagine surgical sex change and seek it for themselves. Such people already had some sense of crossgender identification. Before midcentury they did not yet have the word *transsexual*, but they had the stories in the popular press to give them a language with which to ask doctors for help. They could now articulate their desires as a longing to change their bodies, and they could now reasonably expect that doctors might possibly respond to their requests for self-transformation. They pushed their doctors to recognize the medical means to change the human body and the complex persistence of a gendered sense of self.

Only after World War II did American doctors and scientists seriously address the issue of sex change. In 1949 Dr. David O. Cauldwell, a psychiatrist, used the word *transsexual* to refer to people who sought to change their sex. After the press reports on Jorgensen, Harry

Benjamin, an endocrinologist, publicized the term and the condition it described. Soon other American doctors and scientists joined in a public debate on the pros and cons of sex-change surgery. When the Jorgensen story broke, the press turned to the doctors, who in the postwar era had increasing cultural clout and professional authority. From the start, the doctors and scientists fought among themselves about the explanatory powers of biology and psychology, the use and abuse of medical technology, and the merits of sex-change operations.

In the point and counterpoint of debate, the doctors and scientists gradually shifted their focus from concepts of biological sex to concepts of what they came to call gender. When they tried to explain the desire to change sex, they less often referred to conditions of mixed bodily sex and more frequently wrote of "psychological sex," and later "gender identity," a sense of the sexed self that was both separate from the sex of the body and, some claimed, harder to change than the body itself. The sex of the body, they now asserted, had multiple components— hormones, chromosomes, genitals, and more—some of which could be altered. A few of them began to emphasize the immutability of adult gender identity and to acknowledge the despair of those patients who wanted the sex of their bodies to match their unshakable sense of self. This new understanding of gender was forged and refined in the discourse on transsexuality. With it, more American doctors gradually began to endorse and perform "sex reassignment surgery."

From the doctors' and scientists' point of view, medical examinations and psychological tests could determine a person's sex and verify a person's gender identity. From the point of view of their patients, sex and gender were usually matters of self-knowledge. They had studied themselves, and sometimes they had also read widely in the medical literature. Like the doctors, many of them distinguished between the sex of the visible body and the firm sense of sex that came from an inner sense of self. They had determined for themselves what they were and what they wanted to become. After Christine Jorgensen made the news, hundreds of them approached doctors in order to convince them to recommend or perform surgery. But they ran into constant conflicts with doctors who insisted on their own authority to define sex and gender, diagnose the condition, and recommend the treatment.

For both doctors and transsexuals, the process of defining sex went hand in hand with a process of sorting conditions of bodily sex from conditions of gender identity and conditions of sexual desire. By the end of the 1950s, for example, "hermaphrodites," or people who had both male and female gonads, were more clearly distinguished from "transsexuals," whose gender identities did not correspond with their bodily sex, and also from "homosexuals," whose erotic longings were for members of their own sex. In the early twentieth century many observers, scientists and popularizers alike, had lumped these conditions together. After Jorgensen made the news, American doctors and scientists took up the taxonomic process of sorting out a tangled thicket of varied conditions of sex, gender, and sexuality. On the ground, those who identified as transsexuals, transvestites, lesbians, and gay men sorted themselves out in a parallel social process. Amidst a multiplicity of variations, some of them came to define their conditions not only in contradistinction to the mainstream norm—the heterosexual masculine male or heterosexual feminine female—but also with regard to others on the margins. In everyday life, especially in the cities, they gravitated toward each other, schooled each other in the customs and language of particular subcultures, and developed their own vernacular that delineated finer gradations of gender variance than the language used by doctors.

In the 1960s the complicated process of redefining sex took place within a culture increasingly preoccupied by a "sexual revolution," by more liberal attitudes toward individual choice, and by revitalized human rights movements that insisted on social change in the name of justice. In this climate the doctors and scientists who studied transsexuality began to organize programs, clinics, conferences, and associations to promote study of and treatment for transsexuals, and self-identified transsexuals began to organize to demand their own rights.

In 1964 Reed Erickson, a wealthy female-to-male transsexual, founded the Erickson Educational Foundation, which funded research on transsexuality, and in 1966 Johns Hopkins University Hospital, with funds from Erickson, announced its Gender Identity Clinic to provide sex-reassignment surgery. Soon afterward other major medical centers opened their own gender identity programs that offered sex-change operations. The doctors and scientists involved in the new gen-der identity programs generally saw themselves as liberals. They tried to steer a middle course between those doctors, especially psychoanalysts, who objected to transsexual surgery, and the hundreds of patients who pressured them for operations. As they organized research programs, treatment clinics, and scholarly conferences, they tried to accommo-date a few of their patients, and they also bolstered their own position as authorities and gatekeepers. Eventually, in 1979, they formed their own professional organization, the Harry Benjamin International Gen-der Dysphoria Association.

Meanwhile the birth of a new identity evolved socially and politically into the birth of a new minority. Self-identified transsexuals distin-guished themselves from other "deviants" and saw themselves as mem-bers of a distinct social group. In the late 1960s and early 1970s a few transsexuals began to challenge the doctors' authority and to reject the medical model that cast them primarily as patients. They observed and sometimes joined the 1960s movements for civil rights, feminism, and gay liberation, and they began to organize collectively and demand the right to quality medical care and also the right to live, free from harass-ment, with whatever presentation of gender they chose to express. By the century's end the push for transsexual rights had blossomed into a vocal social movement with local, national, and international organiza-tions and with a new scholarship that sought again to clarify the con-tested meanings of sex.

In this more politicized context, the courts took up the debates on sex, gender, and sexuality that American doctors had entered in the 1950s. From the 1960s on, a few transsexuals asked the courts to define sex legally and to grant them the right to change their legal gen-der status. In response, a few judges followed the lead of the doctors who endorsed sex-reassignment surgery and decided that the law, too, could accommodate sex change as long as it did not entail the radical change of eliminating all legal sex difference. In a handful of courts they came up with a new definition of sex. Instead of determining sex from the genitals seen at birth or from chromosomes, they decided that one's gender identity and the current state of one's genitals could jointly determine one's legal sex. But this new vision—in medicine and in law—came under assault as soon as it was formulated. Other doctors and judges attacked it for going too far, and some transsexual, feminist, and gay activists attacked it for not going far enough.

As this thumbnail sketch suggests, the history of transsexuality engages a number of key trends of the twentieth century. It demonstrates the growing authority of science and medicine, and it points to the impact of sensational journalism. It illustrates the rise of a new concept of the modern self that placed a heightened value on self-expression, self-improvement, and self-transformation. It highlights the proliferation of sexual identities, and it offers a new angle of vision into the breakdown of traditional norms of gender. In the 1970s and 1980s the women's and gay liberation movements eclipsed transsexuality as the sites of public debate over sex, gender, and sexuality. But the history of transsexuality had already laid the definitional groundwork and helps explain the peculiar configuration that sex, gender, and sexuality had already assumed in American popular culture, medicine, and law.

*I*n this book, both *transsexuality,* a term often used today, and *transsexualism,* an equivalent term used more often in the 1950s and 1960s, refer to conditions in which people hope to change the bodily characteristics of sex. (The terms apply whether or not the individual has undergone surgery.) Those who identify as transsexuals often describe their quest to change sex as a deep, longstanding, irresistible longing, an irrepressible desire to live and appear as the other sex. In the United States, no census or register exists to provide precise figures on how many people undergo, seek, or yearn for a change of sex. In the Netherlands, where doctors keep such records, they calculated in 1993 that 1 in 11,900 persons born male and 1 in 30,400 persons born female had taken hormones to change sex. A more recent news report suggests that "at least 25,000" Americans have undergone sex-reassignment surgery.[7] In the past doctors consistently concluded that "male-to-female" transsexuals, or those born with male bodies, outnumbered "female-to-male" transsexuals, or those born with female bodies. Today some doctors in the United States find roughly equivalent numbers of male-to-females (MTFs) and female-to-males (FTMs).

In the popular lingo used today, transsexuals are a subset of "transgendered" people, an umbrella term used for those with various forms and degrees of crossgender practices and identifications. "Transgendered" includes, among others, some people who identify as "butch" or masculine lesbians, as "fairies," "queens," or feminine gay men, and as heterosexual crossdressers as well as those who identify as transsexual. The categories are not hermetically sealed, and to a certain extent the boundaries are permeable.[8] The same person might identify as a butch lesbian at one point in life and as an FTM transsexual at another. Since the 1950s the precise definition of transsexuality has been the subject of debate in popular culture, science, medicine, and law. In general, though, transsexuals today are understood to differ from homosexuals, who rarely wish to change their sex. The longing to change the sex of one's body does not necessarily correspond with any set pattern of erotic behavior or sexual desire. In terms of erotic attraction, many transsexuals identify as heterosexual; that is, male-to-female transsexuals often see themselves as heterosexual women, and female-to-male transsexuals often see themselves as heterosexual men. But some transsexuals identify themselves as (and engage in behavior recognized as) homosexual, bisexual, or asexual. Transsexuals are also understood to differ from transvestites or crossdressers, who dress in the clothes of the other sex but do not necessarily hope to change the sex of their bodies. By the definitions most commonly used today, transsexuals are not *intersexed*, a term used to describe the people who used to be called "hermaphrodites" and "pseudohermaphrodites," people with various physical conditions in which the genitals or reproductive organs do not fit into the standard category of female or male. All these terms have histories, and the distinctions, definitions, and labels provided here are not, as the following pages will show, the distinctions, definitions, and labels always used in the past.

In the United States the discourse on transsexuals came from the people who hoped to change their sex, from the popular culture, and from the courts as well as from the domains of medicine and science. Neither a traditional medical history, which might trace how doctors refined the terms of their predecessors, nor a critical analysis of the science of sex, which might show how scientific experts asserted their power through diagnosis and classification, would do justice to the complex interplay of social, cultural, legal, and medical histories. Those who identified as transsexuals, crossdressers, and homosexuals, doctors and scientists, journalists and readers, lawyers and judges, and feminist, gay, and transgender activists differed among themselves as well as with each other. The experts had more authority than others, but no group projected even the semblance of consensus, and none had the power alone to redefine sex or to dictate the categories and contours of American sexual thought.

*T*oday as in the past, transsexuals often appear as symbols of something larger than their own everyday selves. In the popular culture, various media frequently cast transsexuals as "freaks" or "perverts," and in the more polite language of scholarly journals, doctors and scientists often portray them as mentally ill. The tendency to homogenize, stereotype, and pathologize transsexuals persists, even in an era when it is no longer fashionable, at least in certain social circles, to homogenize, stereotype, or pathologize women, racial and ethnic groups, or gay men and lesbians. Much of the recent literature on transsexuals depicts them as deficient and dangerous if not diseased. Religious conservatives have long accused transsexuals, along with feminists and homosexuals, of defying a God-given and natural order. Recently some California conservatives associated a bill that proposed to outlaw gender discrimination with an alleged "transsexual agenda." They feared "anarchy" and "a complete attack on normalcy."[9] And secular scholars with liberal and radical credentials also invoke transsexuals as symbols of some larger social malaise. Transsexuals, some argue, reinscribe the conservative stereotypes of male and female and masculine and feminine. They take the signifiers of sex and the prescriptions of gender too seriously. They are "utterly invested" in the boundaries between female and male. Or they represent individual autonomy run amok in the late modern age. As self-indulgent technophiles, they "desire to engineer" themselves, taking the injunction to self-transformation to dangerous extremes, and as the ultimate crass consumers, they transform the seemingly immaterial—"fulfillment" and "comfort"—

into "luxury commodities" for sale in the medical market. Or they stand for the phoniness of social frauds. They misrepresent themselves, deceive themselves (and presumably others) as they attempt to pass as something they are not.[10]

On the other side, and less frequently, transsexuals appear as positive symbols of transgression. In response to the negative barrage, some contemporary transgender activists have reversed the pathologizing discourse and portrayed transsexuals as "free spirits" who break the restrictive social rules that mandate living in the sex and as the gender one was assigned at birth.[11] From another vantage point, some theorists identify transsexuals as emblems of liberatory potential. In critical studies of race, ethnicity, colonialism, and postcolonialism, a number of authors have turned to hybridity, syncretism, and border crossing to highlight the ubiquity of cultural mixings that destabilize concepts of racial, ethnic, or cultural purity.[12] For theorists of gender, transsexuals (and, more often, crossdressers) sometimes serve an analogous function as symbols of the mixed-ness or third-ness that illustrates the multiplicity of genders or denaturalizes and parodies the pure oppositions of imagined binaries. "Ambiguous gender identities . . . such as . . . transsexualism," one such account states, "offer a point at which social pressure might be applied to effect a revaluation of binary thinking."[13]

In this book I try to avoid investing transsexuals of the past—a diverse group of people with a wide array of political views—with transhistoric symbolic weight. These various individuals were not, as a group, either the "dupes of gender," who tampered with their bodies in the name of gender ideology, or conscious radicals, who purposefully undermined the categories and destabilized traditional norms.[14] Many transsexuals expressed the desire to live as men or women, and not as something other or in between, but that desire did not distinguish them at all from (or make them more conservative than) the overwhelming majority of Americans in the twentieth century. Their quest to change sex was not necessarily a paean to technology and consumerism, which were usually means to an end, and their varied presentations of gender were no less "authentic," and no more "free," than other sincere attempts to express a sense of self. Like everyone else, they articulated their senses of self with the language and cultural forms available to them. They were neither symbols, emblems detached from social milieus, nor heroes or villains engaged in mythic battles to further or stifle progress. They were instead ordinary and extraordinary human beings who searched for workable solutions to pressing personal problems. In so doing they investigated, debated, promoted, and accelerated new definitions of sex, gender, and sexuality. Their struggles show us how sex changed in the twentieth century.

A note on pronouns: In current English usage, we cannot avoid labeling people as boys or girls, women or men. How should we write about people who lived part of their lives as girls or women and part as boys or men? In most cases I use the pronouns that accord with a person's public presentation of gender. If someone lived as a woman, I use "she," "her," and "hers" regardless of anatomy, and if someone lived as a man, I use "he," "him," and "his." When writing of those undergoing change in bodily sex or presentation of gender, I use the pronouns that accord with the public presentations they ultimately chose rather than the ones they were assigned at birth. In quotations, though, I have not altered the pronouns used in the original texts, and for a few people I change pronouns in the course of the narrative. I write extensively, for example, about Christine Jorgensen's childhood and youth, when she lived as George. In those pages, I refer to her as "him." Some readers, I realize, may find my use of pronouns confusing or even offensive. If the pronouns jar, please consider them a reminder of how deeply we invest our everyday language and lives with constant referents to gender.

SEX CHANGE

1

*I*n 1937 "Miss R. R.," from New York, wrote to *Your Body* magazine inquiring about change of sex. "I have had the feeling," she wrote, "ever since I can remember, that my sex is gradually changing." She located her change bodily in an "unusual lump," which she "imagine[d] to be a masculine organ forming." She had, she said, "an intense desire" to become a man, and she asked the magazine's editor to tell her whether there was "any way of effecting this."[1] Three years later, in the *Journal of Nervous and Mental Disease,* Dr. N. S. Yawger opened his article "Transvestism and Other Cross-Sex Manifestations" with reference to popular reports in newspapers and magazines. "In recent years," he stated, "the following curious public press announcements have appeared: 'Evolution of a Female "Boy" . . . '"Mary" Transformed to Mark, British Surgeon Certifies' . . . 'Girl Transformed into a Man, Plans to Take a Bride.'"[2] It might seem strange that "Miss R. R." wrote to a popular magazine for advice on changing sex or that Yawger, a Philadelphia psychiatrist, drew on the popular press for his scientific essay, but both had correctly identified the cultural location where sex change had made its public debut. In the American popular culture, journalists reported on women becoming men and men becoming women. The question of what constituted sex, and whether and how a person could change it, had entered the public domain.

Before the mid-twentieth century, doctors and scientists did not yet use the word *transsexual.* In the late nineteenth century a handful of sexologists published case studies of crossgender identification, of men and women who felt and acted as if they were the other sex. These early sexologists subsumed crossgender identification under the broader rubric of "inversion" and associated it primarily with homosexuality. In the early twentieth century sexologists Magnus Hirschfeld and Havelock Ellis defined "transvestism" or "eonism" as an independent category that included crossgender identification as well as crossdressing. But "transsexualism," defined in part by the request for surgical sex change, did not appear as a medical category until the late 1940s and early 1950s, when doctors David O. Cauldwell and Harry Benjamin first coined and publicized the English term *transsexual* and when Christine Jorgensen first appeared in the press.[3]

But the concepts of sex change and sex-change surgery existed well before the word *transsexual* entered the medical parlance. In the early twentieth century European scientists began to undertake experiments on "sex transformation," first on animals and then on humans. In Austria in the 1910s, physiologist Eugen Steinach took the lead in changing the sex of animals, and in Germany in the 1920s and early 1930s doctors affiliated with Magnus Hirschfeld's Institute for Sexual Science performed and publicized human sex-change surgeries on patients they labeled "transvestites." The European scientists grounded their medical interventions in a new definition of sex that cast all humans as bisexual, or partly male and partly female. Stated simply, the new definition challenged the more widely known nineteenth-century vision of separate and opposite sexes.

Eventually news of sex-change surgery came to America, not via the medical profession but, as "Miss R. R." and Dr. Yawger knew, through the popular culture. Stories of "sex reversals," "sex changes," and "sexual metamorphoses" appeared in American newspapers and magazines from at least the 1930s on. These stories differed from the relatively frequent newspaper accounts of what historians have called sexual "passing," in which a person known previously as one sex was discovered living as the other.[4] Rather, these were accounts of bodily change, confirmed by doctors, usually involving surgery though sometimes not. In the years before 1950 these sensationalized accounts introduced American readers to the possibility that sex was neither as obvious nor as permanent as it might have seemed.

The American magazine and newspaper stories allowed some nonintersexed readers to envision sex change as a real possibility and to request it for themselves. From the 1930s on, certain readers appropriated public stories of sex change to include the quest for surgical transformation as an expressed component of their sense of self. Through reading, some transgendered individuals—self-identified, in the terms available in their day, as eonists, transvestites, homosexuals, inverts, and hermaphrodites—came to see themselves as part of a group of people who longed to change their sex.

It was in this context of European experiments, American popular stories, and new requests for medical intervention that Cauldwell, a psychiatrist, and Benjamin, an endocrinologist, turned their attention to those who requested sex change. They did not create the category or the diagnosis of transsexualism; rather, they drew on European science, American popular culture, and the life histories related by the transgendered individuals who came to them for help. They assigned the new label "transsexual" to those who hoped to change their sex, and they began to sort it out from the more familiar categories of hermaphrodite, transvestite, and homosexual.

Surgical attempts at changing sex first made it into the public eye in the early 1910s when Eugen Steinach, a physiologist at the University of Vienna, won international acclaim for his "transplantation" experiments on rats and guinea pigs. In 1912 Steinach published an article titled "Arbitrary Transformation of Male Mammals into Animals with Pronounced Female Sex Characteristics and Feminine Psyche," followed in 1913 by "Feminization of Males and Masculization of Females." The essays, soon scientific classics, demonstrated that castrated infantile male rodents, implanted with ovaries, developed certain characteristics, including sexual behavior, associated with females and that castrated infantile female rodents, implanted with testes, developed characteristics, including sexual behavior, of males. In these articles Steinach claimed to have found the specific effects of "male" and "female" hormones. His research belongs in the larger turn-of-the-century scientific project, the new science of endocrinology, that attempted to locate the essence of sex, gender, and sexuality in the secretions of the gonads. In his day, Steinach stood at the forefront of his field. His research convinced Sigmund Freud, among others, of the possible hormonal bases of sexual behavior. But Steinach's research also suggested the medical possibility of transforming sex. As he himself put it: "the implantation of the gonad of the opposite sex transforms the original sex of an animal." Elsewhere in Europe, similar research soon followed, producing various forms of "sex reversal" in does and bucks and hens and cocks.[5]

The research on animals led directly to experimental surgery on humans. At Steinach's urging, for example, Robert Lichtenstern applied the transplantation techniques developed with rodents to human subjects. Beginning in 1915, Lichtenstern transplanted undescended testicles, removed from healthy men, into the abdomens of men who had never developed testicles or who had lost them as a result of injury or disease. Working with Steinach, he also attempted to "cure" a few homosexual men by removing a testicle from each and implanting another taken from a heterosexual man. Other surgeons also undertook testicular transplants, sometimes from sheep, rams, and apes, to men, and ovarian transplants from one woman to another. But the early human transplantation experiments did not attempt, it seems, to transform a man into a woman or a woman into a man.[6]

A few scattered records of surgery for human "inverts" suggest some early efforts at altering sex. These early surgeries simply involved removal of body parts, such as testicles, uteri, and breasts, a form of intervention that did not require advanced medical technology. They took place at the behest of the patients who underwent them. In 1902, for example, New Yorker Earl Lind, a self-proclaimed invert, androgyne, homosexual, and fairy, convinced a doctor to castrate him at the age of twenty-eight. Lind lived as a man but saw himself as a woman and despised his genitalia. He pursued the castration ostensibly to reduce his sexual "obsession" and as a cure for spermatorrhea, the frequent nocturnal emissions that he saw as ruinous to his health. But he also acknowledged that he preferred "to possess one less mark of the male," and he hoped in addition that castration would eliminate his facial hair, his "most detested and most troublesome badge of masculinity."[7] He did not expect castration to transform his body into a woman's, but he hoped it would lessen his male characteristics. Alberta

Lucille Hart, a physician in Oregon, pursued surgery as a means to changing sex. As a child, Hart, reared as a girl, considered himself a boy, and as an adult he wore masculine collars, ties, hats, and shoes along with the requisite skirts. In 1917, at the age of twenty-six, he persuaded psychiatrist J. Allen Gilbert to recommend hysterectomy. As with Lind, the surgery required medical justification, in this case the relief of painful menstruation. In the quest for surgery, Hart also employed a form of eugenic reasoning, advising "sterilization" for "any individual" with "abnormal inversion." Even these arguments, though, did not immediately convince Gilbert, who agreed to the operation only, he claimed, after "long hesitancy and deliberation." After surgery, haircut, and change of attire, Hart "started as a male with a new hold on life," and as Alan Lucill Hart he had successful careers as a radiologist and a novelist.[8]

In contrast to these isolated examples of early surgery in the United States, the quest for sex change was more widely acknowledged in Europe, where the study of sexuality had a longer and stronger tradition. In 1916 Max Marcuse, a German sexologist, published an article on *Geschlechtsumwandlungstrieb,* or drive for sex transformation, in which he distinguished the request for sex-change surgery from more generalized sexual inversion or crossgender identification. The subject of the case study, a male-to-female referred to as "A.," had read in the press about sex-change experiments on animals and requested similar surgery. Around the same time, a few doctors in Europe began to perform transformative surgery. By the early 1920s, two men in England "who aspired to become" women knew of a doctor in Italy "who would remove the male organs," but most of the early human sex-change operations took place in Germany. According to one account from Berlin, a female-to-male "transvestite" had his breasts and uterus removed in 1912, followed by removal of ovaries in 1921, and a male-to-female underwent castration in 1920 and had an ovary implanted in 1921.[9]

In the 1920s and into the early 1930s, much of the sex-change experimentation centered in Berlin at Magnus Hirschfeld's well-known Institute for Sexual Science. From the late nineteenth century on, Hirschfeld, a physician, published widely and campaigned actively on behalf of homosexual rights. In 1910 he published his monumental work *Transvestites,* in which he distinguished transvestites from homosexuals. Hirschfeld identified himself as homosexual, but he did not, it seems, desire to change his sex. For Hirschfeld, hermaphrodites, androgynes, homosexuals, and transvestites constituted distinct types of sexual "intermediaries," natural variations that all probably had an inborn, organic basis. He considered transvestism "a harmless inclination," and he included in the transvestite group those with crossgender identification as well as those who crossdressed.[10] (In an article published in 1923, Hirschfeld used the term *seelischen Transsexualismus,* or spiritual transsexualism, which he associated with a form of "inversion," but he did not use the word *transsexual* the way we use it today. For people who hoped to change their sex, he used the word *transvestite.*)[11] Hirschfeld paid close attention to Steinach's research on animals. In the 1910s he visited Steinach in Vienna and publicized his work, and in the 1920s he pioneered in arranging sex-change surgery for humans. In his work with transvestites, Hirschfeld encountered female-to-males who requested mastectomy and preparations for beard growth and male-to-females who sought castration, elimination of facial hair, the implantation of ovaries, and "apparatus for making the breasts bigger."[12] He listened seriously to the people he studied, and he began to recommend and arrange transformative surgery.

The first complete genital transformation arranged through Hirschfeld's institute was that of Dorchen Richter, a male-to-female, who underwent castration in 1922 and in 1931 had her penis removed and a vagina surgically constructed. Born in 1882 to a poor farm family in eastern Germany, Richter had crossdressed during childhood and longed to live as a girl. She detested her male genitals. At the age of six she had tied a cord tightly around her penis and scrotum in the hope they would fall off. As an adult, her longing to be a woman only intensified. She worked as a waiter at fancy hotels during the summer season and during the off-season lived as a woman. This was the life that Richter wanted, but it was illegal. The police repeatedly arrested her, and the courts sent her to prison. Eventually a judge took pity on her and wrote a letter to Hirschfeld asking his advice. Hirschfeld invited Richter to his institute and helped her obtain an official permit to dress in women's attire. When Hirschfeld offered her surgery, she welcomed the chance to change her bodily sex. After her first surgery, Richter worked as a domestic servant at the Institute for Sexual Science. She remained there as a domestic worker and demonstration patient until the institute's demise in 1933.[13]

In the early 1930s the institute officially publicized its sex-change experiments. In 1931 Felix Abraham, a physician who worked at the institute, wrote the first scientific report on human transsexual surgery. The article appeared in a journal published by the institute and detailed the male-to-female *Genitalumwandlung,* or genital transformation, of two "homosexual transvestites," one of whom was Dorchen Richter. The illustrated account of surgery included castration, amputation of the penis, and creation of a vagina. Abraham believed that countless other patients wanted similar operations but had no way of learning about them. The surgery, he claimed, saved them from self-mutilation. Another surgeon at the institute, Ludwig Levy Lenz, also performed sex-change surgeries, which, he recalled later, the daily newspapers publicized. "Never," he wrote in his memoir, "have I operated upon more grateful patients."[14]

The sex-change surgeries in Germany reached their peak in the early 1930s along with a spate of publicity about one of the institute's patients, Danish artist Einar Wegener, who underwent male-to-female operations to become Lili Elbe. The series of operations began with castration in Berlin, following psychological tests conducted by Hirschfeld. Later, in Dresden, doctors removed the penis and transplanted human ovaries. Elbe died from heart failure in 1931 after a final operation, an attempt to create a "natural outlet from the womb," probably a vagina. Before her death, the story broke in Danish and German newspapers, and after her death her life history appeared in book form, first in Danish and then in German. (In the book version, the pseudonymous Dr. Hardenfeld provides a thinly veiled cover for Magnus Hirschfeld.)[15] Around the same time, Hirschfeld's recommendations for sex-change surgery also won some official support. By one account, a male-to-female had genital surgery in 1932 paid for by the government. Hirschfeld, according to this account, "considered [it] his greatest triumph, for . . . the German government fully accepted and supported his theory."[16] The moment of triumph soon ended. In 1933 the Nazis destroyed Hirschfeld's institute, setting its books and files afire. Hirschfeld, who was Jewish, never returned to Germany. He lived in exile until his death in 1935.[17]

*I*n explaining why transsexuality and sex-reassignment surgery emerged in the twentieth century, one might cite new developments in medical technology, especially new plastic-surgery techniques and the invention of synthetic hormones.[18] Indeed, medical technology played a significant role in the history of transsexuality. But technology alone provided neither a necessary nor a sufficient precondition for modern transsexuality. The earliest transsexual surgeries took place before the invention of synthetic hormones and without the benefit of sophisticated plastic-surgery techniques. The surgical techniques employed in Germany were available elsewhere. In the United States, doctors removed genitals, breasts, and reproductive organs when they were diseased or injured. They performed plastic surgeries, including vaginoplasty for women born without vaginas. For various ailments they administered hormone treatments, through gonadal transplants and hormonal extracts in the 1910s and 1920s and with synthetic hormones by the end of the 1930s. (Surgeons in the United States and Europe rarely attempted phalloplasty, plastic surgery to construct or reconstruct a penis, until after World War II.)[19] Sex-change surgery, then, did not take root when and where it did because of new or unusual medical technology. It took root in part because Germany had a vocal campaign for sexual emancipation. In Berlin, Hirschfeld and others worked to remove the legal and medical obstacles to sexual and gender variance, to enable homosexuals, crossdressers, and those who hoped to change their sex to live their lives as they chose. Equally important, sex-change surgery in Europe relied on a new definition of sex.

We might think of biological sex as a natural phenomenon, with unchanging categories, male and female, universally recognized in all cultures and all centuries. But like gender and sexuality, biological sex has a history. Humans have imagined it differently at different times and in different places. European and American scientists once envisioned sex as a hierarchy of similar beings in which female stood as an inferior version of male. With the Enlightenment of the late eighteenth century, though, they increasingly wrote of two sexes, distinct and opposite. Female less often appeared as a paler copy of male and more often as distinctly different and complementary. Through the nineteenth century, this notion of separate and opposite sexes underscored the dominant social ideals that prescribed sex-segregated social roles which relegated women, focused on reproduction, primarily to the "private sphere."[20]

In the late nineteenth and early twentieth centuries, a growing number of scientists in Europe and the United States began to challenge the notion of separate and opposite sexes. As more women entered the labor force, pursued higher education, and joined social reform movements, a rising women's movement demanded equal access to public participation. Women and men no longer seemed to reside wholly in "separate spheres." At the same time, the increasing visibility of homosexuals, defined in part by gender inversion, called attention to masculine women and feminine men. In this social context, some scientists, like other observers, began to shift their visions of female and male.[21] Some social scientists emphasized what men and women had in common and turned to the environment to explain the perceived differences in their behavior, and some psychologists, especially psychoanalysts, looked specifically to early childhood experience.

Other scientists continued to focus on the human body. Many argued that male and female were ideal types that did not actually exist in reality. All women and men, they said, fell somewhere between the two idealized poles. All males had aspects of the female and all females aspects of the male. They did not refer simply to masculine and feminine traits; they grounded these traits explicitly in what we now call biological sex. They conflated sex, gender, and sexuality, and posed them all as signs of the physical condition. They argued that all humans were to greater and lesser degrees physically bisexual. In every human body, they claimed, one could locate and observe a physical mixture of female and male that created a corresponding mixture of feminine and masculine traits.[22]

Some promoters of this vision traced it back to Charles Darwin. In 1868 Darwin had written: "in many, probably in all cases, the secondary characters of each sex lie dormant or latent in the opposite sex, ready to be evolved under peculiar circumstances."[23] Darwin's early twentieth-century followers described an incomplete process in which sexual differentiation had gradually evolved from hermaphroditic lower animals. Humans still retained some of the undifferentiated traits of their evolutionary forebears. In this view, human bisexuality appeared as a lingering primitive condition that would gradually diminish as evolution progressed.

More often, though, the exponents of human bisexuality looked to embryonic development. In its earliest stages the human embryo did not manifest its sex, and in its later development its sexual differentiation remained partial. The similarities of male and female reproductive organs seemed to reveal their common origins: testis resembled ovary, and penis resembled clitoris. All males maintained vestiges of the female, and all females vestiges of the male. Men had nipples and rudimentary breasts. The embryonic Müllerian duct, which developed into fallopian tubes, uterus, and vagina in the woman, remained undeveloped in the man, and the Wolffian body and duct, which developed into the vas deferens, seminal vesicle, and epididymis in the man, remained undeveloped in the woman. These were not "dead vestiges," one scientist noted, but "latent dispositions."[24]

From the late eighteenth century on, various natural scientists had attempted to measure the bodily differences that distinguished women from men. By the early twentieth century, though, scientists increasingly noted the ways in which women and men overlapped. In various measures of soma and psyche, women differed from one another as much as or more than they did from men. The new science of statistics suggested that women and men did not fall neatly into two separate categories.[25] Some scientists translated these findings into the theory of human bisexuality. For them, sex resulted not in "two antagonistic and profoundly differentiated entities" with "confused conditions of sex regarded as monstrous anomalies," but in "a scale of infinite gradations which extends from flagrant hermaphroditism to forms so attenuated that they merge into normality itself."[26]

From the start the theory of human bisexuality found its strongest proponents in German-speaking nations. Austrian philosopher Otto Weininger developed the theory of bisexuality in his book *Sex and*

Character, originally published in German in 1903. By 1920 the book had gone through eighteen German editions and had appeared in translation in English, Italian, Russian, and Polish. In a recent collection of essays, one scholar has labeled the book "the philosophical bestseller of the first third of the century," and others comment on Weininger's influence on Franz Kafka, James Joyce, D. H. Lawrence, and Ludwig Wittgenstein, among others.[27]

Weininger distinguished his version of sex from earlier theories that posited three categories of sex: male, female, and intermediate. These earlier theories classed hermaphroditism and sometimes also homosexuality as unusual mixed-sex or intermediate conditions. In *Sex and Character,* Weininger explained how the new conception differed:

> I am discussing the existence not merely of embryonic sexual neutrality, but of a permanent bisexual condition. Nor am I taking into consideration merely those intermediate sexual conditions, those bodily or psychical hermaphrodites upon which, up to the present, attention has been concentrated . . . Until now, in dealing with sexual intermediates, only hermaphrodites were considered; as if, to use a physical analogy, there were in between the two extremes a single group of intermediate forms, and not an intervening tract equally beset with stages in different degrees of transition.
>
> The fact is that males and females are like two substances combined in different proportions, but with either element never wholly missing.[28]

Weininger envisioned sex as a continuous spectrum "in which the different degrees grade into each other without breaks in the series." All men and all women stood somewhere in the intermediate span between the two outlying poles.[29]

This concept of sex was not necessarily more egalitarian than the concept of separate and opposite sexes. One might challenge the binary division of sex without overthrowing the hierarchy that assigned male a higher value than female. Weininger defended homosexuals, whom he envisioned as women who physically approximated men and men who physically approximated women. He saw no reason to describe these natural variations as degenerate or pathological. But Weininger's book quickly descended into misogynist and antisemitic rant. He associated the female end of the spectrum with "lies and errors," poor judgment, illogic, and "profound falseness." And then he associated women with Jews. Like women, Jews lacked "deeply-rooted and original ideas" and failed to "share in the higher metaphysical life." Unlike women, however, Jews, by whom he meant Jewish men, had a "definite aggressiveness" and believed "in nothing."[30] Weininger used the theory of universal bisexuality to argue against the women's movement (which he saw as a movement of masculine women) and the relativist politics of racial and ethnic equality. With the concept of the spectrum, one could find women who had enough maleness to achieve success in the world of men, and one could, by analogy, find Jews who had overcome the debased condition of Jewishness (perhaps Weininger himself; he was of Jewish descent). The concept of a continuum of sex or race allowed Weininger to make easy exceptions while asserting the general inferiority of both women and Jews.

Weininger positioned himself as the originator of the new theory about sex, but others disagreed. The Berlin physician Wilhelm Fliess accused Weininger of stealing his unpublished version of the theory of bisexuality, and Fliess blamed Sigmund Freud for leaking it to Weininger. In correspondence Freud eventually conceded the point, and in his published writings he, like Fliess, disputed that Weininger had invented the new conception of sex. "In uninformed circles," Freud claimed, "the assertion is made that the philosopher, O. Weininger, is the authority for the human bisexuality conception since this idea is made the foundation for his rather hasty work, *Geschlecht und Charakter*." Freud cited several earlier formulations by late nineteenth- and early twentieth-century authors, including Richard von Krafft-Ebing and Magnus Hirschfeld.[31] Hirschfeld himself noted that he had suggested the theory of human bisexuality four years before Weininger published his book.[32]

Whatever the origins, prominent European sexologists of the early twentieth century endorsed variations on the concept of universal bisexuality. Freud, for example, agreed that "a certain degree of anatomical hermaphroditism really belongs to the normal. In no normally formed male or female are traces of the apparatus of the other sex lacking." Freud acknowledged this "original predisposition to bisexuality," but he did not extend it, as did Weininger, to the "psychic sphere." Anatomical bisexuality did not, for Freud, explain crossgender behavior or same-sex object choice.[33]

All the key early figures who wrote about transvestism, crossgender identification, and sex change subscribed more fully to this emerging theory. Hirschfeld played a central role in its dissemination. From the late nineteenth century on, Hirschfeld promulgated his theory of sexual intermediaries. In some formulations he portrayed intermediaries—among whom he included hermaphrodites, androgynes, homosexuals, and transvestites—as a "third sex," anomalous exceptions to the male-and-female rule. But from early on he also promoted the concept of bisexuality, according to which all men and women fell into the intermediate categories.[34] In his book *Transvestites* he wrote that "absolute representatives of their sex are . . . only abstractions, invented extremes," and in his article, "The Intersexual Constitution," he included an epigraph: "The human is not man *or* woman, but rather man *and* woman." Historian James Steakley notes that the notion of human bisexuality bolstered Hirschfeld's political campaign for sexual rights. He could remove homosexuals and transvestites from pathologized minority positions and place them as natural variations within the broader stream of humanity "in a world populated entirely, as he ultimately saw it, by sexual intermediates."[35]

In his work on transvestism, British sexologist Havelock Ellis also acknowledged the theory of "universal bisexuality . . . now so widely accepted." Ellis speculated that human bisexuality might provide the biological basis for transvestism, which he called "sexo-aesthetic inversion" or "eonism." (In this category Ellis included people with crossgender identification as well as those who crossdressed. Following Hirschfeld, he distinguished this form of "inversion" from homosexuality.) For Ellis, the biological underpinnings of transvestism included both anatomical predispositions and hormonal influences. "It is now recognized," he wrote, "that the characters of one sex must be latent in the other sex, and we thus have a field in which the various internal secretions may display their stimulating and inhibiting properties."[36]

Other scientists, too, related the new field of endocrinology to the new vision of sex. In the late nineteenth century scientists had relied on gonads as the determinants of "true" sex;[37] but by the end of the century they had begun to include other physical markers, especially hormones. Scientists discovered sex hormones in the late nineteenth century and soon identified them as either male or female. In studying sex differentiation, they focused increasingly on the impact of internal secretions rather than on the gonads themselves or on the morphology of genitals and reproductive organs. In the early twentieth century, scientists acknowledged chromosomes as the initial determinants of sex, but they turned to hormones, as the fluid carriers of sex, to help explain sexual development and the many variations and gradations they saw in the intermediate conditions.[38]

According to the concept of bisexuality, hormones might also explain how male could become female and female could become male. Eugen Steinach, the renowned physiologist who experimented with changing the sex of rodents, wrote: "The line of demarcation between the sexes is not as sharp as is generally taken for granted . . . A one hundred percent man is as non-existent as a one hundred percent woman." All humans, he said, have "the primordial *anlage* or potentiality for either sex."[39] In his experiments on animals, Steinach did not claim to create a male or female wholesale, but he did claim to use hormones to suppress some of the physical characteristics and sexual behavior of the dominant sex and bring out the latent potentialities of the other. Hormones could push the developing animal one way or another along a perceived spectrum of biological sex. Another scientist described the impact of hormones as "the possibility of a mutual transformation, either by furtherance or [by] inhibition."[40] In this view, sex changed quantitatively. Add and subtract glandular secretions, and female slipped toward male or male slipped toward female.

In the 1920s and 1930s new discoveries in endocrinology boosted the notion that male could become female and female could become male. In the 1910s and 1920s biochemists learned to extract hormones from the organs and urine of animals, and in the 1930s they developed chemical tests to detect their presence. They soon discovered that men and women had both male and female hormones. This startling finding suggested that in this respect, too, all women had elements of the male and all men elements of the female. In addition, scientists identified the chemical composition of sex hormones and found that the compounds forming the male hormones closely resembled those of the female. "In this manner," historian Nelly Oudshoorn writes, "they broke with the dualistic concept of male and female as mutually exclusive categories."[41] With the earlier vision of separate and opposite sexes, scientists could not imagine, it seems, how to bridge the chasm dividing female from male. With the vision of overlapping sexes, they could more easily imagine inching sex one way or another across the male-female spectrum. In this sense, the theory of universal bisexuality made sex change seem possible.

The concept of human bisexuality emerged primarily in Europe, but in limited ways it reached the United States. In the 1920s and 1930s it appeared in various forms in American medical textbooks.[42] It also appeared in American scientific studies of homosexuality. Clifford A. Wright, an endocrinologist, wrote several articles on hormones and homosexuality, in which he characterized all humans as bisexual. Homosexuals, he posited, had reversed proportions of the male and female hormones that all humans shared.[43] In his massive study of homosexuality, *Sex Variants,* George Henry concluded: "It is scientifically inaccurate to classify persons as fully male or female."[44] In this view, all men strayed from the abstract pole of male, and all women strayed from the abstract pole of female; "sex variants," or homosexuals, simply strayed farther.[45] By the end of the 1930s the notion of bisexuality cropped up occasionally in more popular accounts. In 1939, for example, an article in *Living* magazine titled "Preparation for Marriage" proclaimed that "every individual is bisexual . . . the man or woman . . . will be only partly male or partly female."[46] The popular magazine *Sexology* also presented the concept in articles in the 1930s and 1940s. One such article stated it as a given: "all human beings are bi-sexual in their makeup."[47]

In the United States, the new conception of sex meshed neatly with broader shifts in social and scientific thought. Biological and social scientists retreated from an older form of taxonomy that focused on dis-

crete categories, moving instead toward an emphasis on individual variation in which categories blended into spectra or continua. They
shifted, that is, from the categorical to the scalar. In this endeavor, the
concept of biological bisexuality paralleled newly emerging notions of
gradations of masculinity, femininity, and sexual behavior.[48] From the
late 1920s on, for example, anthropologist Margaret Mead emphasized
that the "potentialities" and "gifts" of women and men ranged widely
and did not fall automatically into the culturally constructed categories
of masculine and feminine.[49] In the 1930s psychologists Lewis M.
Terman and Catherine Cox Miles noted that "individual differences"
and "gradations of behavior" undermined "the categorical explanation
of any aspect of human nature in terms of well-defined dichotomies."
They constructed an influential quantitative scale that measured the
"range and overlap of the sexes" with regard to personality traits.[50] In
the 1940s sex researchers Alfred Kinsey, Wardell Pomeroy, and Clyde
Martin focused on the wide variation in human sexual behavior. "It is a
fundamental of taxonomy," they wrote, "that nature rarely deals with
discrete categories . . . The living world is a continuum in each and every one of its aspects." They questioned mutually exclusive categories,
such as homo- and heterosexual, and replaced them with graded scales
of frequencies of sexual behaviors.[51]

But Mead, Terman and Miles, and Kinsey and his colleagues did not
adopt the biological correlate that blurred the boundaries of male and
female and posed all humans as biologically intermediate. They maintained the male-female categories and located their scales of individual
variation primarily in the areas of temperament, personality, and behavior. In the context of American social science, they pointed as much to
the effects of culture, environment, and learning as to the effects of
biology. Thus in the first half of the twentieth century, the theory of
human bisexuality had less impact in the United States than it had in
Europe.

*I*n the 1920s and early 1930s most Americans remained oblivi-
ous to the possibility of sex change and to the new definition of sex that
supported it. A few Americans, though, learned about Hirschfeld and
traveled to Germany in search of his help. Florence Winter (pseudo-

nym), female-to-male, went to Berlin, probably in the 1920s, "to find solutions to her problems of homosexuality and transvestism." In Chicago she had felt "isolated from her kind," but in Berlin she found others like herself through her association with Hirschfeld's institute. According to a friend who recorded her story in a letter, Hirschfeld himself agreed to arrange her sex-change surgery. "However, when he warned her that after the operations she would not be either a man or a woman, she backed out." Perhaps Hirschfeld meant that Winter would not have reproductive capacities, or perhaps he referred to the inability of surgeons to create a functioning penis. In any case, after living for "a long time" as a man, Winter left Europe at the outbreak of World War II and returned to Chicago, where she lived again as a lesbian.[52] Carla Van Crist (pseudonym), male-to-female, went through with the genital surgery Hirschfeld arranged. The child of an American father, she grew up as a boy in Berlin and San Francisco, and as a young adult worked as a female impersonator. As she remembered later, she found her way to Dr. Harry Benjamin at his offices in New York, and he suggested she visit Hirschfeld. (Benjamin, however, did not recall the meeting.) In the 1920s she returned to Berlin and worked at Hirschfeld's institute as a receptionist until its destruction in 1933. In 1929 or 1930 she underwent operations, performed by the same surgeon who operated on Lili Elbe. She came back to New York in 1942 and supported herself by "coaching young actors in English diction" and also appeared in "several 'off Broadway' productions." She remembered a number of other male-to-females who underwent surgery in Germany, including another "American boy who had been a female impersonator."[53]

Although only a handful of Americans went to Germany with hopes of changing sex, more began to learn of the new possibilities through the mass media. In 1933 E. P. Dutton published the first English translation of the book recounting the transformation of Lili Elbe. Titled *Man into Woman: An Authentic Record of a Change of Sex,* the book presented its subject as an occasional crossdresser whose female personality had come to predominate. More dubiously, it also depicted her as a form of hermaphrodite, with "stunted and withered ovaries" as well as testicles. It seems highly unlikely that Elbe was intersexed. By the late 1930s Dr. Hugh Hampton Young, an expert in the field, had found only twenty medically confirmed cases of hermaphroditism; not one of them had, as the story of Lili Elbe suggested, two ovaries in the pelvis and two testes in the scrotum. The English-language edition of *Man into Woman* included an introduction by British sexologist Norman Haire, who mentioned Steinach's transplantation experiments on animals but considered it "unwise to carry out, even at the patient's own request, such operations" as those performed on Elbe.[54]

After publication of *Man into Woman,* a few American magazines reported Lili Elbe's story. These accounts downplayed Elbe's transvestism and emphasized her alleged hermaphroditism as a way to explain the surgical intervention. In December 1933, for example, an article in *Sexology* titled "A Man Becomes a Woman" distinguished Elbe from the "purely mental" cases, the more common "disorder of the mind . . . due, perhaps, to unhappy experiences in childhood." The distinction lay in "the surprising discovery" that Elbe's "body contained female organs." After acknowledging that the case was "hard to explain," the article suggested that further investigation might bring "more relief . . . for the 'borderline' cases where the apparent sex and the inclinations seem to be in sharp conflict."[55]

Another account, "When Science Changed a Man into a Woman!," associated Lili Elbe with other alleged cases of intersex. The article related the stories of two females in the process of becoming males, or, as the subtitle proclaimed, "The Cases of Two Girls Who Are Being Transformed into Two Boys Parallel the Extraordinary Drama of the Danish Painter Who Became a Beauty." According to this report, Claire Schreckengost, of rural Pennsylvania, and Alice Henriette Acces, of France, were intersexed, with "organs of both sexes." Both had undergone transformative surgery to correct what was cast as nature's mistake. Likewise, Elbe and the scientists she consulted "became convinced that Nature had intended him to be a woman but, in some wretched way, had bungled her handiwork." With typical reticence, the report refrained from mentioning genitalia or reproductive organs. It did not specify what any of the surgeries involved; it related only that one of Schreckengost's operations was "of the ductless gland type." In the case of Acces, the article suggested that surgery had resulted because Acces "was found to be adhering not at all to her girlish role."

After a series of operations, the French doctor proclaimed, "'Today Henriette Acces has become physiologically a male.'"[56]

These and other American stories of sex change attempted to lure readers with shocking accounts of unusual crossgender behavior, rare biological problems, and astonishing surgical solutions. They tended to appear on the margins of the mainstream press, in sensational magazines and tabloid newspapers, or in publications, such as *Sexology,* which used the cover of science to present sex to a popular audience. (*Sexology* often emphasized the stranger side of the science of sex. Hugo Gernsback, the founder and publisher of *Sexology,* also published the first pulp science fiction magazines.)[57] The popular stories rarely distinguished sex, gender, and sexuality and rarely delineated a theory of sex, such as the theory of human bisexuality, that attempted to explain how the sex of the body might determine gender and sexual variance. Articles occasionally mentioned "sex reversals" of the "purely psychical" kind and presented them as homosexuality, which did not qualify for surgery.[58] For the most part, though, they simply assumed that the sources of gendered and sexual behavior lay in the physical body, and they interpreted gendered behavior and sexual desires as constituent parts and markers of sex. They usually melded a number of phenomena that today we might consider distinct. They covered cases of crossgender identification, intersex, homosexuality, and transvestism, sometimes without distinguishing among them, and they frequently depicted them all as interrelated pathologies in need of medical cure.

The article "SEX REPEAL!," for example, appeared in 1939 in *True* magazine, with the subheading "SCIENCE SOLVES THE RIDDLE OF MAN-WOMEN WONDERS." It noted "51 authentic cases of sex reversal" but focused on the story of Ruth Parrin, a Chicago woman who had once been "beautiful, shapely, healthy, and normal." In 1935, though, as a young adult, Parrin underwent a "mysterious personality change" along with a "more alarming symptom": "She found herself irresistibly attracted to members of her own sex." Then "a radical transformation" followed. Parrin sprouted a beard, her skin coarsened, her breasts shrank, her shoulders broadened, her hips narrowed, and her "pelvic basin" flattened. "Bizarre mental transformations" followed, in which Parrin began to think and feel "like a man." Eventually a surgeon discovered and removed a benign tumor close to her ovaries, and Parrin reverted to her former feminine self. She was, the article stated, "back with her husband . . . soon [to be] a mother." The story of Ruth Parrin did not differ significantly from 1930s medical findings on the "masculinizing" effects of certain adrenal and ovarian tumors. But the article went further. It concluded with a lengthy discussion of historical and contemporary examples of masculine women, crossdressing, "inversion," female impersonation, and surgical sex changes, all of which, the article implied, might have been averted by the excision of tumors.[59]

As in "SEX REPEAL!," other popular press accounts sometimes reported spontaneous metamorphoses wherein a woman or man, perhaps with a glandular disturbance, underwent changes in bodily sex and in gendered behavior during late adolescence or adulthood. Another headline, for example, read, "Boy Prisoner Slowly Changing into a Girl."[60] More generally, though, as in the reports on Lili Elbe, Claire Schreckengost, and Henri Acces, the articles addressed "sex change" accomplished through surgery but failed to specify what the operations entailed. They depicted sex-change surgery as unveiling a true but hidden physiological sex and thus tied the change to a biological mooring that seemingly justified surgical intervention. In this vision of sex, science could and should correct nature's "rare blunders," creating an unambiguous sex, either male or female, from sexual ambiguity, a condition cast and contained as tragic but correctable.[61]

In the second half of the 1930s these features appeared in force in the widely reported accounts of European women athletes who became men. In 1935 or 1936 Zdenka Koubkova, a Czechoslovakian runner, became Zdenek Koubkov, through what one report termed "a delicate surgical operation."[62] Around the same time, British shotput and javelin champion Mary Edith Louise Weston underwent two operations and adopted the name Mark. In 1937 twenty-three-year-old Elvira de Bruijn, a cycling champion from Belgium, had surgery in Paris and began to live as Willy. De Bruijn remembered later, "I read a story about a famous Czech champion who had undergone an operation that changed him from a woman to a man. I decided to investigate." He persuaded his parents "to consent to the operation" after telling them he "felt like a man, never like a woman."[63] In the era when women first participated in public athletic competitions, the press attention reflected the discomfort with female athletes and seemed to confirm popular suspicions that athletic women were, if not actually men, then at least suspiciously mannish. But the stories also provided further publicity about the possibility of changing sex.[64]

The American press covered Koubkov's case extensively, in large part because he came to New York. Considered female at his birth in 1913, Koubkov, according to press reports, grew up as "an utterly masculine youth," who resisted feminine clothes and domestic training. As he aged, "the feeling of masculinity began to assert itself," and he longed for women sexually, "his romantic imagination" supposedly "inflamed by reading French novels." In the 1932 Olympics he competed as a woman, setting a world record in the 800-meter event, but in his early twenties (or, in one account, earlier) "a great light dawned," and he realized he was a man. He consulted a doctor who confirmed his masculinity, and unspecified operations, "the flick of a surgeon's scalpel," followed. Four months later, in 1936, Koubkov came to New York to perform in a Broadway club. In a *tableau vivant,* or living picture performance, he ran on a treadmill, chasing a woman, foreshadowing Christine Jorgensen's later staged performances of gender.[65]

Were Koubkov and the others intersexed (with male organs hidden internally)? Were they what we would now consider transsexual? One quasi-scientific pamphlet, *Women Who Become Men,* published in 1938, suggested that "women-athletes" were "'changing their sex'" through transplants of testicular tissue, but, it claimed, "the press is too delicate to give us exact information."[66] But *Sexology* reported the various stories of sex change—including those of Lili Elbe, Claire Schreckengost, Henri Acces, and the athletes—as cases of unusual intersexed conditions and "arrested development." In one such article Dr. Jacob Hubler admitted that he had no scientific accounts in medical journals on which to rely and expressed reservations about drawing definitive conclusions simply from reading the popular press. Nonetheless, he assumed that popular accounts of sex change referred to surgery for physically ambiguous intersexed individuals, which, by the 1930s, he saw as "nothing new or nothing startling." He explicitly tried to dissuade readers, especially those on the sexual margins, from seeing surgical sex change as anything more. "The average man and woman with homosexual ('third sex') trends and twists," he wrote, "need not think we are on the threshold of new discoveries which will enable any individual to be changed to the sex he or she prefers."[67] His approach differed decidedly from that of the German doctors who saw (and performed) transformative surgery as an option for the patients they labeled "transvestites."

*D*espite the warning, some readers interpreted the stories of sex change in precisely the manner that Hubler hoped to prevent. That is, the publicity about sex-change surgery caught the attention of individuals who identified possibilities for themselves. Sexual identities are "neither innate nor *simply* acquired," Teresa de Lauretis has written, "but dynamically (re)structured by forms of fantasy both private and public, conscious and unconscious, which are culturally available and historically specific."[68] In the history of transsexuality, transgendered subjects used available cultural forms to construct, describe, and reconfigure their own identities. The mass media and reading played critical roles in the articulation of these identities.[69] From the 1930s on, the stories in the popular press provided certain readers, who already had a general sense of crossgender identification, with new and particular ways to describe who they were and new and specific fantasies of what they might become. As they responded to and borrowed from the stories they read, they expressed and reframed their needs with a newly available language.

Sexology published several letters to the editor from readers in search of information. In 1934, for example, one letter writer explained: "I have a peculiar complex—I believe it is called 'Eonism.' That is, I desire to dress as a woman . . . The fact is I have an even stronger desire, and that is—I wish I were a woman . . . I am interested in the Steinach operation in regard to change of sex. I would like more information." And in 1937 another writer, "Miss E. T." from Nebraska, asked: "Is it possible through a surgical operation, or several operations, to change a female into a male? I have read something—not very informative—about such things having been done . . . Could you give me any idea of the method, and also of the cost?"[70]

Sexology acknowledged that the press reports on European athletes, in particular, had "stirred" some of its readers, who now asked "whether it is possible, and if so, how and where." In an article "They Want to Change Sexes," published in 1937, the magazine summarized a handful of letters from both male-to-female and female-to-male writers. The brief and fragmentary presentation of the letters makes it impossible to know to what extent readers used the popular narratives to plot the stories they told about themselves. At least one letter, though, suggests that some readers may have appropriated the stories of intersexed individuals to obtain the information they wanted. A woman who described herself as "nothing feminine" but "apparently of [the female] sex" asked: "If it were true that I have both male and female organs of reproduction, would it not be advisable to undergo what operations are necessary to become the male I wish to be? Can you refer me to a competent surgeon who would be interested in my case?"[71]

More generally, transgendered people used the language available to them to identify their condition. Some described their quest to change sex as a desire or longing. Sometimes they labeled themselves inverts, homosexuals, transvestites, or eonists. Some located the problem in their bodies. They envisioned themselves as hermaphrodites or, in the vernacular, "morphadites," with an emphasis placed on unseen internal organs, or they mentioned their body build or a glandular disturbance to refer to an anomalous physical condition. People who saw themselves as feminine men or masculine women confirmed their crossgender identification by describing the crossgender behaviors in which they already engaged or longed to engage. But mostly they wanted information and medical treatment. They did not need the label "transsexual" or "transgender" to articulate a request to change sex. They tried to identify their problem with whatever labels they had, and then they asked for help.[72]

In the late 1930s and early 1940s, for example, Pauli Murray, a young African-American woman, wrote several documents in which she reflected on her masculine sense of self. She labeled herself homosexual and described her "inverted sex instinct" as including "wearing pants, wanting to be one of the men, [and] doing things that fellows do" as well as "the very natural falling in love with the female sex." Over several years she consulted several doctors and sought "experimentation on the male side." She tried to find "hospitals . . . or medical institutions" where such "experimentation" was conducted.[73] Like other transgendered people, she followed the stories she read in the press. In 1939 she read an article in the *New York Amsterdam News* on the impact of male hormones on feminine men and shortly afterward went to the hospital endocrine clinic mentioned in the article to inquire whether the doctors "would experiment on me with the male hormone." Her "desire to be male" was "so strong" that she could not bring herself to accept the doctor's offer to treat her with female hormones. She rejected psychological explanations of her condition and pondered the possibilities that she had a hormonal imbalance, tumors that made her masculine, or one or both male gonads hidden in her abdomen. This last was "the most radical theory" and also "the one most acceptable" to her.[74] By the early 1950s she seems to have accepted, or at least resigned herself to, her life as a woman. But in the late 1930s and early 1940s she struggled through personal crises and used the prevailing labels, stories, and theories to understand herself, explain herself to doctors, and request medical treatment.

Like many a doctor, the magazine *Sexology* offered little encouragement to people who hoped to change sex. In fact the magazine's editor actively discouraged those who searched for operations. In response to an inquiry about male-to-female surgery, the magazine's editor acknowledged that the letter writer could have "the operation of complete castration" and thereafter live as a woman, but warned that surgery would create a "completely sexless creature." The editor advised the letter writer to see an endocrinologist to "become more masculine" or consult a psychologist to accept the "present masculinity." To a letter writer who requested information on female-to-male sex change, the editor stated bluntly, "There is no operation whereby a *normal female* can be changed to a normal male, or a normal male into normal female. The operations you have read of were performed on 'hermaphrodites.'"[75] Through the 1940s *Sexology* continued to advise such readers, whom it sometimes called "inverts" or "homosexuals," that doctors performed such surgery for cases of intersexuality only. Nevertheless, it continued to run stories about men who became women and women who became men. And letter writers continued to ask for sex-change operations.[76]

As *Sexology* indicated, such surgery was not available in the United States. At least a few American doctors had the same technical expertise as the doctors who performed sex-change operations in Germany. But American surgeons rarely used such interventions on transgendered patients. In his classic book, *Genital Abnormalities, Hermaphroditism, and Related Adrenal Diseases,* published in 1937, Hugh Hampton Young reported several cases in which American doctors had performed surgery to change the assigned sex of their patients, but these patients had had some sort of intersexed condition, with ambiguous genitalia or reproductive organs. In one brief passage, Young mentioned "individuals, apparently not otherwise abnormal . . . [who] assume the attire, mannerisms and habits of the opposite sex." He suspected that such a condition might "possibly be due to glandular and endocrine abnormalities," but he did not suggest or report any medical interventions.[77]

In this context, those who sought to change their sex rarely got the response they wanted from the doctors they consulted. Take the case of Stephen Wagner (pseudonym). Born in 1904, Wagner knew from an early age that he wanted to be a woman. By the mid-1930s he was living as a man in Chicago. A voracious reader, he had learned about surgical sex change and went in search of what he called "feminizing operations." In the 1930s and 1940s he consulted at least eight doctors, mainly psychiatrists, none of whom would help. Wagner read the scientific and popular literature and understood the possibilities for medical intervention, but he could not find doctors who would do for him what had been done for others. In an autobiographical essay, he wrote: "I cannot understand why they make no honest effort to help me whereas in literature I see that so many patients have been helped directly . . . Doctors have given me to understand that such desires as I have are real and basic and that I can not get away from them. Yet, when I ask them to help me realize my desires, they refuse to do so."[78]

By the mid-1940s he had given up, temporarily, on the quest for surgery. He went in search of female hormones and genital feminization, which he hoped to accomplish himself by binding his testicles up into his abdomen, where he thought they might atrophy.[79]

Wagner identified the fundamental dilemma of mid-twentieth-century Americans who hoped to change sex: newspapers and magazines published a stream of sensational stories that hinted at new medical options for transforming sex, but most American doctors refused to offer or recommend treatment unless the patient could lay convincing claim to an obvious intersexed condition. With a few exceptions, American doctors seemed unaware of the German sex-change experiments on "transvestites," and prominent American sexological experts still routinely classed people who hoped to change sex in the same group as homosexuals. In his classic study, George Henry, for example, included as homosexuals men who expressed a desire for sex change, whether or not they had any sexual interest in men. Furthermore, some doctors expressed a chilling hostility to their nonintersexed transgendered patients.[80] Two psychiatrists in Chicago, for example, considered one patient's request for surgery as an example of "his senseless, silly and asinine statements commensurate with mental deficiency." Caught in the middle, a self-identified "true invert" like Stephen Wagner was increasingly aware of the medical possibilities and eager to pursue them, but also increasingly disappointed, frustrated, and depressed. Wagner stated: "I constantly think of suicide as the only way out."[81] But each new bit of publicity offered another shred of hope.

And the publicity continued. In July 1941 newspapers featured the surprising story of Barbara Ann Richards, who had petitioned the Superior Court of California to change her name from Edward and assume the legal status of woman. Sensing a scoop, reporters pursued the story avidly and, repeating Richards' own account in court, presented it as a case of spontaneous metamorphosis. Richards, then twenty-nine years old, told the court in Los Angeles that two years earlier she had "realized that some vital physiological change was taking place." She noted changes in her beard growth, her voice, her skin, and her figure. Adhering to prevalent gender stereotype, she also related that she had become "increasingly fond of cooking and housework." In her petition to the court she described herself as a "hermaphrodite" whose female characteristics had come to the fore, a story strikingly similar to earlier ones on Lili Elbe. In one later account, though, Richards granted that a medical specialist had not found "the organic evidence" for an intersexed condition. Endocrinologist Marcus Graham, who presented her case at a medical conference, attributed the change to hormonal imbalance resulting from childhood illness.[82]

The story remained in the public eye for several months. Newspapers and magazines introduced it with startling headlines, such as "Prank by Mother Nature Turns Los Angeles Salesman into Woman" and "My Husband Is a Woman."[83] In interviews Richards and her wife, Lorraine Wilcox Richards, described Barbara's childhood, their courtship and marriage, and the details of the sexual metamorphosis. Although Richards portrayed herself as a victim of changes beyond her control, she conceded that she was "thrilled at being a woman." Echoing the earlier stories on Lili Elbe, she invoked the imprimatur of nature: "I know now that nature intended me for a girl." As the story unfolded, though, new details suggested that active human intervention may have played a larger role than the stories of passive metamorphosis implied. In October a judge granted the legal change after medical testimony assured him that "the strange transformation from a man to a woman was genuine and permanent." At this hearing a physician's report revealed that Richards was taking "feminine hormone injections" to "stabilize her condition."[84] And in January 1942 another account suggested that Richards anticipated "plastic operations" to make the "outer body conform to . . . inner necessities."[85] (During the publicity blitz, Lorraine Wilcox Richards acted the part of the wife without revealing the common bond that helped sustain the marriage. But later, out of the public view, Lorraine also underwent sex change, female-to-male, through surgery and hormones, and the couple remained together as Barbara and Lauren Wilcox.)[86]

As before, the news reports caught the attention of people who hoped to transform their own sex. Stephen Wagner followed the coverage of Barbara Richards, searching for more details that might explain what exactly had transpired. "In July, 1941," he wrote, "the newspapers had a write up about a man turning into a woman through some freak of nature . . . I have to admit that I have looked through medical literature over and over again for more particulars . . . I am very much frantic over the fact that I have not been able to get the necessary information on this case." A less educated person wrote, with apologies, directly to Barbara Richards: "how did hair disappear from face, and breast grown, this I would really like to have done, and be same as you."[87] Dr. David O. Cauldwell, the editor of *Sexology* magazine's Question and Answer Department, also noted the response to cases such as Richards'. The occasional "legal alteration," he wrote, "leads to . . . proclamations on a wholesale scale that an individual has been medically metamorphosed from one sex into another." Such reports, he claimed, "make a target of my mailbox . . . One question predominates . . . 'Where can I get this done?'"[88]

*A*fter World War II a few popular magazines stated more clearly that doctors could indeed change any person's sex. With the dawn of the atomic age, magazines routinely expressed admiration for the power of science and the wizardry of technology. Medical science in particular seemed poised to find solutions to the most daunting human problems. Perhaps also the wartime shifts in traditional gender roles made the boundaries dividing men and women seem less firm. In this cultural climate, at least a few American magazines, especially of the sensational bent, no longer insisted that sex-change surgery was for intersexed conditions only. As one article stated: "With hormones plus surgery, there's little doubt that, in the not far future . . . doctors can take a full grown normal adult and—if he or she desires it—completely reverse his or her sex." Or as another article, "Would You Change Your Sex?," granted: "The fact that sex is mutable has been illustrated in definite instances of men who have been physiologically turned to women and women to men."[89] Doctors could, as the magazines claimed, alter the bodily sex characteristics of nonintersexed patients; however, in the United States they still generally refused to do so. After World War II, though, two doctors, David O. Cauldwell and Harry Benjamin, took more serious interest in the issue of changing sex.

Born in Cleveland in 1897, David Oliver Cauldwell earned his medical degree at the National University of Mexico and began his career as a general practitioner. During World War II he served as a contract surgeon in the army, a physician for war industries, and a War Department psychiatrist who examined recruits for the armed forces. His wartime work with recruits brought him into contact with, and educated him on, a range of sexual problems. After the war he turned to fulltime writing from his "Farm-Haven" in Alabama. From 1946 to 1959 he served as the letters editor of *Sexology* and, in roughly the same period, as a prolific author for Haldeman-Julius Publications, a small countercultural "freethinking" press located in Kansas.[90] In the 1910s Marcet Haldeman and Emanuel Julius, a married couple, had published socialist tracts, but by the 1930s they had taken a greater interest in sex education, a topic with wider public appeal. After World War II Cauldwell joined the firm's endeavors. By 1951 he had written 140 pamphlets, most of them on sex, published in the popular "Blue Book" series that Haldeman-Julius sold by mail order for thirty-five cents a title. His educational pamphlets included *So You're a Neurotic!*, *Hypersexuality—Is Anyone Oversexed?*, and *Questions and Answers about Cunnilingus*.[91] He hoped to dispel what he considered old-fashioned, guilt-ridden, moralistic attitudes toward sex. In a breezy popular style and with a facetious irreverence, he introduced sexological concepts and terms to his readers, who responded with questions and comments.[92]

In the late 1940s Cauldwell began to write on the subject of altering sex. In a 1949 article in *Sexology* he chose the term *psychopathia transexualis* to describe the case of "Earl," who requested female-to-male surgery for "sex transmutation." (The term *psychopathia transexualis* played on the title of Richard von Krafft-Ebing's famous nineteenth-century sexological treatise, *Psychopathia Sexualis*.) Specifically, Earl asked Cauldwell "to find a surgeon" who would remove the breasts and ovaries, "close the vagina," and construct "an artificial penis." As in earlier writings in *Sexology*, Cauldwell acknowledged that a surgeon could perform such operations, but he refused to endorse them. He stated that the artificial penis would have "no material use" and "no more sexual feeling than a fingernail." Furthermore, he considered it "criminal" for a doctor to remove healthy glands and tissues.[93]

What distinguished this article from earlier ones in the American press was the construction of "psychopathia transexualis" as an independent sexological category. Cauldwell dissociated this request for surgery from cases of intersex and glandular disorder. To Cauldwell, transsexuals were "products, largely, of unfavorable childhood environment and overindulgent parents and other near relatives." And although Earl was sexually drawn to women, the article also distinguished transsexuals from homosexuals. The caption to an accompanying surreal illustration (of a double-headed man/woman binding her/his breasts) stated: "Many individuals have an irresistible desire to have their sex changed surgically . . . These persons are not necessarily homosexuals."[94]

In 1950 and 1951 Cauldwell offered his own definition of sex in pamphlets published by Haldeman-Julius. For Cauldwell, sex referred to the physical body. He wrote of a visible and audible "biological sex," seen in genitals, beards, and breasts and heard in the high and low voices of adult women and men, and he also noted the "sex distinction . . . determined by the gonads."[95] There was, he said, only "a thin genetic line between the sexes." He downplayed sex differences and attributed gender differences primarily to social factors. "Males and females," he claimed, "think differently as a result of social evolution and individualism. There isn't any distinct male way of thinking and there isn't any distinct female way of thinking." Cauldwell pondered the possibility of mixed-sex conditions. A man who inherited "certain genes from his mother and his female ancestors," he wrote, "will look somewhat feminine."[96] But in general he did not posit a universal bisexuality, and he did not envision unconventional gender behaviors or sexual desires as indicators of a mixed-sex condition or as physical problems that required medical intervention. Masculinity and femininity were social and psychological, and when they failed to correspond with biological sex, they indicated an unusual mental condition.

Although Hirschfeld had used the word *transsexualismus* in at least one of his essays, Cauldwell, in *Questions and Answers on the Sex Life and Problems of Trans-Sexuals,* suggested that he himself had coined *transsexual.* He was, it seems, the first to use the word in direct reference to those who desired to change sex. A summary on the pamphlet cover stated Cauldwell's key points: "Trans-sexuals are individuals who are physically of one sex and apparently psychologically of the opposite sex. Trans-sexuals include heterosexuals, homosexuals, bisexuals and others. A large element of transvestites have trans-sexual leanings."[97] In this way Cauldwell separated gender, understood as psychological sex, from biological sex and sexuality. Crossgender identification and the request for sex change were not necessarily linked either to intersexed conditions or to same-sex desire. He endorsed surgery for intersexed conditions "to establish nearer perfection of the true sex," but for transsexuals he advocated "psychological rather than physical adjustment." In *Sex Transmutation—Can One's Sex Be Changed?* Cauldwell continued the process of differentiation. He suggested that transsexuals unconsciously wished "to destroy their sexuality." He was not, he wrote, "in the least critical of either the transvestists or the homosexuals." But his liberalism did not extend to transsexuals. He construed "mutilative operations" as a sign of "lost . . . mental equilibrium."[98]

In constructing his definition, Cauldwell acknowledged and referred to Magnus Hirschfeld's work with "transvestites," but he drew more directly on the letters of those he called transsexuals. By the early 1950s Cauldwell had a voluminous correspondence on issues of sexuality from his work at *Sexology* and at Haldeman-Julius Publications, where, in his pamphlets on transsexuals, he quoted extensively from letters he had received. As earlier, some letter writers already had a sense of the surgical possibilities, and sometimes they explained their knowledge with direct reference to what they had read in magazines, newspapers, and sexological writings. A thirty-three-year-old male-to-female crossdresser who had lived as a woman for fourteen years wrote: "Everything leads to the fact that I have developed a burning desire to be made into a woman. I've read of a number of such instances. The reports were in the daily press and must have been true." Cauldwell expressed annoyance with the persistent requests for surgery. In *Questions and Answers* he blamed medicine for creating "fantastic hopes" and popular magazines for publishing "tales of magic cures and magical accomplishments of surgeons," and in *Sex Transmutation* he denounced the "lurid stories of sex transmutation."[99]

While Cauldwell refused to endorse sex-change surgery, another doctor, Harry Benjamin, began to treat the first of many patients who came to him to change sex. Benjamin, an endocrinologist, came from the German tradition of sexology. Born in Berlin in 1885, he developed an interest in sexual science after reading August Forel's *The Sexual Question* while a university student.[100] Around the same time he met Magnus Hirschfeld and accompanied him on tours of the Berlin bars where homosexuals and crossdressers gathered. He completed his medical studies at the University of Tübingen in 1912 and came to the United States in 1913 to assist a physician who claimed, incorrectly, to have found a cure for tuberculosis. A year later, at the outbreak of World War I, Benjamin attempted to return to Germany, but the British navy prevented his ship from reaching its destination. After a brief stay in England he returned to settle in New York, where he soon established himself as an expert in endocrinology and geriatrics. In the 1920s he spent summers in Europe, visiting Magnus Hirschfeld at the Institute for Sexual Science in Berlin and, into the 1930s, studying with Eugen Steinach at the University of Vienna.

In the United States Benjamin worked to introduce his American colleagues to European sexual science. In the 1920s he publicized Steinach's research, including the controversial "vasoligation" technique, a ligation of the vas deferens, similar to vasectomy, that promised (but failed) to rejuvenate older men. In 1921 Benjamin gave a lecture on Steinach at the New York Academy of Medicine, and in 1923 he showed the "Steinach-Film," a German documentary on Steinach's studies of hormones, to a medical audience in New York. He also published a number of articles on rejuvenation that won him the dubious reputation as "the prime exponent" in the United States of the "Steinachian miracle."[101] In 1930 Benjamin helped arrange Magnus Hirschfeld's visit to the United States. (While in New York, Hirschfeld stayed at Benjamin's home and gave a few "private lectures" in his office.)[102] And in 1932 Benjamin attempted to bring to Chicago the conference of the World League for Sexual Reform, founded in 1928 by Hirschfeld and other sexologists. He also drafted a platform for the World League in which he defended the private sexual behavior of consenting adults.[103]

Benjamin saw himself as "a maverick or an outsider" and an advocate for sexual freedom. By the early 1930s he had emerged as a defender of prostitution and prostitutes. Although privately he considered homosexuality a form of "retarded development," publicly he defended the rights of homosexuals in an era when few other American doctors did. With his radical views on sexuality and his advocacy of experimental forms of rejuvenation, Benjamin, as he knew, stood outside the mainstream of American medicine. He joined a small circle of American sexologists who saw themselves as pioneers and reformers. He expressed contempt for what he saw as prudery and hypocrisy, and he sought out friends and colleagues who agreed with his unorthodox views. He met birth-control advocate Margaret Sanger and anarchist Ben Reitman, and he befriended sex reformer Judge Ben Lindsey and author and gynecologist Robert Latou Dickinson. In 1944 Dickinson introduced Benjamin to sex researcher Alfred C. Kinsey, and Benjamin began to send Kinsey materials for his studies of sexual behavior.[104]

In the 1920s and 1930s Benjamin for the first time offered medical treatment to a crossdressing patient, an elderly German male-to-female, Otto Spengler, who lived in New York. Spengler lived and worked at home as a woman but dressed as a man when outside the house. At Spengler's request Benjamin agreed to administer an extract of estrogenic hormone, marketed as "progynon," developed in part through the experiments of Steinach. "To become feminine," Spengler also underwent x-ray treatments of his testicles, a means to sterilization, under Benjamin's care.[105] Unlike most American doctors, Benjamin showed little reluctance to address issues of sex or to intervene. In the footsteps of Steinach, he placed greater faith in hormone treatments than in attempts at psychotherapeutic cure. Following Hirschfeld's sexological tradition, he suspected, even assumed, that crossgender identification had some somatic cause, thus justifying medical intervention.

In 1949 Benjamin met a patient, referred by Kinsey, who was desperate to change sex. Val Barry (a pseudonym), who lived already as a woman, had spent most of her childhood as a girl. In 1948, at the age of twenty-two, she had entered a hospital in her home state of Wisconsin for psychiatric examination. Like many other transgendered individuals, she had read "several books and articles on operative procedures which feminized men," including the book *Man into Woman* (the story of Lili Elbe), and she now expressed a "desire to be changed surgically." She "refused to consider any other alternative," including "any brain surgery" that might eliminate her "desire to remain a female mentally." More than thirty members of the hospital staff met to discuss her case, and they recommended castration and plastic surgery. For unknown reasons, however, the hospital consulted with the state attorney general's office, which "ruled against the operations as constituting mayhem," a strange interpretation of statutes descended from British common law forbidding the maiming of potential soldiers.[106]

In May 1949 Barry wrote to Benjamin for help. Like many of the patients who crossed Benjamin's path, she learned that he listened sympathetically and went out of his way to offer advice. After reading Barry's medical history, Benjamin told her that he considered her "a woman [who] accidentally possesses the body of a man." Although he had not yet met her, he promised to write to Germany to find out what the law stipulated there. In the meantime he suggested female hormones and tentatively also "x-ray castration" as well as "x-ray treatment of your face to remove the hair growth." In 1949, at his summer office in San Francisco, he began to administer hormones to Barry and to search for surgeons in the United States. He contacted Edmund G. Brown, the state's district attorney (and later governor), about the legality of castration in California. Initially Brown did not envision any legal obstacles to sex-change surgery, but after consulting another lawyer he sent Benjamin a discouraging memorandum. Annoyed, Benjamin replied: "it is difficult to reconcile my common sense with the fact that statutes based on the requirements of English kings in the middle ages should still be valid . . . I do not see how any surgeon anywhere in this country could possibly perform such operation."[107] Soon afterward psychiatrist Karl M. Bowman at the Langley Porter Clinic in San Francisco met informally with Kinsey to discuss Barry's case. Kinsey and Bowman decided not to endorse the surgery. "Sexual desire would remain," they found, "with no possibility for genital outlet if a simple penile amputation were done." Furthermore, they believed, an operation would not resolve "the underlying psychological problem" and would leave the patient "a eunuch."[108] A few months later Benjamin's friend Max Thorek, a renowned surgeon in Chicago, initially sympathetic, refused, on his lawyer's advice, to operate. It was not until 1953, after the publicity about Christine Jorgensen, that Val Barry underwent genital surgery in Sweden.

$\mathcal{B}$y 1950 a handful of American doctors had privately performed sex-change surgery on nonintersexed patients. In 1940 a physician at San Quentin prison related his encounter with a prisoner, "Artie," whom he labeled a "moronic monster." "Artie," he concluded, "had been born a normal male child, and . . . some skilful surgeon, for reasons unknown, had operated . . . and turned him, to all outward appearances, into a woman." In the early 1940s a fulltime male-to-female crossdresser who lived in Utah claimed to have had her "breasts built up by a surgeon," and in 1944, Lauren Wilcox, female-to-male, convinced the doctors at the Langley Porter Clinic in San Francisco to arrange a double mastectomy.[109] These surgeries, though, were clearly exceptions to the rule.

Outside the United States a few surgeons performed occasional sex-change operations. According to Carla van Crist, who had undergone surgery in Berlin, "sex changes became a rather every day occurrence" in Germany during the years of Nazi rule, an era when unusual medical experimentation on human subjects became the norm. In one case, recorded in the scholarly literature, a male-to-female had all her "male sex parts removed," at her own request, in Hannover in 1943. In Switzerland a male-to-female underwent castration in the early 1930s, and another, Arlette Leber, had several operations, including vaginoplasty, in the early 1940s. In England, female-to-male Michael Dillon, an Anglo-Irish aristocrat, began taking testosterone around 1939, had a double mastectomy in 1942, and in the late 1940s underwent a series of operations, performed by the well-known plastic surgeon Sir Harold Gillies, to create a penis and scrotum.[110]

In the United States those who sought sex-change surgery usually found their requests rejected by the doctors they consulted. At midcentury they searched for their own solutions to their sense of crossgender identification and their urgent desire for transformation. One male-to-female hoped "that perhaps in time my genitals will become so useless that I must be castrated. They could operate on my pituitary gland and give me ovarian extract . . . I would prefer to have my penis removed and a vagina made surgically but sometimes at night I get the idea of doing it myself." Desperate thoughts sometimes led to desperate actions. The subject of this case study attempted suicide on several occasions.[111]

If, for all practical purposes, sex-reassignment surgery did not exist in the mid-twentieth-century United States, it nonetheless remained in the public eye. From the 1930s to the 1950s we can trace a transatlantic shift, from Europe to the United States, especially via the popular culture. In the American annals of science, sex change had a subterranean history, virtually invisible in the first half of the twentieth century. But in the 1930s and 1940s sensational stories in the popular press opened possibilities for people who already had some sense of crossgender identification and who recognized themselves in the stories of sex change. For some, the various reports about hermaphroditism, inversion, spontaneous metamorphosis, or hormonal imbalance could be used to account for an otherwise inexplicable sense of being the other sex. For others, the reports suggested ways in which doctors might possibly help them. They did not yet have the label "transsexual," but in the press they found exemplars, however pathologized and sensationalized, who seemed to embody what they knew they wanted for themselves.[112]

In 1952 the press discovered Christine Jorgensen and inaugurated a new era of comprehensive, even obsessive, coverage. In the history of sex change in the United States, the reporting on Jorgensen served as both a culminating episode and a starting point. During the postwar era, with growing attention to science, gender, and sexuality, the Jorgensen story evoked tremendous public response in America. Through the press and her public appearances, she came to embody, literally, the fundamental question raised by sex-change surgery: what makes a woman a woman and a man a man?

"EX-GI BECOMES BLONDE BEAUTY"

2

*A*t the end of March 1959 a *New York Daily News* headline asked: "What's a Woman? City Bureau Baffled by Chris Jorgensen." Since her public debut in 1952, Jorgensen had held the attention of the press in part by raising the question of how to define a person's sex. In 1959 the issue came to a head. With her fiancé, Howard J. Knox, a labor union statistician, Jorgensen applied for a marriage license at the New York City Municipal Building. By the custom of the day, which few questioned at the time, only a woman could marry a man. Where did Jorgensen, who had changed her assigned sex, fit into the categories of female and male? City Clerk Herman Katz, with six staff attorneys, eventually pointed to Jorgensen's birth certificate, which designated her sex as male. Jorgensen, backed by a lawyer of her own, produced her passport, which listed her sex as female, and a letter from her doctor, Harry Benjamin, attesting that "she must be considered female." The city of New York refused to issue the license. On April 4 the *New York Times* described the situation: "Christine Jorgensen, an entertainer, was denied a marriage license yesterday on the ground of inadequate proof of being a female." The more sensational *New York Mirror* announced the news in a front-page headline: "Bar Wedding for Christine."[1] Jorgensen's lawyer promised to petition the New York Board of Health to get the birth certificate altered. Within a few weeks, though, Jorgensen had parted company with Knox, and the questions of how to determine a person's sex and who qualified for marriage vanished temporarily from the public stage.

In the 1950s Jorgensen made *sex change* a household term. She served as a focal point for hundreds of news stories that broached the topic of changing sex and as a publicity agent for the hormones and surgery that enabled bodily transformation. Reporters debated whether Jorgensen qualified as a woman, whether science could create a woman, and how a "normal" woman should behave. And Jorgensen allowed the reporters and the public to satisfy the idle and not-so-idle curiosities that prompted them to observe her. In an interview in the 1960s Jorgensen reflected on her fame. "I was standing at a corner," she said, "when a question was being asked . . . It was because the world was ready for this step . . . the opening of the sexual understanding explosion. If I hadn't been there, someone else would have."[2] As Jorgensen knew, her story highlighted issues that pervaded post–World War II American culture: the limits of individualism, the promise and pitfalls of science, the appropriate behavior of women and men, and the boundaries of acceptable sexual expression. Her story attracted the press, and the public's avid interest in matters pertaining to sex prompted reporters to dig deeply. As the press coverage escalated, journalists and their readers came to distinguish Jorgensen from people with intersexed conditions. The kind of sex-change surgery performed in Europe earlier in the century now took cultural center stage in the United States.

Jorgensen took her public role seriously. Despite the reporters who sometimes characterized her as a "freak" or a "pervert," Jorgensen constructed her own story and her own career in a way that tapped into other cultural sensibilities. She cast her story in a familiar vein as a dramatic success story, and she tried to project a conventional, respectable, mainstream public image. Much of the press's interest, she knew, focused on sexuality, but Jorgensen hoped to separate herself from the lewd jokes about her that circulated into the 1960s. If she could establish herself as a "normal" woman, then she might change the commonplace understandings of what constituted sex, and she might protect herself and others from the ridicule she had endured. In 1954, with a dose of optimism, she told an interviewer from *True Confessions* magazine: "I think that much that has been classified as abnormal for many years is becoming accepted as normal."[3]

With the Jorgensen story, the floodgates broke. A torrent of new stories on other transsexuals made sex change a constant feature in the popular press. Soon sex change made its appearance in record albums, films, and popular novels. And the public responded. Readers bought the newspapers and magazines that carried the sex-change stories, audiences flocked to nightclubs to see Jorgensen perform, and correspondents wrote to the transsexuals whose names made it into the press. As with earlier accounts of sex change, transgendered people responded to the stories, but in Jorgensen's case in particular nontransgendered people responded as well. For at least some readers, Jorgensen had succeeded in making sex change an inspiring story of personal triumph as well as a titillating tale of sexual transgression.

On May 30, 1926, Christine Jorgensen entered the world as George William Jorgensen Jr., the second child and only son of George and Florence Hansen Jorgensen, Danish Americans who lived in the Bronx. To all outward appearances, George Jr. had a relatively uneventful youth. His father, a contractor and carpenter, lost his construction company during the Great Depression but soon found other jobs in the building trades, through the federal Works Progress Administration and in the New York City Parks Department. His mother, a housewife, stayed at home to rear their two children. They managed on short money and held on to their car and home in what Jorgensen remembered as a "pleasant residential area."[4] With grandmother, uncles, aunts, and cousins nearby, George grew up surrounded by relatives in a stable and tight-knit family. Like his older sister, Dorothy, he enrolled in the local public schools, attended summer camp, and went on family vacations.

But as Jorgensen later related it, the seemingly placid childhood hid an inner turmoil. Any recounting of this "inner" life necessarily draws on Jorgensen's constructions of it. In the life histories later presented to the doctors and in various autobiographical writings and interviews, Jorgensen repeatedly told of emotions, wishes, and fantasies invisible to others, of a lonely personal quest to overcome a problem that made life not worth living. In these accounts the plot proceeded from alienation to hope, with science as the solution.

In Jorgensen's telling, George had, from an early age, an aversion to masculine games and masculine clothes. He could not fit in with other boys. "I was unhappy," Jorgensen recalled, "I wasn't like other children . . . I knew something was wrong."[5] Privately, George wanted to play with girls' toys, longed for a doll of his own, and admired his sister's long hair and dresses; and publicly, his sister and others began to note his "outstanding feminine mannerisms," which in the reigning stereotypes included his sense of aesthetics and even the way he carried his books. As a teenager George became "more keenly aware that I was different from other boys."[6] In particular, he found himself with an unrequited attraction to a male friend. "Fear became a part of me," Jorgensen wrote later, "Fear of being wrong. Fear of not fitting into a pattern." In Jorgensen's account, the young George, afraid, ashamed, and confused, comforted himself with books and the study of photography.

As Jorgensen told the story, George's sense of crossgender identification continued to haunt him. In his first fulltime job, in the cutting library of RKO-Pathé News, he tried to "behave like a man, even if I didn't feel like one." Drafted right after the war ended, he served as a clerk in the army for more than a year. "I was underdeveloped physically and sexually," Jorgensen remembered, "I was extremely effeminate. My emotions were either those of a woman or a homosexual. I believed my thoughts and responses were more often womanly than manly." After his stint in the army, Jorgensen moved to Hollywood with hopes of finding a job in photography in the movie industry. There he spoke out loud for the first time about his personal concerns. He confessed to his closest friends, two women, that he had "the emotions of a girl." By expressing what he had seen as isolating secrets, Jorgensen said later, George had "broken through . . . a barrier" and "release[d] the terrifying frustrations."[7] But he still had no solution, and with no prospects of promising jobs, he soon returned to the East, exhausted and depressed.

Jorgensen's story of alienation was not simply a tale reconstructed years after the fact. Around 1945 and 1946, George left some jottings in a pocket notebook. He copied bits of poetry and biblical verses, and he also wrote some of his own musings on love, transcendence, and the barriers dividing humans from one another. At this point Jorgensen already wrote of a private inner life, which he described as a "mystic land of secret hopes and desires" that others could "never know." The melancholic writings include a note of despair. "How can a futureless life go on? Yet it does. Year after year the body lives while the soul dies."[8]

Like others before him, Jorgensen read about sex change in the press and then consulted doctors. In 1948, while enrolled in photography courses, tuition paid by the G.I. Bill, he read about a research scientist in New Haven, Connecticut, who had conducted experiments, in the tradition of Eugen Steinach, by giving hormones to animals. The scientist, for whom Jorgensen later used a pseudonym, was possibly Frank A. Beach, a professor at Yale, who published a book in 1948 titled *Hormones and Behavior.* Jorgensen made an appointment to see him. He wondered whether his own condition might not suggest hormonal imbalance. Years later Jorgensen depicted the encounter as another disappointing episode in the lonely search for answers. The scientist did not suggest the hormone tests or offer the kind of support that Jorgensen sought: "No examination. No questions. No answers. Nothing." Instead, he referred Jorgensen to a psychiatrist who in turn recommended psychoanalysis to eliminate the "feminine inclinations."[9]

Although Jorgensen declined the psychoanalytic treatment, he persisted in his quest to understand his problem. In Jorgensen's story, psychological explanations held little weight. George had, as he saw it, a physiological condition, evident in his "effeminate face and body." The existing photos show a fairly unremarkable-looking young man. He was blond, neat, and slight in build. He had, by doctors' later accounts, standard male genitalia, but with smaller-than-average testicles. His most outstanding features, his protruding ears, did not suggest femininity. Others may or may not have seen Jorgensen as he saw himself, but they did sometimes detect feminine mannerisms in the way he moved his hands or walked. In Jorgensen's understanding of himself, the mannerisms resulted directly from an underlying femininity located in the body and manifest in his physical appearance. Toward the end of 1948 he read a book that solidified his theories about the biological basis of his condition. In the local library he found *The Male Hormone,* by

Paul de Kruif, a popular history of the scientists who extracted, synthesized, and experimented with testosterone. The book suggested that the male hormone created vigor and masculinity and that a lack of manliness denoted hormone deficiency. The author, a middle-aged man, took testosterone himself for rejuvenation.[10]

In American accounts of life-changing conversions, the book that saves is usually the Bible. In Jorgensen's rendition, the book was *The Male Hormone*. In Jorgensen's reconstruction of events, the book marked a turning point. It hit George with stunning impact. It "seemed possible," Jorgensen wrote later, "that I was holding salvation in my hands, the science of body chemistry." The book seemed to confirm that the secretions of the glands—the preponderance of male or female hormones—provided an explanation for feminine and masculine appearance, feelings, and behavior. As Jorgensen later related the story, the new sense of understanding had a catalytic effect. It launched him on a course of study in the available medical literature. At the New York Academy of Medicine he read about intersexed conditions and learned of "conversion experiments in Sweden." To further his studies, he enrolled in Manhattan for training as a medical technician.[11]

With the turn to science, Jorgensen's story moved from passive despair to confident action. George decided to experiment on himself. According to Jorgensen's later accounts, George went to a drugstore in "an unfamiliar section of town" where no one would recognize him and convinced the pharmacist there to sell him estradiol, an estrogenic hormone. He claimed he needed the drug for his work with a doctor who conducted research on animals. Jorgensen's correspondence from the early 1950s, though, hints at a potentially different course of events. One letter suggests that a doctor he consulted, Joseph Angelo, the husband of one of Jorgensen's classmates, supplied him with hormone tablets, perhaps from the start or perhaps at a later date.[12] However he obtained them, George took the hormones orally and soon noted some minor changes. He felt rested and refreshed and also noticed some sensitivity in his breasts. As a medical study later reported, the dose was "too small to produce any marked effect," but the experimentation pleased him, and he began to think more seriously about the possibility of surgery.[13] He consulted with doctors who confirmed that a few surgeons in Europe had performed human sex-transformation operations.

In Jorgensen's telling, George had found his path. He might have chosen to take male hormones, but he had no desire to become more masculine. He might have resigned himself to stay as he was, but he was deeply unhappy as a feminine man. He also refrained from joining the burgeoning gay subcultures in which for decades some feminine men had found a sense of community. Jorgensen noticed the gay life while in the army and afterward, and at the time he assumed he had, as the first medical report on his case described it, "homosexual tendencies."[14] In a later unpublished account, Jorgensen wrote that George, as a boy, had had "the usual experimentations with other little boys," and as a teenager and a young adult had had strong attractions to three different men, what Jorgensen described as "a lot of feeling on my part . . . and most times no feeling at all on the other side."[15] Although Jorgensen denied it repeatedly, it seems that George also had some sexual encounters with men. In an interview in 1979 Jorgensen confessed to an earlier lack of candor and spoke of "a couple" of "homosexual experiences." Still, with or without the encounters, he did not want to live as a homosexual man.[16]

Like many others of his day, George found homosexuality immoral. Jorgensen later reflected that "it was a thing deeply alien to my religious attitudes and the highly magnified and immature moralistic views that I entertained at the time." He also feared the "social segregation and ostracism" that he associated with a gay life.[17] In mid-twentieth-century America, many men who identified as gay reacted with similar fear and shame when they discovered their attraction to men, and some told similar stories of secret longings, alienation, and despair. But few gay men, including those who loathed, rued, resisted, or denied their homosexuality, expressed any sustained desire to change their sex. In contrast, Jorgensen longed to live as a woman, "to relate to men as a woman, not [as] another man."[18]

The yearning to change sex set Jorgensen's story apart from the stories told by gay men. In Jorgensen's accounts, the desire to live as a girl had preceded any attractions to boys. It was the primary driving force that moved him in a different direction. At some point he "yielded," his doctors said, "to his pronounced transvestic tendencies." He "acquired a complete set of women's clothes" and dressed in secret as a woman. Increasingly, he "felt it impossible to continue life as a man."[19] He reported suicidal thoughts. In Jorgensen's story, science offered the only viable solution. George would try to change sex.

In the spring of 1950 Jorgensen left for Denmark to visit friends and relatives and planned to head from there to Sweden in search of medical treatment. He placed his hopes, he wrote friends, in "the possibilities of removing and transplanting," which he acknowledged stood "beyond the acceptance of current medical practice."[20] In Denmark a friend told Jorgensen that he could find what he wanted in Copenhagen and referred him to doctors who promised to help. In late July he found his way to a prominent endocrinologist, Dr. Christian Hamburger, who agreed to experiment free of charge.

Hamburger had never overseen a sex change, and he knew of no such surgery ever performed in Scandinavia. But he had a longstanding research program on the impact of various types of hormone administration on the human endocrine system, and he had at least some familiarity with transformations of sex. According to one newspaper report, he had studied with Eugen Steinach, the Austrian physiologist who had engaged in sex-change experiments on animals, and, in Jorgensen's recollection, he had conducted chemical analyses on Lili Elbe, the Danish artist who had died in 1931 during the course of sex-change operations undertaken in Germany.[21] In Hamburger's proposed plan, Jorgensen would "serve as a guinea pig": he would take estrogenic hormones through injection and ingestion, and in return he would submit to physical examination and provide his urine for medical research. Jorgensen readily assented to the plan and, under Hamburger's guidance, underwent two years of hormone treatments and, with Dr. Georg Stürup, psychiatric evaluations.[22]

In constructing a life history George now had collaborators, scientists who recorded his story as a medical case study. The personal quest, the tale of alienation and hope, had also become a scientific experiment. After less than a year of hormone treatment, the doctors issued their first report. Jorgensen's testosterone secretion had declined, and his testicles had atrophied. His "erective power and sexual libido" had diminished, and pigmentation had darkened the skin of his nipples and genital area. Jorgensen, they found, was "now in a state of mental balance, psychically at ease; he was freed from his mental stress and worked with increased vigor and inspiration" on his photography. Around the same time, Jorgensen sent his own account to friends. Like his doctors, he started with a story of science: "Skin clear and smooth, body contours definitely more feminine." Then he returned to an account of his inner life: "Of course I am my same old self inside only much happier." And he still wanted to change his sex. He had reached the "point of no return."[23]

In the course of the treatment, psychiatrist Stürup asked Jorgensen to write his "life's story" and explain his desire for surgery. In a three-page letter, written in late 1950 or early 1951, George set out the story of alienation and despair, followed by hope, that would serve as the template for Christine's later autobiographical writings. He had not yet heard the word *transsexual* as a label for his condition. He characterized himself as a "homosexual" with "a large amount of femininity." (Within a few years Jorgensen and the Danish doctors would emphasize, as Hirschfeld had earlier, that transvestites and transsexuals differed from homosexuals. At this early stage, they did not.) George wrote of his sense of isolation, of the "wall" he had built around himself "to keep the knowledge of my condition to myself." He hated that others stared at him and sometimes made "cutting remarks." His love for a friend named Jack, he said, had broken down the "wall" that had alienated him from others, but Jack was a "normal man" who did not know, and would never know, that George loved him. "I can never become convinced," George wrote, "that this love for him was wrong for no love is wrong." But in Jorgensen's story, it was science, not love, that surmounted obstacles, and optimism, not tragedy, that shaped the course of his life. He expressed his gratitude for the medical treatment that gave him "reasons to want to live and enjoy life." He told Stürup, "I need desperately to live as a woman."[24]

Stürup soon decided that psychological treatment could not help. His sessions with Jorgensen "seemed futile." Jorgensen wanted "only one thing—an operation," Stürup remembered. "It was impossible to go further psychiatrically." Stürup was not convinced that surgery would make Jorgensen better, but he came to conclude that it would not make him any worse.[25] The Danish doctors had fewer qualms than American doctors concerning genital surgery. Since the late 1920s Danish surgeons had occasionally performed castrations, primarily as treatment for men convicted of sex crimes. The men volunteered, it seems, in the sense that they chose castration over institutionalization. The Danes disagreed with American doctors, who, by the mid-twentieth century, tended to see castration as a cruel form of punishment. As Stürup explained, an American "surgeon can operate on any organ in the body, including the brain. But no, he may not operate on the testes. That is a hypocrisy which the mature society of Denmark refuses to accept." To Stürup, castration was "only for people who feel they need it and need it urgently . . . life, we find, can go on without sex."[26]

In accordance with Danish law, Jorgensen's doctors applied to the national Ministry of Justice for "permission to castrate." Under a 1935 statute on "Permission to Sterilize and Castrate," the ministry could approve castration of an adult not only "when the sexual instincts" made a person "liable to commit crimes" but also when they created "appreciable mental anguish and injury to his standing in society." Although Jorgensen met the latter criterion, it took several petitions to convince the ministry that he was old enough and had lived in Denmark long enough to qualify for approval.[27] Eventually Stürup approached the attorney general of Denmark, Helga Pedersen, who interceded on Jorgensen's behalf. In September 1951, with permit granted, Jorgensen underwent surgery, performed by Dr. Hans Wulff at the Copenhagen County Hospital, to remove his testicles.

The following spring, armed with a letter explaining the treatment, Jorgensen visited the American embassy in Copenhagen and asked to change the name on his passport. At this point Jorgensen still generally dressed as a man in public and went by the name of George. But increasingly he adopted feminine "behavior, gait, and voice." Strangers sometimes read him as a woman and sometimes as a man. He met with the American ambassador to Denmark, Eugenie Anderson, who promised to handle the matter herself. Jorgensen chose the name Christine. She remembered later, "I always liked it . . . Always told myself I would be Christine. Then, after meeting Dr. Hamburger whose name is Christian—the male for Christine—my mind was definitely made up." Late in May, after the State Department approved the passport, she embarked on her new life as a woman.[28]

In June 1952 Jorgensen wrote to her family to explain the change. Although she had stayed in touch with her parents, she had not yet told them anything of her crossgender identification, her medical treatments, or her plans to live as a woman. In this and subsequent letters, she described her problem as hormonal imbalance. She presented her change in the language of popular science and avoided the more dramatic story she told elsewhere of her longings, emotions, and hopes. She briefly acknowledged her fear of homosexuality and now distinguished it from her own condition. She depicted homosexuality as a mental problem, which differed from her own problem, which she characterized as glandular. "I was afraid," she wrote, "for a much more horrible illness of the mind . . . not as yet accepted as a true illness with the necessity of great understanding." Medical treatment offered "the release . . . from a life I knew would always be foreign to me." As in the popular stories from the 1930s and 1940s, Jorgensen portrayed her condition as an error of nature. "Nature," she told her parents, "made the mistake which I have had corrected and now I am your daughter."[29]

By the autumn of 1952 Jorgensen had almost completed her bodily transformation. Under the hormone treatments her breasts had swollen, and through electrolysis her facial hair had mostly disappeared. She had grown her hair long and, to save money, had sewn some of her own clothes. According to her doctors, though, she had "one final ardent wish: to have the last visible remains of the detested masculinity removed." In November she had the operation to remove her penis. At the same time her surgeons, Drs. Paul Fogh-Andersen and Erling Dahl-Iversen, reshaped the scrotum into labia. In 1952 Jorgensen's doctors did not recommend the construction of a vagina. Following Jorgensen's lead, they found "the sexual requirements . . . subordinate to the transvestic impulses." Jorgensen's stated desire was to live as and look like a woman, not to have sexual intercourse. With the plastic surgery, "the genital region," her doctors said, "now had a completely feminine appearance."[30] For Jorgensen, the surgery marked an end to a lengthy ordeal. Her personal tale seemed to have concluded almost miraculously with her rebirth as a woman, and for her doctors the case file seemed to have closed with successful medical intervention. In fact the story had only begun.

While recovering in her hospital bed in Copenhagen, Jorgensen moved irrevocably from private patient to public personality. On December 1, 1952, the front page of the *New York Times* featured stories on the war in Korea, Eisenhower's choice of an ambassador to Britain, and plans for a new coliseum in New York. The *New York Daily News,* however, broke the Jorgensen story with the front-page headline "Ex-GI Becomes Blonde Beauty." The language did not just capture a step from man to woman, but suggested a larger cultural leap, from "ex-GI," the quintessential postwar masculine representation, to "blonde beauty," the hallmark of 1950s white feminine glamour. With pictures of George before and Christine after, the scoop, by *News* reporter Ben White, referred to "a rare sex-conversion" and overestimated the treatment, mentioning, without further detail, "five major operations, a minor operation and almost 2,000 injections." Accompanying the article, the *News* printed the letter that Jorgensen had written her parents the previous June.[31]

How White uncovered the story is still not clear. *Time* and *Newsweek* reported that one of White's friends, a laboratory technician in Copenhagen, tipped him off. In her autobiography, Jorgensen accused an unnamed family "friend," from New York's Danish-American community, who supposedly earned $200 for the information shared. But at least one author, Dallas Denny, has speculated that Jorgensen, despite her expressed surprise, leaked her own story to the press. Historian Vern Bullough, who knew Jorgensen later in her life, confirms that she told the press herself. In any case, however he learned of the story, White allegedly let it sit for a week before he determined to publish it. Although Jorgensen's sex change was obviously sensational, it was not a foregone conclusion that it would qualify as news.[32]

After this initial report, though, other journalists jumped. They swarmed to Jorgensen's hospital room in Copenhagen and besieged her parents in the Bronx. They created Jorgensen's instant celebrity and then reported on its progress, announcing, for example, the offers she received from "night clubs for appearances" and the "bids for a lecture tour, jobs as a fashion model and photographic and magazine articles."[33] And they searched her past for clues to her condition. A neighbor remembered Christine as "a normal boy, but a little effeminate," and the Veterans Administration revealed she was "an 'entirely normal' male" when discharged from the army. After Jorgensen's release from the hospital, the journalists trotted in her wake, reporting on "an offer to star in a Hollywood" movie (titled *Mary Had a Little*), the premiere of the travel film she had made about Denmark, and her parents' visit to Copenhagen.[34]

At the beginning the journalists' key concern was whether Jorgensen looked and sounded like a woman. They commented incessantly on her public presentation, noting every feature of her face, figure, clothing, hair, voice, and gestures. For the most part, the reporters acknowledged Jorgensen's convincing and conventional femininity. They described "her long yellow hair curling on a pillow," her "smooth, low-pitched voice—without a trace of masculinity," and "a slight down on her upper lip, but no sign that she ever had used a razor."[35] They quoted her when she presented herself as a "natural woman" who had "normal womanly" interests. Her authenticity as a woman seemed to rely on her comments, her voice, and her appearance, in part perhaps because her sexual organs were neither visible nor mentionable. With her apparent feminine credentials established, the reporters confessed they were entranced by her beauty. One male reporter admitted, "I Could Have Gone for the He-She Girl," and another story proclaimed, "Beautiful Christine Dazzles Newsmen."[36]

Sexuality clearly served as part of the draw. In Denmark the journalists bombarded Jorgensen with personal questions: Did she hope to marry? Did she have a boyfriend? What did she wear to bed at night? Beneath the surface interest in Jorgensen's sex life lay a lurking concern with homosexuality. Jorgensen had, one article noted, "no vestige of male mannerism in either speech or gesture," and she also seemed "totally without the carefully cultivated mock-feminine gestures often associated with imbalance in sexual equilibrium."[37] She had, it seems, sailed smoothly into the womanly realm of glamour without going overboard into the camp world of gay male drag. But her persuasive femininity could not entirely dispel the hint of homosexuality. For reporters, Jorgensen was still a former man who expressed an interest in dating men, a feature that made her story racier than stories on Hollywood stars. In the first week of coverage, the reporters paid particular attention to Sergeant William Calhoun, a Texan who had dated Christine five months earlier when on furlough from England. Jorgensen insisted he was "just a good friend," but Calhoun admitted he had "kissed her more than once."[38] Perhaps because the stories inched toward taboo, a Catholic newspaper in Boston decried the spate of publicity.[39]

Although the reporters continued to clamor, the coverage took a dip at the end of December, when Jorgensen signed on with Hearst's *American Weekly,* a Sunday newspaper supplement, for the exclusive story of her life. In the midst of "heated bidding from numerous other publications," *American Weekly* agreed to pay her $25,000, plus royalties from syndication, and sent reporter Irmis Johnson to Copenhagen to turn her life history into a popular serial. As part of the deal, Jorgensen promised to refrain from speaking with other reporters, and *American Weekly* promised Jorgensen it would not "make changes of substance" to her story or attribute to her "statements and opinions" that she had "not actually . . . indicated."[40]

American Weekly orchestrated her trip home to coincide with publication of the first installment of its story. Jorgensen arrived at New York's Idlewild Airport on February 12, 1953, with camera shutters clicking and a crowd of around 350 spectators in wait. She wore, as reporters detailed, a brown nutria fur coat and hat, and she carried a mink cape over her arm. In a press room at the airport, she reinforced her womanly presentation. "I'm glad to be back," she told the reporters. "What American woman wouldn't be?"[41] She moved with a "hip-swinging walk" and revealed "a girlish blush beneath her pancake make-up." She held her cigarette in "slender, trembling fingers" and "perched daintily" on a desk while the press questioned her in the airport.[42]

To observe Jorgensen was to search for the markers that connoted feminine and masculine, to articulate consciously the criteria that cast the person-on-the-street as either a woman or a man. One reporter admitted: "Since I knew she had once been a man, perhaps I was looking for masculine traits." This reporter and others took note when Jorgensen teetered in her high-heeled pumps and when her voice sank to "contralto."[43] One mean-spirited story in the *New York Daily News* claimed that she "husked 'Hello' and tossed off a Bloody Mary like a guy," and then commented on the small size of her breasts. The report continued: "If you shut your eyes when she spoke you would have thought a man was talking. But her gestures with a cigaret were gracefully feminine. Her legs . . . were smooth and trim. However, the planes of her face were flat and hard . . . There was no hint of a beard."[44] Once again, the reporting brought the conventions of gender into sharp relief.

Meanwhile, in newspapers across the nation, *American Weekly* advertised its upcoming series, "The Story of My Life." It billed the series as "the story all America has been waiting for." Three days after her return, the first of five installments appeared, "the only authorized and complete account of the most dramatic transformation of modern times." With numerous photos, the series established visually that Jorgensen appeared feminine, respectable, and even glamorous. A few pictures of George allowed readers to contrast before with after, and multiple photos of Christine depicted a daughter with her parents, a young woman in middle-class domestic scenes, and most often a stylish woman out and about in tailored suits, gowns, or furs. Yet, illustrations aside, the series did not dwell on appearances. Rather, the first-person confessional format personalized the story and gave Jorgensen a chance to convey her own voice. She related her life history with an emphasis on her lonely struggles and the saving grace of science. She invited readers to sympathize with her and thereby moved herself beyond the realm of tabloid spectacle. The tale of despair and hope gave her story emotional appeal and reworked a formula already familiar to readers of popular magazines. It universalized her unique history, as *American Weekly* acknowledged, "as the courageous fight of a desperately unhappy person with the fortitude to overcome a seemingly hopeless obstacle."[45]

To explain her sex change, Jorgensen rooted her problem in biology.

She did not adopt the metaphor, common by the 1960s, of a woman "trapped" in a male body.[46] Instead she referred to herself as "lost between the sexes," a phrase that implied a physical condition as much as a psychological one. As in her letter to her parents, she presented her problem as a hormonal disturbance or a "glandular imbalance" that led her to change from "an apparent man to the woman I felt sure Nature had intended." Jorgensen portrayed her doctors as true scientists and spiritual guides, who had offered her medical treatment when she needed it. Her endocrinologist, Christian Hamburger, served as the authority who legitimated her story by cloaking it in the language of science and removing it from the realm of sex. He had reassured her that she was not, as she had worried, a homosexual, but rather had a "condition called transvestism," which was "deep-rooted in all the cells of [her] body." This "wise and gentle man . . . had given [her] hope" and started her on the course of treatment that transformed her body.[47]

In her book-length autobiography, published more than a decade later, Jorgensen remembered the *American Weekly* series as "a somewhat superficial" but "honest, straightforward account." Superficial or not, it recast Jorgensen's story in a way that attracted readers. During the five weeks the series ran, the magazine's distributors reported the greatest circulation boost in memory. Jorgensen recalled later that the series "was translated into fourteen languages" and distributed in seventy nations. More generally, in late 1952 and 1953 the interest in Jorgensen far exceeded that in any previous reporting on sex change. Later the *New York Daily News* announced that the Jorgensen story had been its number-one story of 1953, outpacing in circulation the number-two story on the execution of atomic spy Julius Rosenberg and his wife, Ethel.[48]

$\mathcal{W}$hy did the public show such interest in Jorgensen? The press, we can safely surmise, actively generated public interest in order to sell newspapers and magazines. The reporters saw quickly that Jorgensen's conventional beauty made her a prime candidate for female celebrity status, and they used her instant fame to showcase her as a star. Moreover, Jorgensen demonstrated an affinity for the media that kept her in the public eye. She reinforced her popularity by adopting a particular feminine style that played on the postwar cult of glamour, especially for "blonde bombshells." She also displayed an eye for fashion, an ear for the quotable phrase, and a willingness to engage in repartee with journalists eager for a story. But surely more was at work.

Jorgensen caught the public imagination in part because she embodied tensions central to the postwar culture. Her story, as she told it in *American Weekly,* offered the public an unusual twist on a tried-and-true tale of individual striving, success, and upward mobility. This tale had special resonance in the postwar years. In the popular discourse of the Cold War, a mythic version of American individualism stood in contrast to an equally mythic version of conformist imperatives in "totalitarian" societies.[49] In the story she told, Jorgensen defied the demands that she conform to the social norms of masculinity and embarked instead on a lonely personal quest—"a courageous struggle"—for self-transformation.[50] In the Cold War culture, she could represent an endangered species of American liberalism, the individual spirit that refused to succumb to the strictures of an increasingly homogenized society. But from a more conservative angle of vision, she could also represent a foolish libertarian strain that threatened social order by its obtuse failure to respect the fundamental laws of nature. Jorgensen's story thus straddled the postwar debates over the impact of an individualist ethos.

In the atomic era, Jorgensen's surgery also posed the question of whether science could and should triumph over nature. The *American Weekly* series projected an optimistic postwar image in which science overleapt natural bounds. Jorgensen had refused, as she explained it, to give up her dream to alter her sex. "Impossible!" she wrote. "That word was a challenge to me. How did anyone dare say it in the Atomic Age?"[51] At the same time, though, her story, like that of the atom bomb, could conjure a gloomier Frankensteinian vision, in which scientists tampered with nature and unforeseen chaos followed. The unresolved tension between the twin potential for progress and disaster seemed to encapsulate the postwar hopes and fears about the possibilities of science.

Most of all, Jorgensen captured some of the postwar concerns about gender. During World War II women had temporarily taken on jobs and responsibilities traditionally held by men. And psychiatrists for the armed forces had worried publicly about what they saw as deficient masculinity in surprising numbers of male recruits. In the postwar era the anxieties surrounding shifting gender roles broke into overt cultural contests, with conservatives nostalgically invoking a golden age when women were women and men were men. Popular magazines began to describe a "crisis in masculinity," noted the growing number of women in the labor force, and fretted over the fragility of "sex roles."[52] In this context, the press reports on Jorgensen, with their endless comments on her appearance, enabled a public reinscription of what counted as masculine and feminine. But the story itself, in which an "ex-GI" became a "blonde beauty," inevitably undermined the attempt to restabilize gender through stereotype. Jorgensen posed, more fundamentally, the questions of how to define a woman and how to define a man. The coverage could provoke anxiety about the collapse of the seemingly natural categories of male and female, and it could also incite fantasies of crossing the boundary that divided women from men. Like the female impersonation shows that increased in popularity after World War II, Jorgensen provided convincing evidence of how a person might move from a male persona on one day to a female one on another. In the female impersonation shows, gendered appearance and behavior sprang from performance rather than from biological sex. What did Jorgensen represent?[53]

As homosexual subcultures became increasingly visible in the postwar years and as homophobic reaction intensified, Jorgensen also brought the issue of sexuality into the mainstream news, especially with her confession of her preoperative longings for men. On the one hand, she reinforced the stigma attached to homosexuality when she repeatedly stated that she had not wanted to live as a homosexual man. On the other hand, she undermined the common aspersions when she insisted in *American Weekly* that her youthful love for a man "was something fine and deep and would have been restful had I been in a position to give and accept in the eyes of society." She confounded the category of homosexuality as she attempted to establish a depathologized version of crossgender identification (in which she loved a man because she knew she was a heterosexual woman) and distinguish it from a still-pathologized version of same-sex desire.[54] Her drastic move, involving dangerous surgery, had transformed her into a heterosexual woman, but it had also forced the question of what counted as "normal." Was the very same person more publicly acceptable as a heterosexual woman than she had been when living as a feminine man attracted to men?

In sum, Jorgensen's story linked sensation, celebrity, and glamour with unresolved tensions concerning individualism, science, gender, and sexuality. With this equation, the press coverage attracted readers and then took on a self-perpetuating quality. Journalists jostled one another to win the race for the latest scoop, and each story raised new questions that readers might want answered in the next.

*A*s soon as the Jorgensen story broke, reporters consulted American doctors, most of whom assumed that she was a pseudo-hermaphrodite (with masculine genitals but female organs inside). In an Associated Press story, "Thousands Do Not Know True Sex," one reporter went to the American Medical Association convention and interviewed doctors who immediately associated Jorgensen with such intersexed conditions, which were at this time routinely treated with surgery, sometimes in infancy and sometimes in adulthood. Doctors attempted to contain the confusion surrounding Jorgensen by explaining her away in familiar terms. Another report, for example, noted that doctors "were inclined to minimize the spectacular nature of Christine's switch." One such doctor counted her as a pseudohermaphrodite and noted ten such cases currently undergoing treatment in New York's Presbyterian Hospital. Dr. Elmer Hess, a urologist from Erie, Pennsylvania, told, as one headline stated, of "Hundreds of Boy-Girl Operations." Similar reports rolled in from doctors in California, Maryland, Texas, and Alabama who claimed to have performed operations like Jorgensen's, cases in which "the actual sex had been disguised and was simply released." *Time* magazine soon assessed the commentary as the "expert opinion" of doctors who "pooh-poohed the story as anything new . . . far from a medical rarity . . . [with] similar cases in hospitals all over the U.S. right now."[55]

Nonetheless, from the beginning a few journalists had an inkling that the Jorgensen story might be different. In the first week of publicity, G. B. Lal, the science editor of *American Weekly,* suggested that perhaps Jorgensen "was physically speaking, adequately a male, yet somehow felt the urge to be a woman." Such a situation "would call for drastic alterations—such as no doctor would perform in this country." Lal then referred to Dr. Harry Benjamin and cases of "transvestism." But even this report immediately retreated to a discussion of intersex. "We may assume," Lal wrote, "still without knowing the facts, that Jorgensen was a case of sex confusion—what is known as pseudohermaphroditism, in which one's inborn real sex is hidden."[56]

As in earlier cases, the muddled reporting attracted transgendered readers who wondered about the journalists' claims. Early in December, shortly after the story broke, Louise Lawrence, a fulltime male-to-female crossdresser who lived in San Francisco, wrote Harry Benjamin: "This case, I think, has received more publicity even than Barbara's [Barbara Richards'] ten years ago." She could not, though, "make any concrete decision regarding it because there have actually been no absolute facts given." Still, she wondered why Jorgensen would have traveled to Denmark for "a case of hermaphroditism" that "could be handled in this country very easily . . . from the papers, it seems that such cases are being handled all over the country." In January another male-to-female wrote directly to Jorgensen for clarification: "Were you completely a male physically before your conversion without female organs? Do you think Dr. Christian Hamburger could convert me?" Two months later, a female-to-male wrote: "I have the feelings and emotions of a man . . . Does there have to be anything physically wrong in order to be transformed?"[57]

As the publicity continued, the stories took a new tack. By the time Jorgensen returned from Denmark, there were rumors "that the whole case was a hoax." Shortly before her return, the gossip columnist Walter Winchell claimed to have a "reporter's scoop of the year." On his radio show he announced that "she is a he . . . a few operations were performed . . . but he is a normal male physically . . . he likes to wear feminine clothing . . . Christine is still George, a guy . . . a man with a deep and tragic problem." Soon afterward the *American Weekly* series cast more doubt on the nature of Jorgensen's condition. The trouble stemmed in part from the use of the term *transvestism* to describe Jorgensen's desire to change sex. In the European context, the term had a relatively broad meaning and referred to crossgender identification as well as crossdressing. In the tradition of Hirschfeld, Christian Hamburger, Jorgensen's doctor, suspected that "transvestism," as he defined it in *American Weekly* and elsewhere, had a somatic basis and suspected that "some cases," including Jorgensen's, represented a form of intersexuality. But in the American context of the 1950s, "transvestism" usually meant crossdressing, generally understood as a psychological aberration and often classified as a "perversion," not a physiological condition. Then as now, the term *intersex* referred to hermaphrodites and pseudohermaphrodites. As Jorgensen later related it, the *American Weekly* series, with its use of the word *transvestism*, "created a gross misconception in the minds of many readers." To Jorgensen, it seemed to translate her honest and unshakable sense of herself as a woman into an inauthentic version of female impersonation.[58] For some reporters and readers, though, the term *transvestism* provided the entering wedge to challenge the earlier reports that had classified and contained her as an intersexed woman.

In mid-February one headline asked, "Is Christine Really a Man after All?," and a couple of days later another report quoted one of Jorgensen's surgeons, Erling Dahl-Iversen, denying he had ever called Jorgensen "100 per cent woman."[59] At the same time, Random House backed away from its plans to publish Jorgensen's autobiography as a book, partly, as one radio broadcast claimed, because "the atmosphere of the whole thing was just a little weentzy bit shady . . . no American doctor had said exactly what had occurred."[60] As if in response, the American Medical Association announced in March that it would study the Jorgensen case and requested information from Jorgensen's doctors in Denmark. A number of American doctors had questioned whether "it actually is possible for a man to be changed into a woman." Meanwhile, in Copenhagen Jorgensen's doctors gave a report on the case at a symposium. As the newspaper accounts acknowledged, the

Danish doctors confirmed that Jorgensen was "neither hermaphroditic nor pseudo-hermaphroditic." She had "no vestiges of female organs or female reproductive glands."[61]

Following these leads, the *New York Post* proclaimed at the beginning of April that Jorgensen's sex change was a sham. It ran a six-part series, reprinted in other cities, an alleged exposé, "The Truth about 'Christine' Jorgensen." The opening sentence announced: "'Christine' Jorgensen is a woman in name only"; the quotation marks around Christine suggested that the name, too, was inauthentic. On the basis of interviews with the Danish doctors, *Post* reporter Alvin Davis claimed that Jorgensen had been "physically . . . a normal male" before her treatment, and was now a castrated male, with no added female organs. Davis classified Jorgensen as a transvestite, hinted at homosexuality, and referred to her with male pronouns. He contrasted the outlook of American doctors, who expressed outrage at what they saw as mutilating surgery, with that of the Danish doctors who had advocated the operations.[62]

In the American media, an intersexed person had a legitimate claim to female status, but a male "transvestite," even surgically and hormonally altered, seemingly did not. In the wake of the exposé *Time* magazine declared, "Jorgensen was no girl at all, only an altered male," and *Newsweek* soon followed suit. Jorgensen's doctors in Denmark seemed to confirm these assertions in an article published in May in the *Journal of the American Medical Association,* in which they again described Jorgensen's case as one of "genuine transvestism." Pulp magazine sensationalism followed. *Modern Romances,* for example, ran a story titled "Christine Jorgensen: Is She *Still* a Man?" And *Cavalier,* a magazine for men, reprinted the *Post* exposé under the title, announced on the magazine's cover, "'Christine' Jorgensen is NOT a Woman."[63]

The news reports upset Jorgensen. She had not misrepresented herself as intersexed, but she had also not ruled it out entirely. She clearly preferred organic explanations that presented her problem as a biological disorder, which she usually described as hormonal imbalance. She echoed her Danish doctors, who, following Hirschfeld and others, tended to see transvestism not as psychopathology but as a condition with a physiological cause. The biological emphasis removed her treatment from the grip of psychoanalysts or psychologists and justified surgical intervention. It also helped her cleanse her crossgender identification of the taint of sin or weakness, separated it from "perversion," and underscored how profoundly she felt the need for surgery. Jorgensen bridled at the insinuation that she "had perpetrated a hoax" when calling herself a woman, and she resented the disrespectful tone and "pseudo-scientific commentary" of some of the news stories.[64]

Although the news reports annoyed Jorgensen, they alerted other readers that transformative surgery might take place without claim to an intersexed condition. Louise Lawrence, the San Francisco crossdresser, for example, appreciated the *New York Post* exposé. "I can see how it would disturb [Jorgensen]," she wrote, "but I still think it is the fairest explanation yet published."[65] A European version of sex change, as treatment for "transvestites," had finally hit the American press.

$\mathcal{S}$trangely enough, the news stories, including the hostile ones, did little to damage Jorgensen's popularity.[66] She maintained and even enhanced her public appeal precisely because she remained a controversial figure. Was she a woman, or wasn't she? At the very least, Jorgensen forced a double take. With each new report, she seemed to complicate further the assumptions by which observers commonly categorized women and men. Jorgensen refused to portray herself as either a "freak" or a "pervert," even though others sometimes still attempted to place her in one category or both. She insisted on her place in the mainstream, repeating the popular formula that cast her as an ordinary person who had taken extraordinary risks to follow her own dreams. In this context, the press continued to pass along the details of her everyday life to a public whose curiosity had not yet been allayed.

Jorgensen used the attention to launch a career that kept her in the news and heightened her claim to fame. Soon after her return to New York, Jorgensen began to make public appearances, all duly reported in the press. She attended the ball of the Scandinavian Societies of Greater New York, where she won an award as "Woman of the Year," and she served as a judge at the annual Miss Brooklyn beauty contest. She gave a short speech at Madison Square Garden at a charity benefit hosted by Walter Winchell, and she made an appearance on the television show of dance king Arthur Murray.[67] At the end of April 1953 she acquired a manager, Charles Yates, who had represented Bob Hope, to promote her career. The money from the *American Weekly* series had paid for constructing a new house on Long Island, which she eventually shared with her parents. With little money left and no job in sight, she began to reassess her prospects. Yates pushed her to go on the stage. In the spring, shortly after the *New York Post* published its exposé, she agreed to an engagement in Los Angeles to show the travel film she had shot in Denmark. In early May she flew with her mother to Los Angeles, where a crowd of "more than 2000" met her at the airport.[68] For her weeklong appearance at the Orpheum Theater, Jorgensen allegedly earned $12,500. Although her audiences applauded and wrote her congratulatory letters, the reviewers pronounced the show a bust. One critic called her "a freak attraction" and wrote dryly that the travel film was "not likely to set the show world on fire."[69] But neither the exposés in the newspapers nor the flop on the stage diminished the press attention or the public interest.

Under the guidance of her manager, she used the media to publicize a new show, a nightclub act, which opened at the Copa Club in Pittsburgh in August 1953. For the twenty-five-minute performance, Jorgensen joined with veteran vaudevillian Myles Bell. She appeared in glamorous evening gowns, sang a few show tunes, and told a handful of jokes. The act opened with "Getting to Know You," and after some light patter and another song it took a more serious turn. Bell asked her why she had gone to Denmark, and she tried to explain in a way that would win the sympathies of her audience. She framed her story once again as a lonely struggle, and in the middle of her account she drew on American liberal ideals to assert her right to live as she chose. In the brief monologue she said:

One of the loneliest things . . . is to be born different . . . But many years ago, some very wise men said that every person is born with certain rights, these rights are "Life, liberty and the pursuit of happiness." Well, I didn't have much of a life, because all of my early years were spent in a state of personal confusion and because of social barriers and well—mainly because I was very mixed up. So I decided to go out in pursuit of my happiness . . . nobody knew I was going and no one particularly cared.

She had, she said, overcome "obstacles" with the help of her friends and doctors, and then she launched into another song, "You'll Never Walk Alone."[70] The song's opening line, "When you walk through the storm hold your head up high," conveyed to the audience a sense of her strength and pride. The monologue and the song together placed her both as a lone individual with the right to pursue her own happiness and as a member of a community who would encourage others who had suffered as she had. The political statement asserted a liberal individualism and then tempered it with a sense of solidarity with other troubled souls.[71]

Jorgensen had no real talent for singing or dancing, as she herself admitted, but under careful tutelage she had learned enough to put on a winning show. *Variety* commented: "look for Christine to be more than a once around sensation. The girl has an act."[72] As she took her show on the road, she usually elicited the kind of response she had hoped for. When she performed on Broadway, a reviewer wrote: "for a person . . . suddenly plucked out of obscurity she acquits herself admirably . . . [She] has fine stage presence, her timing is surprisingly good." As before, a handful of critics treated her act as a circus or drag show. In New York, Lee Mortimer of the *Daily Mirror* said the show was "as interesting and educational as a six-legged calf, a Hottentot, or other such carnival midway attractions," and then likened her act to those at the best-known clubs for female impersonation. Jorgensen challenged her audiences to redefine the boundaries of womanhood, and some audience members refused. Mortimer's review reminded the public that it could, if it chose, cast Jorgensen as a "freak" and a "pervert" instead of a woman. But audiences seem to have followed Jorgensen's lead and came away convinced that she was a woman and a star. "She looked radiant," one admiring audience member recalled.

"[Her] voice and stage presence were far better than reported. It was an enjoyable evening by a lady who handled herself well."[73]

*A*fter the exposés of the spring, which had established that she was not intersexed, and her success on the stage, which had confirmed her popular appeal, the press shifted from interviews with doctors and descriptions of her appearance to a heightened concern with issues of sexuality. In September in Washington, D.C., reporters quoted Roy Blick, an inspector from "the Police Morals Division," who threatened to keep Jorgensen from using women's restrooms. In November the newspapers announced her engagement to Patrick Flanigan, a portrait painter, whom she never attempted to marry. And in early 1954 the press reported that the city of Boston had banned her show, which was not particularly risqué. Although Jorgensen tried to hide it, reporters found out about her surgery in New Jersey in the spring of 1954, in which she had a vagina constructed from skin grafts taken from her thighs.[74]

The mainstream press generally recounted her doings in fairly straightforward reporting, but trashy gossip and girlie magazines maintained the titillating edge by printing more dubious stories that involved sex. *Pose* published "The Men in Christine's Life," and *Whisper* printed a peep show, "Christine Jorgensen thru a Keyhole," in which the photos combined "professional models' bodies," semiclad, "with Christine's head." *Confidential,* a gossip rag, presented Jorgensen's "hush-hush romance" with Vanderbilt heir Peter Howard, and later included a tell-all story, "Jimmy Donahue's Private Peek," which related how Jorgensen allegedly stripped for "Woolworth scion" Donahue, a wealthy "scamp" who frequented "Manhattan's . . . swish bars." (Jorgensen later admitted only that she had spent "several pleasant evenings" with Peter Howard and had had a drink in Jimmy Donahue's apartment.) Another pulp magazine published an undeniably phony story, replete with doctored photos, announcing Jorgensen's decision to revert to male. One of the photos showed Jorgensen boarding a plane to return "to Sweden." The caption claimed to quote her saying: "I hope the doctors saved all the pieces."[75]

The caption typified the genre of "Christine" jokes that circulated into the 1960s. The jokes printed in the press included corny comments about "chris-crosses" or dull barbs about her receding hairline, but mostly they toyed nervously with the indeterminacy of her sex, with the uncomfortable recognition that commonplace definitions of male and female no longer seemed to work. "Christine's sister will have a baby," one joke opened. "Does that make [her] an aunt, an uncle or an ankle?" Along the same lines, enlisted soldiers in the demilitarized zone of Korea selected Jorgensen as "Miss Neutral Zone of 1953." "Christine was a wonderful looking couple," another quip went, "and . . . she should be very happy together." For a while the press reported on the "Christine" jokes that prominent comedians seemed unable to resist. When asked whether he planned to return to his homeland, Denmark, comedian Victor Borge, for example, said, "No . . . I might come back as Hildegarde." The jokes were so ubiquitous that one columnist noted that Myles Bell, Jorgensen's partner in her nightclub act, was "the only comedian in the world who doesn't tell Christine jokes."[76]

While the newspapers printed the less risqué jokes, bluer versions circulated orally. Some of these jokes have survived in the private files of comedian Whitey Roberts, who compiled extensive lists of jokes during the 1950s and 1960s. Among the dozens of jokes on Jorgensen and sex change in Denmark, the lewder ones dwelled primarily on her surgery, especially on the amputation of her penis. In one joke, for example, Jorgensen eyes her new husband and says, "I *threw* away more than that." In another, her theme song is "My Johnnie Lies over the Ocean." Vaginas also served as a source of humor. "Christine's story is a live theatrical production," went one joke. "Her whole life began with her opening." In another in the same vein, a book titled "After the Danish Sex Clinic" is authored by Iva Newhole. The privately circulated jokes mentioned what the press could not. They focused on the genitals, the hidden site of sex change, and revealed the anxious sexual undertow of Jorgensen's celebrity.[77]

As entrepreneurs soon discovered, Jorgensen had acquired enough currency that her name and her story promised profit, especially when connected with sexuality. In Memphis an impersonator tried to cash in on Jorgensen's fame. In 1953 officials at the Mid-South Fair banned "a blowsy redhead" who performed in the "House of Oddities," claiming to be Christine. The performer "delivered an unscientific and vulgar recitation of her sex aspirations and the present condition of her anatomy" and then invited viewers, for an extra fifty cents, to an inner tent for "an intimate display."[78] As a gag, someone else packaged "Cristeen," a chocolate bar "without peanuts," sold under the label of a company called HErSHE. In a newspaper advertisement a baldness specialist caught his readers' attention with the headline "Flash! Another Man to Be Feminized into Danish Pastry!" The ad then proclaimed: "Even a Danish doctor can't solve your hair and scalp problems. He hasn't the know-how. I have."[79]

Jorgensen weathered it all with dignity and grace. Although she knew the media interest stemmed largely from prurience, she refused to present herself as a dirty joke, and she also refused, as she put it later, "to put my tail between my legs and go and hide."[80] She charmed the reporters who treated her well, and she cut off the ones who questioned her rudely. Jorgensen tried to craft an urbane image and assert a sense of humor that did not rely primarily on sexual innuendo. In 1954, for example, she wrote a new song, "It's a Change," for her act. The song played on her own status as "a change," acknowledged her difference, and invited her audiences to accept change, and the seemingly strange, as part of modern times. One version of the song began:

> Every hour—every day—we encounter something new
> Electric this—atomic that—a modern point of view
> Now anything can happen—and we shouldn't think it
> strange
> If oysters smoke cigars—or lobsters drive imported cars
> For we live in a time of change.[81]

The song was designed to elicit laughs but not at her expense. It allowed her to associate change with progress, to portray it as modern and entertaining, and to place herself at its vanguard.

*I*n general, Jorgensen crafted her image carefully. She understood that the heightened public scrutiny meant that she operated under different rules from others. "Unlike other women," she said later, "I had to become super-female. I couldn't have one single masculine trait."[82] But within the constraints of her unusual situation, Jorgensen made choices about her public presentation. Femininity came in many guises. Among the styles of femininity available to celebrities, Jorgensen avoided the "sex kitten" image and strove instead for a sharp, sophisticated rendition, which won her comparisons to such Hollywood stars as Eve Arden, Joan Crawford, and Lauren Bacall. She placed herself within the conventions of mainstream femininity, but she did not succumb entirely to all the stereotypes of gender. She presented herself as a woman's woman, who had "many more women as friends than men." She described women as strong and smart and came across as a career woman who did not defer to men. Given the era, neither her style nor her views on women were particularly conservative. In a television interview with Mike Wallace, she spoke of her plans to marry. Conforming to convention, she said she did not think a woman should support her husband financially, but she also would not say that she planned to give up her nightclub act and retreat to domesticity.[83] She presented herself as a cosmopolitan woman who had a life of her own.

Jorgensen understood that her public success had a larger meaning. The autobiographical series in the *American Weekly* had portrayed her as "a pioneer with a message." She wanted medical experts to help others like her, and she wished for the "days of ridicule and emotional torture" to end. But she was neither a social critic who flouted bourgeois convention nor a radical who preferred a place on the fringes of society. She repeatedly posed her longings as conventional and respectable. In an interview conducted in 1957 she said: "We all . . . want to be a part of the group . . . each individual's fight for survival is to be wanted, to be needed, to be part of the mass, and when an individual's segregated out of that . . . it . . . leaves them standing alone."[84] In this way she repudiated an unbridled individualism and spoke to a longing for acceptance and approval, which, she hoped, struck a deeper chord than the jokes about her genitals or the stories about her sex life.

The appropriate public image could establish Jorgensen as a woman, boost her career, and make her a respectable model of sex change. But the public presentation did not necessarily reveal the private person. In the interview with Mike Wallace, she drew a clear distinction between what she saw as the public image and what she was saw as the inner self. "Every human being," she said, "is in a form an exhibition of themselves. We have a physical being which we are constantly showing . . . Inside I believe there is another person. There is the thing which makes you you and me me and each person themselves." Her surgery had helped her to bring a crucial piece of herself—her femininity—to the fore. It did not, though, demolish her sense of a public/private distinction. Jorgensen's friend, the actress Beatrice Lillie, had warned her, "Don't ever tell anyone everything about yourself," and Jorgensen had followed her advice. In a later interview she said she had "always separated very strongly my private life from my theatrical life."[85] In public, she remained on guard.

Jorgensen tried, in particular, to keep her sex life hidden. When the press pried, she sidestepped questions about the men she dated, and she avoided any mention of sexual acts. She asked Sergeant William Calhoun, who had dated her in Denmark, to keep their story private. (Later he wrote to inquire whether "my being quite [sic] is worth . . . anything to you." He claimed the question was "not blackmail in any form," but clearly he hoped for money.)[86] After her return to New York she lived with her parents, which helped situate her publicly more as a dutiful daughter than as a sexually active woman. The attempts to sanitize her image continued into the 1960s. In her autobiography, published in 1967, she portrayed herself as prudish. But she discussed her sex life with her friends. According to friends and acquaintances, her vagina was inadequate—from one report, too short—for sexual intercourse. (According to one account she had reconstructive surgery at Johns Hopkins University Hospital in the late 1960s and again in Oklahoma City in 1980.) But despite the problems with her surgery, she had sexual relations with men from the 1950s on, including, according to one source, actor Lawrence Tierney.[87] Later in her life she renounced the pose of reticence and claimed to be writing a second autobiographical book that told what the first had hidden. "I still enjoy sex," she claimed, "but I'm not a person who has to have it twice a week—I think sex is one of the most overrated things in the world." In another interview she said, "I think people devote too much time to it."[88] Nonetheless, neither in the 1950s nor after did she lead the kind of celibate life she sometimes tried to project.

The more personal side of Jorgensen's life rarely made it into the press. She generally expressed her emotions privately. As in her youth, she still had moments of melancholy. She was, her manager Charles Yates told her, "the type that gets plagued with moods." She also had moments of ire. She vented her anger at the journalists who ridiculed her, at "the heartbreak and smut . . . I had to receive at the hands of the press." (In a letter to Alfred Kinsey she called Walter Winchell a "viper.")[89] Nonetheless, Jorgensen enjoyed the limelight and worked assiduously to maintain her public presence. When her bookings started to flag, she developed new nightclub acts, gave interviews and public lectures, and made minor forays into "legitimate" theater. In 1959 her attempt to secure a marriage license generated another flurry of attention. "Let's face it," Mike Wallace told her, "you have not exactly yourself thrown cold water on publicity."[90]

*W*hile Jorgensen courted fame, the popular culture exploded with new stories on sex change. Reporters produced a flood of sensational copy on sex-change operations, primarily male-to-female. Each new story confirmed that Jorgensen was not alone, that a number of other people hoped to change their sex. The stories came from around the world, but those from the United States and Britain attracted the most attention from the American press. Jorgensen eventually moved from current event to yesterday's news, but as other stories of sex change appeared and reappeared, the media reminded the public that manhood, womanhood, and the boundaries between them were neither as obvious nor as impermeable as they once had seemed.

By 1954 the press had more clearly distinguished transsexuals from people with intersexed conditions, and the newspapers and magazines only occasionally associated the desire to change sex with ambiguous genitals or reproductive organs. But sex change was still tightly linked in various ways with issues of sexuality. In the new accounts of male-to-female sex change, the press struggled with whether or how to distinguish a man who wanted to change sex from a feminine gay man. The distinction drawn today between gender identity (one's sense of oneself as a woman or man or both or neither) and sexual identity (one's sense of oneself as homosexual, bisexual, heterosexual, or some other form of erotic being) was rarely made in the popular press. As much as Jorgensen and some other male-to-female transsexuals tried to distance themselves from homosexuality, and from sexuality in general, they could not in the 1950s escape the associations that equated their femininity when living as men with homosexuality and invested their change of sex with erotic implications. And if they wanted public attention, which a few of them did, then portraying themselves as sexy could attract reporters.

In February 1954 the press discovered Charlotte McLeod, a twenty-eight-year-old native of Tennessee, who had, as a *Time* magazine headline put it, followed "In Christine's Footsteps." Indeed, her life story, as it appeared in the press, echoed the stories on Jorgensen. As Charles McLeod, she grew up "a sensitive boy, quiet and lonely, with a penchant for dressing up in women's clothing." Like Jorgensen, she served in the army briefly after World War II, saw herself as an unhappy misfit, and consulted doctors about her "effeminate" body. Eventually she learned from the press about the possibilities of medical treatment in Denmark.[91] She arrived in Copenhagen in 1953 and discovered that a new law prevented Danish doctors from operating on foreigners. In desperation, McLeod found a renegade doctor whom she described as a drug addict with "an outlaw practice."[92] The doctor castrated her in a four-hour operation performed at night on a kitchen table. After two weeks of bleeding and infection, she got herself to a hospital, and because of her emergency condition the doctors agreed to complete the surgery. They removed her penis and followed up with hormone treatments.

In April 1954, upon McLeod's return to New York, reporters surrounded her. At the Hotel Statler she got into a scuffle with aggressive photographers, took a swing with her umbrella, and landed on the ground. She ended up in the police station with charges, soon dropped, of assault. Not surprisingly, the story, with photos, made the news. In the months that followed McLeod granted a few interviews and appeared in a number of stories that recounted her life history and reported her visit with her father in Tennessee, her breast enlargement surgery, her plans for a nightclub act, and her jobs as a secretary and in a New York beauty parlor.[93]

Like Jorgensen, McLeod tried to explain her condition as physical and to separate it from homosexuality. "I was afflicted from birth," she said, "with a body so effeminate, hair so curly, hands so soft, and a voice so high-pitched that I was never able to do a man's work or take a man's place in society." On the advice of her doctors, she said, she had tried for a while to live "among homosexuals" in New Orleans. She felt, as she described it to reporters, "a great sympathy," but they also "disgusted" her, and she knew she "wasn't one of them."[94] She placed herself within a small subset of feminine men who needed medical intervention. For 95 percent of the "victims of misdirected sex," she called for mental treatment; for the other 5 percent, "surgical procedures."[95]

In the midst of the coverage on McLeod, in March 1954, the newspapers discovered Roberta Cowell, a Briton who had undergone sex change, starting with hormones in the late 1940s. What struck reporters most was that Cowell did not have the same feminine past as Jorgensen and McLeod. As the newspapers noted repeatedly, Cowell had been a "virile, dashing former fighter pilot," a race-car driver, and a rugby player. She had served in the Royal Air Force during World War II and spent six months as a prisoner of war after the Germans downed her plane. Even more strikingly, Cowell had married and fathered two children. One report stated, "British doctors said . . . Cowell's case was unprecedented . . . they knew of no other sex change involving a person who had previously been a parent." With these multiple markers of a masculine and heterosexual past, Cowell's transformation into a woman seemed especially confusing and less tainted by association with taboo sexuality. Her early life did not fit the stereotypes of "effeminate" gay men, and her story suggested, as Jorgensen and McLeod insisted, that the desire to change sex could not be collapsed into familiar categories of sexual variance.[96]

Two months later, though, in May 1954, other reports revived the links between the desire to change sex and homosexuality. The American press, especially on the West Coast, turned its attention to San Francisco multimillionaire John Cabell Breckinridge, heir to the Comstock lode fortune. Breckinridge, fifty years old, announced that he, too, planned to undergo sex-change surgery. Like Cowell, Breckinridge had a history that included marriage and fatherhood. But Breckinridge, known as "Bunny," was flamingly gay and wildly eccentric. He easily fitted and happily flaunted every stereotype of a "fairy." He held a press conference at his luxury apartment, decorated with "pale blue frills and flounces" and "pink and yellow bunnies nestle[d] in . . . the bed." He told reporters that he already had suitors who wanted to marry him after the surgical transformation. A week and a half later Breckinridge entertained the press again, this time in Los Angeles, where he had come, he said, to discuss starring in a film, *Magic Moment,* about a man who changed to a woman. Reporters met him at the airport and noted his "women's shoes," "cloying perfume," "laquered [*sic*] fingernails," and face powder. After the initial publicity Breckinridge faded temporarily from the public scene, but in May 1955 he reappeared. The magazine *Private Lives* featured him in an article, titled the "The She-He Millionaire," illustrated with photos of Bunny dressed in men's clothes but with arched eyebrows, long fingernails, pinkie rings, and other feminine accoutrements. Around the same time, the "odd millionaire who wants to be a woman" made the news when police arrested him in a "routine sweep" of a San Francisco gay bar. If Cowell's story had pushed reporters to separate the desire for sex change from homosexuality, then Breckinridge, who never actually underwent surgery, reconnected the two.[97]

After the initial stories on Breckinridge dwindled, Tamara Rees, born in 1924, added to the confusion. In 1953 Rees had begun taking hormones in Los Angeles and started to live as a woman. Later that year she had traveled to Holland, where she underwent genital surgery in 1954. When her ship arrived in New York, reporters surged to her cabin door.[98] As in the stories on Roberta Cowell, the press homed in on her masculine past, including her wartime career as a wounded and decorated paratrooper and her status as father of two. But Rees tried to dissociate herself from any masculine image. For photographers she struck domestic poses, running a vacuum cleaner and drying dishes.[99] She claimed she had not fathered her ex-wife's children, and she downplayed her warrior image. Her "only motivation," she said, for joining the paratroopers "was my feeling that in joining an outfit noted for its rugged training and manliness, that I would be more generally accepted by society and would thus remove the ridicule and accusations of homo-sexualism." But because of her "mannerism and physical bearing," the ridicule had continued.[100] Like Jorgensen and McLeod, she hoped to convince the public of her lifelong femininity while also separating herself from homosexuality.

But unlike Jorgensen and McLeod, Rees did not shy away from public presentations that emphasized her sexuality. She asserted herself as a heterosexual woman, and she hoped to profit from her allure. Within a few months she began to perform in burlesque clubs. Her act began with a lecture in which she pleaded for tolerance and followed with a striptease in which she peeled to pasties. A 1955 advertisement for her show announced "From GI Paratrooper to Burlesque QUEEN! Plus Bevy of Dancing Girls!" and promised a "lobby display" on her life story.[101] In July 1955 Rees upped the publicity when she married James E. Courtland III, a makeup artist and hairdresser whom she identified as her business manager. One magazine called the wedding "history's first transvestite marriage." (The marrying minister, of the First Methodist Church of Reno, claimed he did not know Rees had changed sex, and the unflappable county clerk, unwilling to serve as a gatekeeper, pronounced: "As long as they come in here with a dress on, they're women.") With her strip show and her marriage, Rees tried to keep herself in the public eye as a heterosexually active woman.[102] But someone who had lived as a feminine man was still too closely associated with homosexual desire for Rees or others to be able to sever the link entirely, even after surgery had altered her body. Furthermore, like Bunny Breckinridge, some of the people who asked for sex change did identify as gay.

These connections were drawn again in 1956 when various newspapers reported that Ray Bourbon, a gay female impersonator, had undergone sex-change surgery in Juarez, Mexico. Bourbon had performed with Mae West on Broadway in the 1940s and by the mid-1950s had won a following for his bawdy record albums, on which he sang such gay-themed spoofs as "Queen of the YMCA" and "I Must Have a Greek."[103] After the news reports of the surgery, advertisements for Bourbon's show in Los Angeles included "a photostatic copy of Miss Bourbon's medical report," signed by Dr. Emerik Szekely and asserting, in Spanish, that Bourbon, after the operation, was more woman than man. Two months later a Los Angeles club advertised Bourbon in a stage revue titled "She Lost It in Juarez." Bourbon told reporters: "I had the operation done just to prevent any charges that I was masquerading as a woman." Still, Los Angeles police arrested him in his dressing room for impersonating a woman.[104] Bourbon used the alleged operation in large part as a publicity ploy. A friend of his noted later that Bourbon still stood to urinate, suggesting that if he had had surgery at all, the doctors had not removed his penis. Later he continued to live as a man (although he enjoyed dressing as a woman) and to work as a female impersonator. But in the popular press of the 1950s, his story seemed to confirm that those who desired male-to-female sex change were akin to gay men who liked to dress as women.[105]

As reporters showcased each new story, a host of other male-to-females made cameo appearances.[106] None attracted as much attention as Jorgensen, and after a while they needed an unusual story to attract much attention at all. Although some of the stories focused on the unresolved issues of sexuality, others won reporters' interest as "firsts." In 1953 *Jet* magazine, for example, announced that Charles Robert Brown, a "shake dancer" in nightclubs, could "become the first Negro 'transvestite' in history to transform his sex." According to *Jet*, Brown had arranged for surgery in Bonn, Germany, after which he planned to marry his boyfriend, a U.S. sergeant stationed in Frankfurt.[107] (In the 1960s other stories presented additional "firsts." One tabloid magazine article noted "a rash of glamorous sex-switchers," including belly dancer Bessie Mukaw, who called "herself the first Eskimo sex-change," and singer Delisa Newton, who had replaced Charles Robert Brown as "the first Negro sex-change.")[108] In the late 1950s a Native

American male-to-female appeared in the press when his life as a woman led to his arrest for defrauding the government. Before his arrest in 1958, John Murphy Goodshot had lived as a woman, married a Navy Seabee, and collected government payments as a dependent wife. Despite his expressed desire for sex-change surgery, the court ordered him, as a condition of probation, "to undergo psychiatric treatment to bring out his masculine qualities."[109]

Although the press showed decidedly less interest, it also reported occasionally on women transformed into men. Some of the earliest stories related accounts of intersexed conditions, in which, among adults, female-to-male surgeries predominated. In early 1953, for example, the *Los Angeles Mirror* ran a sympathetic four-part series, "Strange Case: One Body—Two Sexes," about an anonymous woman who underwent surgery after a doctor discovered internal male organs. Several magazines carried the story of "Joan," who had become "John" in 1949 after Dr. Louis Maraventano, of Yonkers, New York, "freed her obscured penis."[110] But as the press coverage on Jorgensen increasingly distinguished "transvestism" from intersexed conditions, the stories on female-to-male sex change declined.

The brief reports on female-to-males usually came from outside the United States, and compared with the frenzied reporting on male-to-females, their tone approached indifference. With a twist on sexism, the press found men who became women more titillating than women who became men. By the postwar era, men who wore dresses attracted more public notice than women who wore pants. So, too, male-to-female transsexuals drew more coverage from the press. Some of the stories on female-to-male sex change mentioned surgery, and some did not, but in either case they rarely included any details of the medical intervention. Several accounts came from the British Isles. In 1953 the press rehashed the story, originally publicized in 1952, of Scottish physician Dr. Ewan Forbes-Semphill, once Elizabeth, who had married his housekeeper. In 1954 magazines discovered Michael Harford, formerly an English artist's model, who "took to wearing slacks and lost interest in household tasks" before the unnamed "treatment" began. And in 1958 the press revealed that the Anglo-Irish aristocrat Laurence Michael Dillon, now a medical doctor, had lived as Laura Maude

Dillon before his surgical transformation in the late 1940s. Although male-to-female sex change captured more headlines, these briefer stories on female-to-males at least reminded readers that sex change went both ways.[111]

*A*s the cast of characters mounted, magazines and newspapers published more sensational stories. Pulp magazines printed a number of confessional accounts, most of which were probably phony. *True Confessions* published "Man into Woman," the first-person story of "Geraldine," a Hollywood actress who had allegedly undergone sex-change surgery in New York. *HE* magazine presented "I Was Forced into 'Manhood,'" a tale in which "an overambitious medical man" changed the sex of an unwilling girl. Other magazines printed stories titled "Why I Want to Change My Sex," "Sex Surgery While You Wait!," and "The Weird Psychology of Sex Changes."[112] Meanwhile, newspapers published stories on fowl that had spontaneously changed from female to male. One such headline read: "Feathered Christine Causes Amazement among Farm Flock." As the magazine *People Today* announced, "Next to the recurrent hydrogen bomb headlines, reports of sex changes are becoming the most persistently startling world news."[113]

The publicity spread from newspapers and magazines to other popular media. In the early 1950s, television had just entered the competition for the mass national audience, but television producers showed relatively little interest in the sex-change media craze. Jorgensen later claimed that television had barred her in the 1950s. That was not entirely true, given her appearance with Arthur Murray and her interview with Mike Wallace, but it was certainly the case that in the 1950s television shows rarely reported on sex change. Because of its links to sexuality, the topic was considered too risqué for family-oriented entertainment. As late as 1967 the producers of the Joey Bishop Show declined an interview with Jorgensen because they saw it as "too 'touchy' a situation."[114]

But other media were not constrained by the same level of self-censorship. As producers of various forms of mass media competed for an audience, those that targeted "adult" niche markets could profit from the sexual topics that television avoided.[115] In 1956, for example, Ray Bourbon recorded party albums titled *An Evening in Copenhagen* and *Let Me Tell You about My Operation!*[116] In 1957 Christine Jorgensen marketed her own album, an "open and frank" interview, titled *Christine Jorgensen Reveals.* The interviewer, "Mr. R. Russell," who later established himself as the prominent comedian Nipsey Russell, asked slightly racy questions, such as "Are you sexually drawn to a woman?" and "Have you ever been . . . propositioned?" while Jorgensen gave her usual calm and sober answers.[117]

In the 1950s sex change also made its debut in B-grade movies. In 1953 director Edward Wood Jr. made a low-budget motion picture, *Glen or Glenda?*, on transvestism and sex-change surgery. In the film, now a cult classic, horror-movie legend Bela Lugosi plays, as Wood explained, an "all-powerful science-God figure," who introduces the story, scowling and chortling, in an eerie den decorated with skulls and skeleton. The film presents two cases: a transvestite, Glen or Glenda, played by Wood himself, whom a doctor eventually advises against sex-change surgery, and "an extremely advanced case," Alan or Ann, with an intersexed condition, who undergoes hormone treatments and operations. The film drew directly on the early accounts of the Jorgensen story. The advertising poster has the question "Glen or Glenda?" pasted on a collage of clippings on Jorgensen and other accounts of sex change. (Jorgensen refused to act in the movie, and in her record album interview she complained about a "dreadful Frankenstein-like picture about a doctor who does hocus-pocus and changes a man into a woman.") The film was released under various titles, including *I Changed My Sex.*[118] In 1954 *Picture Scope* magazine reported on another film, *Adam Is . . . Eve,* made in France, which combined the stories of Jorgensen and McLeod with "a few spicy embellishments."[119]

Inevitably the topic of sex change made it into cheap paperback novels. Around 1953 Lion Books claimed to have published the first novel on sex change. *Half,* which sold for twenty-five cents, featured a hermaphrodite, but the back cover associated the novel with the news stories on sex change: "You've heard about 'men' like Steven Bankow. You've read about them in your daily newspapers. But here—for the first time—a novelist tackles the problem of a man who tries to change his sex." In 1955 Fabian Books entered the market with *Sex Gantlet to Murder,* a hard-boiled mystery novel that addressed transsexuality. The murderer, a sexy woman named Johnnie, turns out to be a cross-dressing man seeking sex-change surgery and the murder victim an unscrupulous homosexual doctor who promises the operations. The cover shows a voluptuous woman, breasts surging from a clingy strapless gown, assailing a seated man who has surgical instruments at hand. The cover blurb asks, "What happens when a man formulates the desire to become a woman?" The book's answer, murder, helped inaugurate a pernicious popular tradition that associates male-to-female transsexuals with psychopathic violence. The book went through at least four printings, the last of which appeared in 1958 under the more explicit title *The Lady Was a Man.*[120]

In the mid-1950s a few other publishers cashed in on the topic of sex change. After Jorgensen made the news, Popular Library brought out a paperback edition of *Man into Woman,* the story of Lili Elbe, originally published in English in 1933. By mid-decade the first transsexual autobiographies hit the press. In 1954 *Roberta Cowell's Story* came out in England, and the following year, in the United States, Tamara Rees distributed a brief autobiography, privately published, titled *"Reborn."* By the end of the decade a popular science account, *Homosexuality, Transvestism, and Change of Sex,* added to the obsessive publicity.[121]

*T*he onslaught of publicity seemed to capture the popular imagination, but it is difficult to determine exactly how the public responded. A handful of letters to the editor suggest, perhaps predictably, that readers had a range of responses. They expressed fascination and repugnance, curiosity about the details of sex change, and sympathy for the difficult lives of those who underwent surgery. Some denounced the American mores that prevented public discussion of sexual issues and praised reporters for lifting the veil of silence. Others asked reporters to "stop coining . . . sensation . . . for the subway riders and office gossipers" and portrayed the media circus as an undignified frenzy or a cruel assault "on the psychological defenses" of the "unfortunate deviant." A few attacked the American doctors who refused to provide sex-change treatment, and others lambasted the European doctors who had the temerity to perform the operations.[122]

The stories on sex change provoked at least some puzzlement and surprise. "Christine was an epiphany in my youth," the historian Paul Robinson recollects. "I can still remember vividly when the news broke and just how dumbfounded I felt." In his retelling of the events, Robinson recalls: "I had always thought of maleness and femaleness as absolutes, as utterly natural phenomena, so I had the sense that what had happened ought to have been impossible."[123] By challenging the immutability of sex, the publicity invited readers to contemplate more complicated permutations of sex and gender. Soon after the Jorgensen story broke, the *New York Journal-American* stated: "People are now wondering how uncertain and changeable any person's sex can be." For some transgendered readers, the publicity brought comfort; in some other readers it provoked worry. In May 1953 *True Confessions* described the anxiety: "Since the Jorgensen case made headlines, many women have started to worry because of some 'masculine' traits they've noticed in themselves. Likewise, many men have become alarmed about any 'feminine' qualities they have. And parents have become worried about boys who tend to have some effeminate qualities, or girls who seem masculine." Jorgensen herself acknowledged the concerns of parents. She tried, she said, "to direct people to the doctors whom I know and trust and believe in . . . so that they're not walking in the dark."[124]

Whatever the underlying sentiments, the response to the publicity was sometimes overwhelming. In addition to avid readers and gawking crowds, the stories on sex change inspired letter writers who wanted personal correspondence. Virtually every person involved in the sex-change stories reported receiving letters. Charlotte McLeod found "the large number of letters . . . really quite surprising." Within two weeks of the initial news reports on his decision to change sex, Bunny Breckinridge claimed he had received "two or three thousand letters . . . including proposals of marriage from men and women," questions about sex-change surgery, and requests from readers who wanted him "to finance their operations." Tamara Rees also reported "thousands of letters and hundreds of telephone calls," with "the greater percent of expressions of sympathy and encouragement [coming] from women."[125] Jorgensen, of course, received the most mail. In her autobiography she referred to "some twenty thousand letters" in the first few months of publicity. Because of her celebrity, letters addressed simply to "Christine Jorgensen, United States of America," reached their destination.[126]

The Jorgensen story and subsequent news reports brought transgendered people out of the woodwork. As in the 1930s and 1940s, readers who had a sense of crossgender identification sometimes saw themselves in the stories about sex change. But in the 1950s the sheer magnitude of the coverage, the depth of detail, and the public accounting of what the surgery entailed provided more widely publicized, more highly informative, and more inspirational stories. The exposés that called the condition "transvestism" seemed to help transgendered readers, especially those who were not visibly intersexed, find their own stories within Jorgensen's. Many transgendered readers continued to live as part- or fulltime crossdressers or as feminine men or masculine women, and some gay and transvestite readers resented the stories that seemed to suggest a surgical solution to their so-called problems. But other readers pondered or sought the transformation of their bodies. They contacted the magazines that published stories on sex change, and they paid homage to the public transsexuals by collecting news clippings about them. In San Francisco, for example, Louise Lawrence compiled a carefully constructed scrapbook, now housed in the archives of the Kinsey Institute. In Los Angeles crossdresser Virginia Prince stored clippings in notebooks and boxes. In Chicago an anonymous collector created a scrapbook titled "Christine" out of newspaper and magazine articles on Jorgensen. The clipping collections offer tangible testimony to the impact of the popular press. They provided material resources that could give isolated readers a sense of community as well as a sense of possibility.[127] As one male-to-female told Jorgensen, the clippings "assure me that somewhere there are in this world . . . others like myself."[128]

Jorgensen reported a "briefcase full" of letters from people who identified with her and expressed "a seemingly genuine desire for alteration of sex."[129] In the letters that Jorgensen saved, transgendered writers congratulated and praised her and told her of their own attempts to find doctors to help them. A few writers informed her that they, too, had taken hormones or undergone sex-change operations, but many more sought information and advice. A female-to-male wrote: "I thought maybe if I could talk to you, you could help me know what to do." One angry male-to-female found the publicity "distasteful." Jorgensen, she wrote, made it "harder for us that have to live with it . . . Why don't you be quiet?" Mostly, though, the letter writers seemed relieved to find someone else like them, someone who might understand, someone whose poise and pride alleviated the pain and shame that accompanied the daily ridicule of feminine men and masculine women. In 1953 a female-to-male from Poughkeepsie told Jorgensen, "I prayed to God for this day when I could ask someone for help and not be ashamed," and years later, in 1969, a male-to-female from Harlem echoed the sentiment: "You are the only one I can confide in without being embarrassed."[130] The letters ranged from cheery to desperate. Three male-to-female crossdressers wrote a joint letter from Seattle, telling Jorgensen that her story had "thrilled us to our toes . . . We are truly happy to know that someone has at last taken these steps and brought our plight to the attention of the world." Others wrote from the depths of loneliness and despair. A female-to-male confessed, "Suicide has been on my mind ever since I was 10 or 11 . . . You know what I've gone through." A male-to-female wrote, "I . . . feel wretchedly ill at ease wherever I am . . . I had been praying to God that in some way I could be a girl, and then almost like a miracle I read of you."[131] As one male-to-female remembered:

The Jorgensen case appeared in all the newspapers and changed my life . . . Suddenly, like a revelation, I knew WHO and WHAT I was—and something COULD BE DONE ABOUT IT! Christ only knows how much time I spent poring over every last item about Christine I could lay my hands on. Not Christ but Christine, I thought, was my Saviour! Now everything about me made perfect sense, I knew what had to be done, and I had some real HOPE of being able to live a normal life *as a woman!* Talk about your shock of recognition! Man, this was IT![132]

For others, the "shock of recognition" provoked more ambivalent feelings. In Chicago Stephen Wagner, who had resigned himself to his crossgender identification, focused on one sentence in one of the stories in the *Chicago Sun-Times:* "they may have the physical form of one sex and think, act and feel like the opposite." "This seems to describe me to the dot," he wrote. He recognized Jorgensen immediately as "a normal man," not a pseudohermaphrodite, and he tortured himself with the thought that he could not gain access to the surgery that she had managed to obtain. "When I read about Christine's case," he wrote later, "I got terribly upset. I was really very frantic." On the East Coast, Albert Savon (pseudonym) had a similar reaction: "life . . . was bearable, at least it was until the Jorgensen story came out. From then on, I have suffered, because *her* life parallels mine so closely! It is *me* twenty years younger . . . her story is my story . . . I need help, I need relief and I need it soon." On the West Coast, Barbara and Lauren Wilcox had a more practical response to the Jorgensen story. They were interested "from the point of view of 'when and where will the operation be made available to Barbara.'"[133]

The incredible publicity about Jorgensen had helped publicly mark transsexuality as a male-to-female phenomenon, a distinct reversal from the 1930s, when stories of female-to-male sex change predominated in the popular press. "Joe," for example, did not seek surgery until a male-to-female acquaintance gave him his "first hint that the sex change possible for males might also have its counterpart for the female." Many female-to-male transsexuals, though, did see themselves immediately in Jorgensen's story. Several wrote to her, assuming their lives corresponded with hers. "Have had your same problem," one female-to-male wrote, "but in reverse." Another female-to-male sent Jorgensen a long life history. "When things get low," he wrote her, "I can say to myself that here is a human being who pioneered in what I am trying to do." In a later account Mario Martino described his reaction at the age of fifteen, when he first read about Jorgensen: "Over and over I read the news stories I'd secreted in my room . . . At last I had hope. *There were people like me.* And they were doing something about it. Now I had a plan: I must . . . go to Denmark."[134]

In her autobiography, Jorgensen remembered her own response to reading *The Male Hormone.* "Throughout the narrative," she wrote, "there was woven a tiny thread of recognition pulled from my own private theories."[135] In turn, the stories on Jorgensen provided more than a "tiny thread of recognition" to others who came after her. And because she remained a public figure until her death in 1989, her impact continued on successive generations, especially of male-to-female transsexuals. "Jorgensen," one later admirer remembered, "became my idol . . . She always stayed with me—like a goal. When I got to where I wanted to give up, I would say to myself, 'She did it. That's proof—that's all I need to know.'"[136] As the most public and "out" transsexual, Jorgensen starred in the stories on which, for better or worse, other transgendered people could pattern their own desires for bodily transformation.

But the stories of sex change also had wider appeal. Jorgensen, in particular, inspired nontransgendered correspondents. The sheaves of surviving letters attest to her success at lifting herself into the realm of celebrity and provide clues to the array of motives of the people who sought personal contact. Some of the letters have a generic quality: they might have gone to any woman who had entered the world of stardom. Celebrity hounds wanted Jorgensen's photo and autograph, and one admirer hoped to start a Christine Jorgensen fan club. Songwriters asked her to sing their songs in her nightclub act, and employers and entrepreneurs offered her jobs. The manager of a television store asked Jorgensen to work as a receptionist, a manufacturer wanted Jorgensen to model hats, and the performer Evelyn West invited Jorgensen to join her in "a two woman strip show."[137] Lonely men asked to meet, date, or marry her, and well-wishing strangers sent her Christmas cards.

Other letters addressed her particular story. A couple of hostile writers wanted Jorgensen to know they thought her "an insane idiot," a fake, or an exhibitionist. They refused to shift their definitions of womanhood to include someone like her. "Hi 'Neuter,'" one venomous letter began. "Who do you think you are to pose as a woman when it has been proved that you are a man, always have been and always will be." But the vast majority of letters accepted her as a woman, offered encouragement and support, and expressed admiration for her courage and dignity. "Truthfully," one such letter stated, "the majority of the thinking people are rooting for you."[138] A few years later, Jorgensen summed up the flood of mail: "I received thousands and thousands of letters from . . . people with problems . . . an equal number of just congratulatory notes" and "forty or thirty" letters that expressed hostility.[139]

Jorgensen might have been dismissed as grotesque, as a monster or a sinner, but it seems she had shaped her public presentation in ways that evoked a different response. Over and over again, nontransgendered readers identified with her and sympathized with her struggle. They placed her story in the context of their own lives and their own beliefs. She had overcome obstacles, and so could they. "My problem," one man wrote, "seems so insignificant to the hell you had to wade through . . . You've really made me wake up." Like Helen Keller, she served for some readers as a model of how the human will might triumph over adversity. A number of letters adopted religious language to express the inspirational lessons they drew. No doubt the name Christine, derived from Christ, helped some readers cast Jorgensen in religious form. Jorgensen's story, one woman said, "reminds me of the suffering Christ had to go through so we might have salvation." Others referred to Jorgensen's surgery as an example of miracles. "I have seen in Christine," one man wrote, "a miracle of God."[140] A couple of quirky letters suggested that she work as a missionary or dedicate herself to God, in one case to save homosexuals from sin, and in another, to guide women who "trespassed too far into the man's domain . . . back to [their] rightful place."[141] In a more liberal, secular vein, Jorgensen's story also served as a model for struggles for human rights. "I am a Negro," a woman wrote Jorgensen's parents, and "find many obstacles that must be overcome." Jorgensen, too, she said, "belonged to a minority group but she [broke] through its limitations. If more people would face the brunt of the battle I am sure we would all live in a much more pleasant world." Another letter also cast Jorgensen as "a champion of the downtrodden minorities."[142] The letters indicate that Jorgensen's attempt to portray her particular battle as a more common story of human striving had struck a resonant chord.

$\mathcal{T}$he publicity for sex change did not bring direct relief to those who hoped for surgery. It was not until the late 1960s that more American surgeons began to perform sex reassignment surgery. Nonetheless, the ground had shifted. By the mid-1950s the mass media were reporting constantly on sex change. The popular press now acknowledged the European version of sex-change surgery, for "transvestites," not for intersexed conditions. Christine Jorgensen had agreed tacitly to serve as an icon for those who wanted to change sex and also for nontransgendered people who looked to her as a model of persistence, faith, and hope. With ambition and a sense of her mission, she perpetuated her popularity and kept herself on stage. Although she could not control the media, she asserted her presence, and she refused to let the press define her. She told a story that humanized her and defended her right to pursue her own happiness, and she pushed the public to acknowledge her status as a woman.

Jorgensen also pushed American doctors and scientists to redefine their terms. By the mid-1950s they began to adopt the term *transsexual* and to enter into heated debates about the merits of surgical intervention. An American scientific literature on transsexuality, which had not existed before Jorgensen made the news, soon engaged the older European literature that had originated in Germany. The American doctors and scientists returned to the unanswered questions, "What is a woman and what is a man?" and for their answers drew on earlier theories of sex and more recent theories of gender. They published their findings in medical journals and popularized them in magazines and newspapers. The definitions of sex and gender were increasingly scrutinized as closely as Jorgensen herself.

FROM SEX TO GENDER

3

$\mathcal{O}$n the record album *Christine Jorgensen Reveals,* interviewer Nipsey Russell asked Jorgensen a seemingly simple question: "Are you a woman?" Jorgensen gave her standard reply: "You seem to assume that every person is either a man or a woman . . . Each person is actually both in varying degrees . . . I am more of a woman than I am a man." Later in the interview she elaborated: "Society has decreed that there are men and there are women . . . People, both men and women, are both sexes. The most any man or woman can be is 80 percent masculine or feminine." On this occasion and on others, Jorgensen referred to male and female not as mutually exclusive categories but as overlapping ones. The notion that all human beings are both male and female became her mantra. She used it in public, restating it repeatedly in her interviews and writings, and she used it in private when explaining herself to her friends.[1]

In her vision of overlapping sexes, Jorgensen drew on and reiterated the theory of human bisexuality common in early twentieth-century European science. This was the vision of sex held by Jorgensen's doctors in Denmark and also by Harry Benjamin, who treated Jorgensen in the United States. In the wake of the publicity about sex change, Jorgensen and her doctors popularized the theory of human bisexuality and used it to define a biological problem—an unusually highly mixed-sex condition—that justified medical treatment. But ultimately it was not the vision of sex that came to predominate in the United States.

Other doctors and scientists, especially psychologists and psychoanalysts, maintained a vision of separate biological sexes and saw various forms of crossgender behavior and identification, including transvestism and transsexuality, as psychological, not physical, conditions. They recommended psychoanalysis and other forms of psychotherapeutic treatment that might eliminate what they described as mental illness. After Jorgensen made the news, they mounted an offensive against transsexual surgery and denounced the doctors and scientists who supported it. They directly repudiated the theory of human bisexuality. In the United States the psychological position seemed to predominate through the 1950s.

By the end of the 1950s, though, a new position, a compromise of sorts, had started to emerge. In the first half of the twentieth century the theory of human bisexuality had, for some doctors and scientists, redefined sex and legitimated sex-reassignment surgery; in the second half of the century a theory of immutable gender identity came to replace it. In the 1940s and afterward, scientists who studied intersexuality adopted the concept of a deeply rooted sense of "psychological sex." Some of them suggested that hormones or genes created psychological sex, but others considered it conditioned, imprinted, or learned. In any case, they claimed that no one could change an adult's psychological sex. Once established, they asserted, the sense of being a man or a woman remained firmly entrenched, immune to both psychotherapeutic and medical interventions. They applied this conception of psychological sex—which they later labeled "gender role and orientation" and "gender identity"—first to people with intersexed conditions and then to transsexuals. In this view, the mind—the sense of self—was less malleable than the body.

As the doctors and scientists debated, they asked larger questions about sex and gender. Were male and female separate and opposite? Which factors defined who qualified as female or male? Did the physical conditions of sex determine masculine and feminine traits and behaviors? The sexes might overlap or they might be distinct. The essence of sex might reside in the chromosomes, the endocrine glands, the genitals, or the mind. Gendered behavior and gender identity might result from genes, hormones, or neurophysiology, from psychodynamic processes, or from various forms of social learning. Unconventional gender identification could represent a physical disorder, a mental illness, or a benign variation. The doctors and scientists could not agree on the answers to the questions they raised. As they staged their debates, though, they offered new definitions of sex and gender and opened to public vision key issues still contested today.

The debates led to different proposals for programs of treatment. To some doctors, the transformation of the body seemed the best solution to the transsexual dilemma. To others, psychotherapy in childhood seemed to promise a better, and less controversial, result: the prevention of crossgender identification in adults. Through the early 1960s, the doctors who advocated surgery found little support in the American medical profession, while those who called for preventative psychotherapy had greater initial success. They established their first "gender identity" clinic, which aimed to reinforce the traditional norms of gender in children who defied them. By the early 1960s, then, the competing definitions of sex and the new language of gender had resulted in a conservative clinical treatment that attempted to contain unconventional gender behavior and dispel the uncertainties concerning sex.

In the United States the theory of human bisexuality had its popular heyday in the aftermath of the Christine Jorgensen publicity. Soon after the story broke, reporters turned to various medical experts who used bisexuality to explain Jorgensen's condition. A *New York Daily News* reporter, for example, interviewed "a number of specialists." "In reality," he concluded, "all humans remain somewhat bisexual. The male has some vestigial female sex organs, the female some vestigial male organs. Both men and women produce both male and female sex hormones." The very same day, another story in another newspaper drew a similar conclusion: "Scientists recognize this fact: male and female natures are present and blended in each one of us. But the blends are such that, normally, one sex pattern is supreme, the opposite one is subordinate. In the unusual cases, such supremacy of male or female patterns is not clear, or is confused."[2] The theory of human bisexuality helped explain Jorgensen's alleged mixed-sex condition.

In the American press, the theory of bisexuality could offer comfort to readers who did not conform unambiguously to male or female bodily standards or to masculine or feminine roles, but it could also promote an attempt to fortify the stereotypes of gender. In May 1953 *True Story* magazine, which usually published confessional accounts of sex and romance, captured the ambiguity in an article titled "Men and Women: Amazing Truths about Sex Glands." The doctor who authored the piece, Shailer Upton Lawton, used Jorgensen as the starting point for an account of chromosomes, hormones, and sex determination, with an emphasis on human bisexuality. "Male and female sex organs," Lawton explained, "develop out of the same original sex structure . . . every man has within him some undeveloped remains of female sex glands, and every woman has within her some undeveloped remains of male sex glands . . . Men and women secrete *both* male and female hormones." Human bisexuality not only explained Jorgensen; it also helped explain why "*every* man has some feminine traits and *every* woman has some masculine traits." In this way, the theory of bisexuality could push readers to reassess rigid definitions of female and male and feminine and masculine. But the article ended with a different message. If men were not entirely male and masculine and women not entirely female and feminine, then masculinity and femininity had to be taught. Parents, Lawton concluded, "are more important than Nature's own sex glands in giving masculinity to our sons and femininity to our daughters."[3] The article suggested that masculine and feminine were at least in part socially learned constructs, but it refrained from questioning their necessity.

While newspapers and magazines drew social lessons from the theory of bisexuality, Jorgensen and her doctors continued to promote it as the physical cause of her condition. In the autobiographical series published in *American Weekly,* Jorgensen quoted Christian Hamburger, her Danish endocrinologist: "It . . . is impossible to fix any definite borderline between what is normal and what is not. A 100 per cent man, or a 100 per cent woman does not exist. We all have rudiments of the hermaphrodite (dual sex) state within us." In the 1950s and later, Christine Jorgensen used the theory to humanize herself and others like her, to suggest that transsexuality was only one version of a normal, universal mixed-sex condition. She also used it to provide a scientific basis to substantiate her claims to womanhood. Her doctors in Denmark provided the scientific elaboration. In the article they published in the *Journal of the American Medical Association*, Christian Hamburger, psychiatrist Georg Stürup, and surgeon Erling Dahl-Iversen presented Jorgensen not as a pseudohermaphrodite but as a "genuine" transvestite, and, in accord with the theory of bisexuality, they speculated that "the most pronounced transvestites might be intersexes (sex intergrades) of the highest degree." They hypothesized that some humans with male sex organs had female (XX) chromosomes. In their "working theory," this particular variant of bisexuality might result in transvestism.[4]

Harry Benjamin, who became Jorgensen's endocrinologist in the United States, also espoused the theory of bisexuality. In the spring of 1953 Benjamin met Jorgensen at a dinner party at the home of author Tiffany Thayer and soon afterward examined Jorgensen in his office.[5] He wondered immediately to what extent she had the mixed physical characteristics of both female and male. In a letter to Hamburger, Benjamin asked whether Jorgensen had "hypertrophic or hypersensitive feminizing tissue in her adrenals" and whether doctors had examined her abdomen "to discover a possible presence of ovarian tissue." In his first article on the topic, "Transvestism and Transsexualism," published later the same year, Benjamin no longer speculated that "transsexualists" such as Jorgensen had "feminizing" or "ovarian" tissue, but he still echoed the European doctors who had first promoted the concept of human bisexuality. He referred to "the infinite diversity of the male-female scale." "It is well known," he wrote, "that sex is never one hundred per cent 'male' or 'female.' It is a blend of a complex variety of male-female components." The "more or less pronounced irregularities in genetic and endocrine development" resulted in "'intersexes' of varying character, degree and intensity," including not only hermaphrodites and pseudohermaphrodites but also homosexuals, transvestites, and transsexuals.[6]

Benjamin did not subscribe to the Danish doctors' speculative model in which male-to-female transsexuals had male anatomy and female chromosomes. He assumed that male-to-female transsexuals had male (XY) chromosomes. (Later studies confirmed that Benjamin was, for the vast majority of cases, correct.)[7] Benjamin emphasized biological bisexuality, but he could not identify any specific hormonal or genetic factors that might cause transsexualism or even any physical characteristics that marked it. In most other respects, though, Benjamin agreed with the Danish doctors. His term *transsexualism* addressed the same condition they called "genuine transvestism," and with the Jorgensen case in mind he, too, focused solely on male-to-female transsexuals. Like the Danish doctors, Benjamin defined the condition as an extreme type of transvestism, in which men "want to be changed into women, even anatomically." Benjamin had written his article before Hamburger and his colleagues published theirs. "Otherwise," he noted in private correspondence, he "might be accused of plagiarism, so much do our views coincide in certain respects."[8]

In their emphasis on human bisexuality, both Benjamin and the Danish doctors directly challenged psychoanalytic and psychotherapeutic cures. They did not discount psychological origins entirely, but they repeatedly turned to "deeper somatic causes." As Benjamin put it, "the soma, that is to say the genetic and/or endocrine constitution . . . has to provide a 'fertile soil.'" Given the physical basis of the condition, psychotherapeutic interventions could not, they agreed, eliminate the intense desire to change sex. Hamburger and his colleagues wrote: "it is impossible to make a genuine transvestite wish to have his mentality altered by means of psychotherapy." Benjamin concurred: "Psychotherapy, including hypnosis, [has] proven useless in these cases, useless at least as far as a cure is concerned."[9] For the Danish doctors and Benjamin, the physical nature of the condition and the failure of psychotherapy together justified surgical intervention.

For the scientists, the theory of bisexuality could legitimate the surgery and make sex change comprehensible. If all humans had both male and female components that could be inhibited or promoted, if some humans had unusual proportions of maleness and femaleness that did not accord with their genitals, then some apparent women might actually qualify as men and some men as women. Surgery and hormones would just confirm the already existing dispositions. The theory of bisexuality placed transsexuals in the same ambiguous social space as the more visibly intersexed, for whom surgery was already routine. If the patient desired it desperately and if all other treatments had failed, then why not endorse medical intervention? The Danish doctors advocated surgery to "make life easier for such persons." Benjamin also recommended it, but only for a few cases and "only as a last resort."[10]

In the early twentieth century, psychiatrists and psychologists, especially those in the United States, spent relatively little energy on what we now call transsexuality. In the American medical journals a few psychiatrists published descriptive case studies on crossdressing patients who sought sex-change surgery, but they had little to say about the condition itself. In 1918, for example, in his detailed case account of his psychoanalysis of female-to-male Alan Lucill Hart, J. Allen Gilbert simply labeled the condition "homo-sexuality" and did not comment on its causes, except through reference to Hart's "natural male instincts." And in a 1944 case study of a male-to-female "transvestite" who hoped to change sex, D. M. Olkon and Irene Case Sherman speculated that the patient in question, whom they considered a "psychopath," had "an original, constitutional emotional defect."[11]

But as they gradually retreated from biological explanations, psychoanalysts staked out other positions. First in German and later in English, the prominent psychoanalyst Otto Fenichel elaborated on the psychodynamic processes involved in transvestism. In Fenichel's view, the male-to-female transvestite "fantasies that the woman possesses a penis, and thus overcomes his castration anxiety, and identifies himself with the phallic woman." The female-to-male transvestite, whom he took less seriously, displaced "envy of the penis to an envy of masculine appearance." In an early essay, originally published in German, Fenichel noted "cases of actual self-castration by transvestites or of disgust felt by them for the male genital and longing for that of the female," but he refrained from commenting on the patients whom we might now label transsexuals. He needed to analyze them, he said, before he "could make any pronouncement about them."[12]

Meanwhile other psychoanalysts explicitly repudiated the theory of bisexuality. In an influential 1940 article psychoanalyst Sandor Rado examined "the actual status of bisexuality in the biological field" and concluded that "the old speculative notion of bisexuality is in the process of withering away." With regard to "reproductive action systems, individuals are of two contrarelated types." These different reproductive systems constituted "the character of the sexes," and they could be "dissected into a multitude of structures, substances, and functions." Sex was not determined "by the relative percentage of male and female hormones." Rather, sex was a label for the "differential development, directed toward the construction and perfection of the reproductive system." As the embryo developed "under normal . . . conditions," it lost its "original bipotentiality." Rado concluded: "there is no such thing as bisexuality either in man or in any other of the higher vertebrates."[13]

After World War II psychiatry and psychology rose to new levels of prominence and cultural authority in the United States. Psychiatrists and psychologists had played key roles in screening recruits for the armed services during the war and in treating soldiers under stress, and after the war the federal government recognized their growing clout with the National Mental Health Act of 1946, which established the National Institute of Mental Health. Psychiatry, one historian has noted, "moved into the 'mainstream' of American medicine and American society and enormously expanded its claims and its clientele." As their authority escalated, psychiatrists and psychologists turned increasingly to environmental explanations of mental conditions, just as other social scientists increasingly rejected biological explanations of the differences they observed among ethnic groups, races, genders, and socioeconomic classes.[14] It was in this context that David O. Cauldwell, in his popular writings, outlined in briefest form what became a common psychiatric position. In his 1949 article in *Sexology*, he characterized transsexuality as a mental illness resulting primarily from childhood experience, and he portrayed sex-change surgery as mutilation.[15]

After the massive publicity surrounding Christine Jorgensen, other psychiatrists, especially psychoanalysts, explicitly rejected "the biological hypothesis" and refused to redefine sex as a spectrum or continuum. In the case of Jorgensen, they found "nothing in the preliminary physical and hormonal examination" that offered "convincing evidence that somatic, genetically determined factors played a predominant role." They offered instead an interpretation that pathologized crossgender identification by associating it with various other conditions seen as psychogenic sexual perversions. In the *Journal of the American Medical Association*, Mortimer Ostow speculated that Jorgensen was an exhibitionist with "a neurotic aversion" to sexual contact, and George H. Wiedeman saw "features of fetishism . . . homosexuality . . . exhibitionism . . . and masochism," perhaps combined with "an underlying schizophrenic process." They opposed surgery as uncritical compliance with the patient's mental illness. Through analogy, Ostow compared the desire for genital surgery with the desire for death. "If a patient has a wish to die," he asked, "should the physician actively comply with the patient's wish or even condone his suicide?" Ostow and Wiedeman recommended "intensive, prolonged, classic psychoanalysis" or at the least "a deeper going psychiatric investigation."[16]

In 1954 the *American Journal of Psychotherapy* presented the emerging debate. Harry Benjamin opened the symposium, originally held at a meeting of the Association for the Advancement of Psychotherapy. Aware that therapists constituted his audience, Benjamin carefully restated his position. "Organically," he said, "sex is always a mixture of male and female components." Although some milder versions of transvestism, he suggested, were "principally psychogenic," in the most extreme cases, which he labeled "transsexualists," "a still greater degree of constitutional femininity, perhaps due to a chromosomal sex disturbance, must be assumed." In these "extreme" cases, psychological factors were at most secondary, and therapy was "useless as far as any cure is concerned." Psychiatrist Emil Gutheil responded. With a nod to Benjamin, he acknowledged that some as-yet-unknown constitutional factor might well predispose a person toward transvestism and transsexualism, but he noted that "so far, no evidence has been procured to support a biologic concept." He argued instead, with psychoanalytic overkill, that male-to-female transvestism and transsexualism always involved "six psychopathologic factors": homosexuality "with an unresolved castration complex," sadomasochism, narcissism, scopophilia, exhibitionism, and fetishism. He looked to early childhood experience for the origins of the problem and found that "the patient's mother plays a pivotal part." Gutheil advocated psychotherapy.

Its failure thus far, he claimed, resulted in most cases from "patients' uncooperative attitude."[17]

In a medical turf war, the psychoanalysts and psychologists lambasted the doctors who attempted medical interventions instead of psychoanalytic or other psychotherapeutic cures. The battle was not a new one; for decades psychologists and psychoanalysts had challenged medical interventionists in a number of other areas. In the case of schizophrenia, for example, psychoanalysts emphasized early childhood trauma and advocated "talking cures." Some of them disagreed openly with the surgeons who understood schizophrenia as a physical disease of the brain and performed such controversial treatments as lobotomies. In the case of homosexuality, which virtually all medical authorities still considered pathological, psychologists and psychoanalysts increasingly discounted the doctors whose belief in biological origins pushed them to measure bodily parts or to inject testosterone into gay men and estrogen into lesbians. When psychologists and psychoanalysts advocated medical treatments for homosexuality, they tended to prefer electroshock treatments or other aversion therapies that might have an impact on psychosexual conditioning.[18]

The debates over transsexuality were both similar and different. The various doctors posed the same question of origins—psychological or biological—but the medical interventionists took a somewhat different approach to patients. The doctors who performed medical treatments for schizophrenia and homosexuality attempted to regulate and modify the behavior of their patients, and especially in mental institutions they often acted without their patients' consent.[19] In contrast, Benjamin and the Danish doctors followed the leads and wishes of their patients in pursuing medical treatment. They relied heavily on sympathy and showed an unusual tolerance for their patients' unconventional crossgender behavior, which they did not attempt to change.

In the mid-twentieth century the more vocal psychologists and psychiatrists were less inclined to sympathy. As they saw it, transsexuals were not only mentally ill but also willfully annoying. For "Psychological Factors in Men Seeking Sex Transformation," an article published in 1955 in the *Journal of the American Medical Association*, Frederic G.

Worden, a psychoanalyst at the University of California at Los Angeles, and James T. Marsh, a clinical psychologist, interviewed and tested five "physically normal" men who hoped for transsexual surgery. They devoted most of their article to describing transsexuals in pathologizing terms. Their subjects, they said, had "an extremely shallow, immature, and grossly distorted concept of what a woman is like socially, sexually, anatomically, and emotionally." They depicted their subjects as attention-seeking exhibitionists, overly eager for approval. They even held the patients' cooperation with their research against them; to Worden and Marsh, the "offers to be scientific exhibits" fell under the heading of "need for recognition." More generally, Worden and Marsh could not suppress their irritation with subjects who pressured them for surgery. The "state of urgency and impatience," they indicated, was not only "inappropriate" but also "frantic and desperate." The subjects, they concluded, denied the reality of their sex, blamed their problems on "a 'sick' culture that refuses to accept them as women," and refused to acknowledge "the possibility that the wish for surgery might be symptomatic of a disorder within themselves." In their final analysis, Worden and Marsh found that the desire for genital surgery served as "an escape from . . . sexual impulses." The "problem pervades the entire personality" and could not be cured "by amputation of the genitals."[20]

Harry Benjamin immediately objected to the Worden and Marsh study. He wrote to the journal to defend his own position. Worden and Marsh had "badly misunderstood or misinterpreted" his work when they had stated that he envisioned transsexuals as "constitutionally female." Benjamin reiterated the theory of human bisexuality: "sex is never 100% male or 100% female." Male-to-female transsexuals had "a certain degree of constitutional femininity," but that was "not the same as to say that these subjects are constitutionally female." In private correspondence Benjamin criticized the article and also deplored Worden's cold approach to his subjects. In a letter to Alfred Kinsey he wrote: "Worden's sole interest is psychoanalytic research. He is not interested in helping any patients. That is the difference between him and me." In a later letter he returned to the same point. Worden, he said, "is not interested in these people except as material for some research . . . as a physician he has undoubtedly done more harm than good."[21]

The scientific debates made it into the press, in large part because the Jorgensen story had heightened public interest. The newspapers and magazines tended to present the doctors' differences as a national dispute. In her autobiographical series in *American Weekly,* for example, Jorgensen implicitly contrasted her Danish doctors, whom she portrayed as enlightened and understanding, with the American doctors who had refused to help her. She drew a more general distinction between European sexual sophistication and American prurient interest. "Europeans," she said, "look upon matters pertaining to sex as one's own personal affair." In its series "The Truth about 'Christine' Jorgensen," the *New York Post* maintained the national contrast but reversed the valence. The *Post* reporter approvingly quoted a variety of American doctors who expressed outrage "over the employment of so drastic and irrevocable a procedure as castration and penisectomy." Christian Hamburger, according to the *Post,* hoped to "modify the American view." The American doctors, though, did not seem inclined to change their opinions. The *Post* quoted an official from the American Medical Association as saying: "From what we know of it, the imbalance was purely psychological . . . the patient felt like a woman, thought like a woman, and wanted to be one. But castration didn't make him one. I don't see that it did any good at all." In 1955, in a report on the Worden and Marsh article, *Time* replayed the national distinction: "some U.S. doctors feel that surgeons abroad are prompted more by pity for their patients than by facts about their disorders."[22]

Although the most vocal proponents of transsexual surgery did indeed have European backgrounds, the national division emphasized in the press did not account for the many European doctors who publicly protested sex-change surgery.[23] Nor did it mention the handful of American doctors who expressed support. In his syndicated newspaper column Walter C. Alvarez, formerly of the Mayo Clinic, endorsed sex-change surgery, and in his book *Homosexuality, Transvestism, and Change of Sex,* Eugene de Savitsch applauded the surgeons who risked their reputations by performing sex-change operations. "The tragedy of the present-day attitude," de Savitsch wrote, "is that very few people are willing to tackle this problem."[24] But if the press did not capture the nuances of the debate, it did point to its overriding feature: in the 1950s, when a nonintersexed patient requested treatment to change sex, many American doctors simply assumed that she or he was mentally ill.

In a 1957 article psychiatrist Karl M. Bowman and research associate Bernice Engle suggested a few areas of emerging consensus. Like others involved in the debates, they defined *transsexualism* as a term for "the person who hates his own sex organs and craves sexual metamorphosis," and like most other commentators they considered it an extreme form of transvestism. "Theoretically," they granted, "transvestism should occur to about the same extent in both sexes," but like other researchers they focused primarily on male-to-females, who made up the vast majority of the reported cases. They considered transvestism distinct from but related to and "interwoven with other sexual deviations, especially homosexuality, fetishism, exhibitionism, and masturbation." And they also distinguished transvestites and transsexuals from hermaphrodites and pseudohermaphrodites.[25]

Bowman and Engle presented the contradictory research and attempted to navigate between the opposing views. They could find no evidence to support biological origins, but they acknowledged that "a subtle intersex, a gradation . . . [of] human sex types" might, with further investigation, "eventually include some organic base for transvestism." With regard to "psychologic theories," they noted a variety of possible issues, including "castration anxiety," "conflicts over . . . sexual impulses," and a "body image" that included "parts of the opposite sex." Then they drew the obvious conclusion: "The causes and character of transvestism are not well understood." Although they acknowledged the benefits of surgery to the well-being of two of their own patients at the Langley Porter Clinic in San Francisco, they rejected "surgical transformation" because "it plays into the patient's illusions and does not really solve the problem." They expressed qualified support for hormone treatments, although they worried that "prolonged hormonal medication raises the question of the danger of cancer." Their "treatment of choice" was "probably intensive prolonged psychotherapy in suitable cases," even though they admitted that thus far they could not report any "successfully treated cases."[26] In this way Bowman and Engle acknowledged the failure of psychotherapeutic treatment, but, like most American doctors, they avoided advocating surgery.

Bowman and Engle thus summarized the medical literature that emerged in the aftermath to the publicity about Christine Jorgensen. At least a few American doctors had recognized and defined trans-sexualism. They had begun to distinguish it from a more general trans-vestism and also from intersexed conditions, homosexuality, and other "deviations," and they had focused their attention almost exclusively on male-to-female transsexuals. They had not then (and have not now) located the cause of transsexuality. The strongest advocates of surgery tended to endorse a vision of human bisexuality in which transsexualism stood as an especially pronounced version of a ubiqui-tous mixed-sex condition. The loudest opponents of surgery tended to reject the theory of bisexuality and viewed transsexuals as mentally ill.

*A*s the doctors grappled with competing definitions of sex and opposing interpretations of crossgender identification, they also opened a dialogue on the contested sources of what we now call gen-der. For decades sexologists had drawn a distinction between the sex of the mind and the sex of the body. In the 1860s Karl Heinrich Ulrichs, a German lawyer who fought for homosexual rights, formulated his influential concept of a female soul in a male body, expressed in Latin as *anima muliebris virili corpore inclusa*. For Ulrichs, the sex of the soul or psyche, which he envisioned as inborn, explained his own erotic de-sire for men. "Nature," he wrote, "developed the *physical male* germ in us, yet *mentally*, the *feminine* one." In the late nineteenth and early twentieth centuries, a number of sexologists also distinguished physical sex from mental sex. They used mental sex to explain a variety of same-sex sexual attractions, crossgender behaviors, and crossgender identi-fications.[27]

As the medical literature on transsexuals emerged, the doctors and scientists involved drew, as Ulrichs had, a distinction between the sex in the mind, as seen in the sense of self, and the sex in the body, as generally evidenced in the genitals. Cauldwell referred to individuals who were "physically of one sex and apparently psychologically of the opposite sex." Hamburger and his colleagues wrote of a "female personality in a male body" and the "feeling of being a woman." Benjamin borrowed Ulrichs' formulation of "a female 'soul' . . . in [a] male body."[28] Whether they stressed psychological or biological origins, the scientists pointed to and lamented a disjuncture between the sense of self and the visible body. The sex of the visible body, they agreed, should match the sense of self. It was the doctors' goal, if at all possible, to coordinate the body and the mind. The question remained, though, whether they should attempt to change the sense of self or alter the body.

By the 1940s various doctors and scientists used the term *psychological sex* to refer to the sense of being a man or being a woman and to distinguish it from biological sex. In the 1930s and 1940s, much of the research on psychological sex focused on people with visible intersexed conditions. In accord with the scientific thought of the day, doctors assumed they should "correct" ambiguous genitalia. They agreed that surgical methods should be employed to remove the ambiguity, to fit the person as much as possible into the physical category of either female or male. But which sex should the doctors choose? If a person had ambiguous genitalia, should doctors attempt to transform her or him surgically into a woman or a man? At midcentury the medical authorities often advocated choosing "the predominant genetic sex" when surgically altering infants, but for adults they increasingly gave primacy to psychological sex. The sense of self, they said, did not spring automatically from biological sex, and in adults it seemed to be largely immutable. In fact attempts to change the psychological sex of adults "to correspond with the genetic sex" often led to "severe mental conflicts." They argued, as a 1952 summary stated, that "adult patients are usually better adjusted and happier if the genitalia are reconstructed in keeping with their psychological sex, disregarding completely the genetic sex."[29] In other words, the mind, not the chromosomes, should determine the sex.

From early on, this vision of immutable psychological sex appeared in the literature on transsexuality. In an early example published in 1946, Michael Dillon, then a British medical student, directly addressed the issue. Although he did not say so in his book, Dillon was himself a transsexual in the process of transition from female to male. For Dillon, transsexuality—which in the era before the word existed he generally described as a form of homosexuality—had a physical basis. He speculated that feminine men and masculine women had an endocrine disorder, probably inherited. For such people, who had the "psyche" or "personality" of the other sex, Dillon advocated surgery. "Surely," he wrote, "where the mind cannot be made to fit the body, the body should be made to fit, approximately, at any rate, to the mind." Dillon drew in part on the medical literature on intersexuality. "In individuals where the presence of mixed tissue or mixed organs is obvious it is the psychological build that should be consulted and not the predominance of any particular physical structure."[30] The same criterion, he implied, should apply to transsexuals. In determining how one led one's life, the psychological sex should predominate. Doctors could and should alter the body to match the mind.

In Denmark, Hamburger and his co-workers, and in the United States, Harry Benjamin also wrote of transforming the sex of the body to correspond with the sex of the mind. They strove, as they described it, toward "harmony" between the mind and the body. In the case of Christine Jorgensen, Hamburger and his colleagues wrote: "by hormonal feminization and operative demasculinization the patient's soma harmonized with the pronounced feminine psyche." Similarly, Harry Benjamin aimed for "harmony" when he endorsed medical intervention. "If it is evident," he wrote, "that the psyche cannot be brought into sufficient harmony with the soma, then and only then is it essential to consider the reverse procedure, that is, to attempt fitting the soma into the realm of the psyche."[31] By 1960 Benjamin had adopted the term *psychological sex*. "The person in adult life," he said, "should live in the sex of his choice. In other words, the psychological sex should be decisive."[32]

Whereas Dillon, Hamburger, and Benjamin saw psychological sex as a direct result of a hidden physical—genetic or endocrine—condition, other scientists who studied intersexed conditions turned increasingly to environmental explanations. They discovered that, regardless of their genitals, gonads, or chromosomes, intersexed adults reared as boys generally had a sense of themselves as men and those reared as girls usually had a sense of themselves as women. The research tended to show that "environmental factors are frequently more important than the sex of the gonads in the development of sex desires and emotions." The research, then, increasingly suggested that "psychological sex" was not determined by biology. This vision of "psychological sex" corroborated on an individual level the anthropological studies that addressed "sex roles" on a cultural level. From the 1920s on, Margaret Mead and others had argued that "sex roles," which varied across cultures, resulted from social learning.[33] The concept of a socially learned psychological sex foreshadowed the concept of gender that emerged in the 1950s.

In the mid to late 1950s three faculty at Johns Hopkins University, John Money, Joan G. Hampson, and John L. Hampson, published a series of articles on intersexuality that introduced the new vocabulary of gender. For the most part, Money, Hampson, and Hampson simply reconfirmed others' findings on the environmental origins of psychological sex. In intersexed individuals, the sense of being a man or a woman resulted not from hormones, gonads, chromosomes, or other physical variables, they argued, but from the sex to which the infant was assigned and in which the child was subsequently reared. After early childhood, when the sense of sex was established, any attempt to change it resulted in psychological harm. To address these issues they chose the word *gender*. In 1955 Money used *gender role* to refer to "all those things that a person says or does to disclose himself or herself as having the status of boy or man, girl or woman," and *gender* to refer to "outlook, demeanor, and orientation." In later articles, jointly authored, Money, Hampson, and Hampson used the term *gender role and orientation*.[34]

To explain the gender of intersexed persons, Money, Hampson, and Hampson avoided psychoanalytic as well as biological models. They turned instead to a behaviorist model of learning, a model that had increasing currency in the postwar United States. In their influential studies of sexual behavior, for example, Alfred Kinsey and his colleagues had rejected both the theory of human bisexuality and psychoanalytic theories of early personality development. They argued that much of human sexual behavior, including homosexuality and transvestism, resulted from "learning and conditioning."[35] Similarly, in their studies of intersexed conditions, Money, Hampson, and Hampson pointed to forms of social learning as the source of gender. "Gender role and orientation" were neither a result of biological sex nor a sign of mental health or illness. They developed as the child "becomes acquainted with and deciphers a continuous multiplicity of signs that point in the direction of his being a boy, or her being a girl." Money compared gender to a "native language," learned in childhood, deeply ingrained, and "never entirely eradicated."[36] The capacity to learn languages (or genders) was in some sense biological, but the specific language (or gender role and orientation) learned resulted from the social milieu. All three authors speculated that gender role and orientation arose from a process similar to imprinting, in which young animals reacted to specific environmental stimuli that permanently structured their later social behavior. The behaviorist model, at least as applied to the intersexed, presented the sense of maleness and femaleness as immutable, benign variations resulting from early childhood experience.

In 1964 the psychiatrist Robert J. Stoller, in collaboration with his colleague Ralph Greenson, refined the concept of gender with the term *gender identity*, a term that came to dominate the medical literature on transsexuality. Stoller and Greenson used "gender identity" much as others had used "psychological sex," to refer to "one's sense of being a member of a particular sex." Stoller, a psychoanalyst at the University of California at Los Angeles, separated gender from sexuality. He distinguished "gender identity" from "sexual identity," which included "sexual activities and fantasies."[37] The use of "gender identity," as opposed to "gender role," also more clearly differentiated the subjective sense of self from the behaviors associated with masculinity and femininity.

In explaining the sources of gender identity, Stoller attempted to bridge the gap between biological and environmental etiologies. More than many post–World War II psychoanalysts, he looked for a biological substrate of human behavior, and he reminded his readers that Freud, too, had written about biological underpinnings of personality

development. In certain rare instances, Stoller noticed, intersexed subjects had gender identities at odds with their genitalia and the assigned
sex in which they were reared. One of these subjects, reared as a girl,
had always taken on "male roles." When the child reached adolescence,
a physical examination revealed male chromosomes, a penis the size of
a clitoris, undescended testicles, and a prostate gland. Stoller read this
case as evidence of a "biological force," in which an "overpowering
drive" shaped an unshakable gender identity despite the apparent genitals and the sex of rearing. But biology did not play a significant part in
Stoller's assessment of transsexuals. In his early work he focused wholly
on male-to-female transsexuals, who, he speculated, had a "weaker biological push" that did not counteract the "noxious effects of environment."[38] Transsexuals' crossgender identification resulted from damaging psychodynamic processes in early childhood. In a letter to another
psychoanalyst, Stoller explained, "I do not believe that biological factors, other than givens present in all human beings at birth, play a part
in these people who wish to change their sex."[39]

In *Sex and Gender,* published in 1968, Stoller developed a more
specific psychoanalytic rendition of the early childhood influences that
could result in a gender identity at odds with the biological sex. From
his clinical records, he constructed a scenario that resulted in male-to-
female crossgender identification. A bisexual mother, depressed and
beset with penis envy, kept her infant son close to her body in prolonged physical contact, and a distant father failed to protect the son
"from the malignant effect of his mother's excessive closeness." The
son, according to Stoller, did not separate adequately from the mother;
the result was a "core gender identity," established in the first two years
of life, permanently and irreversibly at odds with the biological sex. He
granted "that it is the style these days to blame women when weakness,
passivity, and effeminacy are found in men," but his own psychoanalytic commitments left him little choice but to focus on the mother's
effect on her child. Elsewhere in his book Stoller commented briefly on
female-to-male transsexuals, whom he considered rare, and speculated
vaguely that "too much father and too little mother masculinizes
girls."[40]

Although Stoller emphasized the psychological forces that created
gender identity in transsexuals, he also embraced, as an underlying as-

sumption, the theory of human bisexuality. Like Money, Hampson, and Hampson, Stoller refused to define sex in terms of chromosomes alone. He defined it instead by breaking it down into constituent parts that included "chromosomes, external genitalia, internal genitalia (e.g., uterus, prostate), gonads, hormonal states, and secondary sex characteristics." "One's sex," he wrote, "is determined by an algebraic sum of all these qualities, and . . . most people fall under one of two separate bell curves, the one of which is called 'male,' the other 'female.'" The sexes, then, were not mutually exclusive. "It is well known," he added, "that there is a certain amount of overlapping in all humans." But instead of discounting the impact of the various bodily parts on gender identity, he did not entirely abandon the biological approach. Stoller found "within the sexes . . . degrees of maleness and femaleness (sex) and of masculinity and femininity (gender)," and he noted potential links in which degrees of sex influenced degrees of gender. Referring to studies on animals, he pointed to the impact of hormones on "gender and sexual behavior," and he also speculated on the influence of "neuroanatomical centers and hierarchies of neurophysiological functions." Nonetheless, he repeatedly emphasized that in the development of gender identity "by far the most powerful effect comes from postnatal psychodynamic factors."[41]

As Stoller moved away from biology and toward psychology, John Money moved in the other direction. In the late 1960s and afterward he backed away partially from the environmental model that he and the Hampsons had promoted in the late 1950s. He, too, adopted the term *gender identity,* and he speculated that for both male-to-female and female-to-male transsexuals, it resulted in part from early exposure to hormones and from the neurophysiology of the limbic system and the temporal lobe. At the same time, he reiterated the earlier findings that acknowledged the crucial impact of learning. "The process of achieving a complete gender identity," he concluded, "is a developmental progression, beginning with genetic foundations and terminating with social learning."[42]

Other researchers also adopted the new language, so much so that by the end of the 1960s gender was the dominant concept in explanations of transsexuality. By 1964 Harry Benjamin described transsexualism as "a striking disturbance of gender role and gender orientation." In addition to potential genetic and endocrine causes of transsexuality, he now explored "possible psychological causes," including "imprinting" and "early childhood conditioning." He adapted the new research on social learning to his earlier position by suggesting that "conditioning" might "trigger" transsexuality "if a constitutional predisposition was present," thus maintaining his earlier emphasis on organic causes.[43] "It would," he argued, "stretch the imagination a bit too far to ascribe it all to conditioning."[44]

In 1966, when he published his book *The Transsexual Phenomenon,* Benjamin continued to combine the old and new. He repeated and refined the earlier theory of bisexuality. "Every Adam," he told his readers, "contains elements of Eve and every Eve harbors traces of Adam, physically as well as psychologically." He broke sex into seven component parts: "chromosomal, genetic, anatomical, legal, gonadal, germinal [production of ovum or sperm], endocrine (hormonal), psychological and . . . social sex, usually based on the sex of rearing." Some of the physical parts, he claimed, such as hormones and anatomy, were "never entirely male or female," and some of them could be altered. Although everyone shared male and female characteristics, transsexuals had "the most striking" of the "sex-split personalities." It was the transsexual who most exemplified the mixed-sex constitution. He combined this older vision of bisexuality with the new language of gender. He considered gender, or masculinity and femininity, "a mixture of inborn and acquired." The transsexual, he said, had a "reversed gender role and false gender orientation," which he also labeled "gender disharmony." As before, though, he subordinated the learned, imprinted, or conditioned aspects of gender to those he saw as rooted in biology. He pointed to various studies of humans and other animals that speculated on genetic and hormonal causes of male and female behavior differences, and he looked most hopefully to new studies of the brain. He doubted whether environmental conditions alone could create crossgender identification. "The presence of an inborn, organic, but not necessarily hereditary origin or predisposition," he concluded, "appears more and more probable."[45]

More generally, whatever the labels used—"psychological sex," "gender role and orientation," or "gender identity"—the disjuncture between the sense of self and the visible body increasingly entered into explanations of transsexuality. The concept of gender was widely adopted, in part perhaps because it did not preclude opposing visions of etiology. The gender identity might result from hormones or genes or brain structure, from imprinting or conditioning or other forms of social learning, or from the psychodynamic processes of identification during mother-infant interaction. Participants on all sides of the debate could use the language of gender without undermining their favored position. Gender, then, came to dominate the scientific approach to transsexuality, but it did not resolve the debates about the causes of transsexuality or the definition of sex. Some scientists continued to search for biological causes, while psychoanalysts published case studies pointing to pathological mother-child relationships.[46] Even as Stoller, Money, and others attempted, with varying emphases, to combine biology and psychology, the battles continued unabated.

In the mid-1960s, as today, the scientific theories did not lend themselves to an easy or obvious assessment. To put it another way, neither the psychoanalysts nor the biological scientists made a convincing case. The psychoanalysts relied on their clinical observations and their interpretations of Freud to speculate on the earliest years of their subjects' lives. One early summary of the literature, though, found "no common pattern which allows one to generalize" about the family dynamics of transsexuals. In later works, psychoanalysts continued to disagree among themselves over which unconscious fantasies, defense mechanisms, and psychological defects constituted "the transsexual wish." Furthermore, the psychoanalysts had to concede that neither psychoanalysis nor other forms of psychotherapy had yet relieved a single transsexual of his or her desire to live as the other sex.[47] In short, despite their best therapeutic attempts, they had not altered anyone's gender identity.

Meanwhile the biological scientists failed their own empirical test. They could pinpoint neither a physical cause nor any physical correlates of transsexuality. Measurements of genitals, assessments of physique, and hormonal assays did not reveal any consistently unusual patterns among transvestites or transsexuals. In 1959 the discovery of sex chromatin material in human cells enabled a simple test of chromosomal sex, but here, too, the studies revealed no statistically significant anomalies.[48] With no actual clinical measurements, Harry Benjamin claimed that around two-fifths of his male-to-female patients and almost one-half of his female-to-male patients seemed to have somewhat underdeveloped gonads; but even Benjamin, the strongest proponent of the biological position, had to admit that the "physical examination of the transsexual patients usually reveals nothing remarkable."[49] Without any evidence to back their theories, the biologically oriented scientists pinned their hopes on parts of the body still invisible to the scientific gaze. From the mid-1960s on, they speculated on the genes, prenatal or neonatal exposure to hormones, and the neurophysiology of the brain.

In their continuing battles, then, each side operated on faith, and neither side could win over the other. As a result, the concept of gender contributed simultaneously to calls for different programs of treatment. By the early 1960s Harry Benjamin and a few others used the concepts of psychological sex or gender identity to support transsexual surgery. As one commentator noted: "Those who favor the operation point out that the psychological determinants of sexual role behavior are more significant than the physiological sex." Or, as Benjamin put it, the "gender-feeling" was "so deeply engrained that the morphological sex" had "to yield."[50] But in the same years, some psychoanalysts used the concept of gender identity to call for psychotherapeutic treatment, especially in childhood, when the gender identity was still in the process of formation. Through the early 1960s Benjamin and his allies had less influence on medical practice than did the psychoanalysts who called for psychotherapy.

*A*s the language of gender emerged, numerous doctors repeated and elaborated on their objections to surgical intervention. Some doctors held that sex-change surgery, especially castration of males, was illegal in the United States. They referred to local mayhem statutes, based on English common law that outlawed the maiming of men who might serve as soldiers. In a review of the issue, Robert Veit Sherwin, a friend of Benjamin and a lawyer, wrote there was "little doubt that cutting off of the male genitalia would not be mayhem." The statutes, however, were frequently "cited as the reason why such an operation would be a crime on the part of the doctor." In this legal context, doctors sometimes sought the advice of lawyers and district attorneys. In 1954, for example, Willard E. Goodwin, a urologist at UCLA, asked Rollin M. Perkins, a professor of law, about the mayhem statutes and the legality of sex-change surgery. Perkins acknowledged "the want of any judicial decision on the point," and then advised "caution . . . because of the uncertainty and because of the apparent prejudice in this country." But more often, doctors refused the legal risk before seeking lawyers' assessments.[51] They raised ethical as well as legal concerns about removing healthy organs, especially those involved with reproduction. In *Sexology* magazine, David O. Cauldwell continued to object to sex-change surgery. "No ethical surgeon," he wrote, "will remove healthy organs." Despite the rise of cosmetic surgery, most surgeons still preferred medical indications in the form of disease to justify operations.[52]

But legality and the ethics of removing healthy organs were not the sole or even the primary obstacles to sex-change surgery. The few American doctors who occasionally performed surgery on transsexuals suffered no legal penalty. No one was prosecuted for sex-change surgery under the mayhem statutes or any other laws. In 1962 the attorney general of California, Stanley Mosk, wrote Robert Stoller: "we have not, to my knowledge, ever contended that such an operation with sound medical justification and the consent of the transvestite, is illegal."[53] A few years later the *Journal of the American Medical Association* took up the issue in its "Question and Answer" section. The "legality" of sex-change operations, the author claimed, "would seem to depend on whether or not there was sound medical justification."[54] By the late 1960s doctors stopped citing the law as the reason they could not provide operations. Meanwhile, without apparent qualms, doctors routinely removed the healthy tissue, including genitals and reproductive organs, of intersexed children, even when the patients themselves had not consented to surgery.

Aside from legality and ethics, other issues underlay the doctors' hesitation. Many doctors, it seems, quietly agreed with the more vocal psychoanalysts who proclaimed transsexuals mentally ill, and therefore refused to comply with what they considered unhealthy desires.[55] Others recognized and feared the controversy that surrounded sex-reassignment surgery. One researcher went so far as to claim that "sex-change surgery is the most controversial issue in medicine."[56] Few doctors chose to associate themselves with such procedures. They might damage their standing among their colleagues or win a reputation as mercenaries or quacks. Hospital administrators also shied away from sex-change surgery, which might potentially embarrass their institutions.[57] They feared publicity, and they also worried about liability if they performed risky, irreversible operations without the justification of disease. Disgruntled patients might regret the surgery and institute lawsuits. As Robert Stoller noted, "one would be very vulnerable if sued by a patient."[58]

In the early 1960s doctors noticed the press coverage accorded David Lee Cameron, who filed a five-million-dollar lawsuit against four doctors and the Buffalo General Hospital. Cameron had undergone male-to-female surgery, including removal of genitals, plastic surgery to construct female organs, and breast augmentation. The operations, the suit claimed, had impaired his health. His doctors had experimented on him and "abandoned him" when complications ensued. They had created "a freak and nonentity, without sex or sexual reproduction organs," and they had "led the patient to believe he 'would be able to lead a normal life as a woman and would be employable as a woman and would be cured of his previous psychological problems.'" The case, apparently settled out of court, was the only one of its kind publicized in the United States in the 1950s and 1960s; nonetheless, it put doctors on notice that disappointed patients might return to haunt them.[59]

Doctors and researchers who supported sex-change surgery acknowledged the difficulties involved. In the late 1950s Eugene de Savitsch, for example, granted that any surgeon involved would have to face criticism from "purists" and "moralists," the trouble of "testify[ing] before . . . judicial bodies and committees . . . to change [the] sex officially," and the inadequate financial return for the "time and effort involved and the challenge to his reputation." Such a surgeon, he claimed, would have to "be a missionary content to hope that his reward will be in heaven." In the 1960s, in private correspondence, Harry Benjamin compared the "situation" to "the plastic nose or facial operations for cosmetic purposes . . . 50 or 60 years ago." "I knew a surgeon who did those operations," he wrote, who "was considered a quack and not acceptable for membership in any medical society." He could not, he said, "blame the younger men now who are afraid . . . on account of the possible criticism and danger to their careers." Wardell B. Pomeroy, at the Kinsey Institute, was less diplomatic. "Very few doctors," he wrote in a letter to Walter Alvarez, "will perform such an operation mostly because they are afraid to stick out their necks."[60]

A survey of physicians confirmed that doctors hesitated to grant their approval. In the mid-1960s three researchers at UCLA—Richard Green, Robert Stoller, and Craig MacAndrew—sent a questionnaire on "sex transformation procedures" to American urologists and gynecologists, psychiatrists, and general practitioners. Of 355 respondents, only one-quarter believed that the procedures would harm the patients' mental health. But the vast majority would not themselves approve sex-change surgery.[61] In a commentary on the survey, Richard Green mentioned the specific concerns raised by psychiatrists. They did "not want to have to explain their actions to a local medical society," they worried about legality and "the possibility of a malpractice suit," they considered the procedures too dangerous for "elective" surgery, and they had "moral and/or religious" objections.[62]

Doctors' attitudes toward transsexual surgery bore some resemblance to their attitudes toward abortion. Both procedures posed questions of legality, both raised the issue of patients' control over their own reproductive systems, and both threatened the reputations of doctors who performed them. In both, desperate patients begged doctors for their help, and in both, doctors weighed the needs and rights of their patients against their own convictions and the risks to their careers. Ira B. Pauly, a psychiatrist at the University of Oregon, drew other parallels. Both sex-change surgery and abortion, he wrote, involved "sex and tabooed topics" and evoked strong reactions "with moral and religious overtones." In both, patients required the help of physicians, and rejected patients sometimes turned to "less than optimal and often unscrupulous hands."[63]

In their attempts to argue the merits of surgical intervention, some doctors and researchers took a new tack. In the 1960s they started to publish follow-up reports on postoperative transsexuals to determine "adjustment" and "satisfaction." They studied the psychological state of patients before and after the operations, most of which had been performed outside the United States, and also asked transsexuals themselves whether they appreciated or regretted their surgery. The results pointed to the benefits of medical intervention. Harry Benjamin, of course, used the studies to argue in favor of medical treatment. From his own records on fifty-one postoperative male-to-female transsexuals, he found that 86 percent had "good" or "satisfactory" results. "Most patients," he stated, "no matter how disturbed they still may be, are better off afterward than they were before."[64] From his smaller caseload of female-to-male transsexuals, he also concluded that patients benefited from treatment. Even doctors who expressed doubts about surgery granted grudgingly that the data indicated "apparent success." By the end of the decade, as one summary stated, "the overwhelming majority of cases . . . indicate better postoperative adjustment."[65]

With the data mounting, a few more doctors and researchers began to endorse sex-reassignment surgery. Ira Pauly traced his own change of heart. "In 1961," he wrote, "I felt there was not evidence to support or justify the request for a change-of-sex operation." He had hesitated "to take responsibility for such a serious and irreversible decision." "It is easier by far," he claimed, "to write the patient off as crazy and get on to other matters, or simply recommend psychotherapy." Nonetheless, he came to recommend surgery "reluctantly after soul-searching deliberation, and in view of the fact that no other alternatives are currently available." Donald W. Hastings, a psychiatrist at the University of Minnesota, went through his own process of deliberation in the mid-1960s. He came to justify surgery because he decided it would help patients. "I too," he wrote Robert Stoller, "am concerned about notoriety and by many requests for surgery from all sorts of people, but one has to, in the final analysis, I suppose, balance these factors against . . . the physician's first duty, of trying to help someone who is suffering."[66] But in the 1960s only a handful of doctors joined Pauly and Hastings in recommending surgery.

The more immediate impact of the new research on transsexuality was to reinforce traditional norms of gender. In the early and mid-1960s, several researchers employed the concept of gender identity to point to the need to monitor gender in early childhood. They depicted "childhood transvestism and other cross gender behavior . . . as a potentially malignant symptom" and called for "treatment before the process of gender identification is complete." Stoller, in particular, warned that "authorities" should not take crossgender behavior in boys lightly. He pushed for "early psychiatric treatment." Stoller's work paralleled that of other post–World War II psychologists and sociologists such as Erik H. Erikson and Talcott Parsons, who, as historian Mari Jo Buhle writes, saw successful "psychosexual development principally as the achievement of sex roles."[67]

This preventative model merged with popular prescriptions for maintaining traditional gender roles. Since gender did not necessarily arise directly from biological sex, it required training. Some of the researchers committed themselves to stereotypes of gender difference and urged parents to preserve traditional gender distinctions in themselves and their children. In an early study, "Incongruous Gender Role," Richard Green and John Money saw part of the "successful rearing of a child" as "orienting him, from birth, to his biologically and culturally acceptable gender role" and, to that end, advocated "a relationship between husband and wife exemplifying these respective roles."[68] The new concepts of gender and gender identity led some doctors to engage in heavy-handed attempts to push boys and their fathers to behave in masculine ways and girls and their mothers to behave in feminine ways. Historians sometimes portray the 1950s as the decade demanding strict conformity to traditional gender roles, but it was not until the 1960s that doctors instituted formal "gender identity" programs to teach gender roles to children and their parents. The research on transsexuality contributed directly to the new programs of research and treatment.

In 1962 a group of doctors in the Department of Psychiatry at UCLA inaugurated such programs when they established their Gender Identity Research Clinic (GIRC). Directed by Stoller, the initial group also included, among others, Ralph Greenson as "senior psychoanalytic consultant" and Richard Green, at that time a resident in psychiatry at UCLA. Initially the clinic intended to focus on intersexed patients and explicitly not on "anatomically and endocrinologically normal homo-sexuals, transvestites, or other sexually perverse patients."[69] But two of its earliest meetings addressed "indications for" and "the ethics of sex transformation operations," and by the end of its second year, the clinic's annual report acknowledged that most of its patients were "transvestite-transsexual."[70] For years, the clinic met several times a month. At meetings doctors presented their research and their patients for discussion. Stoller and Green provided the ongoing leadership. Green left UCLA in 1964 to work at the National Institute of Mental Health and as an officer in the U.S. Public Health Service, but he re-turned in 1967 as director of the clinic.

The GIRC provided an institutional base "to study the development of gender identity," but it neither performed nor recommended trans-sexual surgery. The clinic won its professional reputation for its at-tempts to get "sissy" boys (and occasionally "tomboy" girls) to behave in masculine (or, in the case of girls, feminine) ways. Stoller and Green hoped to instill traditional gender roles in children with the explicit goal of preventing transsexuality (and also transvestism and homosexu-ality) in adults. In the mid-1960s Stoller complained that "our society" was "moving all too rapidly toward massive blurring of gender differ-ences."[71] In the 1970s and afterward their approach came under in-creasing fire. The rising feminist movement advocated exactly what Stoller deplored, and questioned whether doctors (or anyone else) should enforce the stereotypes of gender. Gay men, too, protested when "sissy" boys were pushed into conventional masculinity. In the 1960s, though, the doctors' preventative approach allowed them to translate their research on transsexuals directly into clinical efforts to reinforce conventional systems of gender. They tried to contain the threat of changing gender roles by portraying transsexuality as their "malignant" outcome. As the reputation of the GIRC spread, other institutions, including large clinics in New York City and Toronto, created similar "gender identity" programs.[72]

*I*n the United States, the scientific literature on transsexuality did not emerge until after Christine Jorgensen had made the news. From the early 1950s on, though, American doctors made up for their tardy entry into the field with the vigor of their debates. They explained transsexuality variously as a result of human bisexuality, psychodynamic processes of personality development, or immutable social learning. The theories were not necessarily mutually exclusive, but the scientists often argued as though they were.

As they delineated their approaches, they refined their terms and came up with new definitions of sex, gender, and sexuality. They broke sex into constituent parts, including chromosomes, gonads, hormones, genitals, reproductive organs, and secondary sex characteristics, all of which taken together determined whether a person counted as female or male. They distinguished biological sex from the sense of a sexed self, which they labeled "psychological sex" and later "gender." They began identifying component parts of gender, distinguishing gender role from gender identity, and also separating gender from sexuality. In the process of refining their language, they differed markedly from their predecessors, who had often lumped the physical characteristics of male and female, the social and psychological components of gender role and gender identity, and the expression of sexuality all under the rubric of "sex." In 1960, for example, Daniel G. Brown, a researcher in the field, pointed to "three different, independently varying components in the psychosexual development of an individual": "(1) the constitutional composition as male or female . . . (2) the process whereby a child learns how to be masculine or feminine . . . and (3) the process whereby a child . . . acquires a sex-object choice."[73] In this way he separated sex, gender, and sexuality.

As all the researchers knew, the study of transsexuality had broader ramifications. If sex was defined collectively by hormones, genitals, gonads, chromosomes, and more, then no single variable could determine who was a man and who was a woman, and with medical intervention some variables could be changed. Furthermore, lack of accord between the sex in the mind and the sex in the body raised a larger question of how anyone came to a sense of a gendered self. "If we are to understand the normal emergence of such a basic personality characteristic as masculinity and femininity," Richard Green wrote, "we must understand extreme deviations from that norm."[74] In this way the research on transsexuals opened the door to biological and social science research on sex determination, sex differences, and the construction of gender. It provided a new approach to older debates on nature versus nurture that continue to preoccupy those who hope to establish the (biological or social) basis of gender and sexuality.

Today we often associate the concept of gender with feminism. As feminists note, the social construction of masculinity and femininity suggests the artifice of gender roles. If gender is not "natural," then why work to sustain it? But in the early 1960s the concept of gender raised different issues. The doctors, researchers, and commentators—almost all of them men—who engaged in the debates over sex and gender did not question the need to maintain gender differences and failed to critique the particular gender roles that assigned to women a secondary social and political status.[75] Instead, some psychologists and psychiatrists developed treatment programs to instill masculinity in boys and femininity in girls. In their view, gender roles were not constricting, and gender variance was not benign. Through the mid-1960s they seemed unaware of or uninterested in the rising feminist movement that was acquiring greater national visibility. They worried about the changes in men's and women's behavior, and they tried to stop them by intervening in childrearing practice. As the social and cultural climate shifted in the late 1960s and early 1970s, feminists and others would rework the research on and transform the language of gender. But in the early 1960s the new research had its most immediate practical impact on masculine girls and feminine boys.

It had less immediate impact on the adults who hoped to change their sex. Nonetheless, self-identified transsexuals took an avid interest in the new scientific and medical literature. At its simplest, they could side with doctors who portrayed crossgender identification as biological and endorsed transsexual surgery, or they could side with doctors who cast crossgender identification as mental illness and refused to offer the treatment sought. Not surprisingly, they usually chose the former. But theories alone could not satisfy the overwhelming longing to transform one's sex. Transsexuals continued to push for surgery, and a few American doctors responded. As much as the competing theories, the troubled negotiations between transsexuals and their doctors shaped sex-reassignment surgery. The medical practice of "sex change" evolved as transsexual patients insisted on their right to determine their own sex and to alter their bodies to fit their minds.

A "FIERCE AND DEMANDING" DRIVE

4

*I*n the 1950s and 1960s hundreds of people wrote to, telephoned, and visited doctors to inquire about sex-change surgery. A few may have asked for information on a whim or out of curiosity, and a few may have temporarily seen a change of sex as a way out of other personal problems. But most had what they described as deeply rooted, longstanding, and irrepressible yearnings, and they wanted medical treatment, sometimes with an urgency that bordered on obsession. For some of the prospective patients, the growing coverage in the press shaped their inchoate desires to transform their bodies. For others, the news stories renewed their hopes that doctors might actually respond to their already formulated requests. In the 1950s and afterward they used the press and the medical literature to label their longings, to place themselves in a recognizable category, and to find the names of doctors who might help them.

While the doctors and scientists debated the meanings of sex and gender, many transsexuals simply rejected the notion that the bodies they were born with represented their true or permanent sex. For many, the truth of sex lay in the sense of self, not in the visible body. One FTM remembered that as a young child he had refused to wear dresses because "something inside me just told me that I was a boy." Others acknowledged the common late twentieth-century perception that sex resided in the chromosomes. An MTF stated that "sex cannot be changed, and I am painfully aware of the fact." Nonetheless, she said, "external body appearance can be changed sufficiently that a person who is psychologically miserable any other way can safely, happily, and legally assume the status of woman and live and be accepted as such."[1] Sometimes they expressed their desires with the language of "being"—being the sex they knew they were. At other times they positioned their longings as matters of "becoming"—becoming the men or women they knew they ought to be. However they defined the quest, they laid claim to their own sense of authenticity and their own self-knowledge about whether they should or could live and count as women or men.

Their requests to alter their bodies resonated with other trends in modern American culture. In the mid-twentieth century Americans routinely encountered prescriptions for how they might remake themselves in pursuit of self-fulfillment. Humanist psychologists called for "self-actualization"; advertisements for cosmetics and diet aids invited people to refashion their faces and bodies; educators and book publishers promised to improve the minds of students and readers. Democratic ideals, however imperfectly practiced, suggested that all people had or should have equal opportunities to change their station in life, and twentieth-century liberal individualists increasingly insisted on the rights of "consenting adults" to determine their own course as long as they refrained from behaviors that might cause harm to others. In a society that valued self-expression and self-transformation, why not permit people to decide whether they wanted to live as men or as women, and why not allow them to change their bodies in the ways they desired?

In their interactions with doctors, transsexuals dreamed of the new possibilities created by medical science. But as they urged their doctors to enter uncharted territories of medical treatment, they bumped up against the power of medical gatekeepers, the costs of commodified medical care, and the limits of technology. In response, they learned that only persistence produced results. They needed the cooperation of doctors, but as they applied unsolicited pressure, they and their doctors ended up in conflict. It was in this troubled milieu that a few Americans entered the new terrain of "sex-reassignment surgery." In traditional medical histories, doctors often stand as pioneers in science. In the history of transsexuality, doctors, with a few exceptions, lagged behind, reluctant pioneers at best, pushed and pulled by patients who came to them determined to change their bodies and their lives.

In the mid-twentieth-century United States, Denmark looked like a liberal haven to people who hoped to change their sex. Jorgensen had found not one but several doctors who had rallied to her cause and seen her through her bodily change. Her doctors had taken her seriously, acknowledged her sanity, and used their authority and their technical expertise to change her life for the better. To Danish officials, however, Jorgensen stood as an isolated case. Her surgery, they said, would not serve as a precedent for future medical treatment. Although they still supported the Danish law permitting castrations, the officials at the Medico-Legal Council of the Danish Ministry of Justice, startled by a flood of requests for sex-change surgery, soon announced their decision to refuse the petitions of foreigners.[2]

Nonetheless, in the early 1950s transgendered people wrote repeatedly to the Danish endocrinologist Christian Hamburger, whose sympathetic treatment of Jorgensen had appeared in the American press. In less than a year after the Jorgensen story entered the public domain, Hamburger received "765 letters from 465 patients who appear to have a genuine desire for alteration of sex." Of the 465, 180 wrote from the United States. The letters, Hamburger wrote, ranged from "faulty attempts at presentation in writing" to "stylish masterpieces," from "almost undecipherable bits of paper" to "faultlessly typed reports of up to 60 foolscap pages." He read the letters as "a cry for help and understanding."[3]

Hamburger referred his American correspondents to doctors in the United States. Just one month after the Jorgensen story broke, he responded to a male-to-female correspondent who had already sent him "three letters . . . a collection of photos . . . and . . . Christmas greetings." He had received "several hundreds of letters," mostly, he said, from "men, suffering from the same disease as you." The letters impressed him, and he felt he had a "duty to help." He himself, however, could now help "persons of Danish nationality only." He told this correspondent and others to contact Dr. J. W. Jailer, an endocrinologist in New York.[4] Jailer, it turned out, had little interest in transsexual patients. Without providing any details, one MTF described her reply from Jailer as "distressing," and Harry Benjamin noted that others, too, had had "unfortunate experience[s]" with him. Within months Hamburger realized he had sent his correspondents to the wrong doctor. He began to advise them to "get in contact with Dr. Harry Benjamin." He told one letter writer: "If anybody can give you advice or help, it is Dr. Benjamin. I have referred several patients to him, and they have all found an understanding doctor or even friend in him."[5]

Into the 1960s, most roads led to Benjamin. Hamburger sent him patients, and so did the public transsexuals Christine Jorgensen and Tamara Rees, both of whom came under Benjamin's care. From the United States and abroad, other doctors also gave out his name, especially after he published his first articles on transsexualism. Dr. David O. Cauldwell, who coined the English word *transsexual,* and Dr. Walter Alvarez, who wrote a syndicated medical column, told letter writers to contact Benjamin, and later Dr. Robert Stoller, the psychoanalyst at the University of California at Los Angeles, sent him numerous patients. As his name appeared in the press as an expert on transsexualism and especially after his book came out in 1966, the letters snowballed in volume. New patients brought their friends and acquaintances to Benjamin's attention, and each new contact seemed to lead to others.[6]

Would-be patients traveled to meet Benjamin in his offices in New York City and San Francisco. He examined them, counseled them, and prescribed hormones, and he also engaged in voluminous correspondence with patients and nonpatients who asked for his help. The drag queen Margo Howard-Howard, who never seriously considered surgery, portrayed Benjamin as a "charlatan" who encouraged sex change for virtually anyone who crossed his door. "If Joe Lewis, champion fighter, had walked in for a routine examination," she wrote, "Benjamin would have told him he ought to be a woman." But more of Benjamin's patients appreciated his warmth, his concern for their well-being, his old-world charm, and the nonjudgmental way in which he accepted their unconventional desires. In her autobiography *Second Serve,* male-to-female Renée Richards, a doctor herself, remembered Benjamin, whom she first met in the 1960s, as "a likable fussbudget, very much in the tradition of the Old World general practitioner." At first she thought him "kindly and decent" but "hardly one to inspire unreserved confidence." Then she "began to realize that this old man really did understand." In her autobiography *Conundrum*, the journalist Jan Morris, also a male-to-female transsexual, expressed the same sentiment. She remembered Benjamin as "the first person I met who really seemed to understand."[7]

By all accounts, the prospective patients reflected the diversity of the population. They came from "all cultures, ethnic groups, and socioeconomic levels."[8] In one study of letters from 500 people requesting evaluation for surgery at Johns Hopkins Hospital in the late 1960s, 116 reported their race: 103 reported themselves as white, 13 as African Americans. Among 100 FTMs who participated in a counseling group in Yonkers, New York, in the late 1960s, the "ethnic groups" represented included "Irish, Italian, and German," followed by "English, Puerto Rican, Blacks, Polish, French, Greek, Spanish, Swedish, and Welsh," plus one "Canadian, Chinese, Columbian, Cuban, Danish, Hungarian, Indian, Rumanian, Russian, or Turkish" apiece. Case studies of patients in the West include several mentions of Mexican Americans.[9] The letters they wrote came from rural areas, small towns, and cities, and the jobs they mentioned spanned the spectrum from manual day labor and service work to working-class trades and clerical work to middle- and upper-class professions. Some had spent their entire lives in a single location; others had led rootless lives, drifting from job to job and from place to place. But the stories they told rarely dwelled on, and frequently failed to mention, the categories that sociologists tend to use to classify the population. There was no single plot to their stories, no single life trajectory from birth to transgendered adulthood to the request for surgery. But despite the wide disparities in social background, their stories reveal a few common patterns.

In their initial contacts with Benjamin and other doctors, many conveyed a sense of angst that hinted of suicidal despair. In a letter to Jorgensen, Benjamin described the "phone calls and letters" he had received as "frantic." An FTM wrote Benjamin from Florida: "I have reached the point where it is impossible for me to do much of anything constructive . . . Please forgive my extreme feelings of urgency, for I can truly not stand this feeling of being an impostor any longer. I have done all I can to help myself." An MTF wrote from the West Coast: "I find it increasingly difficult to go on living with myself. I am ready *now* to go to whatever extremes . . . necessary to have a 'sex change.' It is the only way I could ever hope of finding my peace of mind . . . I am tired and I am not willing to fight against my real desire any longer."[10]

They told of doctors who had offered every kind of treatment except sex-change surgery. One MTF had "been advised to have psycho ther-apy, [carbon dioxide] therapy, shock treatments, lobotomy, go out and live as a woman, join a homosexual colony, and commit myself to a mental sanitarium." Other MTFs encountered doctors who injected them with male hormones, and psychiatrists or psychologists who pushed them to relinquish their feminine ways. One FTM had "under-gone everything from 'religious training' to self-hypnosis and shock treatments." Others reported lengthy psychoanalyses and months or years in mental institutions. Both MTFs and FTMs found doctors who promised operations and then backed away.[11]

In their exchanges with doctors and researchers, they tried to explain themselves, sometimes guilelessly and sometimes in ways patently cal-culated to convince doctors to recommend surgery. By the mid-1950s they had the label "transsexualism" to describe their longings, but they still needed to make themselves intelligible to doctors and others who dismissed them as insane. One MTF wrote her life history as a way to "clarify" her mind before she tried to persuade her doctor to recom-mend surgery. She understood her mission: "I have to make a person who is without doubt a normal person see my point of view as I, who am not normal, see it and I have to make my abnormal thoughts and conclusions seems as real and logical to him as they are to me."[12]

Many MTFs and FTMs recounted long and arduous journeys to change their assigned sex. Not all told tales of unremitting hardship, but most wrote sad, and sometimes desperate, letters emphasizing the difficulties of their lives, perhaps in part to impress upon doctors the se-riousness of their requests. Some cast their lives in the plots they found in the popular press. Like Christine Jorgensen, they often portrayed themselves as pilgrims or pioneers who struggled against adversity. They vacillated between a persistent optimism in which struggle mer-ited reward and a lurking pessimism in which insurmountable obstacles prevented them from moving on. From the 1950s on, they portrayed themselves as social beings whose outcast status excluded them from the sense of community for which they longed, and they also stressed personal freedom and presented themselves as individualists who asserted their right to live as they chose.

In recounting their lives to doctors, most emphasized a sense of difference that had begun in childhood. From an early age they had played with the toys and dressed in the clothes prescribed for the other sex. "I was eight," an MTF recalled, "when I announced myself a girl and demanded to play with dolls, dress in girl's clothes, and let my hair grow long." An FTM "had always felt that something was wrong." Since the age of four or five, he had "preferred male activities and toys."[13] As they had matured, their feelings had intensified. Some FTMs reported a sense of humiliation or "disgust" as their breasts developed and menstruation began, and some MTFs expressed a feeling of hatred or revulsion toward their genitals. They described a growing alienation from their own bodies, a sense that the body itself was a mistake. A young FTM explained: "Nothing about me seems abnormal, except I have the wrong body."[14]

Many reported years of ridicule for their unconventional presentations of gender. Their parents had misunderstood them, their siblings had teased them, and their peers had taunted and bullied them. One FTM from Arkansas told a doctor he had been "harassed" by "everybody" and called a "'freak,' 'homo,' or 'hermaphrodite.'" His wife explained: "He was always considered a public freak. He has always been scorned, humiliated and ridiculed beyond all measure." A number of MTFs had joined the armed services in a futile attempt, as one described it, to "make a man of myself," but their peers in the military had not necessarily welcomed them. An MTF serving in the U.S. Army wrote Benjamin: "people disrespect and insult me constantly. I would rather die than be a man all my life. It is a life of torture."[15] The stories of ridicule included accounts of violence, "being hit, beat, raped . . . just really being punished."[16]

The police rarely offered protection. Both MTFs and FTMs told doctors about their "fear of arrest and persecution" at the hands of law-enforcement officials. Many worried about being arrested for crossdressing. Through the 1960s, some local governments used vagrancy and other statutes to regulate and restrain those who dressed in public as the other sex. In the early 1950s, for example, an MTF arrested in California served "six months probation. All because her drivers license said male." A friend of hers explained to Benjamin: "Now she is scared."[17] Publicity about arrests could lead to loss of jobs, as in the 1960s case of a male-to-female transvestite, an airline pilot, whose conviction for crossdressing cost him his job and pension a year before retirement. MTFs could expect harassment, and sometimes assault, when they were booked, and unless they went in the "queens' tank," the cells reserved for feminine men, time in jail could result in rape by other inmates. By the mid-twentieth century the police more frequently arrested male-to-female crossdressers, who appeared more shocking in dresses than FTMs appeared in pants. But FTMs who lived as men also knew, as one described it, "the apprehension of risking discovery and imprisonment." Another described his fears when using public restrooms: "In using a men's room, when dressed in male attire, I subject myself to possible apprehension as a 'male impersonator.' In using a women's room, other women there might possibly regard me as a man invading their privacy." He had, he said, "an insoluble and potentially dangerous problem."[18]

The doctors' records also report arrests for running away from home and other infractions. Transgendered youth sometimes tried to escape their unhappy pasts and to lose themselves in the anonymity of larger cities, where they might also find doctors and friends to help them. One FTM with "fanatic religious" parents was arrested en route from Tallahassee to San Francisco to meet with Harry Benjamin. Sometimes family members called in the police. The mother-in-law of another FTM had him arrested for taking money on false pretenses, but she objected primarily to his "unnatural" marriage to her daughter. The arrests often led to referrals to psychiatrists and sometimes to incarceration in jails or mental institutions.[19]

They might avoid such conflicts, but only, they said, at a psychic cost. The transsexual child, one MTF believed, had a choice: "whether to flaunt his desire . . . and launch himself on a defiant life of nonconformity and endless conflicts with society and the law—or to bury deeply his feminine inclination . . . no matter what the cost to mental well-being." Before her surgery, she chose to hide her femininity. She had, she said, "few friends," and her "tolerable world was the world of fantasy." She secretly dressed as a girl, and she had fantasies of "exotic surgical operations in which my brain would be transferred to the body of a beautiful girl." She contemplated suicide before eventually finding her way to doctors who agreed to help her.[20]

Whether they exposed themselves to ridicule and arrest or hid their desires protectively, they often portrayed themselves as misfits. Their stories, like Jorgensen's, were frequently tales of isolation, of people who may have had family and friends but still lacked and longed for a sense of belonging. By the 1960s more of them came to know and rely on other transgendered people, especially in the cities.[21] But even as they developed their own sense of community, they frequently presented themselves as seekers who looked for a place in the world where they might feel at ease and at home. Although they asked the doctors for surgery to change the insignia of sex, the quest itself was not solely or even primarily about breasts or ovaries or penises or testicles. In a letter to Robert Stoller, one FTM described it as "yearnings for release from . . . bondage." "A more complete transformation," he wrote, would provide "enough freedom to find . . . a real identity and a dignified existence." He did not want either "a temporary refuge" or a life "alone and apart."[22]

The request for surgery, though, was not just a strategy for self-protection or an attempt to escape from ridicule, violence, arrest, and isolation. It was also an active form of self-expression. Transsexuals often presented their personal quest as an overwhelming commitment to an unshakable sense of an authentic inner self. Increasingly they used a modernized variation of Ulrichs' nineteenth-century formulation, "a female soul in a male body." They spoke of "a female trapped in a male's body" or "a male entity . . . somehow imprisoned in a female body."[23] By the 1960s, this became a shorthand rendition for a particular life history in which the desire to change sex reflected the assertion of an inner self.

Among postmodern academics today, it is decidedly unfashionable to speak of a "true self," an "inner essence," or a "core" identity beneath a surface appearance. But transsexuals, like most people, had a deeply rooted sense of who they were. We need to attend, as psychoanalyst Lynne Layton reminds us, to "the specificity, construction, and experience of an individual's inner world and relational negotiations." Layton refers to a core identity as "something internal that recognizably persists even while it may continuously and subtly alter." For many late twentieth-century transsexuals, the "true" or "inner" or "trapped" self referred to this core identity and provided the dominant metaphor to summarize a "life-plot" of crossgender identification.[24]

Those who were more educated sometimes explained this sense of self with the modern language of psychology. Stephen Wagner referred directly to the "self-actualization" of postwar humanist psychology. He "had a hunch that the reason why some of us choose to become women is because of the basic pioneering spirit which is very essential in all of us . . . It is related very closely to the principle of nonconformity as well as to that of creativity." In this view, crossgender behavior and sex change were bold forms of self-improvement, creative acts of "individuality and individual freedom" that pushed against the limits of conventional mores. Others used the more traditional language of religion. The desire to change sex came from God or resided in the soul. An FTM told Robert Stoller: "God created me a girl, so maybe I should be. But I couldn't be, and which is more important, your mind or your body? God created my mind too, and if my mind is working that way, He created that." From a different spiritual angle, an MTF speculated on past lives and reincarnation and concluded, echoing Ulrichs, "maybe once in a great while a female spirit or soul accidentally incarnates in a male body."[25]

While some adopted the language of psychology and religion to express their understandings of themselves, more turned to biology to explain the source of their unconventional desires. Their crossgender identification felt so substantial and their desire to change their bodily sex so firmly rooted that most could not perceive the condition as anything but physical. Despite the publicity about Jorgensen, some transsexuals, especially FTMs, still presented themselves to doctors as hermaphrodites and pseudohermaphrodites. Several FTMs believed they had testicles hidden internally. One imagined his testicles in a lump in the groin and another in "swellings on either side of the vaginal outlet." They diagnosed themselves as biologically male and "rejected any

other interpretation." To convince their doubting doctors, they sometimes requested (and occasionally underwent) exploratory surgery in
an attempt to prove the existence of hidden male gonads.[26]

MTFs also favored a biological approach. Like FTMs, some portrayed themselves as intersexed, hoping perhaps, as one psychiatrist
phrased it, to "substantiate a biological basis for their condition, and
thus obtain the change of sex operation." A few who knew otherwise
presented themselves as hermaphrodites because this seemed a more
convincing story. "I realize my own condition perfectly," one MTF
told Benjamin, "but to quite some few people . . . the idea of
hermaphroditism is easier to explain and understand."[27] Others focused on hormones. One MTF explained herself to her children with
the theory of bisexuality: "in each man and each woman there is a rem-
nant of the opposite sex, and . . . the balance between the two is not always at the same point." Like Jorgensen, she explained her problem
"in terms of hormones and ductless glands." Another MTF wrote to
Benjamin: "All of us feel that there is something different about our
chemical make-up."[28]

Some acknowledged the possibility that the desire to change sex was
not a physical condition, but they insisted that the longing for transformation was too compelling and too authentic to eradicate. One MTF
insisted: "I still feel that somehow . . . there must be a physical reason
for the way I feel. It is such an overpowering feeling." Another MTF
explained:

> At first I thought that there might be some organic cause or rea-
> son for my feelings, but now I'm not so sure. My family doctor
> and a psychiatrist that I went to told me that it was not organic
> but psychological. The psychiatrist wanted to rid me of the feel-
> ings but they are so strong and intense that I have no desire to
> change them . . . I can't imagine just why I feel as I do but the
> feelings are real and not put-on.

Another MTF "had no idea" why she had "always wanted to be a girl,"
but she considered it "a form of mental suicide," the death of her self,
to abandon her femininity.[29]

1. In the 1910s Eugen Steinach, a physiologist in Vienna, attempted to change the sex of rodents by transplanting gonads. In this "masculization series," he showed how a castrated infant female guinea pig with an implanted testicle grew to the size of a male. Left to right: "masculized sister, castrated sister, normal sister, normal brother."

Paris 1929
Vor der Operation

Dresden 1930
Nach der Operation

2. In the 1920s and early 1930s a number of human "sex change" experiments took place under the auspices of Magnus Hirschfeld's Institute for Sexual Science in Berlin. Danish artist Lili Elbe, formerly Einar Wegener, was one of Hirschfeld's patients.

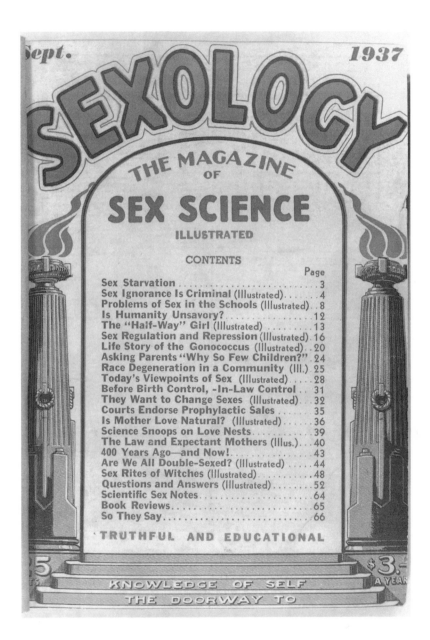

Sept. 1937

SEXOLOGY

THE MAGAZINE OF

SEX SCIENCE

ILLUSTRATED

CONTENTS

TRUTHFUL AND EDUCATIONAL

5 $3.-
ts A YEAR

KNOWLEDGE OF SELF
THE DOORWAY TO

3. From the 1930s on, the popular magazine *Sexology* carried articles on sex changes, including the article "They Want to Change Sexes" in this September 1937 issue.

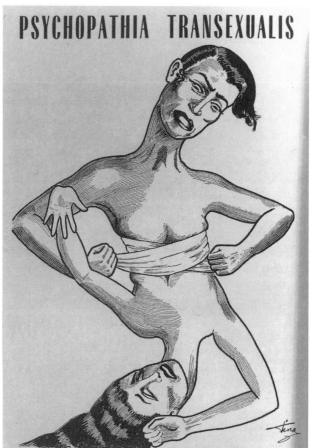

PSYCHOPATHIA TRANSEXUALIS

Many individuals have an irresistible desire to have their sex changed surgically. Some females want to become males, some males want to change into females. These persons are not necessarily homosexuals. Our surrealist artist vividly illustrates the case of a young girl who violently insisted to become a male. She wore only male clothing and in a desperate effort to change her sex she bound her breasts so they would take on a more male-like appearance. The dual personality is shown in the two figures, merged into one. The top represents the "masculine" female, the bottom the real-recessive female. Individuals of this type are psychopathic, i.e., sick persons. This condition is by no means rare. Many medical men have had such cases.

4. A 1949 article, "Psychopathia Transexualis," in *Sexology* magazine used the word *transexual* to refer to people who hoped to "live as the opposite sex."

5. Harry Benjamin, a German-born and German-trained endocrinologist, was the first doctor in the United States to specialize in and publish scholarly articles on transsexualism. For decades he served as a sympathetic advocate for his patients.

DAILY NEWS

NEW YORK'S PICTURE NEWSPAPER®

Vol. 34. No. 136   Copr. 1952 News Syndicate Co., Inc.   New York 17, N.Y., Monday, December 1, 1952   4¢ IN CITY LIMITS | 5¢ OUTSIDE CITY LIMITS

4¢

EX-GI BECOMES BLONDE BEAUTY

Operations Transform Bronx Youth

—Story on Page 3

(NEWS foto Copyright 1952 by NEWS Syndicate Co. Inc.)

A World of a Difference

George W. Jorgenson Jr., son of a Bronx carpenter, served in the Army [▲] for two years and was given honorable discharge in 1946. Now George is no more. After six operations, Jorgenson's sex has been changed and today she is a striking woman [◄—], working as a photographer in Denmark. Parents were informed of the big change in a letter Christine (that's her new name) sent to them recently. —*Story on page 3*

6. On December 1, 1952, the *New York Daily News* broke the Christine Jorgensen story with a front-page headline, inaugurating a media frenzy.

HERE IS A CLOSEUP of blue-eyed, blonde Christine as she meets the barrage of questions hurle
her by reporters on her flying arrival from Denmark, via Scandinavian Airlines.

7. After surgery in Denmark, Jorgensen returned to New York City on
February 13, 1953. This photo—with journalists swarming around a glamorous Jorgensen—shows the aura of celebrity that already surrounded her.

PEOPLE IN MEDICINE

NEW SEX SWITCHES

Behind the Sensational Headlines Loom Unpleasant Medical Facts

Next to the recurrent hydrogen bomb headlines, reports of sex changes are becoming the most persistently startling world news. Latest U.S. case in point is Charles—Charlotte McLeod (*below*). But similar stories crop up elsewhere: In Teheran, surgeons help a 16-year-old girl turn into a soldier of the Shah. In London, a dashing fighter pilot and father readjusts to life as a sophisticated lady. In Naples, 13-year-old Adrianna becomes Andrew.

What are the facts behind these tales? How can a man turn into a woman, and to whom does this happen? PEOPLE TODAY herewith presents the latest authentic information about these secrecy-shrouded phenomena.

News reports generally avoid medical details and precise classification of sex changelings, but each case falls into one of the following groups. ▶

Charles McLeod (*l.*), 28, went to Denmark for surgery in '53. He's back as Charlotte (*r.*), counts on final operation in '55 for "a normal life."

8. In the mid-1950s the American press frequently reported on sex-change surgery. This article from the May 5, 1954, issue of *People Today* magazine begins: "Next to the recurrent hydrogen bomb headlines, reports of sex changes are becoming the most persistently startling world news." The photos are before and after shots of Charlotte McLeod, a male-to-female who followed in Jorgensen's footsteps.

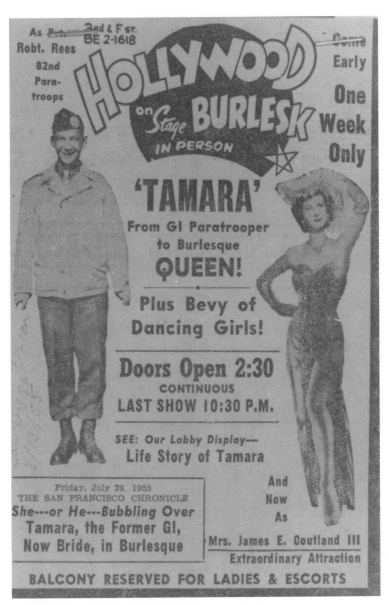

9. In 1955 Tamara Rees, a male-to-female, went on the stage in a burlesque show, projecting a more risqué image of transsexuality.

10. Louise Lawrence began to live fulltime as a woman in 1944 but never underwent surgery. In the 1950s she worked with Harry Benjamin, Alfred C. Kinsey, and other researchers to educate scientists about transvestism and transsexuality.

11. Coccinelle, a French male-to-female performer at Paris' famous nightclub Le Carrousel, promoted a more overtly eroticized image of MTFs.

12. *"I Changed My Sex!,"* the autobiography of the male-to-female stripper Hedy Jo Star, exemplified the more titillating approach to transsexuality that appeared regularly in the 1960s.

From Man To Woman

By Delisa Newton

This is the first of a two-part series on the life of Delisa Newton. Miss Newton tells how she underwent an operation which changed her from male to female. In her own words, she describes her frustrated existence as a boy, her homosexual experiences as an adult before the dramatic sex-change that turned her into what she always wanted to be — a woman.

'I was a complete misfit — I had the mind and soul of a girl and the body of a boy'

On this crowded planet where billions of people live, I am the one and only Negro sex change!

It took many years before I could claim this famous first, years of heartache, tears and pain. But now, at last, I'm a woman, really a woman.

You men who feel at home in your muscular, strong bodies — you'll never know what I have undergone.

You women who were lucky enough to be born female and soft, you'll never understand what a blessing your natural femininity is!

But I know, because I struggled for years to achieve it.

Let me tell you what it was like to realize even before I became a teenager that I was born the wrong sex.

Let me go back to the beginning and picture for you the life of a complete misfit — complete because I had the mind and soul of a girl, but the body of a boy.

I was born in New Orleans 32 years ago. New Orleans, a town of mixed blood, mixed languages and mixed desires. Some of that exotic mixture may have rubbed off on me.

My mama is from Haiti, a beautiful mulatto woman who speaks both French and English fluently in her soft, musical voice.

My father, a Baptist minister, I never knew well. He and my mama separated when I was three.

The doctors say I had no father figure to pattern myself after, so I identified with my stern, no-nonsense mother. Maybe.

But I did have brothers, one of them 14 years my senior. And he had as much author-

13. An article on Delisa Newton, billed as "the first Negro sex-change," from *Sepia*, an African-American magazine, 1966.

14. In 1967 Christine Jorgensen revived her career with the publication of her autobiography.

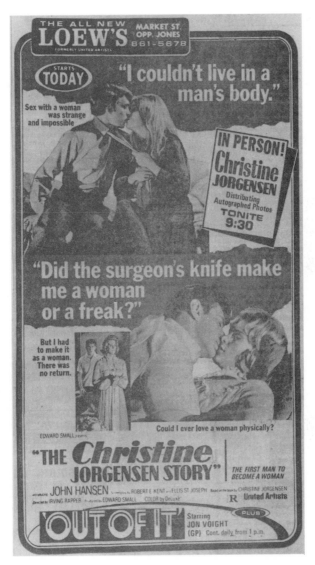

15. Advertising for *The Christine Jorgensen Story* (1970) tried to make the movie sound sexy, but the film actually had little erotic content. Jorgensen consulted on the film and took pride in it even though it flopped.

16. In 1964 Reed Erickson, a wealthy female-to-male transsexual, founded the Erickson Educational Foundation, an organization that promoted research and education on transsexuality.

17. John Money, a psychobiologist at Johns Hopkins University, conducted research on transsexuals. He was a key figure in establishing the Johns Hopkins University Gender Identity Clinic, inaugurated in 1966, the first university medical center to conduct sex-reassignment surgery.

18 and 19. Robert Martin was the sole female-to-male transsexual in COG, a San Francisco group founded in 1967. It was the first formal organization of self-identified transsexuals. Wendy Kohler, a member of COG, served as the first director of the National Transsexual Counseling Unit, a San Francisco organization that grew out of COG in 1969.

20. In 1986 Louis Sullivan organized a support group for female-to-male transsexuals in the San Francisco Bay Area. The group eventually became FTM International, the largest FTM organization in the United States.

As they related their life stories, they hoped for a sympathetic ear. For some, simply writing or talking to a humane doctor was "in itself a tremendous relief."[30] But usually they wanted more. Some sought doctors' advice on various treatment options, but many came already convinced that they wanted surgery. The surgery promised real benefits. They might live legally as the sex they desired without fear of arrest, assault, or exposure. "I desire to work and live openly," one MTF told Benjamin, "with assurance of freedom from prosecution by law." Also, with bodily transformation, others might see and treat them as the men or women they knew or wanted themselves to be. An FTM who had lived as a man for twenty-three years explained to Benjamin: "I have to live in fear all the time . . . whenever it came to lite [sic] that I wasn't a man as they thought but a woman, then I would lose my job. I have suffered years of embarrassement [sic] and ridicule." With surgery, they hoped, they might "just liv[e] without the feeling of being a misfit."[31] But surgery was also symbolic. It was the coup de grâce that ended a "sham existence" or "a life of deceit." Surgery was not the only part or even the most important part of the quest for authentic self-expression. For some, however, it became a defining event. An MTF told Benjamin: "I think of nothing else but the operation."[32]

*O*perations, though, were not easy to obtain. First, they required money. In the American market economy, the quest for self-expression increasingly involved the purchase of goods and services that promised a better life. For the American transsexual, surgery was such a commodity, a desperately desired consumer item, available only to those who could afford it. The United States did not (and does not) have a national health plan that covered surgery, and private medical insurance would not cover "elective" procedures, especially ones that had not won the approval of mainstream doctors. Christine Jorgensen had found doctors who treated her for nothing as part of their medical research. Those who followed often hoped for similar treatment. "Maybe," one MTF said, "some doctor might want to operate . . . as a sort of experiment."[33] But transsexuals without substantial savings rarely found doctors in the United States or abroad who responded positively to requests for surgery. In 1955 Harry Benjamin wrote to urologist Elmer Belt: "Those who have no money or too little of it are simply out of luck. I feel a bit ashamed of the medical profession to allow such a state of affairs to exist." Ten years later Robert Stoller responded to a request for a "sex transfer": "I would say that your chances of getting such help are small, especially if you do not have a lot of money."[34]

Even patients with money had difficulty finding surgeons who would perform transsexual operations. Through the 1960s, the demand for sex-change operations well outpaced the supply. In 1966 Johns Hopkins Hospital announced its program to perform sex-reassignment surgery. Over the next two and a half years the doctors there received "almost 2000 desperate requests" for surgery. They turned almost all of them down, performing surgery on only 24 patients, just slightly more than one percent of the total.[35] In this bottleneck situation it took money, persistence, and unwavering will to find a doctor who would agree to surgery.

Facing obstacles at every turn, some transgendered people gave up. Stephen Wagner, for example, had searched for male-to-female surgery since the 1930s. After the publicity about Christine Jorgensen, he wrote Alfred Kinsey, "If I had the money, I would fly to Denmark at once!"[36] He renewed his efforts to find an American surgeon, corresponding with Christian Hamburger, Walter Alvarez, and Harry Benjamin, among others. Meanwhile, in his hometown of Chicago he visited doctors who he thought might offer operations. Dr. William S. Kroger, Wagner recounted, promised surgery and then changed his mind. According to Wagner, Kroger advised him "to move away from Chicago and live as a woman without . . . operations." Another doctor gave him injections of male hormones "to become more masculinized," which Wagner stopped against the doctor's wishes.[37] But aside from the doctors who failed to give him what he requested, Wagner expressed concerns of his own. When Harry Benjamin offered to see and treat him in New York, Wagner wondered how he would find a job and a home and worried how his sister and brother-in-law would react. He longed for operations to change his sex, but he also "hate[d]" himself "for being so overwhelmed by that horrible desire." And he did "not relish the idea of being a 'weak facsimile' of a woman." The lack of local doctors to help him conspired with his own anxieties and kept him from acting on his stated desires. In 1958 Harry Benjamin annotated his correspondence with Wagner: "Never met him. Not operated."[38]

For other transsexuals, the obstacles to surgery only strengthened their resolve. Debbie Mayne (pseudonym), an MTF with few financial resources, tried every possible avenue to find herself a surgeon. She wrote to Christian Hamburger, Harry Benjamin, and other doctors, convinced a reporter to help her find a surgeon in Europe, asked a transsexual friend to castrate her, and cooperated with the research of Drs. Frederic Worden and James Marsh in Los Angeles in the hope that they would recommend her for surgery. By the end of 1954 all her attempts had failed. Yet she told Benjamin: "I am *extremely confident* and determined . . . This drive is [so] fierce and demanding that it frightens me." She determined to "find me a quack in Mexico" who would perform the operation.[39] Others sought underground practitioners in the United States. An FTM had his breasts removed on his sister's kitchen table. According to one report, other transsexuals "resorted to abortionists, in the belief that these criminal operators would do anything for money."[40]

With or without surgery, transgendered people sometimes experimented with other forms of bodily change. Some FTMs bound their breasts to flatten their chests and decided to live fulltime as men. Tom Michaels (pseudonym), an FTM, described his transformation: "In a matter of months I progressed from my usual jeans and shirt to flannel slacks and tie to completely masculine attire and 'passing.'"[41] Some MTFs began the painful and lengthy process of electrolysis to rid themselves of their facial and body hair, and some crossdressed in public despite the risks of violence and arrest. Caren Ecker (pseudonym) lived for a while as a woman in Mexico City until the experiment ended "in disaster" when a "pawing drunk" discovered her secret. A few MTFs attempted other forms of self-induced physical change. In the mid-1960s one MTF bought "female hormone facial cream" and ate it, and also attempted "to push my testicle back up inside my body." Another attempted to create breasts by injecting "air, hand cream, mother's milk and water" into her chest.[42]

FTMs and MTFs usually took hormones under the care of doctors such as Harry Benjamin, but some managed to obtain solutions and tablets on their own. After a few months of testosterone injections, FTMs underwent visible, audible, and permanent changes. Their voices dropped to a lower pitch. Gradually their clitorises increased in size, their skeletal muscles developed, and their facial and body hair multiplied. Some FTMs also noticed weight gain, acne, a slight shrinking of the breasts, or male-pattern balding. As long as they took the hormone, it enhanced their libido and inhibited menstruation. It could also produce a surge of energy akin to the jolt from caffeine. For MTFs the visible changes were subtler. After taking estrogen, often combined with progesterone, MTFs noticed swelling in their breasts, sensitivity of the nipples, and sometimes softer hair and smoother skin. Their testicles atrophied, their libido declined, and their erections and ejaculations diminished or ceased. With prolonged doses, they experienced a more visible redistribution of subcutaneous fat and more pronounced growth of the breasts. For many, estrogen also seemed to have a soothing or calming effect. To quicken the process of change, some exceeded the recommended dosage, despite the risks of heart disease and liver damage for FTMs and thrombosis for MTFs. For this reason, Harry Benjamin warned against "self-medication."[43]

For some, binding their breasts or crossdressing or taking hormones was sufficient. Louise Lawrence, born in 1913, had lived fulltime as a woman since 1944. By the 1950s she saw surgery as one possible way of accommodating crossgender identification, but she did not seek it for herself. A friend said Lawrence considered herself "to [sic] old" for surgery, and Lawrence told a correspondent: "As in most everything else in life there are numerous ways of achieving a given result." Still, she recognized the urge to change sex and told Harry Benjamin: "I firmly believe that MOST transvestites have that same urge but in varying degrees and areas." She lived as a woman until her death in 1976, and under Benjamin's guidance she experimented with hormones.[44]

Others moved in fits and starts toward surgery. After he decided to don men's clothes, Tom Michaels spent years living as a man, some of them in "grossly anti-social behavior" with criminal associates, "the first social grouping which accepted me on my own terms." Ashamed of his life, he eventually decided to pursue "professional ambition" and earned a bachelor's degree in zoology. He reverted to living as a woman and spent a year in medical school. But he could not relinquish his desires. In the mid-1960s he contacted Robert Stoller in search of "a more complete transformation." It "would be infinitely easier," he wrote, "with medical help rather than opposition." He wanted the "necessary alterations" and also hoped for "moral support." He began taking testosterone and looked forward to surgery.[45]

For MTFs the search for surgery often began with castration. As doctors rebuffed them, some MTFs reached the point of desperation and cut off their own genitals. According to one review of the medical literature, published in 1965, 18 of 100 MTFs had attempted to remove their own testicles or penises, and 9 had succeeded.[46] At the age of forty-three, for example, Caren Ecker, now living in northern California, gave herself local anesthetic, removed her testicles, and, in her own words, "almost bled to death." Eventually Dr. Karl Bowman, of San Francisco's Langley Porter Clinic, recommended additional surgery to remove the penis. At the end of 1953 Dr. Frank Hinman Jr. performed the surgery at the University of California at San Francisco. As in cases of botched self-induced abortions, doctors sometimes felt more comfortable cleaning up afterward than providing medical care from the start.[47]

Annette Dolan (pseudonym) sent Harry Benjamin an autobiographical account of her self-surgery. (Later a different version of it appeared in print, under a pseudonym, in *Sexology* magazine.) "For years," she said, doctors had told her "there was no 'help' for me, and I accepted this [as] gospel." After Christine Jorgensen made the news, though, she made up her mind to undergo surgery. Initially hesitant, her doctor, probably Benjamin, eventually suggested she go abroad for castration, after which he could help her find a surgeon in the United States to perform the rest of the operations. Lacking funds for surgery overseas, she decided to perform the operation herself. She read medical texts outlining the operation and bought the surgical equipment needed to perform it. "I learned to ligate, suture and anesthetize," she said; "I studied the surgical procedure step by step and memorized its sequence." She excised her testicles successfully in an hour and later presented her doctor with the fait accompli. With any legal obstacles literally removed, she found a surgeon to complete the work. In 1954 Elmer Belt, a urologist at UCLA, performed the rest of her surgery, including construction of a vagina.[48]

Like many surgeons, Belt had a certain bravado. He took pride in his technical skills and saw new forms of surgery as a challenge to his expertise. He had, as he told Benjamin, "a strong sense of compassion for these poor devils" and also "an intense curiosity." He considered himself a "softie" who found it hard to turn away desperate patients.[49] In the 1950s he operated on other MTFs, including Barbara Richards Wilcox, who had made the news in the early 1940s when she had gone to court to change her legal gender status. Belt used a procedure in which he preserved the testicles, pushing them through the inguinal ring out of the scrotum and into the abdomen. He thought it medically best to preserve the testicles and the hormones they produced, and thereby managed to avoid whatever legal liability castration might potentially involve. At the end of 1954 Belt temporarily ceased his work when a committee of doctors at UCLA, including urologist Willard Goodwin and psychiatrist Frederic Worden, decided against the surgeries. In the late 1950s he quietly resumed his sex-reassignment practice, but in early 1962, under pressure from his wife, son, and office manager, he decided to stop for good. He complained about searching for hospitals that would let him perform sex-reassignment surgery, he feared that a dissatisfied patient would sue him and ruin his practice, and he groused about the impoverished patients who failed to pay their bills. When he learned that Dr. Georges Burou, a French surgeon with a clinic in Casablanca, was doing good surgery, he opted out.[50]

Other MTFs found a handful of other surgeons, mostly abroad, who would perform the operations. In 1954 and 1955 several of Benjamin's patients had operations in Holland. But European doctors were not as accepting as some transsexuals had imagined. After initial surgery in Holland and plastic surgery in Denmark, one MTF told Benjamin: "The 'favorable' doctors . . . are in the minority in Europe." And most of the "favorable" doctors refused American patients after 1955. In the mid-1950s other MTFs, including Debbie Mayne, went to Mexico for surgery with Dr. Daniel Lopez Ferrer. In the early 1960s Burou replaced Belt as the surgeon of choice for those who could afford his fees and the costs of international travel. For years afterward his widely acclaimed surgical skills brought him a steady stream of patients from Europe and the United States. In the early and mid-1960s operations were also occasionally performed "rather secretly," according to Benjamin, in the United States, as well as in Japan, Mexico, and Italy.[51] Dr. Orion Stuteville did "a few such procedures" in Chicago, as did Drs. Jaime Caloca Acosta and Jose Jesus Barbosa in Tijuana and Professor Francesco Sorrentino in Naples. By the end of the 1960s a few university hospitals—Johns Hopkins, University of Minnesota, Stanford, and University of Washington—had begun to provide surgery for a small number of MTFs.[52]

The techniques differed from place to place. Some surgeons removed only the testicles and penis, or one or the other, but most also performed plastic surgery to create labia, usually from the scrotum. Increasingly surgeons also created vaginas at the same time. Doctors had performed vaginoplasty since the nineteenth century, when they experimented with various methods for constructing vaginas for women born without them or for women with deformed or damaged ones. By the mid-1950s the most common method used skin grafts from the thigh, buttocks, or back. Occasionally surgeons used mucosal tissue from the intestine, but this entailed more-invasive surgery. By the late 1950s a few doctors preserved the sensitive skin of the penis, turned it inside out, and used it to line the vagina. In Morocco, Burou attracted patients by perfecting this method. In the late 1960s a handful of American doctors adopted his technique.[53]

The surgery itself was painful and harrowing. For Patricia Morgan, who underwent surgery with Elmer Belt in 1961 and 1962, the first operation lasted around eight hours. Belt removed the penis and pushed the testicles into the abdomen. When Morgan woke up, she saw "all the wires and tubes and catheters." "I was just a glob of aching flesh," she wrote later. After two and a half months Morgan returned for eight more hours of surgery to create a vagina. After the second operation, "the pain inside was even worse than before." After three days Belt removed the bandages. "I was sickened by the stench of the blood and the dead flesh," Morgan remembered. "There was swelling something fierce down there. I couldn't look." For two more weeks in the hospital, "the pain remained unbearable," and for a while after her release she still could not walk and bled profusely from her vagina.[54]

Before and after genital surgery, some MTFs sought other operations. Some wanted to enlarge their breasts. In New York in the 1950s Dr. Else K. La Roe, a German-born surgeon, gave breast implants to a few MTFs, including Charlotte McLeod. Other MTFs hoped to change the shape of their noses or shave off the more prominent cartilage on their "Adam's apples." Their goal in general was to appear as nontranssexual women, and the additional surgery often helped keep strangers from reading them as men. Faced with repeated requests for surgery, some doctors complained of "the tendency of these patients to desire polysurgery" and advised restraint in offering additional operations. But MTFs persisted, and occasionally their requests outstretched the medical technology. A few patients hoped that doctors could reduce their height or enable them to bear children. "In the most successful operation we ever had," Elmer Belt wrote, "the patient came in after all was done expressing dissatisfaction because there was not a uterus with tubes and ovaries . . . and she could therefore not have a baby." Another MTF approached Else La Roe in tandem with an FTM. They asked for "a mutual transplantation of their sexual organs," a request they may have borrowed from the realm of science fiction.[55]

$\mathcal{A}$lthough doctors today usually posit equal numbers of FTMs and MTFs, in the 1950s and 1960s they believed that MTFs far outnumbered FTMs. The ratios (MTF:FTM) offered by various studies in Europe and the United States ranged from 8:1 to 2:1. They reflect the numbers of MTFs and FTMs that doctors encountered in their practices or in reviews of the medical literature. By the mid-1960s, for example, Benjamin had diagnosed and treated 152 MTFs but only 20 FTMs. At the end of the decade, when Johns Hopkins Hospital reported almost 2,000 requests for surgery, only one-fifth came from FTMs.[56] As a result of the numbers, some researchers considered transsexualism in the same way they considered fetishism or transvestism, as a largely, if not wholly, "male" condition. They sometimes speculated that sex differences in neuroendocrine development or in the psychodynamic processes in which the infant separated from the mother led to a skewed sex ratio in the prevalence of crossgender identification.[57]

For this reason, FTMs sometimes had trouble convincing doctors to take them seriously as candidates for surgery. In 1954, before he had FTM patients, Harry Benjamin did not know what to make of a correspondent who asked about female-to-male surgery. "There is no operation possible," he responded, "that would change a female into a male. In some rare cases a male has been operated on so that he later on resembles a female, but nothing like that is possible if the patient is a normal girl." At the end of the 1960s doctors at UCLA's Gender Identity Research Clinic debated privately whether FTMs even qualified as transsexuals. From 1968 to 1970 they held at least fifteen meetings devoted to FTMs. Robert Stoller wondered "whether there should be such a diagnosis as 'transsexualism' for females." After twelve years of treating FTMs, he could not find "etiological events which hold from case to case or even a very consistent clinical picture, other than the raging desire to become a male." His colleague Richard Green disagreed. He attempted "to convince the world (or at least our microcosm) of the existence of a syndrome of female transsexualism."[58] But the interest at UCLA was somewhat unusual. In the main, doctors focused their research and their attention on MTFs.

For their part, fewer female-to-male transgendered people asked doctors for surgery. They may not have seen examples in the press of successful surgical transformations, and they may have avoided a surgical solution that still could not produce a functioning penis. The subordination of women may also have played a role. Those who had grown up as girls may not have had the same sense of entitlement to medical services as did MTFs or the same insistent attitude with doctors, and those who lived and worked as women may have had fewer economic resources to finance medical intervention. The diverging constraints of masculinity and femininity may also have entered into their decisions. Female-to-males could dress as men with less risk of arrest. By midcentury, women frequently dressed in pants. On the streets, onlookers often treated a masculine or butch woman with hostility and contempt, but police rarely arrested her simply for her attire. Furthermore, in the postwar era some highly masculine women could find an accepting community in butch-femme working-class lesbian bar networks, but highly feminine men were increasingly reviled, even among gay men.[59] In addition, with hormone treatments most FTMs could live as men without arousing suspicions. If they grew facial hair they could usually expect casual observers to see them as men. For these and other reasons, female-to-male transgendered people often stopped short of surgery.

Still, some FTMs begged doctors for surgery and took it where they could find it. If they could not convince American doctors, they sometimes went to Europe or Mexico in search of operations.[60] In the early 1960s, for example, a twenty-six-year-old South American FTM came to the United States in search of surgery. In one "eastern medical center," operations were "advised but . . . not available"; in another, surgery was refused. He then "travelled to Denmark," where doctors refused to treat him because he "was neither a citizen nor a resident." Eventually he found doctors in New York who promised what he wanted. He began testosterone injections. In 1965 he underwent "bilateral mastectomy," and in 1967 he had "all internal genitalia" removed and his vagina closed.[61]

In most cases, surgery for FTMs meant removal of breasts and internal reproductive organs. These were procedures that surgeons performed routinely on women. They did not require unusual technical skills. Patients could sometimes convince doctors that painful menstruation, cysts, or other ailments justified the surgery. For many FTMs, mastectomy came first because breasts, especially large ones, made it difficult to live as a man. A 1968 study of six FTMs found that "they all hated their breasts and found them . . . mortifying." All six subjects gave "precedence to flat-chestedness over cessation of menstruation, much as they were repelled by the idea of having to menstruate."[62] Next they sought excision of the uterus, fallopian tubes, and ovaries, which would not only remove their reproductive organs but also end their menstrual periods (if they were not already taking testosterone) and eliminate their chief source of estrogen.

Through the 1960s, FTMs rarely underwent phalloplasty. The procedure was technically difficult, and few doctors attempted it. Surgeons first reported on phalloplasty after World War I, when they attempted to reconstruct penises for men whose had been amputated. By midcentury the favored technique was a "tube-within-a-tube," in which the internal tube served as the urethra. In the late 1940s the plastic surgeon Sir Harold Gillies described the technique, developed in part by others, in an article on men with "congenital absence of the penis."[63] In Britain, Gillies himself constructed a penis for at least one FTM in the late 1940s.[64] In the United States, though, there is no evidence of phalloplasty for transsexuals until the early 1960s, when Seth Graham (pseudonym) underwent surgery with Dr. D. Ralph Millard Jr. in Miami, Florida. Millard knew Gillies' work well: in the late 1950s they had coauthored a landmark book, *The Principles and Art of Plastic Surgery,* which included an illustrated description of the surgical procedure. In the case of Graham, Millard performed thirty operations over the course of three years as he attempted to perfect the penis and scrotum he had constructed. Eventually Graham refused to come back for more, even though Millard still wanted to "put a corona atop the terminus." By his own account, the medical treatment cost Graham around $10,000, only about $1,000 of which went directly to Millard. The remainder, he said, paid for two earlier unspecified operations, perhaps mastectomy and hysterectomy, and "the high cost of hospitals and drugs."[65] In the late 1960s surgeons at Johns Hopkins Hospital began performing phalloplasties on a handful of patients, and by the mid-1970s a few more surgeons, such as Ira Dushoff, in Jacksonville, Florida, and Donald Laub, at Stanford University, had experience with the operation.

As Seth Graham's account suggests, phalloplasty involved multiple stages of surgery, performed over a course of weeks, with unpredictable results. In the "tube-within-a tube" pedicle procedure, doctors created two tubes, usually from the skin of the abdomen. They incorporated the smaller tube, with skin surface turned inward, within the larger tube pedicle, with the skin surface outward. In a pedicle, the flap of skin, sutured into a tube, remained attached at both ends to the body, looking, as one FTM described it, like a "suitcase handle."[66] This supplied blood to the raised tissue, which was gradually moved end over end to its new position. Doctors implanted one end of the tube-within-a-tube on the clitoris and later freed the other end. The complicated procedure also involved skin grafts to the abdomen, and required extending the original urethra so it could reach the new urethra in the tube. Doctors aimed for "a satisfactory esthetic appearance . . . that would allow the patients to stand while voiding."[67] But even after multiple surgeries, the constructed penis did not necessarily look normal, and it sometimes failed to take. For erections, doctors might use cartilage or other implants to create a permanent stiffness, or they might leave the penis flaccid.

Some FTMs were "entirely pleased with the results of hormone therapy, breast amputation, and hysterectomy," but others hoped for genital surgery despite the dearth of doctors, the multiple surgeries, the expense, and the imperfect results. Without a penis, some continued to fear "discovery" and exposure.[68] But equally important, a penis, like a flat chest, provided one more sign that the body approximated the male sense of self. In the late 1960s Mario Martino took hormones and underwent operations to remove his breasts and reproductive organs, but he still wanted phalloplasty. "To have my body reflect my image of myself as a male," he wrote, "I would pay any price, do anything within honor." He had heard "vague rumors about surgeons . . . overseas" who created penises, but "nothing could be verified." Eventually he found a surgeon in the United States. The first attempt, from a tube pedicle on the thigh, failed because of infection. Four years later, Martino found another surgeon in the Midwest, who created a penis from a tube pedicle on the abdomen. Despite the pain and the problems, Martino expressed his satisfaction with the "new part of me," which he had "always conceived of myself possessing." "It completes outwardly," he said, "a picture of myself which I have always carried in my head." It served as "an acknowledgment" of his "maleness."[69]

Other FTMs sought additional forms of surgery. In 1969 Rob Dixon (pseudonym) began to live as a man while receiving hormone injections. A year later psychiatrist Richard Green reported: "This patient still insists on having surgery and feels that he hates the female aspects of his body." Dixon wanted "to have both breasts removed . . . as well as the uterus and ovaries." He also hoped for the surgery suggested by the UCLA urologist Willard Goodwin: an operation "to free up the enlarged clitoris and redirect the urethral orifice" as well as "insertion of prosthetic testes."[70] In the former operation, more common today, the doctor cuts the ligaments around the clitoris, enlarged by testosterone, to create an organ resembling a small penis. (It does not today involve repositioning of the urethra.) In the latter operation, the doctor constructs a scrotum from a skin graft and follows it up with implants in the shape of testicles. In 1960, for example, Lauren Wilcox, one of Benjamin's patients, had plastic testicles implanted at the time of hysterectomy. In a few cases doctors also closed the vagina when operating on FTMs. Of Benjamin's first twenty FTM patients, at least fourteen had some kind of surgery, but only one had his vagina closed.[71]

*B*efore and after surgery, transsexuals engaged their doctors in a complicated give-and-take, fraught with trouble and conflict. On one side, patients felt angry at doctors who dismissed their desires for bodily change. The difficulty of finding surgeons who would perform the operations, the doctors' brusqueness, ignorance, or condescension, the expense of the treatment, and the complications attending surgery fed the frustrations of patients. On the other side, doctors bristled at the demands of patients who pressured them for treatment. They felt betrayed when patients tailored their stories in order to qualify for surgery and angry when patients failed to express gratitude for the risks taken on their behalf. More fundamentally, the conflicts brought up questions of control. Who could decide whether a person was or should be a man or a woman? Who could decide whether to change the bodily characteristics of sex? Transsexuals hoped to decide for themselves, but they needed the consent and cooperation of doctors.

The conflicts involved issues of knowledge and authority. Transgendered people often had more knowledge about their own condition than the doctors they approached. They had their firsthand stories of crossgender identification, and many of them had also read widely in the medical literature. They had their own compelling reasons to follow newspaper stories, track down case studies, and follow them up for leads on the impact of hormones and new surgical techniques. "Why," one MTF wondered, "did I know about the [sex-reassignment] procedure and doctors didn't?" Yet the doctors had the cultural authority, whether or not they had ever encountered, studied, or thought about transsexuality. Journalists turned to the medical profession to define the problem publicly and propose solutions. On a more personal level, doctors also had the power to determine exactly who would qualify for treatment. From the start, patients protested the clout of doctors "who do not know anything on the subject."[72]

In this situation, some transgendered people worked to educate the doctors. In San Francisco, Louise Lawrence devoted herself to teaching medical authorities and scientists about transvestites and transsexuals. From the mid-1940s, when she started to live as a woman, she worked with Karl Bowman at the Langley Porter Clinic to help doctors there understand transvestism. In the late 1940s she met Alfred Kinsey and began to send him letters, clippings, photos, books, and manuscripts. Eventually Kinsey paid her for her efforts.[73] He introduced her to Harry Benjamin, with whom she corresponded frequently to discuss reports in the medical literature and the popular press. Both Kinsey and Benjamin relied on Lawrence as a key source of information on transsexualism. Lawrence, for example, informed Benjamin of David O. Cauldwell's earlier writings on transsexuals. Benjamin, as two of his former colleagues noted, used her "as a sounding board for . . . many of his ideas." And Lawrence appreciated Benjamin as "one of the few medical men in this country who has any understanding of this problem."[74]

After the Jorgensen story broke, Lawrence redoubled her efforts. She saw the negative response of American doctors as an example of their "rigid attitude toward the acceptance of new and progressive ideas." In correspondence with an MTF, she speculated that the doctors who repudiated sex-change surgery had their own form of castration anxiety. "If only some of these American medical men could . . . not continually imagine that their own penis was removed when Christine's was, maybe we would see some sound thoughtful, imaginative progress made in this field." With Benjamin as her liaison, she corresponded and met with Jorgensen. She hoped to reply to the letters that Jorgensen did not have time to answer and to use them for scientific study. Jorgensen would not relinquish the letters, but she did refer some correspondents to Lawrence. Lawrence told one such letter writer that she was "trying to gather as much information . . . as possible in order that medical men . . . will be able to help people who come to them."[75]

The patients understood that they themselves provided the raw data that doctors and researchers used to formulate their descriptions and their theories. Debbie Mayne told Benjamin that after reading his article "Transvestism and Transsexualism," her mother had commented, "why you have been telling me this right along." "Of course I have," Mayne said she replied; "where do you think the doctor gets his information?" For this reason many early transsexuals agreed, and even sought, to participate in research projects. In the late 1940s and early 1950s Alfred C. Kinsey took an avid interest in transvestites and transsexuals. With the encouragement of Louise Lawrence and Harry Benjamin, several transsexuals agreed to cooperate with him. Caren Ecker gave her life history to Kinsey "in hopes that any information . . . may in its small way eventually be of help to others of my kind." Like Ecker, others hoped to shape the scientific literature, with the long-term goal of increasing knowledge and public understanding. After reading *Sex and Gender*, an FTM wrote Robert Stoller: "perhaps in the same spirit one donates one's body to a medical school for the good of posterity, I would like to offer my psyche-soma to your group for what you could make of it."[76]

Caren Ecker referred to her educational efforts as "missionary work for our cause." While recovering from her surgery in San Francisco, she gave the curious doctors offprints of Benjamin's article, with the goal of "promoting interest and tolerance." Later she worked with Louise Lawrence for public education, and cooperated with Frederic Worden and James Marsh in their research project at UCLA. She was "trying to sell" Worden and Marsh, she said, "the true idea that I'm happy with my new life, and the idea that for suitable subjects it is right to make these changes."[77] These early, unorganized efforts to educate doctors

and scientists were precursors to an organized transsexual rights movement that emerged in the late 1960s. From early on, though, transsexuals discovered how difficult it was to convince the doctors to treat
them in the ways they wanted.

They quickly learned that researchers had their own agendas. For the
MTFs interviewed by Worden and Marsh, the lesson came as a painful
blow. In letters to Benjamin, four of the five subjects expressed outrage
at their treatment. From the start, they resented the clinical attitude of
Worden and Marsh, who wanted to test them but failed to listen to
what they had to say. After psychological testing, Carla Sawyer (pseudonym) wrote: "I feel as if I have been flattened out, and rolled up and
pushed through a knot hole and I told them so, too." When Marsh interviewed her, she said, he "didn't even seem to know about what my
case concerned," and when Worden interviewed her, "he hadn't even
taken the time to look at" a six-page letter she had given him. "I told
them," she said, "I was getting pretty tired of it."[78]

Of the five MTFs interviewed, three had already had surgery, but
two others, Carla Sawyer and Debbie Mayne, hoped their participation
in the research would convince the doctors to recommend operations.
Apparently Worden held out some possibility of surgery at UCLA. Despite her misgivings, Sawyer stuck with the research project. She told
Benjamin: "there is not much else that I can do except make myself
available to them . . . the only thing I care anything about is having my
sex changed."[79] Debbie Mayne, the most volatile of the group, spent a
year working with Worden, waiting impatiently for approval for surgery. Louise Lawrence told her "NOT to blow [her] top." "I will
agree," she wrote, "that Dr. Worden is probably a very young man who
has a lot to learn . . . [but] for the sake of all of us try and hold your
emotional reactions in check." With a heavy dose of paternalism, Harry
Benjamin also tried to keep Mayne calm. "It isn't very wise and very
diplomatic of you," he warned, "to antagonize Dr. Worden . . . Do try
hard to give the impression of a well-balanced sensible person . . . you
must not expect everybody . . . to understand this problem . . . do be a
sensible girl." Not so easily reined, Mayne replied: "This girl is going
to keep on raising hell until I get my operations." Ultimately, though,
Worden refused to recommend surgery, leaving his subjects more frus-

trated and angry than before. Worden, Mayne concluded, "has never recommended anything for anybody . . . he doesn't know too much to begin with."[80]

Other participants in the research expressed their anger after Worden and Marsh published their article in 1955 in the *Journal of the American Medical Association*. They objected to the way the doctors had used their interviews to cast transsexuals in a negative light. The article, Janet Story (pseudonym) told Benjamin, "certainly was a cruel thing." Annette Dolan went into greater detail. She sent her objections to the *Journal of the American Medical Association*, Elmer Belt, and Harry Benjamin as well as to Frederic Worden. "In general," she said, "my words were twisted to suit their purpose." Point by point, she disputed their interpretations of her own responses and more generally of their understanding of transsexuals, and she wondered how they could draw conclusions from interviews with only five subjects. But mostly, she expressed her outrage at the cold approach and condescending tone of the researchers. Worden and Marsh, she wrote, had not "made a genuine attempt to establish a rapport with their subjects"; they had tried "to milk scientific information from them in the approximate manner laboratory animals are used." As she told Elmer Belt, she could "sense the subtle ridicule heaped by the authors on their subjects." Worden and Marsh had rewarded her willingness to participate in their research with a damaging portrayal of transsexual pathology, and she rightfully resented it.[81]

The episode with Worden and Marsh reflected ongoing conflicts. For decades to follow, both transsexuals and doctors confirmed the troubled relations between the patients who sought surgical sex change and the medical authorities who hesitated to recommend it. In the mid-1950s, Robert Stoller, then new to the field, "tried to reverse" Carla Sawyer's "sexual tendencies" and thereby "antagoniz[ed] the patient." Other doctors responded to would-be patients with the rankest of prejudice. In her autobiography, Vivian Le Mans remembered doctors "who threatened to have [her] arrested" for requesting sex-change surgery. "One doctor," she recalled, "even had his janitor chase me out of the office with a mop! He said he didn't want to contaminate his hands."[82]

In order to qualify for surgery, patients sometimes stuck, at least temporarily, with doctors whom they disliked and distrusted. In the late 1960s, Phoebe Smith went to a psychiatrist who attempted to kiss her to see, he said, how she would react and later tried to burn her with a cigarette to find out, he claimed, whether she would defend herself. Eventually she concluded that "the doctor had problems of his own." Around the same time, Mario Martino found a doctor who administered hormones and conducted monthly group therapy sessions where Martino gladly met other FTMs. But the doctor, Martino found, "took no real personal interest in me as a patient . . . nor in any of his patients." "One by one," Martino recalled, "his patients began to mistrust him," especially after the doctor could not refer them, as promised, to a surgeon. Martino began to wonder, "Was I patronizing a quack?" His skepticism rose as the doctor showed excessive interest in "sex and the sex act." Eventually Martino turned to other FTMs for the referrals, counseling, and advice he wanted.[83]

Increasingly, patients kept their guards up and avoided the kinds of self-disclosure that might damage their chances for surgery. Those who hoped for surgery had to tell their stories to doctors, but they soon learned to censor themselves as well. Patients tried to tell the doctors what they thought the doctors wanted to hear. Even with sympathetic doctors, they sometimes tailored their accounts to make themselves fit into the recognized diagnostic categories, to convince doctors that they were not just garden-variety homosexuals or transvestites, and to reassure doctors that they would not bring trouble after the operations were done. In order to impress their doctors with their need for surgery, MTFs attempted to demonstrate conventional femininity, and FTMs masculinity. They tried to persuade the doctors that they would lead "normal" and quiet lives after surgery. And they tried to convince doctors of their sense of urgency. "In order to get surgery," one MTF claimed, "you have to tell the doctor that if you don't get it you will commit suicide."[84]

Before the "sexual revolution" of the 1960s, many transsexuals refrained in particular from expressing overt interest in sexual relations. After her surgery, Debbie Mayne told Harry Benjamin that she wanted "the sex life of the woman . . . I would not admit this before because I thought it might prevent me from getting the operation and I lied."[85] The surgeon may well have applauded Mayne's heterosexual interest, but she saw it as dangerous to mention any sexual interests at all. Transsexuals knew that "normal" meant heterosexuality after surgery, but if they expressed such interests, they might appear as overly interested in sex or they might come across, in the preoperative state, as homosexuals who did not qualify for surgery. This reticence about sexuality appeared in various records. Take, for example, the 1953 case study of an FTM, hospitalized against his will. "I never had any desire," he told a doctor. "I've never had any sex relations of any kind in my life. My wife said it never bothered her, that she could take it or leave it." He wanted "that operation," he said, but it did not have to do with sexuality. As if to underscore the point, he repeated later, "Sex isn't important to me." Or take the letter an MTF, hoping for surgery, wrote Harry Benjamin in 1955: "You can rest assured that all I ever want from life is something moral and right, and marriage and men are only minor things, because the really important thing is to dress as a woman and be accepted by society."[86] Perhaps these particular patients had little interest in sex, but maybe they saw the double bind and simply omitted, as did Debbie Mayne, the sexual acts or interests that they imagined would trigger the doctors' disapproval.

By the 1960s, doctors realized that their transsexual patients often structured their life histories to maximize their chances for surgery. The well-publicized story of "Agnes" served as a key case in point. In 1958, Agnes came to the UCLA Medical Center, seeking genital surgery. She met with a number of doctors, including Robert Stoller, and convinced them all that she qualified for surgery as an intersexed patient. She was, as the researchers recalled, "a 19-year-old, white, single secretary," living as a woman, but with male genitalia.[87] She had grown up as a boy in a Catholic working-class family, but she had always seen herself as a girl. During puberty, she had developed female secondary sex characteristics, including breasts, and at the age of seventeen, had begun to live as a woman. Earlier tests, conducted in Portland, Oregon, had shown that she had male (XY) chromosomes and neither a uterus nor ovaries nor a hypothesized tumor that might have produced estrogen. After exhaustive examinations, the doctors at UCLA recommended the surgery she sought. In 1959 a team of surgeons, including Elmer Belt, removed her male genitals and constructed labia and a vagina.

With her male genitals, feminized body, and high levels of estrogen, Agnes was wholly unlike any other intersexed patient that the doctors had encountered in their own observations or in the medical literature. The doctors pondered, publicly and privately, what she represented, and they used her case study in scholarly presentations and publications. Three medical doctors joined Stoller in authoring "Pubertal Feminization in a Genetic Male." They hypothesized that Agnes had "a diffuse lesion of the testis" which had produced the estrogen which had, in turn, produced her breasts. To Stoller, Agnes's bodily changes during puberty seemed to confirm the usually hidden "biological force" underlying gender identity. A congenital physical factor, which manifested itself later in the growth of her breasts, explained why "the core identity was female" even though "the child was an apparently normal-appearing boy and . . . also genetically male."[88] Stoller presented his findings on Agnes in 1963 at the International Psychoanalytic Congress in Stockholm and also published them in scholarly journals.

But all along, Stoller and his colleagues noted some suspicious evidence. During the seventy-odd hours of interrogation, Agnes refused to engage a number of topics, and she also refused to allow the doctors to interview her family. Furthermore, from the physical evidence gathered, the doctors had to acknowledge a "clinical picture that seemed to suggest the superimposition of an excess of estrogen upon the substratum of a normal male."[89] They discussed among themselves whether perhaps Agnes had given herself estrogen to induce the growth of her breasts. In the end, they convinced themselves that she had not. She herself denied that she had ingested estrogen. More important, her conventional feminine presentation impressed the doctors as genuine and ran counter to their stereotypes of "caricature" and "hostility . . . seen in transvestites and transsexuals." "It was not possible," they wrote, "for any of her observers, including those who knew of her anatomic state, to identify her as anything but a young woman."[90] Elmer Belt, impressed by the size of her breasts, remembered her in private correspondence as "very beautiful—well stacked."[91] The other doctors also suspended their disbelief in the face of contradictory anatomical evidence and convincing gender presentation.

Then, in 1966, seven years after her surgery, Agnes confessed. She told Stoller that her body had changed during puberty because she had taken estrogen tablets since the age of twelve. She had stolen the hormone from her mother, who had used it after her hysterectomy. As Stoller later reported, "The child then began filling the prescription on her own, telling the pharmacist that she was picking up the hormone for her mother and paying for it with money taken from her mother's purse." Posing as a unique example of an intersexed condition, Agnes had convinced her doctors to give her the surgery they routinely denied to male-to-female transsexuals. In the wake of her confession, Stoller wondered about his theories. Richard Green attempted to reassure him. "Do not despair about the biological force behind gender identity," Green wrote Stoller. "I am sure there is one somewhere and there are other cases to consider which are supportive of the idea."[92] Still, an embarrassed Stoller had to admit that Agnes "is not the example of a 'biological force' that . . . influences gender identity . . . rather, she is a transsexual."[93] He retracted his earlier findings at the International Psychoanalytic Congress in Copenhagen in 1967 and also published Agnes' revelations in 1968 in the *International Journal of Psycho-Analysis* as well as in his book *Sex and Gender*.[94]

The lesson was not lost on the doctors. Various researchers had already concluded that transsexuals were "unreliable historian[s] . . . unable to recall very well, or inclined to distort."[95] By the end of the 1960s, the medical literature on transsexuals regularly noted that transsexuals shaped their life histories and even fabricated stories that might convince doctors to help them. As a few more American doctors began to perform sex reassignment surgery, candidates less often portrayed themselves as intersexed, as had Agnes, but instead "as textbook examples of 'transsexuals.'" They presented "their personal histories," one article suggested, "to conform to the prevailing 'scientific' fashions." If they could prove to the doctors that the diagnosis fit, then perhaps the doctors might recommend the surgical treatment. As the doctors acknowledged the medical context that encouraged patients to coordinate their autobiographies with scientific accounts of transsexualism, they increasingly questioned "the extent to which the patient's stories and self-descriptions can be trusted."[96] In short, the patients mistrusted the doctors, and the doctors mistrusted the patients.

*F*or transsexuals, the problems did not end when they convinced doctors to recommend and perform surgery. The fees, as Mario Martino remembered, were "staggering." In the mid-1950s, Harry Benjamin wrote: "I have my hands full with patients . . . who should have the operation but do not have the necessary funds." The funds needed varied, depending on the doctor and the surgeries performed, but in the 1960s, they generally ran a few thousand dollars. In some cases, disappointed patients, accepted for surgery but unable to afford it, talked of suicide or self-surgery. A number of MTFs engaged in prostitution to raise funds for their operations. Others tried to negotiate the costs. In the mid-1950s, with Benjamin's help, Debbie Mayne had the "extravagant fees" for her surgery in Mexico reduced and then agreed to pay on the installment plan. In 1970, Lyn Raskin convinced Georges Burou to reduce his $4000 fee to $1500.[97] Such arrangements required confrontations with doctors who generally did not expect patients to bargain with them for their services. The fees not only alienated the patients, but led, as one doctor described it, to "unpleasant experiences."[98]

In the doctors' offices and at the hospitals, wary patients observed the behavior of doctors and staff members who treated them unprofessionally. At Elmer Belt's clinic in Los Angeles, Annette Dolan sensed "an undercurrent of uneasiness caused by our presence." She also noted that her confidential records lay out on the business manager's desk, used, she said, "in the same manner as a best seller."[99] A few years later, at the same clinic, Aleshia Brevard remembered, Belt himself was "condescending and rude." In other cases, hospital staff treated the patients as oddities. When Mario Martino, with a full beard, entered the hospital for a hysterectomy, "everyone outside the department," he remembered, "lined up to take a look at the new specimen: *me*."[100]

Pain at the hands of doctors also heightened patients' discomfort. For months after surgery, MTFs had to dilate their vaginas frequently to keep them from closing. The first dilations were particularly painful. Carla Sawyer noted the "rough physical treatment" she received at the clinic of Elmer Belt, and a few years later, Patricia Morgan also recounted the pain. She said it took Elmer Belt and his son, also a doctor, fifteen minutes to force "a piece of plastic shaped like a man's penis" into her new vagina. "I grabbed the bars on the bed," she recalled, "and gritted my teeth."[101] While some patients accepted the pain as a necessary evil, others questioned the competence and motives of their doctors. The pain he endured during a routine pelvic examination made Mario Martino "suddenly apprehensive." He wondered: "Was this doctor as professional as he first appeared? Was he just impersonal? Or did he enjoy inflicting pain?"[102]

Given the less-than-perfect medical technology, the operations themselves often created additional sources of frustration. For both MTFs and FTMs, there were infections, grafts that failed to take, and scar tissue that changed the appearance of the chest or labia. It was not unusual for new vaginas to close, new penises to wither, and urethras to constrict. FTMs who had phalloplasty regularly encountered post-surgical problems. In his first attempted phalloplasty, Martino reported how the tube pedicle failed: It "was shriveling, curling in on itself like a snail." In the second attempt, the head of the new penis "turned dark, signifying death of the tissue." Three months later he returned to the surgeon for another skin graft and "repairs."[103] Even after successful phalloplasty, FTMs often had "urinary problems in the form of fistulae, . . . infections, and incontinence." Frustrated patients, both FTMs and MTFs, returned to their doctors again and again with post-surgical problems. They sometimes underwent additional surgery to "correct a small vagina, a tender urethral stump, or a deformity of the labia," "to release strictures," to remove infected implants, or to attempt another graft after the first one had failed.[104]

The disappointments mounted when the bodily transformations did not have the appearance or the functions the patients wanted. One follow-up study on nine MTFs showed that all expressed "some dissatisfaction with the physical results of their surgery," especially with the size of the vagina or the "appearance of the labia and external genitalia." The doctors, aware of the limits of medical technology, acknowledged the "conflict with the surgeon." They admitted that "duplicating either sex in a perfect anatomical way is impossible."[105] Some tried to forewarn patients to lower their expectations about what the technology could accomplish. Harry Benjamin wrote one patient: "Please . . . do not expect either one-hundred per cent success, or one-hundred per cent happiness. There is no such thing."[106]

On top of it all, the patients knew that the doctors often saw them as mentally ill, irritating, or hostile. In the published medical literature, some psychiatrists, in particular, pathologized their transsexual patients. As Richard Green and Howard Baker noted, "the psychiatric literature is replete with deprecatory descriptions." Many doctors had, it seems, little experience with patients whose sense of urgency led them to insist on unusual forms of medical treatment. They seemed perplexed by the "extreme impatience" and the "anger" of patients who pushed them to stretch the boundaries of acceptable medical practice.[107] Accustomed to deference, they encountered patients whose determined demands surprised and annoyed them. Even the more sympathetic doctors sometimes lambasted their patients. In a letter to Willard Goodwin, Elmer Belt wrote: "These patients are simply awful liars. They lie when there is no need for it whatever." In letters to Harry Benjamin, he occasionally referred to his transsexual patients as "queers" or "nuts."[108] Robert J. Stoller considered MTFs "dissatisfied," "exhibitionistic and unreliable." "Some of these patients," he wrote to another doctor, "can be a real pain in the neck . . . even after surgery some of them can be quite persistent."[109] In his published writings, Harry Benjamin, the most sympathetic of the crew, wrote of the "selfishness, unreliability and questionable ethical concepts of some male and female transsexuals." A benevolent paternalist, he responded graciously to those who expressed "gratitude and loyalty" in response to his efforts.[110] But in a moment of pique, after a patient accused him of lying, he wrote, "You have been unappreciative and ungrateful."[111]

Those who underwent sex-change surgery encountered a range of daunting problems that went well beyond their dealings with doctors. Before and after surgery, they had to deal with families and friends who did not necessarily approve of the change of sex. They could choose to sever contact and move to a new life in which no one knew of their pasts, or else they could confront, and risk rejection by, anyone who knew their histories. They needed to find employment in their new gender status, often without the benefit of references from previous employers. They worried about the "apparent handicap they [had] in finding someone [who] will offer them employment," and they feared "being detected on the job."[112] As they changed their lives, a few transsexuals courted publicity, especially MTFs who hoped to follow in Jorgensen's footsteps, but most feared exposure in the press and also in daily life. Caren Ecker worried that the newspapers would print stories about her surgery. "I could see nothing of the financial good that came to Christine," she told Benjamin, "and only confusion to the plans I have made to continue my nursing career . . . publicity at this time would wreck all my chances." MTFs, in particular, worried about "passing," especially when their height, voices, facial features, or facial hair defied conventions of femininity. If they did not appear to be women, they risked the same harassment and arrest after surgery that they had faced before.[113]

The more sympathetic doctors did what they could to help their patients through the transition. Harry Benjamin tried to take care of "his girls." Aleshia Brevard, whom Benjamin treated in the early 1960s, remembered, "He really went to bat for me." Benjamin "talked to [her] parents" and "set up everything that there was to be set up, the meeting with the psychiatrist . . . all the legal rigmarole . . . it was all relatively painless because of him."[114] Benjamin, Belt, and others provided patients with letters attesting to the surgical change of sex. A typical letter, written by Elmer Belt in 1956, read: "This is to certify that a surgical operation performed for _____ has altered the genitalia of this patient, converting the sex from male to female, and that _____ in my opinion should legally be considered as belonging to the female sex."[115] The patient could show the letter to police if picked up for crossdressing or to skeptical bureaucrats who hesitated to change the name and sex on a driver's license, passport, or social security record. Benjamin also worried about the employment prospects of his patients and tried to encourage them in the job search. Mario Martino's surgeon hired him as a nurse, but few doctors went so far as to find jobs for their patients.

As the doctors advised their patients, they also inadvertently encouraged their dependence, which ultimately fueled frustrations. Benjamin and others urged post-operative patients to hide, and even to lie about, their past lives as the other sex. This placed the doctors among the few confidantes to whom the patients could turn. When the doctors failed to provide assistance, the patients felt betrayed. In Los Angeles in the mid-1950s, Annette Dolan, for example, hoped that Frederic Worden and Elmer Belt would help her and another MTF find jobs. "We are of the opinion," she wrote, "that an all out effort should have been made to give us a new start in life." When she asked Willard Goodwin for help, "he was," she said, "cold as ice."[116] Benjamin told her not to "expect anything from others" and also warned her that her "tactless" behavior might "rob" her "of some friends and sympathies." But she explained her sense of urgency: "What you fail to realize is that I literally am fighting for my life."[117]

For a few, the long struggle did not seem worth it in the end. In the available records, a handful of transsexuals expressed regrets about their new lives. One MTF failed to find employment as a woman and had to revert to living as a man. "I am not doing this," she told Belt, "because I desire to go back to an unhappy life, but I have to survive. It is a bitter pill, the bitterest I ever took, but there is nothing left to do." Another MTF decided after surgery that she had "a man's mind," that her "new body was all wrong." She made a good living as a "Latin Bombshell" stripper, but she disliked the aggressive men who expected her to have sex with them. She had lost her interest in sex with either men or women, and she found her life "lonely beyond belief."[118]

On the whole, though, those who managed to obtain surgery rarely regretted it. They overwhelmingly endorsed medical treatment, even though they had disappointments with the arduous process and imperfect results. Despite their persistent conflicts with doctors, they expressed their appreciation. In an article on FTMs, one doctor noted: "the patients demonstrate an attitude of extreme gratitude." In letters to Harry Benjamin, MTFs gave their thanks for the ways he had helped them fulfill "a life long dream" and find "peace of mind." "Nothing else in the world," one MTF wrote, "means or could ever mean so much to me as accomplishing this goal."[119] Surgery, of course, could not solve everything. "I guess that loneliness is the thing in this life that I now dread the most," Caren Ecker explained. "Still, I am grateful that my biggest problem is so well solved, that is, as well as it is possible to solve such a problem, and much better than I would have ever believed possible a few years ago."[120]

By the end of the 1960s, then, transsexuals had persuaded at least a few American doctors to move from theory to practice. They insisted that they could determine their own rightful sex and gender, and they convinced a handful of doctors to make their bodies accord with their minds. The request for bodily change distinguished them from other sexual "deviants." Homosexuals and transvestites did not have the same longings for medical intervention. For the most part, they wanted doctors to leave them alone. Doctors noted the differences, and so did transsexuals themselves. In the medical literature, the doctors engaged in and elaborated on the differential diagnoses that created the scientific classifications of sexuality, and in daily life, self-avowed transsexuals staked out their claims to identities of their own.

SEXUAL REVOLUTIONS

5

*I*n 1968 Classic Publications published the tellingly titled *Take My Tool,* the autobiography of a postoperative MTF. Unabashedly pornographic, the book related sexual escapades before and after surgery, with enough insider details of medical treatment to convince the reader that the author was indeed transsexual. "Sexual surgery," the back cover blurb stated, "made him a complete woman capable of the ultimate in unbridled sexual desires." In the pornographic imagination, it was female genitalia that made "a complete woman" and distinguished her from a man. Both femaleness and femininity were defined by a woman's anatomy and by her capacity for and engagement in heterosexual acts. "Today's modern medical miracles has [*sic*] made me as much a feminine female as any Sophia Loren," the author claimed. "And in bed performing sexually, I can finally fulfill myself and my male partner as much as can any other women—and probably better than most!"[1] This sexualized definition of womanhood emerged more publicly in the 1960s as changes in censorship laws accompanied a new sexual ethos.

From the earliest publicity in the 1930s, much of the public interest in and anxiety surrounding sex change had stemmed from its implicit connection to taboo forms of sexuality. Through the 1960s, both transvestism and homosexuality stood well beyond the pale of mainstream propriety, and to some observers transsexuality seemed to compound the transgression by combining the two. No matter how they behaved, transsexuals could not entirely dispel the aura of illicit sexuality. Christine Jorgensen, for example, worked concertedly to present herself as a lady, but at least some observers read her as a crossdressing man who dated other men. The burden of proof seemed to lie with her and her doctors: How did she differ, before or after hormones and surgery, from transvestites and homosexuals?

In the years after Jorgensen entered the public domain, two different "sexual revolutions" transformed the associations between transsexuality and sexual transgression. In a taxonomic revolution, doctors, homosexuals, crossdressers, and transsexuals redefined the sexological categories and sorted out a multitude of sexual and gender variations. To a certain extent, they tried to desexualize transsexuality by separating it from transvestic fetishism and homosexual desire. But in the other, more familiar sexual revolution, as seen in *Take My Tool,* a more publicly visible sexuality led to the open eroticization of MTF transsexuals.

In the taxonomic revolution, some doctors and transsexuals worked to separate gender and sexual variations. From early on, doctors engaged in differential diagnosis. Those who chose to recommend or offer surgical treatment wanted a clearer sense of who qualified as a bona fide transsexual and who did not. In the face of opposition, especially from psychoanalysts, they created and refined a new schema of sexological classification that elaborated distinctions between transsexuals and more familiar "deviants." While the doctors attempted to redraw the boundaries, those who identified as transsexuals, transvestites, and homosexuals also engaged in their own social practice of taxonomy. They tried to distinguish themselves from one another. In fact they often defined themselves by what they knew they were not. They were not, they granted, typical men and women, but they also were not exactly the same as other classes of "deviants."

The process of sorting and separating sometimes included a shift in self-identification. In the 1950s and especially the 1960s, social networks emerged that served as training grounds of sorts for transsexual identity. In major cities would-be transsexuals increasingly learned about the possibilities of hormones and surgery through circles of MTF crossdressers, professional female impersonators, drag queens, and, later, butch lesbians. A deeply rooted sense of crossgender identification could express itself in different forms at different times in a single person's life. Often people came to see themselves as transsexuals only after they had entered the emerging subcultures of gay men, lesbians, or MTF heterosexual transvestites. The medical distinctions blurred when a butch lesbian came to identify as a transsexual man or when an MTF crossdresser shifted from occasional transvestism to a profound desire to live and look like a woman. In everyday life, the borders between unconventional gender identities and unconventional sexualities seemed permeable at best.

In popular culture and in everyday life, the connections between crossgender identification and sexual transgression—and between gender and sexuality—remained and even multiplied. The sexual issues took center stage in the 1960s with the rise of the other "sexual revolution." In the emerging countercultures, more sexual nonconformists chose to assert a flamboyant presence. Some MTF transsexuals projected a more sexualized persona and rejected the coy image that Christine Jorgensen had invoked in the 1950s. In print and on stage, the eroticized MTF captured the public eye and confirmed that sexuality still played a central role in popular conceptions of what made a woman a woman and a man a man. In fact, in *Take My Tool* the very definition of womanhood seemed to rely on heterosexual acts.

*F*rom the late nineteenth century on, European and American sexologists had "medicalized" sexuality, transforming unconventional sexual behavior from sins requiring redemption to pathologies inviting cure. In the process they created and refined classification schemes to define distinctions among the various forms of sexuality they considered abnormal.[2] In the early twentieth century, homosexuality increasingly referred to same-sex object choice, as opposed to gender "inversion," and transvestism came to refer to crossdressing only. But with the new definitions, the "inverts" who described themselves as men with female bodies or women with male bodies stood in taxonomy's limbo. In the mid-twentieth century doctors began to define transsexualism as a new sexological category that included some of the inverts left out by the narrower definitions of homosexuality and transvestism. The new taxonomy created new debates. In the medical literature, doctors argued among themselves about how or whether to distinguish transsexualism from homosexuality and transvestism.

Into the early 1950s, a number of doctors and scientists tried to fit their transgendered patients into the older categories used to describe unconventional sexuality. In the first case study of Christine Jorgensen, for example, published in 1951 before the press had discovered her, Christian Hamburger, Jorgensen's endocrinologist, described her as "suffering from homosexual tendencies."[3] By 1953, though, he and his colleagues had changed their diagnosis. They now placed Jorgensen in the category of "genuine transvestism" or "psychic hermaphrodism" or "eonism." "Eonists," they found, "are persons with a fundamental feeling of being victims of a cruel mistake—a consequence of the female personality in a male body." In these cases, "the sexual life generally plays but a minor part." Hamburger and his colleagues noted that others often "confused or identified" eonism "with homosexuality," but this conflation, they concluded, prevented society from "grasp[ing] properly the problems" of eonists.[4]

Other scientists and doctors went through similar processes of classification and reclassification. Initially they tended to associate transsexualism closely with homosexuality, and later they drew greater distinctions. In the late 1940s and early 1950s, for example, Alfred C. Kinsey began to amass data on transvestites and transsexuals. With the help of Louise Lawrence and Harry Benjamin, he collected life histories and autobiographical writings. According to his colleague Paul Gebhard, Kinsey at first saw MTF transsexuals as effeminate homosexuals.[5] In 1950, when Kinsey met with psychiatrist Karl Bowman to discuss Val Barry (pseudonym), an MTF under observation at Bowman's Langley Porter Clinic in San Francisco, they "encouraged" Barry "to undertake homosexual relations as a means of learning to value his genitals." In 1951 Kinsey advised another MTF "to find a homosexual colony."[6] Likewise Bowman, in a 1951 report on sex offenders, included transsexuals as a subset of homosexuals. He had cases of two MTFs and two FTMs who had asked for sex-change surgery. "Male homosexuals of this type," he wrote, "are called 'Queens' and seem to differ markedly from the main group of homosexuals who are more nearly like the average man."[7] But as they studied transsexuals both Kinsey and Bowman gradually retreated from their earlier position. By the time of his death in 1956, Kinsey no longer envisioned MTFs as self-denying homosexuals who tried to avoid their sexual orientation by changing their sex.[8] By 1957 Bowman, too, no longer cast people who sought "sex transformation" as homosexuals; like Hamburger and Benjamin, he included them instead as an extreme type of transvestite.[9]

Following the lead of Magnus Hirschfeld, Sigmund Freud, and other early twentieth-century sexologists, the scientists and doctors gradually came to separate gender from sexuality. In part they acknowledged sexology's newer, narrower definition of homosexuality. In 1957, for example, Daniel Brown reminded his readers of the "importance of differentiating between sex-role inversion and homosexuality."[10] Feminine men and masculine women, transsexual or not, were not necessarily homosexual, and homosexuals were not necessarily feminine men or masculine women. One's object of sexual desire was not necessarily a defining characteristic of one's gender identity, and one's gender identity was not necessarily a defining characteristic of one's sexuality. The sexologists increasingly placed transsexualism and transvestism together as forms of crossgender behavior and identification, and homosexuality as a distinct but related condition concerned with sexual object choice.

In part they listened to the people they observed. Before and after surgery, many MTFs spoke of sexual attractions to men and FTMs presented themselves as attracted to women, but they almost always portrayed themselves as heterosexual women and men, respectively, and not as gay men and lesbians. "I know I'm not a homosexual," one FTM said. "I knew a lot of lesbians . . . I was too masculine for them."[11] Furthermore, in their correspondence with scientists and doctors, transgendered people described their sexuality in a variety of ways. A few MTFs said they felt sexually drawn to women or to both men and women, and on rare occasions an FTM expressed sexual interest in men. (In the 1980s doctors and therapists adopted the term *transhomosexuality* to refer to MTFs who identified as lesbian and FTMs who identified as gay men.) Others said they felt attracted to no one or had no sexual desire. As self-description, one MTF used the word "bisexual" and another "asexual."[12] For some, sexuality followed gender presentation: when they lived as men, some MTFs had sexual relations with women, but when they lived as women, they found themselves attracted to men. In the 1960s a few doctors began to grapple with this complexity. When MTFs denied they were gay men, Robert Stoller considered it "too glib" to say they were simply covering over their real homosexual feelings.[13]

Other doctors, especially psychoanalysts, were not convinced. They continued to portray transsexuals, especially MTFs, as anxious, guilt-ridden homosexuals. In the early 1960s Ralph R. Greenson, Stoller's colleague at UCLA, interviewed an MTF, almost certainly Tamara Rees, and diagnosed her as a type of homosexual. For certain people, Greenson claimed, the prospect of their own homosexuality provoked such dread that it undermined their sense of gender identity. The patient in question reacted "according to the formula: If I love a man then I must be a woman." Heterosexuality proved itself "more precious than genital organs, and even . . . gender." Later in the decade Charles W. Socarides, a psychoanalyst in New York, took a similar stand. In 1969, in the *American Journal of Psychiatry,* he concluded that transsexuals were "either transvestites, homosexuals, or . . . struggling against intense homosexual urges." He focused especially on homosexuality. Like Greenson, he found "transsexualism . . . in the homosexual who, in attempting to resolve the emotional conflicts of his homosexuality, hits upon the idea of changing his sex." The "recasting of identity," Socarides claimed, "alleviates . . . guilt for his homosexual object choice." In response to a critical letter, he reiterated his position a few months later with the additional claim that "only the most ill homosexuals resort to the desperate course of offering their bodies for mutilative processes."[14]

In the face of such opposition, the doctors who supported surgery defended their position. To convince the medical community of the merits of surgical intervention, they needed to dispel the concern that they endorsed risky, irreversible procedures at the behest of homosexuals or transvestites who were too disturbed to assess their own real needs. (Although most doctors still considered homosexuality and transvestism mental illnesses, they no longer recommended surgical interventions as treatment, especially when the interventions came at the request of their allegedly ill patients.) The doctors who endorsed surgery repeated the distinctions they drew: transsexuals had an overwhelming sense of crossgender identification, transvestites crossdressed, and homosexuals desired same-sex sexual partners. In terms of sexuality, they distinguished homosexuality from transvestism, often seen as a form of fetishism, and transsexualism, which a few doctors portrayed as "an escape from genital sexuality."[15]

By 1966, when Benjamin published his magnum opus, *The Transsexual Phenomenon*, he devoted an entire chapter to the "attempt to define, diagnose, and classify" transvestism, transsexualism, and homosexuality. In Benjamin's schema, transsexuals differed from transvestites in that they desired "to be and function as members of the opposite sex, not only to appear as such." "The homosexual," he wrote, referring to gay men, "is a man and wants to be nothing else." Homosexuality primarily involved the desire for same-sex sexual partners; in contrast, transvestism was a "completely solitary act, requiring no partner at all for its enjoyment." Male-to-female transsexuals desired "sex transformation," after which the desire for a "male sex partner" was "often enough dispensable and by no means constant."[16]

Much as they may have wanted to delineate distinctions, though, the doctors could not entirely separate the conditions they described. They confronted the difficulties of diagnosis and sometimes acknowledged that "sex reassignment . . . may be requested by persons considered to be primarily homosexuals or transvestites."[17] They came up with a compromise position. Some patients who requested sex-change surgery did not, they granted, fit the textbook definition of transsexual. In 1965 psychiatrist Ira B. Pauly separated genuine transsexuals from "pseudotranssexuals." For genuine MTF transsexuals, any preoperative homosexual longings were "secondary," a by-product "of the well-established primary gender role inversion." A "small percentage" of those who requested surgery, though, seemed "to seek the operation as a means of rationalizing their homosexuality." Others adopted Pauly's schema and used it to concede that a few patients might request surgery "to justify their homosexuality." By the end of the decade Harry Benjamin, too, stated that at least a few of his patients "could be more homo- than transsexuals." These MTFs sought surgery "more . . . to gratify a heterosexual man than to appease their own gender role distress."[18] Benjamin and other doctors considered these patients less suitable candidates for surgery.

As usual, the doctors focused substantially more attention on the more numerous MTFs, but a few doctors also addressed the complexities of diagnosis for FTMs. Ira Pauly, for example, attempted to differentiate FTMs from lesbians by their sexual activity. Although most preoperative FTMs had sexual relations with women, they tended to avoid "pleasurable genital stimulation," including masturbation, because it reminded them of their "female anatomy." Robert Stoller pondered the issue at greater length. He attempted to draw distinctions between patients he considered genuine transsexuals and lesbians who sought to change their sex. In one case he distinguished butch lesbians from FTMs by their attitudes toward men. "Female transsexuals" had "good" relations with men "as with colleagues," while many butch lesbians, including the patient in question, evinced "barely disguised hatred." Although the "rather masculine" patient had begun taking testosterone and requested surgery to change sex, Stoller was "not convinced of her being a clear-cut transsexual." A few years later, in correspondence with another doctor, Stoller admitted that he still had trouble with diagnosis. He was "uncertain whether what I call transsexualism in females is not in fact an ultimate form of homosexuality."[19]

If the doctors' distinctions between homosexuality and transsexuality sometimes blurred, then the lines they drew between transvestism and transsexualism scarcely existed. By the 1960s many of the doctors who wrote on the topic agreed with Hamburger and Benjamin, both of whom saw transsexualism as an extreme version of transvestism. Although they distinguished crossdressing from crossgender identification, the doctors could not draw the boundary as firmly as they might have wanted. For MTFs, Benjamin noted "an overlapping and blurring of types." He created a six-point "Sex Orientation Scale," modeled explicitly on Alfred Kinsey's continuum of hetero- and homosexuality. On one end of the scale Benjamin included the "pseudo" transvestites who had "only sporadic" interest in crossdressing and the "fetishistic" and "true" transvestites who derived sexual pleasure from crossdressing. On the other end he established three categories of transsexuals, culminating in the "high intensity" transsexuals with "total 'psychosexual' inversion." The transsexuals generally had low libido.[20] "Occasionally," Benjamin noted, "one condition seems to develop out of the other, so that a sharp clinical separation cannot always be made."[21] Other doctors adopted Benjamin's concept of a scale, with some patients pegged at a particular spot and others moving over time along the continuum from occasional crossdressing to an avid desire to change sex. The concept of a continuum allowed the doctors to distinguish conditions without creating mutually exclusive categories or snapshot pictures of unchanging patients.

The doctors simultaneously defined the categories and undermined them with "transition zones" that they admitted were "blurry." To underscore the overlaps, they wrote of the "transvestitic male transexual," who moved from the urge to crossdress to the desire to change sex, or of "effeminate-homosexual transsexualism," marked by a history of homosexual behavior. Or they wrote, as in the case of one FTM, of "successive stages of homosexuality, transvestitism, and transsexuality." Ultimately, they acknowledged, their diagnoses relied on their interpretations of their patients' self-descriptions. Without any physical measures to guide them, the doctors often returned to the request for surgery itself as the primary distinguishing feature of the transsexual condition. Although they noted exceptions, they reconfirmed, as Benjamin wrote, that "the request for a conversion operation is typical only for the transsexual and can actually serve as definition."[22]

From the outside, the doctors debated the boundaries of transsexualism and marked it as a recognizable place on the sexological map. From the inside, homosexuals, transvestites, and transsexuals also laid claim to particular spots in the landscape of gender and sexual variance. While the doctors wrestled with definitions and diagnoses, self-identified homosexuals, transvestites, and transsexuals engaged in a parallel practice in which they tried to distinguish themselves from one another. They hoped to make themselves intelligible to others and also to convince doctors, courts, and the public to accord them dignity, rights, and respect. Some chose to align themselves with other sexual and gender variants or wondered out loud which of the existing categories best embraced their sense of themselves. But mostly, it seems, they hoped to explain their differences. In a sense, they constructed and affirmed their own identities by telling themselves and others how they differed. For some, the social practice of taxonomy involved a "politics of respectability."[23] Those who identified as homosexual, transvestite, or transsexual sometimes attempted to lift their own group's social standing by foisting the stigma of transgression onto others. They lived in a social order in which status derived in part from upholding norms of propriety. Asserting one's upstanding middle-class status meant rejecting other behaviors tainted as vulgar, lower class, or deviant.

When the Jorgensen story broke, some gay men and lesbians took an immediate interest. According to one testimony, "many homosexuals" were "fascinated" by Jorgensen's story, and according to Jorgensen herself, she served as "a cult figure . . . among the gays."[24] From 1953 on, the issue of "sex change" appeared in the "homophile," or early gay rights, movement. The American homophile movement had emerged with the founding of the Mattachine Society in 1950. In the hostile postwar climate, the movement aimed to protect the civil rights of homosexuals, to educate the public, and also to foster a sense of community. From 1953 into the 1970s, the various publications of the homophile movement sporadically addressed the emergence of transsexuality.[25] Much of the interest seemed to reflect a basic curiosity, but sometimes it also expressed tensions.

In 1953, for example, *ONE* magazine published a debate among its readers as to whether gay men should denounce Jorgensen. In the opening salvo the author Jeff Winters accused Jorgensen of a "sweeping disservice" to gay men. "As far as the public knows," Winters wrote, "you were merely another unhappy homosexual who decided to get drastic about it." For Winters, Jorgensen's story simply confirmed the false belief "that all men attracted to other men must be basically feminine," which, he said, *"they are not."* Jorgensen's precedent, he thought, encouraged the "reasoning" that led "to legal limitations upon the homosexual, mandatory injections, psychiatric treatment—and worse." In the not-so-distant past, scientists had experimented with castrating gay men. The publicity about transsexuals, Winters implied, might inspire doctors or courts to advocate castration as a cure.

The public might "applaud" Jorgensen's "solution," he wrote, but "eunuchism" was "not a solution for those who are homosexual." "There are hundreds of thousands of male homosexuals," he claimed, "who would rather die than lose their genders."[26] Winters affirmed a homosexual identity that was not tied to crossgender identification and at the same time positioned those who desired to change sex as dangerous sellouts.

In the ensuing months two readers wrote letters critiquing the article. They asked homophiles to refrain from condemning other outcasts. The goal of the homophile movement, one letter claimed, was "tolerance for the deviate." Jorgensen, the writer said, had "never urged similar treatment for all sexual deviates." Another letter considered Jorgensen a "transvestite" and implied that homosexuals should not condemn her decision to change sex or her right to do what she pleased: Jorgensen "succeeded in getting what he wanted. Who is going to throw the first stone?" Jorgensen's doctors, the letter continued, combined "the most humane considerations with the essence of liberalism, that of the right to self-determination . . . Again, who is hurt?"[27] The debate centered on the question of whether Jorgensen was an embarrassment to the homophile movement or whether she was a fellow outcast of a different species whom homophiles should defend.

Among the homophile activists, the mixed reaction to Jorgensen went hand in hand with a broader debate about gender transgression among gay men and lesbians. Some gay men and lesbians believed that homosexuals would win respect more readily if they refrained from challenging the norms of gender. They should love whom they wanted quietly and in private, but they should not, some argued, engage in publicly offensive "swish" or "butch" behavior. "Face it, butches," one lesbian wrote, "there is absolutely nothing to be gained by living our lives in farcical imitations of men."[28] For the most part, the disparaging comments about "swish" and "butch" reflected debates internal to the homophile movement and may have involved class differences among the homosexual subcultures. Historians have suggested that fairies and butches often found their homes in working-class communities.[29] Some gay men and women seemed to associate public gender transgression with what they saw as undignified, low-class behavior.

Such attempts to dissociate lesbians from masculinity and gay men from femininity also sometimes included an attempt to distance homosexuals from transsexuals. As early as 1948, a lesbian denounced the "types of homosexual women" who "actually believe they are men in women's bodies." These individuals, she said, "sow the seeds of the harvest of ridicule and contempt that all must reap. This does not endear them to . . . [lesbians] who are trying to live naturally and with dignity, on a parallel with heterosexual society—not as freaks within it."[30] After the publicity about Jorgensen, the same sentiments led some gay men to pose "sex-change headline-hunters" along with "female impersonators" as groups that "brought discredit" to homosexuals.[31]

But even those gays who readily broke the social rules governing gender drew a line between homosexuality and transsexuality. For some, transsexuality posed a threat, an unwanted alternative to a gay life. As Margo, a drag queen, recalled recently, the Jorgensen story "really scared me, because as a gay young teenager I did not want to be a woman, and here it is in the paper that this may be what I have to do." In the documentary film *The Queen*, made in 1968, several gay drag queens denied any interest in changing sex. "I know that I'm a drag queen," said one of the group; "I've been a drag queen for a long time, I've been gay for a long time, but I certainly do not want to become a girl."[32] The initial publicity about transsexuality and later the increasing availability of transsexual surgery pushed them to stake out their own identities and to state, to themselves and sometimes to others, whether or not they wished to change sex. They defined themselves not just with reference to their differences from the mainstream but also with reference to other "deviant" options they rejected for themselves.

Transvestites engaged in a similar form of identity politics. In the early 1950s, MTF crossdressers expressed an ongoing concern with dispelling the commonly held view that transvestites were homosexuals. In 1952 a small group of crossdressers in southern California put out two issues of a mimeographed newsletter, titled *Transvestia: Journal of the American Society for Equality in Dress*. The newsletter qualifies as the opening act of a fledgling transvestites' rights movement. One of its key concerns was to distinguish transvestites from homosexuals. The first issue stated: "Transvestism should not be confused or compared with sex deviates . . . Transvestism is merely and simply an aesthetic expression and manifestation of artistic appreciation for true beauty and charm." The second issue made the distinction more clearly: it categorized transvestites as "aesthetic and innocuous" but placed homosexuals among "deviates of psychopathic origin."[33] Just as the early homophile activists sometimes condemned gender transgressors, so conversely transvestites often attempted to establish their own respectability by denying sexual deviance. They downplayed the fetishistic sexual pleasure that many MTF transvestites derived from wearing women's clothes and also the fantasies of bondage and discipline found in much of the fiction geared to transvestite readers. But even more, they hoped to remove from themselves the stigma attached to homosexuals.

When transsexuality made the news, it added another wrinkle. Some MTF crossdressers identified with Jorgensen and wondered whether they would "have the courage and desire to follow in her footsteps."[34] "I understand," one inside observer noted, "that the whole 'sorority' is quite thrilled at the recently head lined 'sex transformation' case and there have been serious discussions by several in regard to investigating the possibility of such action upon themselves."[35] Most transvestites ultimately decided against surgery, but some hoped the publicity about transsexuality would create a more tolerant climate for transvestites. Enid Foreman (pseudonym), an MTF crossdresser, was a retired lawyer who lived in southern California. In the early 1950s she advertised in *Billboard* magazine, offering "personalized instruction" in impersonation. In return for a fee, she sent her correspondents fifty or more "lectures," most of which provided instruction on how to sound and appear like a woman.[36] In 1952 she worked on the two issues of *Transvestia*. Foreman objected strongly to transsexual surgery. By 1954 she had heard about Elmer Belt's surgical procedures in Los Angeles. "Naturally," she wrote, "one might be aghast at this sort of surgical adventuring." She worried about the medical complications after transsexual surgery and considered the results "artificial and superficial." She also lamented the potential loss of libido and "orgiastic relief." Still, she expressed hope that the publicity to Jorgensen might "redound to the benefit of transvestites in general." It might "arous[e] the lethargic public mind to better understanding of eonism," and it might "result in more tolerant regard on the part of law enforcement agencies toward anyone who indulges in 'crossdressing.'"[37]

Others worked to create a transvestite identity that explicitly excluded both homosexuals and transsexuals. Virginia Prince emerged as the chief spokesperson for this position. Prince, a chemist, was part of the network of MTF crossdressers who socialized in southern California. In 1952 she wrote under the name "Muriel" for the original *Transvestia* newsletter, and in 1960 she launched a new magazine, also titled *Transvestia*, which quickly became the centerpiece of the transvestite movement. The magazine aimed "to provide expression" for crossdressers, "to provide information" to the ignorant, and "to provide education for those who see evil where none exists."[38] By this time Prince had adopted the first name Virginia, and in 1968, at the age of fifty-five, she began to live fulltime as a woman. From the start, Prince used the pages of *Transvestia* to delineate differences among transvestism, homosexuality, and transsexualism. The very first issue hinted that she hoped to rid transvestism of its public association with homosexuality. "Educating society to look for the differences that set groups apart," she wrote, "would reduce the number of incidents where individuals are . . . made to bear stigma that they do not deserve."[39] For Prince, transvestism was "gender expression," not "sexual deviation," and transsexual surgery was a "tragic mistake" for transvestites, who were "biologically males and heterosexually orientated."[40] A letter advertising *Transvestia* summed up the claim to respectability: "Transvestism occurs in normal, hetero-sexual men who are otherwise quite masculine and aggressive."[41] *Transvestia*, it seems, hoped to dissociate MTF transvestites from the taint of both sexual deviance and effeminacy.

Prince did not define transsexuality as the request for surgery; in fact she thought that the great majority of those who requested surgery were not truly transsexuals. "Those of you toying with the idea of surgery," she wrote in one issue of *Transvestia*, "should forget it." "If you are a TV [transvestite]," she stated, "if you have in the past functioned successfully with a female sexually, had a fairly decent job and were able to get along with boys as one of them, it is very unlikely that you are really a TS [transsexual]."[42] In the same issue she published an article by someone who had and regretted surgery, another by a crossdresser who pondered and rejected surgery, and a third by a transvestite who denounced other transvestites' "obsession" with surgery as "the expression of a most childish, immature, superficial and retarded . . . personality development."[43]

It is hard to pinpoint the source of Prince's push to distance transvestites from transsexuals. In the mid-1950s she had been, she claimed later, "envious" of Jorgensen and other early publicized transsexuals. "If I had had the money at the time," she wrote in her autobiography, "I would have taken the boat to Europe." Later, though, she envisioned surgery as "a very expensive, painful and dangerous trip to take to a destination I didn't want to go to."[44] She used her own story to convince other crossdressers to refuse the surgical interventions she had already rejected for herself. She had "a missionary complex," as she told Jorgensen in a letter written in 1953. She hoped "to alleviate the lot of our kind in the social scheme."[45] But by the 1960s she no longer included transsexuals among her kind; instead she hoped to stop the conversions of transvestites to another denomination. Prince continued to publicize her message for decades, not only in *Transvestia* but also through the other publications of her publishing house, Chevalier Press, through the national organization for MTF crossdressers she founded, and through the steady stream of books and articles she authored.

Although gay men, lesbians, and MTF crossdressers saw themselves as different from, and sometimes defined themselves in opposition to, people who wanted to change sex, they were in general more accepting of transsexuals than the mainstream medical profession. In the mid-1960s three researchers at UCLA—Richard Green, Robert Stoller, and Craig McAndrew—sent a questionnaire on transsexuality to gay men and lesbians affiliated with organizations of the homophile movement, transvestites on "the mailing list of a nationally circulated transvestite magazine," most likely *Transvestia,* and various doctors. They compiled the responses of 169 noncrossdressing male homosexuals,

115 lesbians, 83 MTF heterosexual transvestites, and 355 doctors. The "deviant groups," they found, had more positive views of transsexuals than did the doctors. Less than 2 percent of transvestites and homosexuals considered transsexuals "psychotic," in contrast to 14 to 17 percent of the doctors. The great majority of transvestites, gay men, and lesbians did not find transsexuals "morally depraved" or a "threat to society," and many more of them than doctors approved of surgery. Nonetheless, the survey also recorded a less-than-positive image of transsexuals. Almost half of transvestites and more than two-thirds of gay men and lesbians considered MTFs who asked for sex-change surgery "severely neurotic."[46]

For their part, self-identified transsexuals expressed their own ambivalence about homosexuals and transvestites. Some, including Jorgensen, found friends among gay men, lesbians, and crossdressers. On her record album interview, Jorgensen acknowledged her gay friends and said they had more understanding of her problem because of their own experience. She also defended the rights of homosexuals, an unusual public stance for the late 1950s. "I don't personally believe," she said, "that homosexuality is a problem to society in any way or form." But there was, she told an interviewer in the 1960s, a "great psychological difference" between her own desires and those of homosexuals. "I identified myself as a female," she said, "and consequently my interests in men were normal." Her use of the word *normal* implicitly stigmatized homosexuality as "abnormal" desire, a position she confirmed in private through "disapproving" comments about gay men and lesbians.[47] Jorgensen also attempted to distance herself from crossdressers. In her 1967 autobiography she insisted that she had "never worn, or wanted to wear, feminine clothing" before her sex change. (Here she contradicted her own doctors, who had written in 1953 that she had indeed acquired and worn women's clothes.) In a review of the book in *Transvestia,* crossdresser Sheila Niles thought "this insistence on complete dissociation from the TV's seems a little exaggerated." While Niles agreed that "TV and TS are separate phenomena," she found Jorgensen's "tone . . . a little less than friendly."[48]

Other transsssexuals distinguished themselves from homosexuals and transvestites even more pointedly. An MTF who had lived as a woman for seven years before surgery and "dated men only" said: "I was never a homosexual in any form. I went to gay bars twice in my entire life. I was not accepted by gay society, nor did I wish to be." In his autobiography, FTM Mario Martino discussed the sexual relationships he had had with women while still living as a woman himself, but he insisted: "I was definitely *not* a lesbian!" He understood himself instead as a heterosexual man. Along similar lines, Gayle Sherman, an MTF, separated herself from crossdressers: "I wasn't then and I'm not now a transvestite. I don't get sexual pleasure out of dressing as a woman."[49]

Like some homosexuals and transvestites, some transsexuals expressed scorn for those they considered beneath them. They repeated derogatory stereotypes, and they tried to establish their own health and authenticity through invidious distinction.[50] Some transsexuals expressed the desire to live as a "normal" woman or man as opposed to living as a "queer" or a "freak." In this sense, transsexual surgery occasionally had overtones of upward mobility. Jorgensen's rise to fame suggested that transsexual surgery could lift a person not only from "queer" to "normal" but also from working-class obscurity to celebrity and fortune. Any astute observer could understand that Jorgensen was unusual: sex change rarely led to lucrative offers. Still, it might permit an escape from the déclassé and difficult life on the sexual margins, and it might allow transgendered individuals to fit quietly into the mainstream. In the late 1960s, in an interview for a documentary film, an MTF in San Francisco said that she wanted to live her life as "a respectable, normal, ordinary woman—period." She resented that others "classified" her as "a common queen." A few transsexuals spoke of their efforts to remove themselves from the stigmatized sexual fringe. An FTM made the issue of class standing explicit. He hoped "to become either a teacher or a lawyer," and, he feared, "either of these careers would be closed" if he lived as a lesbian.[51]

The multiplicity of subgroups on the sexual margins complicated both the private search for identity and the public demands for dignified treatment. People who decades earlier might have been grouped together as "inverts" were now sorting themselves out. In each group, those who sought respectability hoped to avoid the label of freak or the status of outcast. They adopted strategies that might make them appear "normal," strategies that sometimes involved rejecting "abnormal" others. In this climate of mutual aversion, they sometimes made disparaging comments about other sexual minorities, and they also noted the hostile attitudes that they perceived, rightly or wrongly, among others. In the late 1950s, in her record album interview, Jorgensen remembered one letter writer who had sent her a razor blade with the message "Why don't you cut your throat? You're making it hard for the rest of us." Jorgensen commented: "What 'us' was I don't know." But others guessed. At least one MTF, who had surgery in the early 1960s, assumed that "us" was people "from within the gay community . . . sending her rusty razor blades in the mail." Gays resented, she believed, the "negative attention," the way the publicity about Jorgensen put homosexuality in the spotlight. Such hostility, she remembered, "was very prevalent."[52]

*E*lsewhere, though, mutual tolerance prevailed. From the 1950s on, the sporadic border skirmishes between sexual and gender minorities did not preclude friendships and cooperation. To some extent, the overlapping social circles of the sexual subcultures belied the avowed divisions among the various groups. In the 1950s and 1960s the social lives of transsexuals were invisible to the general public and usually also to the doctors, and today they are only barely visible to the historian trying to reconstruct them. Nonetheless, we have enough evidence to know that people who came to call themselves transsexuals did not necessarily live in isolation from or engage in battles with other sexual and gender nonconformists.

For the 1950s, the best evidence of these social circles comes from the San Francisco Bay area, where Louise Lawrence acted as a one-woman social hub. Since the late 1930s, Lawrence, who identified herself as a "permanent transvestite," had corresponded and met with dozens of other transvestites. But she also made a point of engaging with a wide range of other people she considered "interesting."[53] Earlier in life, when she had lived as a man, she had experimented with homosexuality but discovered that she "derived absolutely no satisfaction" from it.[54] She continued, though, to socialize with gay men and lesbians. She knew gay female impersonators who performed at the famed Finocchio's, and she attended gay drag parties at the Beige Room in San Francisco. She worked with the homophile movement as well. According to Don Lucas, head of the San Francisco Mattachine Society, she came to his office "quite frequently." She also invited Lucas, as he recalled, to a meeting of around twelve "transsexuals or crossdressers."[55] Lawrence saw herself as a champion of transvestites, but she took an ecumenical approach to the various subgroups on the margins.

In the 1950s Lawrence placed herself at the center of, and to some extent created, a transsexual social network. Even before the news of Jorgensen's sex change, her social circles included people seeking surgery, such as Barbara and Lauren Wilcox, whom she had befriended in the 1940s. After Jorgensen made the news, Lawrence had Harry Benjamin introduce her to his patients, and she made contacts on her own. She corresponded with them, introduced them to one another, invited them to her home, and counseled them informally. The trail of correspondence now at the Kinsey Institute archives shows that by the mid-1950s Lawrence had befriended at least seventeen people who sought or had surgery. Most of them visited or stayed with her, sometimes in groups of two or three. Among the early publicized cases of people seeking surgery, Lawrence avoided only the wealthy San Franciscan Bunny Breckinridge. Friends and acquaintances described Lawrence as "elegant, reserved" and "dignified."[56] Her style clashed with Breckinridge's high camp fey flamboyance, and her need for privacy—she risked arrest for crossdressing—conflicted with Breckinridge's penchant for publicity. "I have a feeling," she told Benjamin, "that he is very unstable and probably psychotic . . . I might be leaving myself open for trouble should I contact him." Benjamin agreed.[57]

Lawrence's concerted efforts to bridge the social gaps among sexual and gender minorities were unusual in the 1950s. But the overlapping subcultures were not. Many transsexuals gravitated to the sexual margins in their search for a social home. The stigma associated with gender variance made it difficult for them to feel at home in the social mainstream. Regardless of class, racial, or ethnic background, they often found themselves ejected from the families and social milieus in which they were reared. They found comfort among others who might understand them or at least accept that their unconventional longings did not disqualify them as worthy friends and decent human beings. In the medical literature, one article noted that "many male and female transsexuals describe migrating to the homosexual society because they feel 'accepted and understood.'"[58] Under such circumstances many transsexuals came to know transvestites or homosexuals, and vice versa. In fact many transsexuals went through phases in which they identified themselves temporarily as lesbian, gay, or transvestite.

Identities were neither entirely fixed nor entirely fluid. People who had a longstanding, deeply rooted sense of crossgender identification sought out the social groups that best fitted their sense of themselves. As they encountered new social options, they sometimes changed the ways they envisioned themselves and the categories in which they placed themselves. In major cities, certain sexual subcultures seemed particularly inviting. Once they had entered these social settings, some MTFs engaged in a chain migration of sorts, following newfound friends and acquaintances who had already identified as transsexuals and embarked on their search for surgery.

In the 1940s and 1950s a number of MTFs, who later sought genital surgery, first found their ways to the social networks of transvestites. In 1949, for example, Carla Sawyer's arrest for crossdressing in Los Angeles introduced her to other transvestites. "I didn't think there were any other transvestites in the world," she wrote, "until after my arrest." Because of publicity in the press, she received a number of letters from "people with similar interests."[59] Traumatic as it was, her arrest drew her into a social world that ended her isolation. It was only after she met other transvestites that she learned of the possibility of changing sex. A few years later Louise Lawrence encouraged her to write to Harry Benjamin, who eventually helped her obtain surgery in Mexico. The social networks of MTF crossdressers also served as launching pads for other transsexuals. They corresponded, met, and socialized with other transgendered people with whom they could debate and share information on transsexual surgery. As Lawrence recalled: "I was soon to find that a number of my friends whom [sic] I was certain were transvestites actually went through with this . . . sort of operation."[60]

By the end of the 1950s and even more so in the 1960s, the gay male circles of professional female impersonators also served as communities for emergent MTFs. In the early 1950s Coccinelle, an impersonator who worked at Le Carrousel, a well-known Paris nightclub, began to take hormones, and in 1958 underwent surgery in Casablanca. Soon afterward a number of her colleagues followed in her footsteps. In fact by 1964, according to one account, all but one of the impersonators at Le Carrousel had had "the operation."[61] In the United States and elsewhere, the press publicized the "sex changes" of the French *travestis*, especially Coccinelle and Bambi. Coccinelle, in particular, inspired dozens of magazine and newspaper stories that associated her with the world of celebrity. One illustrated story showed her seated between Bob Hope and Aristotle Onassis, and promised a follow-up story on "Coccinelle with Debbie Reynolds, Marlene Dietrich, Anita Ekberg, and other stars." After Coccinelle, Bambi appeared in the press as the "latest in the crop of glamour guy-gals."[62]

For American MTFs, the French example served as a draw. In the 1960s Renée Richards traveled to France in search of Coccinelle. At Le Carrousel she met with Bambi for "about twenty minutes," a conversation "packed with information." "I was left with the feeling," she remembered later, "that [surgery] was within reach, that it could be done if I wanted it badly enough." Other American MTFs imagined themselves in France but never made the trip. As a teenager Suzan Cooke "clipped stories about Bambi and Coccinelle." She planned on leaving her parents' home to "work at the Carrousel Club and figure out how to get my operation."[63]

Within the United States as well, the circles of female impersonators provided a haven for certain MTFs. In the late 1950s Aleshia Brevard, living as a gay man, visited Finocchio's in San Francisco. One of the performers, teasing her from the stage, introduced her as "one of my star pupils" to audience applause. "And that was it," she recollected. I "knew that it was me." Young, pretty, and happy in the spotlight, she won a job as an impersonator, performing under the name Lee Shaw. Finocchio's, she recalled, "was the only place I could find total acceptance of me." But it was also a place in which she transformed herself. In her classic *Mother Camp*, an anthropological study of female imper-

sonators, Esther Newton notes that "the effect of the female impersonator subculture is to socialize individual deviance so that it is brought
under group control and legitimized."[64] Female impersonators taught
each other the particular customs that earned them a living, a fan following, and the praise of their peers. They schooled one another in
how to dress, how to move, and how to perform onstage as glamorous
women. Some of them also taught one another how to take hormones
or offered encouragement to pursue a woman's life offstage.

While she worked at Finocchio's, Brevard began to consider transsexual surgery. Another performer, Stormy, took her under her wing
and introduced her to "this little purple pill," hormones that would
make her breasts grow. Brevard borrowed a pill immediately and soon
went to Harry Benjamin to get her own prescription. She read about
the surgeries of Coccinelle and Bambi. "That transsexuals were very accepted," she remembered, "in fact even lauded . . . in France, was a real
incentive for me." Eventually Stormy and she decided to castrate themselves. She went first and bled so heavily that Stormy refrained from
following suit. A year or so later, in 1962, Elmer Belt completed the
surgery in Los Angeles. Stormy had her surgery later, performed by
Georges Burou in Casablanca. At the time, the other transgendered
performers at Finocchio's rejected transsexual surgery. Stormy and she,
Brevard remembered, represented a "new generation."[65]

By the mid-1960s more members of the "new generation" moved
from female impersonation to transsexuality. Another MTF, who had
worked as a female impersonator in Los Angeles, described the change.
"When I first began work as an impersonator, I only very rarely met
anyone who wanted to have the sex change operation." But by the
time of her interview, in the early or mid-1960s, one year after her own
surgery, she said, "almost every impersonator" knew "someone, or several someones" who had "made the change." She knew "half a dozen
impersonators who, some years back, denied that they had the slightest
desire to become women." "Now," she said, "they are saving for the
operation." Because they knew others who had had surgery, she believed, they were no longer "so afraid."[66]

Offstage, the subcultures of "street queens" also attracted MTFs. In
the urban geography of the gay underworld, drag queens congregated

in certain neighborhoods. They took on a feminine style publicly, on the streets. Some also performed onstage as female impersonators in bars and clubs, but many more earned money through prostitution. In San Francisco, street queens congregated in the center city neighborhood known as the Tenderloin. Brevard remembered it as "sort of the underbelly of society . . . you were safe to a degree because you were all outcasts. So you could look a little strange, without the fear." In Chicago, the North Side's Old Town was a gathering place for queens. Major started hanging out with the queens as a high school student in the late 1950s. "There were other girls to back you up and be with you," she said. There was "a sense of unspoken unity in the community" and a certain power in numbers. "You might get beat up," she said, "but you probably weren't going to get murdered because you had this force with you." In New York, 42nd Street was the heart of street queen prostitution, and the West Village served as the unofficial social center for the queens. In the mid-1960s, Holly Woodlawn recalled later, "all the 'girls' in the West Village were starting to come out of their closets." She shared an apartment with other queens and frequented "the bars and the coffee houses" of the neighborhood. The Stonewall Inn, a bar in New York (and in 1969 the site of the famous riots that helped launch the gay liberation movement), drew "people going through major gender changes," and another bar, the Washington Square, had primarily street queen clientele.[67]

The social circles of street queens attracted mostly poor and working-class transgendered MTFs, from an array of racial and ethnic backgrounds. In San Francisco's Tenderloin, Tamara Ching remembered, "there were very few Asians and Pacific Islanders" until the 1980s. But in 1969, soon after she entered the drag queen scene, "there was an invasion of black girls from Chicago, St. Louis, and Detroit. The next year, Mexicans came from Texas and Colorado and from across the border." Major, who is African American, remembered Chicago's drag queen circles as racially mixed. When she was young she lived on the South Side, where most blacks lived in Chicago, but she came to the North Side to hang out with other queens. In New York, too, black, white, and Latina drag queens stood side by side on the streets and in the bars. "The black 'girls,'" Holly Woodlawn recalled, "tried to look like the Supremes and the white 'girls' . . . like the Shangri-Las."[68]

The street queens were part of the gay male social world, but they differed from the gay men who projected a masculine image. As middle-class gay men increasingly asserted their own respectability by avoiding feminine or "swish" behavior, the drag queens, like earlier working-class "fairies," endured the brunt of public and police hostility.[69] But they also stood out as a beacon of sorts for at least some MTFs. In the late 1960s, Regina Elizabeth McQuade remembered, she had hoped to find "a support network" at a gay bar. But the gay men she met there were "anti anything different." Drag queens, though, welcomed other transgendered people. They "were fun," she recalled, "and they were supportive."[70]

By all accounts, many street queens experimented with hormones from the late 1950s on. Major began taking hormones in the late 1950s after other queens introduced her to a Chicago doctor who dispensed them on demand in return for immediate cash payment. "There weren't a lot of queens who wanted to be women at that time," she said. "They were on hormones to soften their skin and their appearance, not because they wanted sex reassignment . . . It was a craze . . . everybody admired what Christine Jorgensen had done. There was this sense of 'she was pretty before and gorgeous after, and the hormones were the reason for this look' . . . Everybody wanted to go for this look, from being attractive or pretty to being gorgeous." Those who did not take hormones often disparaged those who did. The "gay boys," Holly Woodlawn remembered, "gave us the derogatory label 'hormone queens' . . . I hated the term." Despite the ridicule, a "very significant proportion" of queens found their way to hormone pills or shots as well as other drugs.[71] As Major said, the queens who took hormones did not necessarily identify as transsexuals. Woodlawn seriously considered surgery but ultimately rejected it along with the transsexual label. So did Sylvia Rivera, a teenaged street queen in New York. In the mid-1960s she and her friends obtained hormones from a doctor on the Lower East Side. Once she learned she was getting monkey hormones, she switched to a Dr. Stern. "If you let him play with you for a little while," she recalled, "he'd give you anything for free." In the end, Rivera decided to stop the hormones. She did not want sex-change surgery. "I came to the conclusion," she said later, "that I don't want to be a woman . . . I like pretending. I like to have the role." And she wanted to keep her penis.[72]

Other MTFs moved step by step from the subcultures of feminine gay men and drag queens to transsexuality. In New York, Patricia Morgan started hustling in the mid-1950s as a feminine boy. Through a friend, she met "gay boys who dressed in drag." One of them showed her how "he hid his penis and had sex with men—without their realizing he was a boy." Eventually she, too, engaged in prostitution with customers who never discovered her male genitals. But she did not want a life in drag. She had read about sex-change surgery in the newspaper, and in a New York restaurant a friend had introduced her to an MTF who had had "the operation." "Vera took me home," she recalled, "and took off her clothes and showed me. I couldn't believe it. The biggest dream of my life was to become a woman." After two of her friends had surgery in California, she started saving her money. Morgan, who had run away from an impoverished home, lacked the financial resources to cover the costs of expensive surgery, but her work as a prostitute enabled her to pay for medical treatment otherwise out of her reach. Her friends told her "how to go about getting the operation" from Elmer Belt in Los Angeles. She underwent surgery in 1961 and 1962.[73]

By the end of the decade a few researchers began to comment on this social process in which MTFs followed friends and acquaintances into genital surgery. In the late 1960s James Patrick Driscoll spent a month in San Francisco's Tenderloin interviewing MTF transsexuals for his master's thesis at San Francisco State. He interviewed twenty-one MTFs, seventeen of whom he classified as transsexuals. All of them, he found, had come to transsexuality via "the gay world." They had lived for a while as "hair fairies," feminine gay men who "wear their hair long and tease it." From "hair fairies," they "decided to come out" as "drag queens," who dressed as women and acted "in as feminine a fashion as possible." Like Patricia Morgan in New York, most of them supported themselves by engaging in prostitution. They lived in the Tenderloin and had "an active social life among themselves."[74]

The MTFs Driscoll interviewed did not stay queens for long. Within a few months they met transsexuals and learned of the possibilities of surgical sex change. The increasing availability of hormones and surgery made it easier to see and meet self-identified transsexuals. "Once they have heard of the conversion operation and know that there is such a thing as a transsexual," Driscoll wrote, "the self concepts of the girls seem to change." They came to describe themselves as women, not as fairies or queens, and they took hormones and underwent electrolysis if they could afford it. In the Tenderloin, Driscoll located four apartment houses and hotels that regularly rented rooms to transsexuals. One such hotel on Eddy Street had mostly MTF inhabitants. The MTFs who lived there advised one another on how to talk, walk, and dress in ways that made them appear womanly. "They learn from each other and the newcomer has a ready made classroom and teacher."[75]

As part of the journey toward sex change, those who came to identify as transsexuals gradually separated themselves from other forms of queer identity. They redefined their sense of themselves as they discovered and found themselves drawn to specific subcultures. They did not define themselves solely in the lingo of medicine or psychology but also in the gay vernacular, a language that had a broader range of labels for different renditions of femininity. "We didn't use psychspeak," one MTF recalled, "our language was the language of the queers and queens." While the public may have lumped them all together as "effeminate" outcasts and the doctors struggled to define them in medical terms, they themselves saw finer social distinctions in which "TVs" differed from professional female impersonators, "hair fairies" or "flame" queens differed from "drag queens," and "hormone queens" differed from MTF transsexuals. The labels reflected a spectrum of gender variance on the sexual margins, and for those in the know, they implied different feminine styles. Hair fairies, Driscoll noted, wore "a little makeup, a bulky sweater, and tight trousers," drag queens looked "like whores," MTF transsexuals modeled their femininity on the "high fashion showgirl," and those who wanted to leave the Tenderloin pat-

terned their look after "college students or the ordinary working girl."
Most of those who had surgery did leave their former lives behind.
Some "paired off," Driscoll found, to find apartments together outside
the Tenderloin in a residential area, and some wanted nothing to do
with other transsexuals. Surgery seemed to offer an escape route for
those who hoped to leave the dangerous nightlife of prostitution and
also for those who hoped to rid themselves of the stigma attached to
drag queens. As one observer put it, "transsexualism was a way of settling down."[76] For others, like Patricia Morgan in New York, prostitution remained the most viable means of self-support after surgery as
before.

In the 1960s, the overlapping networks on the sexual margins
flourished. Increasing numbers of young people advocated and engaged more openly in sexual experimentation. The underground circles of crossdressers, female impersonators, drag queens, and butch-
femme lesbians occasionally came up to surface as the popular culture
showed a new interest in publicizing the sexual fringe. The new hippie
subculture, with its unisex style and its freewheeling approach to sex
and drugs, attracted primarily middle-class, white youth who rebelled
against the sexual ethos of their parents, and it served as a refuge for
some transsexuals who felt excluded from the "straight" world. MTFs
could experiment with long hair and FTMs with jeans and T-shirts
without anyone's suspecting that they hoped to change their sex. For
Suzan Cooke, the counterculture provided a temporary refuge. Even
in high school in upstate New York, she had her "own little band of
freaks," who played guitar and supported the civil rights movement.
Later, in California, she lived as a gay, androgynous hippie in San Francisco's Haight-Ashbury district and then as a transsexual radical in a
commune in Berkeley. When she started dressing as a woman publicly,
in part "to avoid the draft," she anticipated "rejection." "I thought,"
she said later, "I was going to have to go off and live with the queens.
And I didn't." In the 1960s, for a few years at least, she found acceptance in the counterculture with its general tolerance for unconventional behavior. When Angela Douglas started to crossdress in Los Angeles in the late 1960s, her countercultural "friends took it with a grain
of salt, viewing it as just another weird trip." As another MTF recalled,

the counterculture "wasn't about your crotch or your color. You were cool or not cool."[77]

Like MTFs, many FTMs found temporary shelter in the urban subcultures that welcomed various types of nonconformists. In particular, many FTMs spent months or years as lesbians, sometimes participating in the butch-femme social networks of working-class lesbian bars. But through the 1960s, their move to transsexuality tended to happen in isolation. At the age of sixteen, in the late 1940s or early 1950s, for example, Tom Michaels, living as a girl, "joyously discovered the homosexual world and thought I was no longer singular in the universe." He was, he recalled later, "quickly disappointed." He soon decided that lesbians "were not like me, not at all." He began to live as a man, and then again as a woman, and only years later sought transsexual surgery. A medical case study from the 1960s described a similar process. The patient, D. L., "wondered," in the doctor's words, "if she were homosexual" and began "to frequent various homosexual haunts." "She soon decided," though, "that she was not a homosexual" and then went through a phase in which "she led an almost solitary existence." Eventually D. L. "moved to another city," assumed a new name, and lived as a man. A few years later he had a bilateral mastectomy and began taking hormones.[78] Through the 1960s, FTMs, like Tom Michaels and D. L., rarely had friends and acquaintances who coached or guided them on how to move from butch to FTM. By the end of the decade, a few met other FTMs after they had decided to take hormones or undergo surgery. But it was not until the 1980s that the process of transition increasingly occurred in social settings in which individuals watched their friends undergo the shift from butch lesbian to FTM, admired the process, and followed suit.

As transsexuals sorted themselves out from other queer subcultures, the sorting process itself showed how difficult it was to maintain the boundaries. People who had spent months or years identifying themselves as transvestites, butches, or drag queens had trouble explaining that they differed substantially from other members of those groups. In general, they insisted on their difference, on the temporary or provisional nature of their prior identifications. "They all explain their homosexuality," one observer commented, "in terms of the fact that they had no knowledge of transexualism at the time. Had they known about transexualism they would not have pursued a career in homosexuality." One MTF characterized it as "a stage that I was going through, the homosexual stage . . . and after that I would go into another stage." But some acknowledged that the lines dividing the subcultures, identities, and stages were rarely so clear-cut. An FTM believed that "many of the so-called lesbian butches . . . are really female transsexuals" who had simply become "resigned" to their status as women. Suzan Cooke also recognized an overlap between the diverging groups: "I had trouble seeing any vast separation between trans and queens. I mean, to me, queens were just sisters who didn't get whittled on downstairs."[79] Increasingly, gender and sexuality—and transsexualism, transvestism, and homosexuality—were analytically distinct, but in everyday practice they were still socially linked.

*T*he sexual revolution made it even more difficult to sanitize transsexuals and move them from the margins of sexuality. Some doctors and transsexuals defined transsexuality as a condition of gender and attempted to desexualize it, but most transsexuals, like most other adults, engaged in sexual acts. Transsexuality was not homosexuality or transvestism, but it had its erotic components. For transsexuals, as for many others, the sexual revolution of the 1960s brought sexual acts and sexual representations to the forefront of popular culture.

In the 1960s some MTF transsexuals engaged in their own sexual revolution. That is, a number of MTFs began to take on a more sexual style. A younger generation rejected the model offered by Christine Jorgensen, in which transsexuals proved their respectability by keeping their sex lives private and their appearance conventional. Those who came to transsexuality after living as drag queens or hippies had often already adopted a more defiant attitude in which self-expression included sexual expression. They saw themselves as rebels and flaunted their rejection of mainstream mores. Jane Fry, an MTF transsexual, identified with the youth counterculture. Jorgensen, she wrote, "had to be supermiddle-class conservative . . . she had to convince the majority of people that she was all right . . . She could have never walked the road that I am walking, which is the freak life." To some younger MTFs, Jorgensen seemed to hail from a different generation. As Suzan Cooke put it recently, "Christine Jorgensen was almost like my parents. [She] was in her mid-twenties by the time I was born." The drag queen Holly Woodlawn expressed a more general sentiment. Jorgensen, she recalled, "was such a nice lady, but hardly a role model for me. I wanted to be notorious and gorgeous, not prim and proper."[80]

By the end of the 1960s doctors noticed, and denounced, their more flamboyant patients. They identified two distinct groups of MTF transsexuals. One group had "a long history of petty and sometimes major criminal offenses" and "a history of homosexuality" and presented themselves as "hysterical males dressed in dramatic and seductive female clothing." They had exhibitionist tendencies and seemed "prone to seeking jobs as entertainers." These "antisocial" patients differed from the patients who had tried "to deny and suppress their cross-gender feelings." In the doctors' view, this second group was more reliable and less "flagrantly manipulative." Some of them had married women and fathered children. They "report[ed] considerable chronic depression" and suicidal tendencies, but despite their distress some of them had obtained college degrees and "attained a significant position in the community life."[81] The doctors seem to have distinguished between those patients who had come through the gay or hippie subcultures and borrowed from the more sexual styles of female impersonators, fairies, or drag queens and those patients, like Jorgensen earlier, who lived lonelier and quieter lives. The doctors clearly preferred the repressed and depressed group, whom they cast as more respectable and higher in class status. They used the distinction to separate good patients from bad. The "antisocial" patients annoyed the hospital staff with their "quarrelsome, demanding behavior" and their "boisterous and exhibitionistic" visitors. In contrast, the ward staff saw the other group "as more cooperative and 'better patients.'"[82]

The more outrageous MTFs also appeared, in different form, in the popular press. From the early 1960s on, tabloid newspapers and pulp publishers produced a stream of articles and cheap paperback books on MTFs who had worked as female impersonators, strippers, or prostitutes. They often illustrated the stories with pin-up style photos that revealed breasts, legs, and buttocks. The more sexualized MTF showed up in the sensational press in the stories on Coccinelle, the MTF who worked at Le Carrousel in Paris. While Jorgensen chose a feminine style that resembled Eve Arden's or Lauren Bacall's, Coccinelle adopted the more explicitly sexual femininity of Marilyn Monroe and Brigitte Bardot. The English translation of her biography, titled *Reverse Sex,* by Mario Costa, came out in the early 1960s, with sixty-four photographs, some of them nude. The cover itself, emblazoned "Strictly Adult Sale Only," had a nude profile of Coccinelle with buxom breast and nipple showing.[83] In tabloid newspaper articles, too, Coccinelle appeared nude or nearly so.[84] In her youth, Jorgensen posed occasionally in relatively conservative bathing suits, but she avoided the softcore pornographic conventions adopted by Coccinelle, who performed striptease onstage and posed for photos with her mouth pouty or open, legs spread (with genitals covered), and breasts and buttocks bared.

The eroticized pictures of Coccinelle exemplified a new approach. In the early and mid-1960s popular stories on MTFs included accounts of sexual encounters, and photos revealed the MTF's feminine body, though not yet her genitalia. In the United States the *National Insider,* a tabloid published in Chicago, led the way with numerous stories on sex change. In late 1962 and early 1963 it published an autobiographical series by Hedy Jo Star, an MTF who had worked for years as a stripper on the carnival circuit. Star began her career in the late 1930s as a "half-man, half-woman," soon became an exotic dancer, and eventually managed her own show. In the mid-1950s, in Augusta, Georgia, another MTF approached her while she rehearsed and told her about a doctor who could change her sex. The series included stories of Star's love life with men and photos of her, after she had her breast implants, in stiletto heels, fishnet stockings, and pasties. Taken together, the heterosexual love life and the revealing photos of her body made sexuality the centerpiece of her life as a woman. The series soon came out as a paperback book titled *"I Changed My Sex!,"* which the tabloid sold by mail order. The book, illustrated and "for adults," promised that "even Christine's bizarre experiences cannot compare with" Hedy Jo Star's. Its publisher, Novel Books, claimed that it sold out "in five days."[85]

At some point in the publicity blitz, Star agreed to write an advice column, "Both Sides of Love," for the *National Insider*. In 1964 Novel Books reprinted the columns, along with an article by Star's fiancé, in a lackluster sequel to her book. Here, in an exchange from her advice column, Star elaborated on a sexualized definition of womanhood that accompanied the stories of love and the sexy photos. "Dear Hedy," a letter writer began, "you say you are a woman but I don't think so because you cannot have a baby, so you are not really a woman. To me you just dress like a woman and have female sex . . . You are just a man to me, a man in a dress." In response, Star shifted the definition of womanhood away from procreation and toward sexuality. "It is quite true," she wrote, "that I can't have babies, but that doesn't mean I'm not a woman. After all, there are hundreds of women in America who can't have babies, but I doubt seriously if their husbands consider them men!" It was the marital relationship—and presumably the intimate acts within it—that convinced the husband of the womanhood of his wife. In that scenario, Star counted as a woman.[86]

After its success with Star, the *National Insider* published additional series, replete with risqué photos, on other MTFs. In 1963 it printed an autobiography of female impersonator Gayle Sherman, titled "I Want to Be a Woman!," and in 1964, of former female impersonator and fashion model Abby Sinclair, titled "I Was Male."[87] These serials, too, came out again as cheap paperback books. Beyond the photos and confessional tales, the books added supplemental features to attract readers. Gayle Sherman's book included the story of the life and loves of a British man, raised as a girl, whose male genitals developed in late adolescence, and Abby Sinclair's included a short account, "I Want to Be Male Again," by Latina Seville, a former female impersonator who underwent surgery and then regretted it. Like earlier stories on Jorgensen, the new pulp autobiographies constructed their life stories through narratives of isolation, alienation, and striving, but the newer stories also relied heavily on accounts of passion and sex. In the mid-1960s the *National Insider* featured another series, this time on nurse and jazz singer Delisa Newton, billed as "The First Negro Sex Change." Newton had not worked as a stripper or a female impersonator, and she did not pose disrobed. But sex change alone, even "The First Negro Sex Change," was no longer enough, it seems, to grab the reader's attention. The sensational headlines for Newton's series, "My Lover Beat Me" and "Why I Could Never Marry a White Man!," promised stories of sexual violence and interracial sex.[88]

In other pulp publications, too, the articles had increasingly outrageous headlines, the books had racier titles, and the pictures bordered on pornography. An article on Bambi in *Candid Press,* for example, announced in its headline, "'I Once Had a Penis!,'" and a front-page article in the *National Mirror* carried the banner "Sex-Changed Son Raped by Father," next to an obviously staged photo of the alleged attack. Accounts of transsexuality appeared in cheap paperbacks with provocative titles, such as *Sex Perversions and Taboos* and *Transvestite 69.*[89] New photo magazines of female impersonators included nude and seminude pictures of MTFs. In the early and mid-1960s, *Female Mimics* featured spreads on Coccinelle, Bambi, and Abby Sinclair. A similar magazine, *Female Impersonators,* carried racy photos of Coccinelle and, later in the decade, Lily St. Clair, a female impersonator who had sizable breasts and planned to undergo "the rest of the operation."[90]

The new approach reflected in part the growing number of MTFs and their wider range of backgrounds and experience. But more to the point, the stories and photos reflected the changing sexual ethos. More MTFs proved willing to talk about their sex lives and to pose for erotic photos. And more publishers jumped at the chance to cash in on the phenomenon. From the late 1950s on, the courts had slowly chipped away at obscenity laws and opened the way for more erotic films, books, and magazines to escape legal challenge.[91] The sexualization of MTFs went hand in hand with the legalization and commercialization of sexual expression. In this changing sexual climate, the tabloids and pulps presented their stories as less concerned with what the mainstream press dubbed "desperately unhappy lives" and more concerned with titillating adventures. The opening sentence of an article in *Newsweek* read: "The transsexuals lead a tortured life." In contrast, Abby Sinclair's autobiography, which is fairly bland, proclaimed on the cover: "A story that makes Christine Jorgensen's and even Hedy Jo Star's read like Dick and Jane."[92] In the mainstream press, issues of sexuality still lurked in the background of transsexuality; in the sensational press, they stood upfront and center.

The eroticization of MTFs in print had its counterpart on the stage. In France, Coccinelle, Bambi, and others continued to perform at Le Carrousel after they had their surgery. But in the United States, those who had genital surgery usually left the world of female impersonation. The owners of Finocchio's, for example, fired those workers who opted for hormones and surgery and refused to hire postoperative MTFs.[93] By the mid-1960s, though, a few urban nightclubs engaged MTFs as strippers and topless dancers. In New York, Abby Sinclair worked as a stripper. "The customers know I was formerly a man," she wrote, "for the ads publicize this fact." In San Francisco, Roxanne Lorraine Alegria performed for years in a number of clubs, billed at first as "The First Topless Sex-Change Dancer." A preoperative MTF, Vicki Starr, also performed topless in clubs in San Francisco as well as New York. Like other topless dancers, she bared her breasts, enlarged by hormones and implants, and kept her genitals hidden.[94]

By the end of the decade the genitals, too, were unveiled. Publishers could legally print more sexually explicit books, and new autobiographies of MTFs reflected the change. Most explicit by far was *Take My Tool,* in which the sexual episodes overwhelmed the transsexual narrative. The author, who used the pseudonym Vivian Le Mans, began her story with pornographic descriptions of oral and anal sex that illustrated her homosexual life before she had her surgery and ended with graphic accounts of postoperative heterosexual intercourse. Chapter titles included "Sex Is a Pulsing Jet," "My First Female Sex Act!," and "Mixed Sex Partners." Wedged between the sex acts were brief, rich, and compelling descriptions of the author's childhood as a "sissy," her working-class youth, her search for a doctor, her surgery in Los Angeles, and her first days living as a woman. But transsexuality served as a subtext, maybe a pretext, for the book. Sexuality drove the story, and sexual acts defined and legitimated the new woman. "I felt that magnificent shaft with the crimson crown," one typical passage stated, "nudging the sex lips of my new femininity."[95]

The new trend in autobiographies continued in later publications, although none surpassed *Take My Tool* in pornographic content. In 1972 Olympia Press published Lyn Raskin's *Diary of a Transsexual,* in which she, too, described her sex life as a gay man and later as a woman. And around the same time, Lyle Stuart published *The Man-Maid Doll,* Patricia Morgan's account of her life as a prostitute. On the second page Morgan announced: "Let's face it—I'm a whore . . . I've hustled men as a boy, as a guy in drag, and as a woman." Her book, she wrote, was "life in the raw."[96] It was almost as if the truth of sex change lay in the sexual acts.

In photography, too, the sexualization proceeded apace. At the beginning of the 1970s the photos of MTFs moved from soft-core to hard. In 1970 Command Publishing Company produced at least two issues of a magazine called An "Intimate" and Gay Diary. The cover of the first issue asked: "When Is a Girl a Boy?" and showed a photo of an MTF or drag queen with hormone-enlarged breasts, and no genitals showing, in the embraces of a man. The cover of the second issue, graced with a similar photo, asked: "Panties or Jockey Shorts?," raising the question again of whether the body displayed was male or female, as defined by the hidden genitals.[97] In the same year another magazine, HeShe, provided an answer by introducing photos of genitalia. The magazine, labeled "collector's item," featured four preoperative MTFs, with hormone-enlarged breasts, revealing, or sometimes tucking, their male genitals. In the text of the magazine the editors explained that they had conceived of the publication around September 1969 and then placed ads for models in magazines and newspapers. "Two of these 'girls,'" the text announced, had since gone "to Scandinavia for the operation." The magazine's editors hoped for a later issue on postoperative transsexuals.[98] The next year, Screw magazine followed HeShe's lead, publishing an interview with postoperative MTF Debbie Hartin. The accompanying photos, all fully nude, included one with Hartin seated, legs spread, and genitals revealed. "From Punk to Pussy," the caption announced, "transsexual surgery rescued this woman from a life of tragedy and frustration."[99]

*B*y the late 1960s the sexualization of MTFs had seeped into the mainstream culture. In 1967, for example, Esquire magazine ran a long and informative article on "The Transsexual Operation." One of the MTFs interviewed, a topless dancer, described her past life as a prostitute. In 1970 Look carried a similar piece that mentioned, without details, the sex lives of postoperative MTFs "picking up men in bars and charging for their favors."[100] By this time, sex in general permeated the popular culture, and mainstream mass-circulation magazines printed, in milder form, some of the same kinds of stories told in detail, with illustrations, in the tabloid press and pulp paperbacks.

In 1968 the eroticized MTF made her biggest mainstream splash with Gore Vidal's bestselling novel *Myra Breckinridge*. Vidal's protagonist, Myra, formerly Myron, was a power-hungry transsexual out to destroy men. Myra presented herself as the "New Woman," the crowning achievement in the decline of manhood and the rise of woman. Her mission was "to re-create the sexes and thus save the human race from certain extinction." Vidal used Myra as a mouthpiece for barbed commentaries on Hollywood, movies, television, psychoanalysis, youth, and masculinity. But sexuality propelled the plot more than Myra's wit did. With "tyrannous lust," Myra aimed to avenge the wrongs she had faced as the homosexual Myron. Her schemes to humiliate men culminated in a thirty-page scene in which Myra, armed with a dildo, raped a masculine man.[101]

Vidal appropriated the MTF confessional autobiography and reworked it as a social satire and a saga of sexual conquest. He may or may not have read the transsexual autobiographies available at the time, but the story he wrote scarcely resembles them. Vidal did not tell a tale of a lonely child, alienated and vulnerable; instead, he created a protagonist who asserts her power with a megalomaniac's assurance. He did not relate an arduous transition in which an uncomfortable man embarked on a new life as a woman; rather, he began with a self-made woman who reverts happily to male at the novel's end. He redrew the eroticized MTF as a caricature that allowed him to skewer American sexual mores and to construct, through a single character, scenes of gay male, heterosexual, and lesbian sex.

With its wicked wit and its sexual content, *Myra Breckinridge* was an instant hit. To give the book an "underground" appeal, the publisher, Little, Brown, refrained from advance advertisement and withheld the book from advance circulation for review. The marketing ploy worked. The cover of the paperback edition provides a thumbnail history of the book's success: "With *no* advance advertising, *no* advance copies offered to book reviewers, *no* advance publicity fanfare—*within two weeks of its hardcover publication*—Gore Vidal's *Myra Breckinridge* became A SKYROCKETING NATIONAL BESTSELLER!" In *Look*, a reviewer called it "an ingenious story, rich in wit, irony and the crudest of comic invention," and in the *New York Times Book Review* another proclaimed: "only a really queasy reader will fail to be amused."[102] Many transsexuals, though, found it wholly offensive. One MTF called it "the worst possible publicity for the transsexual cause," and another wrote, "I burn every copy I can get." Christine Jorgensen seethed. In a radio interview she said: "my first reaction was absolute terror." The book threatened that "fifteen years of progress" would go "down the drain based upon garbage." Vidal, she said, "had no scientific knowledge of his subject." Jorgensen had a litigious side. She discussed the possibility of legal action with her lawyers, who, as usual, discouraged her. "Most times," she reported, "my attorneys say, 'Chris, don't get involved,' but I said . . . there is a point in life when you must stand up and be counted . . . Is there no limit to this degradation?"[103]

$\mathcal{B}$y the late 1960s Jorgensen no longer wowed the public as she had fifteen years earlier. After a brief foray in summer stock theater, her nightclub career had petered out. At her peak in 1953 and 1954, she had often earned $5,000 or more per week for nightclub appearances; in the 1960s she accepted $1,000 to $1,500 a week and occasionally less.[104] In the 1960s the nightclubs themselves closed in droves, and Jorgensen did not engage in the kinds of sexualized performance—topless dancing, for example—that might have kept her on the stage in the changing market. By mid-decade she had lost interest in the nightclubs but still looked to them for money. In 1965, when the Honolulu entrepreneur Jack Cione offered her a starring role in his proposed Las Vegas lounge show, titled "Boys Will Be Girls," which would feature "several sex changes," Jorgensen responded, "your project sounds interesting . . . good taste I hope." When the show fell through, she expressed relief: "I had the feeling that it might be the type of show which would not do my career any good." She was, she acknowledged, willing to use her transsexuality to earn her living but not to steep it in sexuality. For Jorgensen, the public proof of her womanhood lay in her feminine appearance, not in revealing her body or recounting her sexual acts. "Exploitation yes," she wrote, "vulgarity no."[105]

With less time on the road, Jorgensen finally completed her autobiography, aided by ghostwriter Lois Kibbee. The book maintained the same prim confessional tone Jorgensen had cultivated in her autobiographical series in *American Weekly* in 1953, and it supplemented her earlier story with an account of her subsequent career. Her agent, Warren Bayless, offered it to a number of major publishers before the small press Paul S. Erikkson, Inc., agreed to print the hardcover edition. It came out in 1967 to positive reviews, and the next year in a Bantam paperback edition. The publishers launched an all-out campaign to turn it into a major seller: a twenty-city book signing tour, a big author's party in New York, radio interviews, the Merv Griffin Show, the Steve Allen Show, and other television appearances. To a certain extent, the publicity worked. The paperback sold almost 450,000 copies.[106] Still, Jorgensen expressed disappointment in the sales and wondered why major newspapers like the *New York Times* failed to review the book. "I know," Bayless wrote her, "there have been great and even severe disappointments about the hardcover situation and also the softcover sales . . . The only answer I can gain is that we may have been a year or two late." In 1967 and 1968 her story was "noble and acceptable" but not, he implied, provocative or startling. Jorgensen must have resented that Vidal's mocking novel on transsexuality won more attention and acclaim than her own sober account. Indeed, she wrote to a Chicago newspaper protesting Vidal's book and asking why her own had not been reviewed.[107]

In 1970 both Jorgensen's autobiography and Vidal's novel came out as Hollywood films. Jorgensen, who consulted on her film, wanted Mia Farrow for the lead, but the director, Irving Rapper, chose a chunky unknown male, John Hansen, to play the part. Rapper cut the twists and turns from Jorgensen's book to make a simpler film, and he made only minor attempts to spice it up. He added, for example, a fictional scene in a brothel, in which the young George Jorgensen Jr. proves unable to perform the expected heterosexual act.[108] The film's distributor,

United Artists, tried to heat up the movie, to Jorgensen's dismay, with posters and ads that asked: "Could I ever love a woman physically?" and "Could I ever love a man?"[109] These feeble attempts to add some sex could not save the film, which plodded clumsily through Jorgensen's childhood, her medical treatment, and her public debut. It was by most accounts an embarrassing flop, and it never recovered the cost of production. One reviewer called it "too boring to be disgusting" and labeled it "a dreadful piece of sexless sexploitation." Nonetheless, the *New York Times* reviewer praised *The Christine Jorgensen Story* as a "dignified little picture." He contrasted it directly with "a glittery garbage pail like 'Myra Breckinridge.'"[110] In that film, the sex symbol Raquel Welch played Myra to the hilt, and the emphasis on sexuality ensured a larger audience. In print and on the screen, in fiction and nonfiction, in the mainstream and in the sensational culture, the sexualized MTF stole the scene from those transsexuals, like Jorgensen, who still believed that sex change with only hints of sex made an interesting story.

*I*f the sexual revolution bumped Jorgensen from center stage, it pushed FTMs offstage altogether. In the 1960s the popular press printed even fewer stories on FTMs than it had in the 1950s. Newspapers rarely commented on FTMs, and pulp publishers did not print their autobiographies. Fewer FTMs than MTFs underwent surgery, but that fact alone does not explain the dwindling coverage. As the interest in MTFs shifted toward the more overtly sexual, the interest in FTMs seemed to diminish accordingly. FTMs did not come out of communities of stage performers and prostitutes; they did not exhibit their bodies. And in the sexual revolution, they did not qualify as sexy. In the 1960s, the eroticization of MTFs had no equivalent among FTMs.

Still, FTMs, like MTFs, felt the impact of change. The doctors had differentiated transsexuality from other sexological categories, and transsexuals, both FTMs and MTFs, had distinguished themselves from other sexual and gender minorities. The delineation of the new category "transsexual" and the assertion of new identities laid the groundwork for institutionalizing what Harry Benjamin called "the transsexual phenomenon." In the 1960s the doctors who worked with transsexuals began to organize into networks, clinics, and associations, and transsexuals themselves began to organize as a minority group to support one another and demand their rights. As an institutional structure emerged, transsexuals confronted a legal system that had neither redefined sex nor redrawn the borders of sex, gender, and sexuality. They asked the courts to define transsexuals and to answer the legal question "What makes a woman a woman and a man a man?" In the 1960s and 1970s, sexuality was part of the answer.

THE LIBERAL MOMENT

6

*I*n 1968 Judge Francis N. Pecora, of the Civil Court of the City of New York, accepted the application of an MTF transsexual, an exotic dancer known as "Naughty Lola," to change her legal name from the "obviously 'male'" Robert to the "obviously 'female'" Risa. The judge could have decided the case without any public comment, but as a liberal judge in an activist era, he decided to write a decision. The petitioner, he noted, had undergone "surgical corrective sex change" in Casablanca in 1966 in which "all male organs were removed." She was "now capable of having sexual relations as a woman although unable to procreate." Pecora posed the issue as a question of individual rights. "Is the gender of a given individual," he asked, "that which society says it is, or is it, rather, that which the individual claims it to be?" To side with society, he answered, "would be to disregard the enlightenment of our times." He came up with a new definition of sex. "A male transsexual who submits to a sex-reassignment," he wrote, "is anatomically and psychologically a female in fact . . . Should a person's identity be limited by the results of mere histological section or biochemical analysis . . . ? I think not." Pecora thus rejected the immutable chromosomes as defining facts of legal sex, and relied instead on genitals, which could be altered, and gender identity. A person's sex might legally change. The case set a precedent for transsexual civil rights. "It could be as important to sex changers," a tabloid newspaper proclaimed, "as the 1954 Supreme Court decision is to black people."[1]

Pecora's decision followed and built on several years of organizing and advocacy. In the 1960s both doctors and transsexuals formed associations that brought attention to and services for transsexuals. The doctors who supported transsexual surgery began to create more formal networks and to find institutional backing for research committees and associations. Just as some doctors pushed to legalize abortion in the 1960s, so a few also attempted to liberalize the medical treatment of transsexuals. By the late 1960s they succeeded in creating clinics to perform sex-reassignment surgery in the United States and in establishing their own professional standards to guide, delimit, and codify the medical treatment of transsexuals. While the doctors created and legitimated a medical model for the treatment of transsexuality, a few transsexuals began to organize as a minority and demand their rights. With the rise of 1960s social movements, transsexuals met for mutual support and came to see themselves as a distinct social group. They pushed for access to medical treatment and employment and also for freedom from police harassment. The new associations registered the triumph of a liberal sexual ethos and the first stirrings of more radical demands for transsexual rights.

As the doctors and transsexuals organized, they also went directly to the courts. In the era after *Brown v. Board of Education,* more individuals chose to pursue their civil rights in the courts, and by the 1960s, with the rise of judicial activism, they had some expectation that they might find judges to back them. As a few transsexuals petitioned the courts to allow them to assume the legal status of the other sex, the lawyers involved called on doctors to testify as expert witnesses. In the late 1960s and the 1970s a few judges, like Pecora, followed the lead of the doctors who endorsed transsexual surgery. They took on the task of defining the legal meanings of sex and gender, of who counted legally as a woman and who counted legally as a man. The public process of redefining sex, seen earlier in the press and the medical literature, had found its way into the law.

A new era of organizing and advocacy began in 1964 with the founding of the Erickson Educational Foundation (EEF), a nonprofit entity incorporated in Baton Rouge, Louisiana. The EEF, as a mission statement read, existed to fund research in "areas where human potential was . . . limited by adverse physical or mental conditions or because of public ignorance or prejudice." It eventually provided money for a variety of unconventional projects. It funded research on the use of medicinal herbs in Mexico, on "mystical states induced by hypnosis," and on lunar cycles and telepathy.[2] It also contributed hundreds of thousands of dollars to establish and support the Institute for the Study of Human Resources, based in Los Angeles, for education and research on homosexuality. But its foremost order of business, its raison d'être, was to promote research on, understanding of, and assistance to transsexuals.

In an era when mainstream funding agencies rarely touched the subject, the EEF sponsored medical research, conferences, and symposia on transsexuality, and subsidized scholarly publications. It worked with journalists on newspaper and magazine articles on transsexuality, scheduled television and radio interviews, and arranged educational presentations at medical schools, hospitals, colleges, and churches. In San Francisco it supported a counseling service for transsexuals, in Miami community conferences, and in New York the production of a documentary film. In the late 1960s and early 1970s it published informational leaflets and pamphlets and also served as a clearinghouse providing transsexuals with referrals to doctors. From 1964 to 1977, when it closed most of its operations, it spent, according to one account, around $2.4 million.[3]

Behind the EEF was Reed Erickson, its founder, funder, and executive director and the sole voting member of its board. He was a female-to-male transsexual. Born in 1917, Erickson grew up in Philadelphia as a girl named Rita, the child of a Jewish mother and German father. From an early age he defied gender stereotypes. As a teenager he attended a girls' high school in Philadelphia, where he played the trumpet, an instrument more often played by boys. In the late 1930s he attended Temple University, where he fared poorly in the secretarial courses intended for women. In the early 1940s he studied engineering, a traditionally masculine pursuit, at Louisiana State University and later worked for a while as an engineer. He was, according to one account, "a rather misplaced girl." But his parents did not reject him, and they held lucrative properties, including a lead-smelting business, that ensured his financial well-being.[4] In the 1950s Erickson worked in the family business and started new companies that produced seats for stadiums. Through the 1950s he lived as a lesbian.

Before he founded the EEF, Erickson had some minor political involvement with the American left. In 1942 an informant told the Federal Bureau of Investigation that Erickson had "been recruited" into the Communist party. In the Cold War climate of the era, any association with the left provided grounds for extensive FBI surveillance. The FBI began watching Erickson in 1944 and continued its observations sporadically into the 1970s. Although the investigators generated a 171-page file, they could not uncover much. In the early 1940s, the records suggest, Erickson purchased Communist party literature. In the late 1940s he may have joined or attended a few meetings of Communist party front groups, such as the American Association of Scientific Workers, and worked as a poll watcher in 1948 for the liberal Progressive party. The investigators had to grant that Erickson was not particularly active in Communist party work. In fact one informant found Erickson "not the least bit interested in politics or social reforms." The FBI investigators did note, though, that Erickson had a "masculine appearance and . . . masculine mannerisms." They also noted that Erickson "underwent a sex change in 1962" and obtained a new passport under the name Reed.[5]

In the early 1960s Erickson met Harry Benjamin, and in March 1965, a year after founding the EEF, he underwent a hysterectomy in New York. Later that year he had a mastectomy at Johns Hopkins University. Erickson rewarded the doctors who helped him. He funded the research of Harry Benjamin and his associates, and he also provided grants to doctors at Johns Hopkins. Like Louise Lawrence, he had faith in science and chose to work with and encourage doctors who supported sex-change surgery. He hoped, he wrote, to replace "ignorance" with "some real, detailed knowledge . . . to counter the prejudice that remains." Some of the researchers he funded never met him, but others remember him as an "engaging" man, a bit eccentric, who wanted recognition for the EEF.[6]

Erickson hired Zelda Suplee, a warm woman with an "apple-cheeked smile," to serve as assistant director of his foundation. Suplee had a wide circle of friends, who knew her from her long career as the "queen of the nudists" and an advocate of psychic healing.[7] From her office in New York she managed the daily operations of the EEF and the everyday contacts with transsexuals who came to her for help. Erickson positioned himself as the benefactor behind the scenes. By the early 1970s he spent much of his time in Mexico, where he lived with his wife, two children, and pet leopard. He kept himself out of the limelight, but he made the ultimate decisions about whom and what he funded.[8]

In the late 1960s and early 1970s Suplee and Erickson had tremendous influence in promoting studies of, services for, and publicity about transsexuals. Together they brought an unusual array of interests to their work: transsexuality, left-liberal leanings, sexual libertarianism, a concern with health and psychic phenomena, and a faith in mainstream medicine and alternative healing. In their support for research, treatment, and advocacy, they helped transform transsexuality into an acknowledged medical specialty and a serious social issue. In an era abounding in social movements, they could build, as Erickson wrote Christine Jorgensen, on "the cornerstone" she had laid.[9]

*A*fter World War II, medical research grew at an unprecedented pace. Wartime innovations such as the use of penicillin enhanced public faith in the potential benefits of research and promoted the rise of government plans, as President Roosevelt had asked, to help "the war of science against disease." From the late 1940s on, the Cold War competition with the Soviet Union spurred the race for new scientific discoveries. From 1945 to 1960 the research budget of the National Institutes of Health shot from $180,000 to $400 million, and the Hill-Burton Act, passed in 1946, provided federal aid for the construction of hospitals. With the influx of funds, hospitals hired more workers, treated more patients, and equipped themselves with the latest technology.[10]

The doctors who studied transsexuality reaped few of the benefits. They had lesser status in their profession and little access to research money earmarked for disease. Those who advocated sex-reassignment surgery could not expect support from other doctors, hospitals, the American Medical Association, or the public agencies and private foundations that provided money for research. In fact both inside and outside the United States the controversy surrounding transsexuality could hurt their professional standing. Christian Hamburger, for example, said his role in the treatment of Christine Jorgensen had brought him "enormous troubles." He believed that the publicity about his work had damaged his "reputation as an honest scientist."[11]

Still, even without grants to fund research, clinics, or conferences, the doctors and scientists who studied transsexuality worked with one another. The cultures of medicine and science encouraged collaboration and communication, and the controversy surrounding transsexuality promoted special bonds—the camaraderie of kindred spirits—among the doctors and scientists who had not chosen conventional and prestigious areas of specialization. In the 1950s a few clusters of researchers worked together on issues of transsexuality. In San Francisco, Karl Bowman and his colleagues at the Langley Porter Clinic worked with transvestite and transsexual patients and helped arrange a couple of surgeries. In Los Angeles, Elmer Belt consulted with other doctors, including his colleague at UCLA Willard Goodwin and his partners at his urological clinic, his son, Bruce Belt, B. Lyman Stewart, and Norman LeTourneau. In Bloomington, Indiana, Alfred Kinsey and his associates Paul Gebhard and Wardell Pomeroy jointly collected data on transvestites and transsexuals. In New York, Harry Benjamin referred his patients to the psychiatrist Robert Laidlaw and the psychologist Albert Ellis and worked with the lawyer Robert Veit Sherwin on the legal issues of changing sex. The central figures—Bowman, Belt, Kinsey, and Benjamin—also worked with one another, although they had no national organizations devoted specifically to the study or treatment of transsexuals. They understood themselves and respected one another as liberal pioneers in a conservative profession.[12]

It was only in the 1960s, though, that the doctors who studied transsexuality joined the move toward organized research programs in major medical centers. The founding in 1962 of the Gender Identity Research Clinic (GIRC) at UCLA launched the trend. The doctors in the GIRC guarded their professional reputations by avoiding the dangerous waters of transsexual surgery. They focused on the gender identity of children and refrained from using their clinic to provide public

endorsements of sex-reassignment operations. According to Richard
Green, Robert J. Stoller, the first director of the clinic, was "conservative." Stoller would not recommend surgery, but, in his own words, he
"never discouraged" patients from "seeking it somewhere else in the
world." "While I feel that some of the people who have had these operations have been happier," he wrote a colleague, "this is by no means
always the case." He worried about the process of selecting proper candidates for surgery, and he also feared the potential legal liabilities.[13]
Green, the second director of the clinic, disagreed. He told Stoller in
1965 that his "contact with a few" postoperative transsexuals had made
him "more sympathetic toward the surgery." Green wrote letters recommending operations for transsexual patients, and in one case, in the
late 1960s, one of his patients underwent surgery at UCLA. (Willard
Goodwin performed the operation.) But this was the private exception
rather than the public rule. The doctors at UCLA repeatedly told in-
quirers that "no transsexual operations are done at UCLA."[14]

In New York, Harry Benjamin took the first steps toward creating a
formal program with a network of doctors and psychologists who were
willing to recommend and arrange surgery. In the mid-1960s Benjamin shared his practice with gynecologist Leo Wollman, and at the end
of the decade he invited internist Charles L. Ihlenfeld to help him with
his patients. He also worked with the sexologist Robert E. L. Masters,
with whom he coauthored a book on prostitution, with endocrinologist Herbert Kupperman, and with psychologists Wardell Pomeroy,
formerly of the Kinsey Institute, Ruth Rae Doorbar, and Henry Guze.
In 1964 the Erickson Educational Foundation enabled Benjamin to organize his friends into the Harry Benjamin Foundation. The EEF
promised to finance the effort for three years with "a minimum of
$1500 per month."[15] Benjamin held meetings in his New York office
and eventually laid out a plan of research. He and his colleagues would
conduct psychological, endocrinological, and neurological tests on
transsexual patients and interview them before and after surgery. They
hoped to "prove or disprove a possible genetic and/or hormonal and
neurophysiologic basis" of transsexuality and try out new therapeutic
techniques. Benjamin provided his patients as research subjects;
Pomeroy headed the "psychological investigations."[16]

The grant from the EEF helped Benjamin enhance his professional status. It allowed him to court the academic researchers who did not regard him as an intellectual peer. In 1964 Robert Stoller told Richard Green that Benjamin's "reputation is not as savory as it might be." When pressed to elaborate, Stoller praised Benjamin's "thoughtfulness" but concluded that some doctors "looked at" Benjamin "askance because he is not psychiatrically trained and because he does not always publish in the most reputable journals." In 1965 Stoller politely declined to serve on the advisory board (and have his name on the letterhead stationery) of the newly formed Benjamin Foundation. Stoller, Green remembered, did not consider Benjamin's work "scholarly."[17] In 1966, when Benjamin published *The Transsexual Phenomenon*, the book that solidified his place at the center of the field, Stoller started to come around. After meeting with Benjamin, he now told Green, with faint praise, that Benjamin had "not only a good heart but plenty of good clinical data."[18] In 1967 the Benjamin Foundation made its scholarly debut, and Stoller agreed to participate. Benjamin arranged to have his associates present their preliminary findings at the prestigious New York Academy of Sciences and to have the proceedings published in the Academy's *Transactions*. Stoller presented the first paper. In this way, funding from the EEF allowed Benjamin to extend his national networks and, in a limited way, elevate the professional standing of his own study of transsexualism.

But in 1967 and 1968 the Harry Benjamin Foundation began to fall apart. Benjamin and Erickson had a series of disagreements, primarily over money. Benjamin resented what he saw as Erickson's attempts to dictate how the money was spent, and he also resented spending his own funds on items he thought the EEF should cover. Eventually minor disputes led to a major falling out. In the spring of 1967 the EEF reduced its grant from $1,500 to $1,200 a month, and in the fall of 1967, after the initial three-year grant expired, the EEF stopped funding the Benjamin Foundation entirely. A final round of negotiations failed after Benjamin refused to accept a small monthly grant (around $250 to $300) from the EEF. He told John Money that he had to preserve his "emotional health" and "peace of mind." Erickson was "too petty, too small in money matters, too paranoid . . . and too unreliable in his promises." Erickson, Benjamin claimed, had "a childish craving for authority, for power, and 'being in charge.'" "Quite a number of my transsexual patients," he groused, "suffer not only from gender, but also from moral, disorientation."[19] The EEF soon asked Benjamin to vacate the offices it subsidized. A year later, Benjamin still fumed over what he perceived as Erickson's "flagrant ingratitude."[20]

When the dust settled in 1969, Benjamin reorganized his research as the Harry Benjamin Research Project, funded by "personal friends," and a few years later as the Benjamin Gender Identity Research Foundation. At the end of the 1960s he conducted this research under the auspices of the Society for the Scientific Study of Sex, a group he had helped found more than twenty years earlier.[21] Benjamin still hoped to conduct follow-up tests on postoperative male-to-female transsexuals, and he also worked with his longtime secretary, Virginia Allen, and parapsychologist Stanley Krippner, who directed the Dream Laboratory at Maimonides Medical Center, to compile statistical analyses by computerizing the case records of his transsexual patients.

Despite the organized programs of research, Benjamin and his associates never attained the scholarly cachet that Stoller and the doctors at UCLA enjoyed. Few of them had affiliations with the institutions that conferred academic credentials, and few of them had ongoing access to the research facilities that such institutions provided. Many of Benjamin's associates focused more on their private practices than on serious research, and some of them tended toward research that had a 1960s countercultural flair. Leo Wollman, for example, had a special interest in hypnosis, an interest shared by Zelda Suplee. The EEF encouraged the less conventional research interests in Benjamin's circles. Even after his battles with Benjamin, Erickson funded the research of Stanley Krippner on dreams and of the husband-and-wife team R. E. L. Masters and Jean Houston on mind-altering devices. (Krippner and Masters already knew Zelda Suplee through their common interest in "altered states of consciousness and psychical research." In fact they had urged Erickson to hire her.) With EEF support, Krippner eventually published an article on the dreams of male-to-female transsexuals, using Benjamin's patients.[22] In the late 1960s Masters also worked with Benjamin's patients, helping "decide which patients to recommend for sex change surgery." As Masters remembered later, he "guided LSD sessions for transsexuals." "Neither in LSD sessions, nor in prolonged hypnotic trances," he recalled, "did the façade ever crack in the ones we both [Benjamin and Masters] felt to be authentic transsexuals."[23] The use of hypnosis, dreams, and psychedelic drugs further isolated Benjamin's crowd from the doctors who dominated the medical profession.

Richard Green claims that many of the American doctors who took an early interest in transsexuality were "offbeat." The label seems especially apt for Benjamin and his friends, many of whom had quirks and experiences that gave them off-center perspectives on issues of sexuality. As some of his patients and colleagues knew, Harry Benjamin was a hair fetishist who found long hair on women sexually arousing.[24] Charles Ihlenfeld later came out as gay. Ruth Rae Doorbar, who was white, had an African-American boyfriend in an era when interracial marriage was still illegal in some states. Wardell Pomeroy had "a prodigious sexual appetite." He was, according to historian James H. Jones, "relentless in his pursuit of sexual partners of both sexes, though with a decided preference for women."[25] Benjamin and his friends saw themselves as advocates of sexual liberation. Benjamin, as his longtime friend Albert Ellis later remembered, "always was solidly on the side of sexual liberty." Benjamin took pride in his radical sexual stance, but he knew it detracted from his scholarly status.[26] Even with EEF funding, he and his friends could not obtain the kind of institutional backing that could launch or sustain a program for sex-reassignment surgery.

In the mid-1960s transsexual surgery had not yet won acceptance as an area of medical specialization. More than a decade after the Christine Jorgensen media madness, no major medical centers in the United States had endorsed transsexual surgery. In 1964, when the University of California at San Francisco (UCSF) announced that its doctors had performed a few sex-change operations, it released the information solely as a defensive move. In a letter, the chancellor admitted that he had issued a press release only because "local reporters had gotten wind" of the operations and "wished to build this into another Christine Jorgensen piece of sensationalism." He wanted "to forestall the attendant unsavory publicity." The seven-page press release began with five pages on intersexed conditions, with the discussion of transsexuality tacked on discreetly at the end. It emphasized how few transsexual surgeries—three in a decade—the doctors had performed and stated that they had agreed to perform surgery only on the advice of "expert consultants" who had "concluded after prolonged study that no alternative course of treatment would suffice." The press release did not suggest that UCSF had or planned a program for the treatment of transsexuals. As the chancellor's letter suggested, the officials at UCSF found the topic of sex-change surgery embarrassing.[27]

In 1966 Johns Hopkins Hospital, in Baltimore, made the move that finally accorded a certain professional legitimacy to sex reassignment surgery. In November it announced its program to perform sex-change operations. For decades Johns Hopkins University had served as a center for the study and treatment of intersexed conditions. It took a relatively small step to open its doors to transsexuals. For both intersexed and transsexual patients, standard treatments involved issues of gender identity, and in both, the typical medical interventions often involved hormones and surgery on genitals and reproductive organs. John Money spearheaded the campaign to treat transsexual patients at Hopkins. A native of New Zealand, Money had come to the United States to pursue graduate studies in psychology. He earned his Ph.D. from Harvard with a dissertation on hermaphroditism, for which he used case records from the hospital at Hopkins. He joined the Hopkins faculty in 1951 while completing the dissertation. Eventually he served as head of the psychohormonal research unit.[28]

As Money himself noted, his "experience in hermaphroditism had singled him out, over the years, for requested consultations on cases of transvestism and transsexualism." Other doctors at Hopkins, the gynecologist Howard W. Jones Jr. and the plastic surgeon Milton T. Edgerton, had also encountered transsexual patients. In the late 1950s the doctors at Hopkins had evaluated a female-to-male patient and in 1960 performed a bilateral mastectomy on him. But typically they rejected such requests. Hedy Jo Star, for example, underwent five days of examinations at Johns Hopkins in 1959 with the hope that she might convince the doctors there to perform genital surgery. The tests suggested that her "basic structure" was "anatomical male," with no evidence of any intersexed condition. In a unanimous decision, the team at Hopkins turned her down.[29]

Like Benjamin and his friends, John Money saw himself as a pioneer who rejected the vestiges of Victorian prudishness and championed sexual liberty. Some people saw him as brilliant and charismatic, and others disliked him with a certain intensity. He was confident to the point of arrogance. He had a "need," Robert Stoller said, "to continually search," and he was also stubborn and persistent. By the mid-1960s he had set his mind on convincing his colleagues to perform transsexual surgeries at Hopkins. "I can recall," Howard Jones remembered, "that for a number of months, maybe even *years,* John kept raising the question of whether we shouldn't get into the transsexual situation." After much debate, Money, who served on the Harry Benjamin Foundation's advisory board, brought three of Benjamin's postoperative patients to Hopkins to meet with Jones and Edgerton. Finally, they agreed to perform sex-reassignment surgeries.[30]

In 1965 Money and his colleagues at Hopkins formed a committee that met monthly. They worked closely with the Harry Benjamin Foundation, which provided them with patient referrals. The more liberal sexual climate of the 1960s probably made sex-reassignment surgery seem less outrageous to the doctors at Hopkins, and so did the growing familiarity of other forms of bold operations, such as organ transplants. But as is often the case, funding also played a critical role. From the start, the EEF subsidized the Hopkins program. In May 1965, before their falling out, Harry Benjamin told Reed Erickson that the doctors at Hopkins had agreed to perform their first complete genital surgery on an MTF, Avon Wilson, an African-American patient whom Benjamin had referred to them a few months earlier. The surgery, Benjamin wrote, "will certainly make history and will be a real break-through." The next month Erickson visited John Money in Baltimore and agreed to pay $500 toward the costs.[31] Later Erickson provided funds to support an ongoing program. In July 1966 the doctors at Hopkins established their formal program, the Gender Identity Clinic, with John E. Hoopes, a plastic surgeon, as chair of the clinic staff. By November 1966 the doctors at Hopkins had performed surgeries on ten transsexual patients, five FTMs and five MTFs.[32]

With funds and staff in place, the doctors at Hopkins neither needed nor wanted publicity. In the year before it went public, the committee (and then the clinic) already had more than a hundred referrals, and the doctors planned to evaluate only two patients per month and to perform surgery on even fewer. Once again, though, the popular press pushed the doctors into the public eye. Avon Wilson made it into the news. In October 1966 a gossip columnist in the *New York Daily News* discovered her. It reported that "a stunning girl who admits she was a male less than one year ago . . . underwent a sex change operation at, of all places, Johns Hopkins Hospital in Baltimore." The hospital confirmed the report, and the doctors decided to try to forestall "a sensational, inaccurate account" by sending a sober press release to the *New York Times.* A *Times* reporter, Thomas Buckley, had already contacted Harry Benjamin for a magazine article on transsexuals. The doctors at Johns Hopkins decided to work with Buckley in the hope that "the prestige of the *New York Times* would then set the tone for all other papers copying the story." The plan succeeded "exactly as hoped."[33]

The Johns Hopkins team issued its press release on November 21, and on the same day the *Times* published its front-page report. The article, authored by Buckley, referred to the Johns Hopkins Hospital as "one of the most eminent teaching and research institutions in the country." It was "the first American hospital," the article noted, to give transsexual surgery "official support." The story was front-page news in papers across the nation. In San Francisco, for example, the *Chronicle* announced it the same day with a banner headline: "Sex Change Surprise." A rush of publicity followed. The major news magazines—*Time, Newsweek,* and *U.S. News & World Report*—all carried informational articles with much the same message: "One of the nation's most reputable medical institutions" had "risked its reputation" and given "official medical sanction" to transsexual surgery.[34] The press reported a few objections to the Johns Hopkins program. *Time,* for example, published a couple of letters from protesting readers. A doctor from South Carolina decried "the irresponsible tampering with the body," which he deemed "unethical" and "vicious," and a woman from Boston objected to surgery that turned people "into freaks." As before, the "main opposition" in medical circles, as one newspaper reported, seemed "to spring from psychiatrists." Mostly, though, the press reported that "attitudes have changed." A Baltimore newspaper asked local clergy about transsexual surgery and "failed to produce any moral objections to the physical change of sex." The Catholic archdiocese declined to comment, but thirteen Protestant and Jewish leaders expressed support for the Johns Hopkins program.[35] As reported in the mainstream press, sex-reassignment surgery, now sanctioned by Johns Hopkins, had won a modicum of respect.

Among transgendered people, the announcement of the Johns Hopkins program represented a decisive break with the past. Finally an American medical center had placed its imprimatur on transsexual surgery. The day after the *New York Times* published its article on Hopkins, Christine Jorgensen wrote Christian Hamburger in Denmark: "It has taken my country many years to progress to the point where an organization such as Johns Hopkins would recognize the problem." She saw the decision to perform surgery as the "verification of our beliefs."[36] The news also had an impact on other transgendered people, who now envisioned surgery as a more viable option. It seemed to have special impact on poor and working-class transsexuals, who lacked the resources to pursue surgery abroad. "All of a sudden," one MTF recalled, "being a transsexual went from something you had to go off to Europe to do, and being a vaguely fairy tale-ish dream . . . to being something that was very concrete." The doctors at Johns Hopkins fielded hundreds of requests for operations. Two and a half years later, they still reported receiving letters from twenty potential patients per week.[37]

As a symbol, the program did indeed make a difference; in practice, it scarcely made a dent. Hopkins turned away almost all the applicants for surgery. Stoller saw the problem from early on. "They are going to build up a very large backlog of ill will," he wrote Willard Goodwin, "among the thousands of people they will not be treating." He considered it unethical, as he told Richard Green, to "excit[e] so many transsexuals" when they knew they would "operate on practically none of them."[38] In 1968 Renée Richards, for example, met with John Money "for hours" and underwent "several psychological tests." At the end of

the long session, Money told her that Hopkins was not accepting any
additional transsexual patients at the time. She came away, she said,
with a renewed sense of "hopelessness."[39]

The program at Hopkins, though, produced results in another way:
it cleared a way for other medical centers to follow. After almost two
years of discussion and planning, the University of Minnesota Medical
School established a Gender Committee in October 1966. The committee built directly on the work of the Harry Benjamin Foundation
and the Johns Hopkins Gender Identity Clinic. It sent two members to
New York to examine MTFs, a visit arranged by Harry Benjamin, Leo
Wollman, and Wardell Pomeroy. Soon afterward a University of Minnesota surgeon, John Blum, went to Hopkins to observe transsexual
surgery there. As elsewhere, the doctors at Minnesota hoped to avoid
publicity but found the press at their door. "Within minutes of sched-
uling the first patient in the operating room (under a false name and
operative procedure)," Donald W. Hastings, the psychiatrist who
headed the Minnesota program, recounted, "a reporter was on the
telephone asking for full information." The positive publicity accorded
Johns Hopkins encouraged the doctors to work with the press. In December 1966 the Minnesota program went public with no significant
adverse response. Over the next three and a half years it conducted
twenty-five sex-reassignment surgeries on male-to-female Minnesota
residents.[40]

Soon other medical centers set up programs of their own. In 1967
Northwestern University Medical School, north of Chicago, established a study and treatment program, started by Orion Stuteville, who
had already performed several sex-change surgeries. In 1968 Stanford
University, south of San Francisco, inaugurated its Gender Reorientation Program, later renamed the Gender Identity Clinic. Within a decade it ran the largest university program performing sex-reassignment
surgery. Shortly afterward the University of Washington in Seattle
opened a Gender Identity Research and Treatment Clinic, headed by
John Hampson, formerly of Johns Hopkins. By the end of the 1970s
more than a thousand transsexuals had undergone surgery at the hands
of doctors based at American universities, and fifteen to twenty "major
centers" conducted transsexual surgery in the United States.[41]

While various institutions founded programs and clinics, the doctors consolidated their hold on the field—and warded off their critics—with new national networks. In the mid-1960s Richard Green served as a key link drawing the earliest programs together. From 1957 to 1961 Green had attended medical school at Johns Hopkins, where he worked with John Money on issues of crossgender identification in young boys, and in the early 1960s he had worked as a resident physician at UCLA with Robert Stoller. When he returned east in 1964 he began to collaborate with Harry Benjamin, whom he admired. He went to New York weekly to have dinner with Benjamin, see his patients, and attend meetings of his foundation. He also spent one evening a week working with Money in Baltimore. He kept Stoller apprised of the developments in New York and Baltimore and also of the financial support from the Erickson Educational Foundation.[42] Green had the connections and credentials that enabled him to work easily with academics like Stoller and the offbeat personality that allowed him to fit in with Benjamin and his friends. In a letter recommending Green for psychoanalytic training, Stoller, who saw himself as a family man, noted Green's "rebellion," "nonconformity," "ambition," and "unsettled" personal life. "He strikes me," Stoller wrote, "as an intelligent and nice person who has a fine-edged uneasiness."[43] But connections, credentials, and personality were not enough to promote the kinds of publications and institutions that legitimated the doctors' professional move into transsexual surgery.

The Erickson Educational Foundation provided the extra boost to the national and international networks that had begun to coalesce. In the late 1960s it provided funds to Richard Green and John Money for the publication of a major anthology on transsexualism. Green and Money edited the volume, Erickson wrote the foreword, and Benjamin wrote the introduction. More than half of the thirty-two articles came from researchers affiliated with the UCLA Gender Identity Research Clinic, the Harry Benjamin Foundation, and the Johns Hopkins Gender Identity Clinic. Published in 1969, the book, as the editors wrote, did not offer "a forum for the many critics of sex reassignment surgery." Instead, *Transsexualism and Sex Reassignment* provided detailed outlines of how to treat transsexual patients with hormones and surgery. It served as a handbook for doctors who chose to treat transsexual patients. The same year the EEF cosponsored the first International Symposium on Gender Identity, a three-day meeting held in London in July. Richard Green and John Money participated in the conference.[44]

The EEF and the researchers reciprocally benefited each other. The EEF provided funds, and to a certain extent the science followed the money. The EEF accelerated the research agendas, enabled some of the publications, and promoted the clinical practice of the doctors and scientists who endorsed sex-reassignment surgery. In turn, the researchers and publications raised the status of the EEF. Robert Stoller's shifting views illustrate the change. In 1964, when Richard Green first mentioned the EEF, Stoller thought it "a little strange" and said he "would be leery of taking money" for his research. A few years later, though, he agreed to supervise a researcher funded by the EEF. In 1970 he provided a qualified endorsement. A psychologist in Florida asked him whether the EEF was "reputable." "Their commitment to transsexualism is perhaps a bit intense," Stoller replied, "but nonetheless their support has been in legitimate channels." The EEF had supported the research, and the research had legitimated the EEF and, more generally, the medical treatment of transsexuals.[45]

As transsexual surgery acquired some institutional backing, the doctors began to publicize their emerging model for the medical treatment of transsexuals. At each institution they formulated criteria for assessing patients and selecting a few for surgery. The guidelines allowed them to steer a liberal course between what Richard Green called "quagmired conservatism" and "reckless unsystematic abandon," which was also a course between the critics who opposed transsexual surgery and the transsexuals who pressured the doctors for treatment.[46] The criteria demonstrated professional standards to those critics who cast the doctors as charlatans. They helped the doctors select patients carefully and thus avoid potential lawsuits from those who might regret the surgery. They also allowed doctors to figure out how to choose a handful of patients from the hundreds who asked for surgery. Different institutions devised slightly different criteria, but several key elements united them. By the end of the 1960s the doctors required psychological evaluation to ascertain that patients had longstanding crossgender identification and no severe mental illness. The doctors also wanted patients to live as the other sex and take hormones for a number of months or years before undergoing irreversible surgery. They looked for patients with the intelligence to understand what the surgery could and could not do, and with what they considered realistic plans for the future, especially employment.[47]

The criteria summed up the doctors' accommodation with transsexual patients. While other doctors rejected surgery outright, the group that endorsed surgery set up a gatekeeping system that allowed them to control access to treatment. Under pressure from their patients, they provided a safety valve through institutions that offered relief to only a few patients. To a certain extent, the doctors' safeguards revealed their own biases. They preferred patients who avoided "exhibitionism" and promised to live "quietly." They hoped to avoid patients who might "publicize, notorize [*sic*] or capitalize on" their transsexual surgery. They had explicit preference for those who could pass as the other sex. They hoped their patients would look and behave like conventional women or men. With MTFs, Harry Benjamin wanted to know that "a reasonably successful 'woman' could result," and he defined success as "outward appearance and the impression of the total personality." Regardless of how deeply they longed for surgery, large and balding MTFs with heavy beards seemed less qualified for surgery than smaller MTFs with more typically feminine distributions of hair.[48] Some of the doctors actually required their patients to undergo training in conventional gender stereotypes. At the Stanford clinic, for example, the screening process included a "rehabilitation" period with workshops on appropriate grooming. Along the same lines, the doctors also expected their patients to live as heterosexuals and, better yet, to marry after surgery. A preoperative MTF who had sex with women did not qualify for treatment as readily as a preoperative MTF who had sex with men, sex alone, or no sex at all. At a meeting in 1971 Harry Benjamin and his associates "all agreed that a large amount of heterosexual activity [before surgery] did not indicate a good surgical candidate."[49] In sum, the doctors rejected candidates who would not conform after surgery to the dominant conventions of gender and sexuality.

In the early 1970s Norman Fisk, a doctor at Stanford, admitted that he and his colleagues had devised their criteria to screen candidates "so that the overall program could or would be continued." That is, they tailored their medical model to enhance the public image of the program. They chose patients who would best exemplify success and rejected patients who did not fit neatly into the categories they devised. But the doctors soon learned that transsexuals had "a very effective grapevine." The patients coached one another on what they needed to say and do to qualify for operations. The doctors discovered that their patients "were carefully preparing and rehearsing" for what amounted to auditions for surgery. By the late 1960s, for example, some MTFs had adopted a casual, unisex, hippie style, but their transsexual friends told them they had to dress up as conventionally feminine women in order to convince the doctors to approve their surgery. They also warned one another to refrain from mentioning certain details about their sex lives, especially if they took sexual pleasure from their genitals or intended to live as homosexuals after their surgery. They "felt it necessary to tell the evaluating psychiatrists a certain, standard story," one FTM confessed to Benjamin, "because we all knew that the truth would shock them." Once the doctors discovered the grapevine, they saw that transsexuals, too, had organized among themselves.[50]

From the first publicity about Christine Jorgensen, some transsexuals had longed for peer groups for support. "It would be a great relief," one MTF wrote Jorgensen, "if some of us could get together, and discuss our mutual problems among ourselves, without fear of ridicule by the outside world." Along the same lines, an FTM suggested that "some of us . . . talk to one another or perhaps write each other." He imagined "a companionship in which there would be no need for subterfuge and fear of embarrassing questions." Another letter writer called for "some sort of organization to co-ordinate the ideas and actions of the various Trans-sexuals who have contacted you, perhaps something similar to A. A. [Alcoholics Anonymous]."[51] They longed to meet with others who might understand their hardships and who might share advice on how to navigate daily life and how to find medical treatment.

To that end, Harry Benjamin introduced his patients to one another, and Louise Lawrence also brought transsexuals together. By the mid-1950s about a dozen MTFs visited and corresponded with one another. They shared information on doctors, traveled together for surgery, compared surgical results, helped one another when unemployed, and occasionally lived together. By 1955, for example, Carrie Jordan (pseudonym) was corresponding with at least six other MTFs. After her surgery in the Netherlands she moved from New York to Los Angeles and stayed at the Barbizon, a hotel for women, where another patient of Benjamin's already resided. Later she lived in Phoenix, San Francisco, and Seattle with another MTF friend, who came along with her when she went to visit her brother and sister for the first time after her surgery. Her friendships with other transsexuals, she told Benjamin, made "a cruel problem easier to bear."[52]

By the 1960s transsexuals met more easily. In the cities, MTFs in particular found one another in the social circles of crossdressers, female impersonators, or street queens, and sometimes found friends who supported them through the painful process of surgery and recovery. Some also met other transsexuals through their doctors or electrologists or through Zelda Suplee of the EEF. By the end of the decade group therapy sessions, in vogue among psychologists, provided another forum where transsexuals came to know one another. Some doctors, like Leo Wollman in New York, offered such sessions for their patients. Mario Martino attended monthly meetings of FTMs. The participants, he recalled, "exchanged experiences, ideas on male attire, how and where to have clothes made to order, the feelings and facts of our new anatomy."[53]

Toward the end of the 1960s a few transsexuals began to organize more formally. New peer-led discussion groups resembled both older support groups, like Alcoholics Anonymous, and newer rap groups of the 1960s youth movements. They attracted mostly preoperative transsexuals who shared information on obtaining surgery and coping with the everyday problems that confronted people who hoped to change sex. In the late 1960s a group of MTFs met weekly in a brownstone in Brooklyn where *Turnabout* magazine, a publication for crossdressers, was produced. Renée Richards attended the group for a short while and characterized its members as "withdrawn," "glum," and "downbeat." A well-heeled doctor herself, she had both the financial resources and the connections to find herself medical treatment. Nevertheless, she said, the group gave her "a realistic perspective" on her "fellow transsexuals and the problems they faced." Around the same time, Mario Martino started his own group for FTMs, "a select few" who met at his home in Yonkers, New York. They helped one another through the bureaucratic maze of changing their names on transcripts and birth certificates. The support group seemed to encourage a sense of community. "It was good," Martino remembered, "to be with our people."[54] But the new groups lacked the institutional backing enjoyed by the clinics or the independent resources that sustained the EEF. They tended to come and go rapidly.

Gradually the search for community became an organized movement, albeit a small one, for social change. The first organizations for transsexuals appeared in the late 1960s and early 1970s. They grew out of and borrowed from the other social movements of their day. The "search for authenticity," to use Doug Rossinow's phrase, characterized the more general youth rebellion of the 1960s and made it particularly welcome to transsexual activists. Who could lay better claim than transsexuals to a sense of "estrangement . . . from their own real selves"?[55] For many transsexuals, the demand for surgery represented the quest to express outwardly what they described as their inner, true, or authentic selves. The more militant transsexuals rejected the medical model that cast transsexualism as a disease or disorder. As they shifted from informal discussion and support to collective and organized activism, they began to forge a minority movement in which transsexuals asserted their rights to express themselves, to live as they chose, and to participate fully, without harassment, in American society. In these goals they had much in common with other 1960s social movements that called for an end to discrimination and the right to self-fulfillment.

In the late 1960s, San Francisco stood at the forefront of the emerging movement. The Tenderloin, the impoverished neighborhood in the city center, had long served as a home, as one minister described it, for "social outcasts," including "youth with sexual problems." In the mid-1960s more gay youth, drag queens, and transsexuals arrived in the Tenderloin, pushed in part by the urban renewal that forced them out of other neighborhoods and pulled by the district's reputation as a home for runaway teens. As the Tenderloin changed, the police engaged in crackdowns, raiding bars and arresting MTFs for prostitution and female impersonation. On the streets the police harassed crossdressers and sometimes beat them with billy clubs or demanded free sexual services. In the latter half of the 1960s the street youth in the Tenderloin, as historian Susan Stryker has shown, organized against police harassment. In 1966 a new group, Vanguard, called for "street power," to bring together the disempowered youth of the central city. Initially sponsored by Glide Memorial Methodist Church, a haven for radicalism in central San Francisco, Vanguard provided a social space for young gay men and transgendered MTFs. Eventually the tensions peaked in a confrontation between police and the transgendered youth who congregated at Compton's, a twenty-four-hour cafeteria in the Tenderloin. Compton's attracted the impoverished youth of the district and also gay hustlers, hair fairies, street queens, and MTF prostitutes, some of whom were saving their money for surgery. One night in August 1966 the police came in, as they had before, to arrest the crossdressers at Compton's, and this time the transgendered customers fought back. They broke out the restaurant's windows, and the fighting spilled into the streets. "There was just a lot of street life going on," one MTF remembered, "and . . . the police . . . were losing their grip."[56]

In the same year, the publication of Benjamin's book *The Transsexual Phenomenon* and the announcement of surgery performed at Johns Hopkins University made transsexuality seem an achievable goal rather than just a fantasy embodied by Christine Jorgensen and a few like her. In San Francisco, transsexuals were suddenly more visible, especially in the Tenderloin. The street queens, Suzan Cooke remembered, "were just transitioning into being trannies, a lot of them, right about this time . . . this is all in response to the 1966 announcements [about treatment at Hopkins]. Because prior to that people were content to be hair fairies, they were content to be drag queens, even if it wasn't a very good life."[57] Elliot Blackstone, an officer with the San Francisco Police Community Relations Bureau, assigned to the Tenderloin, had already established himself as the sympathetic police liaison to gay men and queens. In late 1966 he met his first self-identified transsexual, Louise Ergestrasse Durkin, who lent him a copy of Benjamin's book, and he began to arrange social services, including legal and financial assistance, for "the outcasts among the outcasts," transsexuals in the Tenderloin.[58] As part of these efforts, Blackstone asked the Center for Special Problems, a radical enclave in the San Francisco Department of Public Health, to provide services for transsexuals. Soon afterward the center began a program that offered hormones and provided counseling and referrals. The director of the center, Dr. Joel Fort, befriended Benjamin, who came there to train the staff.[59]

In this conducive setting, transsexuals began to organize more formally. In 1967 a group of MTFs founded COG, an acronym that stood, in various accounts, for Conversion Our Goal or Change: Our Goal. According to one account, COG was "probably the first formal organization of self-defined transsexuals in the world." It attracted white, "lower class," preoperative transsexuals, most of whom lived in the Tenderloin and worked as prostitutes. A year or so after its founding it had seventeen members, all but one MTF. (The sole FTM, Robert Martin, fell to his death from a YMCA window in 1969, a sharp reminder of how unbearably difficult transsexual lives could be.) COG distinguished itself from other transsexual groups not only by its formal organization but also by its overtly political goals. It offered mutual support to its members and also called for freedom from police harassment, legal rights to change sex, "job opportunities," "equal housing at equal rates," and "equal services at equal prices in stores, restaurants, etc." Aware of the new program at Johns Hopkins, its members also sought access to inexpensive surgery in the United States.[60] COG members were clearly inspired by the civil rights movement. In a mimeographed newsletter, they expressed their political goals as a combination of individual and minority rights. "Now, as never before," an unsigned editorial began, "the individual is coming to terms with the mass. Members of minority groups are being recognized as people first, with perhaps a different way of life." The editorial ended with a denunciation of police harassment and a plea: "Just give us a chance to earn a decent living and a clean place to live!" COG met twice a month in Glide Church. It also met with police, made public educational presentations, and appeared occasionally in the press, on television, and on radio.[61]

A tiny group without any funds, COG survived for two years because it had the support of other 1960s social service programs. Lyndon Johnson's "War on Poverty" had encouraged urban community organizing and provided funds for neighborhood groups. In 1966 a San Francisco neighborhood organization, the Central City Citizens' Council, led by homophile activists, fought successfully to have the Tenderloin designated a poverty program target district.[62] This move enabled COG and other Tenderloin groups to tap into federally funded social service programs. COG worked with the Central City Economic Opportunity Council, which offered facilities for putting out COG's newsletter and provided training and jobs for a few MTFs. It also cooperated with the Center for Special Problems. Mostly COG worked with police via Elliot Blackstone. He encouraged the organization of COG, attended its meetings, and served as "informal counselor" to its members. With Blackstone's active support, COG convinced the police not to arrest transsexuals simply for dressing as women or for using women's restrooms.[63]

By the end of the decade, COG dwindled and fell apart, prey to the transience of its members as well as its lack of funds. In 1968 a short-lived splinter group, California Advancement for Transsexuals Society (CATS), claimed to take a more vocal stand than COG, but it had only two or three members. Its key leaders were Louise Durkin, a "very forceful, very outspoken" MTF, who had already befriended Elliot Blackstone, and her husband, Gerard. Like COG, CATS worked with Blackstone, but it failed to attract other transsexuals, who backed away from the Durkins. Suzan Cooke met the Durkins in 1969. They were, she said, "into controlling people" and also "sleazy." (Gerard Durkin, Cooke recalled, demanded oral sex before he would give her information about resources for transsexuals.)[64] In 1969 a new group, the National Transsexual Counseling Unit (NTCU) rose out of the ashes of COG and CATS.

By this time Zelda Suplee of the EEF had discovered COG and CATS and established contact. The EEF decided to fund the new initiative. It hired Wendy Kohler, a twenty-seven-year-old MTF formerly involved in COG, to work as research coordinator for Elliot Blackstone and invited Blackstone to give presentations in other cities on transsexuals. Kohler became the first director of the National Gender-Sexual Identification Council, soon renamed NTCU and a few years later Transexual Counseling Service. She opened an office, rent paid by the EEF, in the same building that housed two homophile organizations, the Mattachine Society and the Daughters of Bilitis. She consulted with a number of doctors, including Harry Benjamin (whom she called "a cute little devil"), and she tried to convince them to establish a gender-identity clinic in San Francisco. She organized a well-publicized seminar on transsexuals at Glide Church and hosted a radio program twice a month. Kohler left in 1971, and the NTCU continued with a succession of preoperative MTFs working as counselors alongside Blackstone, who held the titles of treasurer and consultant. In the early 1970s the EEF paid the salaries of the NTCU counselors and publicized the NTCU in its national newsletters. With the added publicity, the NTCU began "dealing with as many people by mail as on a walk-in basis." It offered guidance, advice, and referrals to doctors and engaged in educational work, visiting college classes and meeting with police.[65]

The first transsexual organizations emerged amid the heightened radical demands among youth. At the end of the 1960s, the larger social movements of the era—the movements of African Americans, Chicanos, and Native Americans, the women's movement, the antiwar movement—turned toward increasingly militant rhetoric and confrontational tactics. In San Francisco, as Suzan Cooke remembered, there was "an intense radicalization" at the end of the decade.[66] Gender issues stood at the forefront of the radical challenge. Antiwar activists rejected the masculine warrior ideal, and feminists led a frontal assault on cultural injunctions that demanded feminine behavior among women.

To a certain extent, the counterculture popularized and celebrated the questioning of gender conformity. The fashions of the era broadcast a new willingness for men and women to break with traditional masculine and feminine styles. "All of a sudden," Cooke recalled, "there were girls wearing jeans that zipped up the front. There were girls wearing black leather jackets. There were guys in beads with long

hair . . . and bell bottoms with velvet."[67] Other evidence also points to
a rising countercultural interest in transgendered behavior. On New
Year's Eve in 1969, for example, the Cockettes, a genderbending hippie theatrical group, performed the first of its outrageous drag "mid-
night musicals . . . at a run-down San Francisco movie theater." By the
time of their last performance in 1972, they had won a national following. In 1970 the Kinks produced their hit song "Lola," which tells the
story of a man who "almost fell" for a drag queen. Lola "walked like a
woman, but talked like a man." Some of the song's lines, such as "girls
will be boys and boys will be girls," hint at broader challenges to traditional configurations of gender.[68] In the early 1970s, Andy Warhol's
films gave fifteen minutes of fame to Holly Woodlawn, Candy Darling,
and other transgendered performers. Around the same time, the "glam
rock" scene, inspired in part by the Cockettes, elevated genderbending
performers like David Bowie to cult status.

In San Francisco, the transsexual movement shifted in response to
the trends. The early transsexual activists in COG and the NTCU came
from what Suzan Cooke called the "first wave." Wendy Kohler and
other "first wave" activists, Cooke recalled, believed that women
should marry or work in traditional women's jobs. They did not consider themselves radicals, feminists, or hippies, and they dissociated
themselves from gays, even though most of them had flouted sexual
and gender conventions in their earlier lives as street queens. They attempted, as observers noted of COG, to project an image of "middle-
class respectability."[69] Cooke placed herself in the "second wave." She
came to NTCU in 1971. By that time she had participated in the Students for a Democratic Society, antiwar demonstrations, the gay liberation movement, and the women's movement. She saw similarities in
the civil rights struggles of blacks, gays, and transsexuals, and she saw
herself as "a radical feminist" and a "less traditional sort." She took
pride in her unconventional stance, radical politics, and hippie style.
The split reflected class differences as well. Cooke came from a working-class background, but she had attended college for a year and a
half. She had more education than Kohler and other Tenderloin residents. When she prostituted, she worked as a call girl, not as a street-
walker. In fact she found the street queens frightening. "I was scared of

the Tenderloin at that point," she remembered, "scared of the queens, because the few that I had met in jail were very rough."[70]

In the early 1970s, the "second wave" took over the NTCU. In 1971 Cooke and Janice Maxwell, another MTF, changed the organization. "We radically infused it," Cooke recalled, "with some pretty intense feminism and pretty intense trans consciousness."[71] In 1973 Leslie St. Clair and Wendy Davidson, also "second wave" activists, codirected the NTCU. They emphasized a depathologizing message. St. Clair, a flamboyant and charismatic MTF, wanted "people [to] know . . . that TS's [transsexuals] are people with a specific gender problem and not a mental illness."[72] In this way, the shift from the "first wave" to the "second wave" also represented a shift away from the medical model that defined transsexualism as a disease and gave doctors the sole authority to diagnose and treat it. Around this time the NTCU changed its name to Transexual Counseling Service. For some 1970s activists, the use of *transexual* with one *s* marked a self-conscious departure from the medical term *transsexualism* (although in fact some of the key scientific authorities, such as John Money, also preferred to use *transexual*). Like other activists of the era, transsexual activists questioned the reign of experts, who seemed to collude with the status quo. In the do-it-yourself, be-your-own-expert style of the counterculture, Wendy Davidson tried to organize her own treatment clinics, in which transsexuals counseled their peers and referred them to surgery. She worked with the renegade doctor John Ronald Brown, who offered cut-rate surgery on demand.[73]

By the early 1970s the city's activists covered a wider swath, from those who provided professional health care services to those who protested in the streets. Laura Cummings, for example, worked as a therapist in San Francisco with transsexual clients. An MTF herself, she established a "gender counseling program" in 1971 at Fort Help, a social service center and health clinic run by the radical doctor Joel Fort, who had earlier directed the Center for Special Problems. She distanced herself from the more militant activists and tried to distinguish MTF transsexuals from homosexual men, whose "love object is [their] genitalia," and drag queens, "who are just looking for a way to get hormones." In 1973 she opened and directed the San Francisco Gender and Sexuality

Center.[74] Other activists worked to unite transsexuals, drag queens, and gay liberationists into a single more powerful movement. The Reverend Ray Broshears, the controversial president of San Francisco's Gay Activist Alliance, helped organize transsexuals and drag queens in San Francisco's Tenderloin. He called a meeting to protest the arrests of "46 persons, mostly transsexuals," in a sweep of the Tenderloin in 1971 and led a picket line to protest housing discrimination after a Tenderloin hotel evicted thirty-three drag queens in 1973.[75] Broshears also directed the Helping Hands Center, a Tenderloin counseling service that catered to gays, drag queens, and transsexuals. He cooperated at various times with CATS and NTCU.

The radicalizing trends accompanied the emerging sexual liberation movements in other cities as well. In the late 1960s, gay men and lesbians organized more militant groups than the earlier homophile organizations. The politics of confrontation had replaced, or at least joined, the politics of respectability. A national gay liberation movement, as seen in the Gay Liberation Front (GLF), sprang up in 1969 after gay and transgendered people rioted against police harassment at the Stonewall Inn, in Greenwich Village. Radical queens, self-proclaimed fairies, and androgynous lesbian-feminists made gender transgression part of their political movements. "Many of us in GLF," one publication proclaimed, "are traitors to our sex, and to this sexist society. We reject 'manhood,' 'masculinity,' and all that."[76]

In the factional battles that followed, various subgroups soon split apart. The shift from umbrella coalitions under gay liberation to separate organizations reflected the process of self-sorting on the sexual margins. In New York in 1969, Sylvia Rivera, a seventeen-year-old street queen from the Bronx, founded Street Transvestites for Gay Power, later renamed STAR, or Street Transvestites Action Revolutionaries, and in 1970 Lee Brewster started Queens, later known as Queens Liberation Front. QLF published the magazine DRAG, which claimed a circulation of 3,500 by 1972.[77] The queens felt alienated from the gay activists, who found them embarrassing. Offended by the "uptight professional" gay men who "make a point in the media to say that they are not swish, faggoty mad screaming drag queens," they organized among themselves. The QLF demanded the "right to congregate" and the "right to dress as we see fit," and it had some success in getting New York City officials to permit crossdressing in public.[78] Few drag queen activists identified as transsexual. (One supporter of QLF referred to sex-change operations as "so 1950s.")[79] But *DRAG* published a number of columns on and by transsexuals who saw themselves as part of the movement.

Amidst the genderbending, militancy, and infighting, new transsexual groups appeared and disappeared in short order. In September 1970, for example, Judy Bowen, an MTF, organized Transsexuals and Transvestites, or TAT, in New York City. TAT lasted for only a couple of months. From the few available records, it seems to belong in the "first wave" of transsexual activism. Bowen, who served as TAT's president, found the transvestites, probably drag queens, "too politically radical" for her tastes. Transsexuals, she claimed, did not want gay liberation or other radical change; they wanted MTFs accepted as women. Bowen also tried to organize transsexuals as a separate group. She called the first meeting of Transsexuals Anonymous, held in early 1971 in the office of plastic surgeon Benito Rish. About twenty transsexuals attended, most if not all MTFs. Rish held out the promise of transsexual surgery, and Deborah Hartin, a postoperative MTF, talked about her difficult life, including her problems with "her family, her neighbors and her daughter."[80] Zelda Suplee of the EEF tried to encourage the new groups. In 1970, when Angela Douglas, an MTF visiting from California, handed Suplee a leaflet announcing a demonstration on Sheridan Square for "Transvestite and Transexual Liberation," Suplee changed her weekend plans in order to attend. (The rally flopped; only one organizer and Suplee showed up.) And she personally invited an FTM, who hoped "to start an organization," to "attend the Trans[sexuals] Anonymous meeting." Despite Suplee's support, the New York groups fell apart. According to one source, Bowen had genital surgery and then "lost interest" in organizing transsexuals.[81]

Other groups had more success in providing services or attracting members or publicity. In Yonkers, Mario Martino and his wife set up Labyrinth Foundation Counseling Service, the only group of the era specifically for FTMs. They began their service in the late 1960s as a "halfway house" for postoperative FTMs just released from a nearby hospital. Soon they had doctors refer patients to them for counseling. They hoped "to bring transsexualism out into the open," but they discovered that newspapers refused to carry ads for their service.[82] More radical groups sought publicity in the underground press, such as the *Berkeley Barb,* the *L.A. Free Press,* and publications like *DRAG* that targeted a transgendered audience. In Belmar, New Jersey, UTTS, or United Transvestite and Transexual Society, run by Sussie Collins, published its own magazine, *Female Impersonator News.*

An array of other ephemeral groups left little record of their activities. In the Los Angeles area alone, several such groups made brief appearances in the early 1970s. In 1971 a group called AND/OR, "The Androgynous Organization," set up "a transsexual help center" sponsored by the city's Gay Liberation Front. Headed by an eighteen-year-old MTF, David Feldman, also known as Lee Ann Charlotte, AND/OR planned "to locate legal and medical aid for transsexuals as well as housing, jobs, and counseling."[83] AND/OR soon disappeared from the historical record, but other groups followed in quick succession. By the mid-1970s, transsexuals in the Los Angeles area had grouped and regrouped as the Transexual/Trans-Gender Rap Group, Transvestites and Transexuals, National Organization of Gender Identity Dysphoria, Transexual Guidance Clinic, and the Transvestite, Transexual, Female Impersonator and Gender Identity Program of the Gay Community Services. In Detroit the Black Alliance of Transexuals, in Honolulu Hidden Life, in Seattle the Empathy Club, in Menlo Park the Salmacis Society, and in San Diego the Jorgensen Society showed up briefly on the rosters of transsexual organizations.[84] Some of the groups grew out of the circles of MTF crossdressers, others grew out of gay liberation, and some sprang up independently.

Aside from the EEF, only one transsexual organization had a national presence in the early 1970s. Angela Douglas was the force behind the group.[85] From the mid-1960s Douglas, still living as a man, had scraped by as an aspiring rock musician and gadabout hippie, frequently high on various drugs. In 1969, shortly after she began to dress publicly as a woman, she joined the Los Angeles Gay Liberation Front, even though she did not consider herself gay. (She considered herself transsexual. Both before and after she lived as a woman, she was attracted primarily to women.) She traveled around the country and participated actively in gay liberation protests and demonstrations. She split with GLF when she discovered the "antitransvestic" attitudes of the gay men she encountered and when she found that GLF ignored the transsexuals who wanted to push for a clinic in Los Angeles. "I'd had my fill," she wrote, "of insults from gays, all demanding I be a man and stop dressing as a woman."[86] As the sexual liberation movement splintered into distinct groups for gay men, lesbians, drag queens, and transsexuals, Douglas started her own militant organization, TAO, in Los Angeles, first for transvestites and transsexuals and then for transsexuals only.

At its founding in 1970, TAO stood for Transvestite/Transsexual Action Organization, and a year later for Transsexual Action Organization. It used the same militant tactics found in gay liberation and other radical social movements. With her countercultural style, Douglas had an outspoken, in-your-face approach to political activism, and under her leadership TAO called for confrontational protests and street demonstrations. In an early action, Douglas and another transsexual "blocked the entrance" to the theater showing the film *Myra Breckinridge* to protest the exploitative and ill-informed portrayal of a transsexual and also the use of a nontranssexual actor (Raquel Welch) to play the transsexual role. TAO also protested when Los Angeles welfare officials refused to continue aid to men who dressed as women.[87] In 1970, according to Douglas, TAO persuaded the California Peace and Freedom party, a leftist political party, to include in its platform "The right to determine the uses of one's body, as in sex change operations and others," and convinced the Socialist Workers' party to call for an end to arrests for crossdressing.[88] As part of the more radical "second wave," it spoke out against sexism and worked with women's liberation groups, and also maintained contact with the Gay Liberation Front. "As I progress as a transsexual," Douglas wrote Harry Benjamin, "I find myself more attune[d] to Women's Liberation, in particular, the demands and ideas of gay women." In a letter to *Playboy* magazine, published in 1970, Douglas explained that TAO supported "both gay liberation and women's liberation: we believe that all victims of prejudice and discrimination must work together to change this society."[89]

In 1972 Douglas moved to Miami and set up a new branch of TAO, with several Latina (Cuban and Puerto Rican) members. She published a newsletter, *Moonshadow,* and later a magazine, *Mirage,* that reported on TAO's activism and on national news of interest to transsexuals. In Miami TAO focused especially on police harassment. In 1973 it set up a "security force" to stop "police and public abuse of transsexuals and gays."[90] It publicized the arrests of transsexuals and their mistreatment by police who beat them or coerced them into sexual acts. In its magazine TAO objected to the emphasis the mainstream media placed on the "medical aspects" of transsexuality. There were, it argued, "more severe problems" confronting transsexuals, including "transsexuals in prison," various laws, "the exploitation by surgeons, psychiatrists and 'gender identity clinics,'" as well as "extortion and persecution by police." In Miami transsexuals could obtain surgery, the TAO said, but "police harassment of *both* pre and post-op TSs" was "severe . . . one horror story after another."[91]

Like other militant activists, Douglas opposed the medical model, which cast transsexuals primarily as patients who should turn to the expert care of doctors. She did not envision doctors "as the final authority," to use philosopher Judith Butler's words, but as "one instrument or resource to be deployed." She also deplored the pathologization of transsexuals. In 1973 the American Psychiatric Association, under pressure from gay activists, announced that it no longer considered homosexuality a mental illness. Soon afterward TAO "called on the American Psychiatric Association to remove transexualism from its list of mental disorders."[92]

Douglas came to dislike the Erickson Educational Foundation, which devoted much of its effort to working with and supporting its advocates in the medical profession. She described Zelda Suplee, whom many others admired, as an "old lad[y] who viewed transsexuals as mentally ill at best." She came, she said, "to loathe the EEF and everyone involved with it." The confrontational TAO avoided the EEF, which tried to attain mainstream respectability. Indeed, in its newsletter the EEF repeatedly named the doctors with whom it worked but rarely mentioned the militant transsexual organizations and never mentioned TAO. Nonetheless, the EEF attempted to work behind the scenes with Douglas. By 1974 the EEF had noticed the growing success of TAO.

According to Douglas, Suplee offered her $20,000 to "place the TAO within the EEF's framework." Douglas declined, believing that "every cent would have strings attached."[93]

Douglas had a difficult personality and came into frequent conflict with those around her. Her "second wave" radicalism put off many transsexuals whose politics differed from hers. Canary Conn, an MTF, remembered TAO in Los Angeles as "a gathering place for a bunch of drag queens who were mostly interested in running pink flags up poles and picketing college campuses as well as having sex with anyone who walked by, male and female. It was a fiasco." For her part, Douglas lambasted the people who disagreed with her and made increasingly strange accusations that put off virtually everyone else. She suspected the Central Intelligence Agency of setting up the program at Johns Hopkins and publicly associated the EEF with the alleged government plot. And she linked Donald Laub, a founding surgeon of Stanford's Gender Identity Clinic, with a bizarre plot among doctors to transplant the brains of transsexuals. She saw conspiracies everywhere and believed that others were trying to steal her name and her ideas. She soon won a reputation as a disruptive figure who fostered dissension within the radical wing of the movement. Suzan Cooke, the San Francisco activist, had little tolerance for Douglas, even though she generally shared her political views. Cooke thought that Douglas "was nuts" and "didn't much care for her."[94]

Still, by 1974 TAO was, as Douglas described it, "the loudest and . . . most radical" of the various small transsexual groups scattered across the nation.[95] In the United States it had, at various points, chapters in San Francisco, Philadelphia, Chicago, Atlanta, Orlando, and Jacksonville, as well as Miami Beach, and abroad it had chapters in England, Canada, and Northern Ireland. By this time it included a few FTMs as well as MTFs. At its peak in the mid-1970s, the organization had, according to Douglas, about a thousand members.[96]

In 1974 Douglas stepped down as president of the TAO, and another MTF, Barbara Rosello, took the helm. Rosello issued a statement that suggests how far the movement had come. "TAO," she said, "is an organization for transexuals only . . . We have many goals which can only be accomplished by our own efforts." She did not make an appeal to the doctors, and she did not dwell on transsexuals as patients; instead, she called for an end to "the persecution" and "ignorance." She demanded changes in the law. "We should be able to marry," she said, "and adopt children if we wish." She protested the high costs of surgery in the United States and criticized the medical treatment in which transsexuals were "forced to be guinea pigs for crazy doctors doing ridiculous experiments." And she referred to the problem of employment discrimination. "I have lost many jobs myself," she noted, "once it was found out that I am a transexual."[97] The movement had gone well beyond mutual support, counseling, and referrals. In the more militant organizations, activists challenged the doctors, organized among themselves, and called for social and legal change in the name of civil rights. "In the emergence of organized political and cultural groupings around sexuality in the late twentieth century," Jeffrey Weeks has written, "the long process of definition and self-definition may be said to have reached a qualitatively new level." Such was the case in TAO.[98]

While doctors and transsexuals organized, the courts began to address the question of whether a person could legally change sex. The cases arose when individual petitioners showed up in court asking to change their names or the sex on their birth certificates or to find out whether a marriage was legal. In response, the courts tried to determine whether a male-to-female transsexual counted legally as female or a female-to-male as male. The petitioners thus forced the courts to state explicitly what male and female entailed. Amazingly, the courts had few precedents to follow. For decades various courts had come up with shifting definitions of race, acknowledging implicitly that categories that might seem biological were in fact social designs. But they had never before had reason to spell out a legal definition of sex. They had simply assumed that male and female were readily apparent and immutable.[99]

From early on, the more sympathetic doctors backed their patients in court. In 1960, for example, Harry Benjamin went to Chicago to give a deposition for a judge in a small midwestern town on behalf of an

FTM named Tommie who hoped to change the sex on his birth certificate. The issue involved more than the birth certificate alone, because an altered certificate might, in various locales, enable Tommie to change his name, change his driver's license, and marry without legal interference or bureaucratic hassles. He could, in short, live legally as a man. Benjamin hoped to persuade the judge with his scientific definition of sex. "I explained," Benjamin wrote Elmer Belt, "that there are all kinds of interpretations of 'sex': the genetic sex, the anatomical one, the endocrine one, the psychological one, the social sex, and the assigned sex of rearing. I explained that after Tommie's treatment, only the genetic sex could still be called completely female while all the others would be considered either totally or partially male." The judge deferred to Benjamin's expertise and granted the change on the birth certificate. "Isn't it encouraging," Benjamin wrote, "that occasionally we encounter an intelligent judge."[100]

In the late 1960s and early 1970s a few cases made it into the legal record with published decisions that other courts could read. In most of these cases the lawyers called in doctors as expert witnesses. The judges involved fell roughly into two camps. Some turned to the doctors who opposed transsexual surgery and rejected the petitions in the name of preserving the status quo. Others cited the doctors who endorsed transsexual surgery and tried to provide "relief" to the individual petitioners. The two camps came up with different definitions of sex. Neither, though, paid any attention to the transsexual activists who rejected the medical model, and neither questioned the need for the legal categories of female and male. In fact they went out of their way to maintain them.

The first precedent-setting case was *Anonymous v. Weiner*, a case decided in the New York County Supreme Court in 1966. An anonymous male-to-female transsexual petitioned the court to have the sex designation changed on her birth certificate.[101] The case actually began a year earlier, in 1965, when the anonymous petitioner asked the New York City Department of Health to issue a new birth certificate with sex designated as female. The Commissioner of Health, Dr. George James, took the question to the prestigious New York Academy of Medicine. He asked the academy to convene a special group of doctors to consider the issue. In response, the academy created a committee comprised of fifteen men, including one lawyer and fourteen doctors from various medical fields. The academy wrote a report, used directly by the court and quoted in its decision.

The report and the subsequent court decision reveal the conservative stance that still reigned in the mid-1960s. The EEF had already begun to fund research on transsexuals, Harry Benjamin had started his research foundation, and the doctors at Johns Hopkins were just hatching their plan to offer transsexual surgery. But they had as yet little support from other doctors, bureaucrats, and judges. From the beginning, the Department of Health and the New York Academy of Medicine stood predisposed against the transsexual petitioner and her allies. Although the committee of medical experts invited Harry Benjamin to advise its members at one of its meetings, it ignored his views entirely. The committee's deliberations, saved in the archives of the academy, show why and how the experts rejected legal change.

There were no federal laws to guide the Department of Health, the New York Academy of Medicine, or the New York Supreme Court. By 1960 the U.S. Army had decided to exclude transsexuals from enlistment, but otherwise the question of transsexuals' legal status was decided piecemeal in the states.[102] By 1965 ten other states had allowed changes of sex on birth certificates under existing legislation, and New York City officials in the Department of Health had already quietly changed the certificates of three other transsexuals. But the special committee of the New York Academy did not want to leave the issue for administrators to decide on a case-by-case basis. The committee members regarded transsexuals as "sick" or "psychotic," and they did not condone transsexual surgery, which they tended to see as dubious science.[103] In addition, they had specific worries that fell loosely under the headings of sex, gender, and sexuality.

The committee viewed sex as an immutable biological fact, ultimately determined by chromosomes. "Most psychiatrists," one committee member stated, "would consider it illegal to alter the biological facts on the birth certificate."[104] It would interfere, as the doctors saw it, with honest recordkeeping and record linkage. But if records were their sole concern, then they might have agreed to keep and seal the original record and append another for public use. (Some states already used such procedures for births out of wedlock or for adoptions.)[105] Furthermore, the doctors knew that chromosomes did not always determine the sex, legal or otherwise, of intersexed individuals, some of whom had, for example, XY chromosomes but lived legally as women. They saw transsexuals differently. The committee opposed changing birth certificates "as a means to help psychologically ill persons in their social adaptation." It might encourage "what might be regarded," according to one doctor, "as operations of mutilation."[106]

The committee had other concerns, though, than transsexuals, surgery, and biological sex. The committee considered a letter from a federal official, at the Division of Vital Statistics (in the Public Health Service), who noted that "in certain agencies, benefits to women differ from benefits to men." If a person changed legal gender status from man to woman or woman to man, then various agencies would have to "decide how to accommodate these situations."[107] In other words, a change on the birth certificate would force consideration of the policies, laws, and practices that distinguished women and men. In the mid-1960s the stroke of a pen on a birth certificate could in some circumstances affect access to a job, eligibility for jury duty, or the amount of a pension. As the lawyer on the committee put it, the case could possibly involve "every law which establishes a different standard for the sexes."[108] The case also raised the specter of homosexuality. As the commissioner of health asked: "Would it [change of sex on a birth certificate] not be countenancing marriage between individuals of the same biological sex and the enormous psychological, legal, and biological implications of that action?" And in the committee's private deliberations, one doctor concluded that "the primary concern" was "whether a statement by the Academy would be used in many other ways relating to the whole question of homosexuality."[109]

The case arose at the very moment when feminists and gays were beginning to organize increasingly vocal social movements to demand their rights and when older traditions of family and marriage law were beginning to crumble in the courts.[110] As the authorities seemed to recognize, the right to change sex legally threatened to undermine the established system, not only with regard to transsexuals, but also with regard to other issues of sex, gender, and sexuality. The doctors backed out of the dilemma. In their report they recommended against changing the birth certificate. The Board of Health accepted the committee's recommendation. When the case made it to court, the presiding judge found that the Board of Health had not "acted in an arbitrary, capricious or otherwise illegal manner."[111] He rejected the petition. In this way, the authorities not only prevented the legal change of gender status of one anonymous male-to-female transsexual; they also reaffirmed a legal system that maintained women's secondary status and the heterosexual norm. *Anonymous v. Weiner* revealed the stakes involved in legal change. A particular vision of social order underlay a legal system that insisted on the immutability of sex and gender. When transsexuals asked for a new definition of sex or a new legal gender status, they threatened to overturn it all.

As a few American universities created gender-identity clinics and as some transsexuals formed advocacy organizations, more liberal sentiments surfaced among some judges and lawyers. In 1968, just two years after *Anonymous v. Weiner,* Judge Francis Pecora permitted Robert Parisi to change her name to Risa Bella.[112] Instead of deciding the case quietly, Pecora took an activist stance and used it, as a later analysis found, to offer "ammunition for possible departure from the rule of *Weiner.*"[113] "Perhaps the easiest method of disposing of this application," he noted, "would be merely to deny the petition." He suggested instead that new situations "perhaps merit new rules and/or progressive legislation." He thus distinguished himself from conservatives, who preferred to maintain the status quo. But Pecora was not a radical. He accepted the categories of male and female and distanced himself from what he considered outlandish views. "It has been suggested," he wrote, "that there is some middle ground between the sexes . . . Yet the standard is much too fixed for such far-out theories." He also refused to let individuals determine their own legal sex. As Pecora redefined legal sex, genitals and gender identity trumped chromosomes as defining criteria. He supported the individual's will but only if surgery had made "anatomical sex . . . conform with . . . psychological sex."[114] His new definition of sex allowed postoperative MTFs to change their legal sex but excluded anyone who had not had genital surgery, including implicitly the many FTMs who never underwent phalloplasty.

The Erickson Educational Foundation, with its main office in New York, took immediate interest in the local case and its redefinition of sex. As the EEF framed it, the law lagged behind science in redefining sex. Scientists now had "eight criteria for determining" sex: "chromosomal, gonadal, internal sex organs, hormonal pattern, external genitals, habitus, sex of rearing, and gender role and orientation." (In this, the EEF drew on the writings of John Money and Harry Benjamin—and ignored the doctors and scientists who opposed them.) In the view of the EEF, the law generally did not consider the complexity of sex and gender. Judge Pecora, however, had "revealed his careful study of the problem." The EEF applauded the decision as a "landmark opinion."[115]

In the late 1960s and early 1970s three articles in law reviews called, as Pecora did, for a new definition of sex. At least two of the authors had direct connections with the EEF or with the doctors who supported sex-change surgery. John P. Holloway, who published "Transsexuals—Their Legal Sex" in 1968, researched his article with the cooperation of doctors at Johns Hopkins, and Richard Green and John Money appreciated the article enough to reprint it in their anthology. Douglas K. Smith, who published his essay three years later, had assistance from the EEF and advice from Harry Benjamin. All three articles sympathized with transsexuals and hoped to accommodate their needs. Like Pecora, they accepted the categories of sex and redefined them in such a way as to admit transsexuals legally into their postoperative gender. Smith considered it "impractical for the law to abandon the two-sex assumption." He called for "an administrable and equitable legal standard by which to test a person's sex while preserving the traditional sexual dichotomy."[116] To that end, he and the others all rejected chromosomes as the basis of defining sex and called for relying on postoperative anatomy and gender identity as the deciding criteria. For Holloway, such a version of legal sex would help the transsexual and not harm anyone else. In the view of the anonymous author of "Transsexuals in Limbo," published in the "Notes and Comments" of the *Mary-*

land Law Review in 1971, the new definition of legal sex would acknowledge "the rights of the individual" and "the privacy and dignity" of citizens. It would treat transsexuality as "any other curable defect or disease" and permit the patient to "achieve a productive role in the social order."[117] For Smith, it represented "the best interests of the transsexual," which were not, he said, in conflict with "the interests of society."[118] As the EEF undoubtedly knew, these law review articles could (and would) be used strategically in the courts as external sources in support of legal change. This was a tactic that other civil rights organizations, most notably the National Association for the Advancement of Colored People, had already successfully developed.[119]

Meanwhile, more lawyers with transsexual clients began to realize that a chromosomal definition of sex hindered their cases. In 1970, as he forged his own legal strategy, James A. Plessinger, a Connecticut attorney, wrote Harry Benjamin: "It would appear from my very limited exposure to this problem that the chromosome test is not only unfair to a person having undergone this operation but is inadequate and unsuitable to determine the true and obvious sex of an individual." For the most part, Benjamin agreed. He considered "the so-called chromosome test" an accurate measure of "genetic sex," but genetic or "chromosomal sex" had "merely theoretical significance." "To insist upon diagnosing the sex of a person from the chromosomes," he wrote, "may do a very great injustice." Six months later Benjamin restated his point. Chromosomal sex, he found, was "merely of abstract, scientific and theoretical interest." It should not, he concluded, serve as the basis for legal classification of sex.[120]

In the early 1970s other developments suggested that transsexuals might win more support for a redefinition of legal sex. In the 1970s (and continuing into the 1980s) various courts struck down local crossdressing laws that had made it illegal for men to dress as women. The rise of unisex fashions made the laws seem increasingly irrelevant and difficult to enforce. Judges expressed irritation with police who filled their courts with hippies and transvestites.[121] Meanwhile the American Civil Liberties Union began to recognize transsexuals, and to provide legal aid to them, as part of its larger vision of rights and liberties. In New Jersey an ACLU attorney worked with Paula Grossman, who was suspended without pay from her job as a schoolteacher when she started to live as a woman. In New York the Sexual Privacy Project of the ACLU came out in support of transsexuals' rights.[122]

The EEF stayed abreast of the new legal developments. In 1970 it published *Some Legal Aspects of Transsexualism*, which it billed as its "first pamphlet of advice." The pamphlet advised transsexuals on crossdressing laws, changing names, and altering official records. It included the names of four sympathetic attorneys, serving on its Legal Advisory Board, who had agreed to work with transsexuals. The EEF also provided identification cards to transsexuals undergoing medical treatment. Transsexuals could show the cards to police who might stop them for crossdressing or to officials who might wonder why they should change a name on a driver's license or bank account. This practical support could help transsexuals navigate their public change of sex while the courts debated legalities.[123]

The practical approach was especially important because the legal support for transsexuals' rights had not necessarily affected administrative practices. As more government agencies encountered more transsexuals, some officials tried to help transsexuals, but many did not. In some cases, policies hardened. The Passport Office, for example, actually reversed its earlier liberal policy. Since Christine Jorgensen had changed her passport in 1952, the Department of State had issued new passports when it could certify that surgery had changed the anatomy of the person in question. (A letter from a doctor generally sufficed.) In 1971, though, the deputy director of the Passport Office told the *Cornell Law Review* that it now required a court decree attesting to the change of name and identity.[124] A similar process occurred with regard to public funds for transsexual surgery. In Connecticut the Division of Rehabilitative Services provided funds for surgery on the grounds that it improved "the employability of 'handicapped individuals.'" After a few such cases, the director of the program asked the U.S. Department of Health, Education and Welfare (HEW) for guidance. In 1973 HEW officials reversed the earlier practice. "Federal funds," an official wrote, "should not be used to provide surgery to accomplish an alteration of sex since surgical intervention has not reached the status of a professionally accepted or recognized . . . treatment."[125]

In the courts, too, transsexuals and their allies often failed to win their cases. In 1973 Deborah Hartin went to the New York County Supreme Court to request a new birth certificate with sex designated as female. By this time the New York City Department of Health had agreed to issue transsexuals new birth certificates with no sex designation at all. But Hartin wanted proof that she could live legally as a woman. The judge cited the *Weiner* decision and turned her down. Pecora's more liberal sentiments, one analysis concluded, had "failed to convince his brothers on the bench."[126] The next year the Superior Court of New Jersey turned down Paula Grossman's attempt to win back her job as a music teacher in an elementary school. The court posed the case as one of competing interests, balancing Grossman's individual rights against the alleged needs of schoolchildren. The two sides lined up opposing medical experts. For the Board of Education, psychoanalyst Charles Socarides, one of the most vocal opponents of transsexual surgery, argued that Grossman's presence in school would harm children psychologically. On behalf of Grossman, Charles Ihlenfeld, who shared a practice with Harry Benjamin, and psychiatrist Robert Laidlaw, who worked with Benjamin's patients, argued that Grossman's change of sex "would have no significant effect" on her students. Ihlenfeld claimed that any child who found Grossman deeply disturbing already had "a potential for developing a problem" and needed counseling anyway. The court awarded Grossman back pay but refused to reinstate her.[127]

In the 1970s the less-than-liberal view generally prevailed in the few cases pertaining to marriage. Most states did not require proof of sex before allowing marriage. The marriage cases arose with divorce or annulment, when a husband claimed that his wife was not a woman or a wife claimed that her husband was not a man, in an attempt to invalidate the marriage. Although the laws rarely specified it, marriage was generally understood as a relationship between a female and a male. But here, as in other areas of the law, the courts had not considered what male and female meant. In the 1960s the U.S. Supreme Court had reconsidered marriage—and the state's right to restrict such unions—in another area. In 1967, in *Loving v. Virginia,* the court struck down a state law prohibiting interracial marriage. With the transsexual cases, the courts considered once again who could legally marry whom. The only direct precedent was a 1970 British case, *Corbett v. Corbett,* in which the judge stated that marriage was "a relationship between man and woman," and then decided that April Ashley, the MTF in question, was "a biological male from birth." Sex, he found, "cannot be changed." The marriage was therefore invalid.[128]

In New York four years later, the Kings County Supreme Court heard a similar case involving a female-to-male transsexual. In March 1972, Mark B. underwent mastectomy and hysterectomy, and in April he applied to change his name and married. He had, according to his wife's complaint, "fraudulently represented" that he "'was and is a Male person.'" His wife, Frances B., sued for annulment, claiming her husband was female. In response, Mark B. sought a divorce, on the ground that his wife had abandoned him. The court found that "marriage is and always has been a contract between a man and a woman." Was Mark B. a man? The court defined sex in terms of reproductive and sexual capacity, not in terms of chromosomes, but the result was the same. Marriage, it said, "exists . . . for the purpose of begetting offspring." Mark B. did not have a functioning penis (he did not have a penis at all), he could not engage in sexual intercourse, he could not produce offspring, and for purposes of marriage he was therefore not a man. "While it is possible that defendant may function as a male in other situations and in other relationships," the judge wrote, "defendant cannot function as a husband by assuming male duties and obligations inherent in the marriage relationship." He could not "function as a man for purposes of procreation." The court did not consider the obvious issues of fraud and deception; instead, it offered a strange definition of legal sex that would have excluded any man who was sterile or impotent from the category "male."[129]

A different view came to the fore in 1976, when the Appellate Division of the Superior Court of New Jersey redefined sex for purposes of marriage. This was the only case of the era in which a judge elaborated explicitly and extensively on the liberal legal vision, pioneered by Judge Pecora, and its limits. The case considered the failed marriage of M. T. and J. T., who had met in 1964. In 1971 M. T. underwent male-to-female genital surgery, and in 1972 she and J. T. married. Two years later J. T. left, and M. T. filed for support. J. T. refused to pay support on the grounds that his wife "was a male and that their marriage was void." In the trial court Charles Ihlenfeld, M. T.'s doctor, testified on her behalf. He explained to the court that his patient had a "feminine gender identity" he could not alter and that she had a vagina "the same as a normal female vagina after a hysterectomy." She was no longer a male "since she could not function as a male sexually either for purposes of 'recreation or procreation.'" Charles Annicello, a psychologist from the Johns Hopkins Gender Identity Clinic, also testified for the plaintiff. She qualified as a female, he said, because she had a "female psychic gender" and had undergone "a sex reassignment operation." On the other side, J. T. called his father, a medical doctor, as an expert witness. Dr. T. claimed that "anatomy alone . . . determined the real sex." He discounted gender identity and pointed to the plaintiff's lack of female reproductive organs.[130]

In a victory for male-to-female transsexuals, three judges affirmed the lower court's decision that M. T. qualified as female. "For purposes of marriage under the circumstances of this case," they decided, femaleness was determined not by chromosomes or reproductive organs, but by gender identity plus "sexual capacity," which included "both the physical ability and the psychological or emotional orientation to engage in sexual intercourse" as a female. In the wake of the sexual revolution and in a case focusing on marriage, the decision foregrounded sexuality in ways that Pecora's earlier decision had only implied. Judge Alan B. Handler, who delivered the opinion of the court, explicitly shifted the purpose of marriage away from reproduction and toward heterosexual intercourse, moved the anatomical criterion for sex away from reproductive organs and toward genitals, and also insisted that gender identity played a key role in determining legal sex.[131] For purposes of marriage, genitals, gender, and heterosexual capacity determined who qualified legally as a woman or a man.

In *M. T. v. J. T.*, the judges relied directly on liberal medical experts and also on the liberal law review articles, two of which Handler cited in the decision. But they were unwilling to undercut the dominant system of gender and sexuality. The decision stated explicitly that "a lawful marriage requires . . . two persons of the opposite sex." "Marriage between persons of the same sex," Handler wrote, "cannot be fathomed." With the new definition of sex, a postoperative male-to-female transsexual could marry a man (if the transsexual identified as a heterosexual woman and had a penetrable vagina), but a preoperative male-to-female transsexual, a male crossdresser, or a gay man could not. Conversely, a lesbian could not marry a woman, nor presumably could a female-to-male transsexual (because surgeons could not construct a sexually functioning penis). Furthermore, Handler noted that in other areas "where sex differentiation is required or accepted" different definitions of sex might apply. The judge specifically mentioned public records, military service, participation in sports, and eligibility for some occupations. He thus carefully contained the impact of the decision. It would, he concluded, "promote the individual's quest for inner peace and happiness, while in no way disserving any societal interest, principle of public order or precept of morality."[132] In sum, the liberal position accommodated the requests of the transsexual petitioner but tried to preserve intact the rest of the legal apparatus concerning sex differences, gender, and sexuality.

In 1977 the New York County Supreme Court reaffirmed the liberal redefinition of sex. The United States Tennis Association had refused to allow Renée Richards, a postoperative MTF, to play professional tennis as a woman unless she could pass a sex chromatin test that showed she had female (XX) chromosomes. Richards turned to the court, with the backing of her surgeon Robert Granato as well as Leo Wollman, John Money, and tennis player Billie Jean King. In support of her case, Judge Alfred M. Ascione called using the chromosome test as the sole criterion of sex "grossly unfair, discriminatory, and inequitable."[133] After the court decision, there was no indication that any MTFs changed their sex in order to compete with women athletically, thus allaying concerns that Richards had started a trend to undermine women's sports. And Richards herself soon lost in tournaments in which she played against nontranssexual women, dispelling fears that her size or strength gave her an undue advantage against XX females.

In a 1975 law review essay, Edward S. David wrote: "A fundamental classificatory scheme, male and female, is breaking down." But he was wrong. In the discussions of legal sex in the 1960s and 1970s, hardly anyone questioned the necessity or utility of legal sex classifications. In response to critical comments from Robert Stoller, one lawyer who worked with transsexual clients, Richard Levidow, a friend of Harry Benjamin's, wrote: "I do not think it sophistry to consider a human being solely as a human being." He was willing, he suggested, to "destroy the conceptual ramifications of a Birth Certificate's gender identification." For the most part, though, the liberal position redefined sex but failed to do away with the legal categories underlying it. The liberal judges both accommodated transsexuals and contained the threat. "While sex differences may serve to 'ground' a society's system of gender differences," anthropologist Judith Shapiro has written, "the ground seems in some ways to be less firm than what it is supporting."[134] The law could, it seems, respond to transsexuals and redefine sex without overthrowing the basic taxonomic scheme (male and female) or undermining the dominant codes of gender and sexuality.

In the mid-1970s the liberal stance seemed in ascendance. The *Erickson Educational Foundation Newsletter* reported regularly on the mass media, on the dozens of newspaper and magazine articles and radio and television shows featuring transsexuals or their doctors. The *New York Times, Cosmopolitan* magazine, and NBC News, among others, provided positive publicity about the clinics and the doctors who ran them.[135] With the growing press coverage, the EEF expanded its newsletter and hired more clerical help to answer correspondence. In 1970, when *Look* magazine published a lengthy feature article, with the EEF listed as an "excellent source of information," the foundation reported a "flood of inquiries."[136] And in 1975, when the syndicated advice columnist "Dear Abby," who was friends with Harry Benjamin, printed the name and address of the EEF, "hundreds of letters . . . came in response, seeking information and help." By mid-decade the EEF mailing list had hit twenty thousand.[137]

The doctors and scientists who supported transsexual surgery expressed optimism. In 1975, at a celebration of Benjamin's ninetieth birthday, John Money proclaimed: "The public has begun to learn to be more open-minded about the ethics and personal rights of self-determination regarding social and legal gender status." But self-determination for transsexuals was not the first item on the doctors' agendas. Their sense that the public approved allowed them to move away from a defensive pose and actively expand their own authority in a growing medical field. In the early 1970s they adopted *gender dysphoria syndrome* (and later *gender identity disorder*) as an umbrella term covering a broader range of crossgender identifications that might ultimately lead to surgery. The new diagnostic category, as originated by Norman Fisk, allowed "the liberalization of previously rigid and truly unrealistic diagnostic criteria," which in turn "liberalized the indications and requirements for sex conversion surgery."[138] In other words, some of the doctors expressed a new willingness to expand their diagnostic turf and their clinics and to approve more patients for surgery.

By the mid-1970s the doctors had bolstered their authority. They had their own clinics and research programs, and they had increasing clout in the courts and positive coverage in the press. The clinicians and researchers continued to hold regular national and international meetings, and in 1973 they started to plan a national organization. In 1975, at the Fourth International Symposium on Gender Identity, held at Stanford University, they appointed committees to draft guidelines to serve as medical standards for the diagnosis and treatment of transsexuals. In 1977, at the fifth international conference, held in Norfolk, Virginia, they selected a Standards Committee, composed of six doctors, and voted down a proposal to include a transsexual on it. Meanwhile Richard Green began to draft a section on transsexualism for the next edition of the American Psychiatric Association's *Diagnostic and Statistical Manual of Mental Disorders*.[139] The liberal doctors seemed to have contained the longstanding threat posed by the doctors who opposed sex-change surgery and the more recent challenge posed by the radical activists who wanted transsexuality viewed as benign variation rather than as illness or disorder. But they had not silenced their critics, and they had not yet felt the full force of the women's and gay liberation movements, which increasingly countered the doctors' versions of gender and sexuality. The liberal triumph hid years of unresolved tensions beneath an appearance of surface calm.

THE NEXT GENERATION

7

$\mathcal{B}$ y the end of the 1970s, the liberal triumph had culminated in the professional recognition of transsexualism and professional guidelines for its treatment. In 1979 the physicians, therapists, and researchers who worked with transsexuals formed the Harry Benjamin International Gender Dysphoria Association (HBIGDA). At its founding, the members of HBIGDA approved its standards of care, which gave "official sanction" to standardized criteria for diagnosis and treatment. The standards explicitly authorized medical treatment, under certain conditions, but disavowed surgery "on demand" and required recommendations from two licensed psychologists or psychiatrists before surgical intervention.[1] The following year transsexualism found its way for the first time into the American Psychiatric Association's *Diagnostic and Statistical Manual,* the volume routinely used to diagnose mental disorders. For better or worse, "transsexualism" was now an officially recognized "gender identity disorder."[2]

But the official recognition of transsexualism did not quiet the battles that had augured its birth. By the late 1970s the first transsexual advocacy organizations had disintegrated. The National Transsexual Counseling Unit, the Transsexual Action Organization, and the Erickson Educational Foundation had all shut down, and the transsexual activists had lost most of the allies they had had in the gay and women's movements. In a sense, the temporary decline of activism cleared the field for the professionals in HBIGDA. They could now put forward their guidelines for diagnosis and treatment without organized counterclaims from transsexuals themselves. As it turned out, though, the doctors found themselves no less beleaguered than before. The rise of the women's movement introduced a different formulation of gender, and feminist and gay activists increasingly pointed to the political implications of treating gender variance as a mental disorder. And from within the doctors' ranks, psychoanalysts once again raised vocal objections to transsexual surgery.

More quietly, other trends transformed the field. In the 1970s and 1980s a number of private doctors discovered a lucrative practice in transsexual surgery and began to specialize in sex-change operations. With surgery more readily available, the number of people obtaining medical treatment increased. In the same years, new activists emerged from the ranks of transsexuals. They advocated changes in local, state, and federal policies, offered peer counseling, and began to form new organizations to replace the old. For the first time, FTMs took a more public role. In the popular culture, too, transsexuality reappeared in new form. In the 1970s and 1980s transsexual themes appeared in feature-length films, and transsexuals themselves routinely spoke to a national audience on new tabloid television talk shows. The changes opened another chapter in the medical, social, and cultural history of transsexuality. In the late 1980s the deaths of Harry Benjamin and Christine Jorgensen seemed to confirm that one era had ended, and in the early 1990s the rise of the contemporary transgender movement suggested that another had begun.

*T*he early transsexual activist groups had been fragile from the start. They faced the same problems as other identity-based social movements. The members shared one constituent part of their senses of self—their transsexuality—but not necessarily others. Transsexuals differed from one another in gender, class, race, religion, and ethnicity. They had different personalities, and they held diverse political views. They did not necessarily agree on whether biological forces or early childhood experience had shaped their gender identities or on the versions of masculinity and femininity they expressed. They had different sexual preferences and varying degrees of participation in, comfort with, and tolerance for other forms of gender and sexual transgression, such as transvestism and homosexuality. Moreover, most transsexuals showed little desire to participate publicly in militant organizations that pushed for political change. Many wanted to live quietly, to blend in comfortably unnoticed after years of standing out as misfits. In the early 1970s the changing political climate further weakened the transsexual organizations. The Vietnam War ended, and so did the antiwar movement. Government repression of radicals damaged the civil rights and other social movements, and disillusionment with drugs gutted the counterculture. The women's and gay liberation movements survived, but with greater separatist impulse and fewer active coalitions with other social movements. The major social movements shifted from a push toward activism to a pull toward retreat.

In this climate, the early transsexual organizations fell apart. In 1973 the San Francisco police arrested Suzan Cooke and Janice Maxwell, who ran the National Transsexual Counseling Unit, for selling drugs. The police, it seems, set up the bust to damage the organization. Maxwell's boyfriend, it turned out, was a police informant, who convinced her to buy some drugs and sell them to him. The police stepped in for the arrest and then used it to undermine their colleague Elliot Blackstone, whose liberal sympathies for transsexuals, gays, and lesbians offended other members of the San Francisco force. According to Blackstone, the arrests damaged the NTCU and his own career. Within two years the NTCU had disappeared, and Blackstone had retired.[3] The Transsexual Action Organization also declined in the mid-1970s. In 1976 its founder and former president Angela Douglas moved from Miami to Berkeley, taking with her the energy that had sustained the organization. In 1978 she formally disbanded it. "Life is like quicksand," she wrote a few years later, "and if you're a transsexual, there is no firm ground at all."[4]

Around the same time, the Erickson Educational Foundation suspended most of its operations. In 1976 Zelda Suplee closed her New York office and moved to Galveston to start the Janus Information Facility (JIF), a referral service affiliated at first with the gender clinic at the University of Texas Medical Branch, directed by Paul Walker. Walker, a psychotherapist, had worked earlier with John Money at Johns Hopkins University. He helped found HBIGDA, helped draft its standards of care, and served as its first president. The JIF took over the educational functions of the EEF. It moved to San Francisco at the end of the 1970s when Walker opened a private practice there.[5] The EEF thus merged with the organized professionals, with Walker as its chief liaison. The waning influence of the EEF followed Reed Erickson's personal decline. In the 1970s he succumbed to drug addiction, which contributed to an "acute psychotic episode" in late 1976. In 1983 police in Ojai, California, arrested him for possession of cocaine. He jumped bail, and after two more arrests he retreated to Mexico and gradually deteriorated mentally. By the end of the 1980s he was paranoid and delusional, and in 1992 he died.[6]

The tragic decline of Erickson occurred in the same years that transgender styles and transsexuals themselves came under attack in the gay and women's movements. In the 1970s and 1980s gay men, lesbians, and feminists increasingly cast transsexuals variously as irrelevant, out of style, invasive, or conservative. The gay liberation movement moved away from its earlier embrace of gender transgression. Among gay men, the "cult of the macho," with its "close-clipped mustache [and] shaved head looks," celebrated masculinity and rejected the more feminine long-haired look of queens, fairies, and hippies.[7] As drag queens and radical fairies found themselves displaced from the center of gay liberation, transsexuals lost their strongest allies in the heart of the movement. In women's organizations, a number of feminists engaged in more overt rejection of transsexuals. In the early 1970s a few MTFs joined the feminist movement. Like other feminists, they had come to a new assessment of the subordination of women, sometimes as a result of seeing firsthand the privileges they lost when they started to live as women. "I think women need to have more rights," one MTF said, "I don't really enjoy a second-class status as a woman, not at all. I had more rights as a man."[8] But not all feminists welcomed transsexuals into their organizations. As some lesbian-feminists called for separate "women-only space," in which women organized and engaged with one another separately from men, they portrayed MTFs as interlopers who brought male privileges with them even when they lived as women. Less frequently, they also addressed FTMs, whom they described as self-hating lesbians who had given up the struggle for liberation in favor of living as men or as benighted women who believed in male superiority.[9]

The conflicts with feminists arose in part from clashing styles of gender presentation and diverging personal histories. Many MTFs and FTMs rejected the androgynous style in vogue among 1970s feminists. Some transsexuals admired and longed to express the femininity or masculinity denied them in their youth, while increasing numbers of feminists critiqued femininity as a sign of women's oppression and masculinity as a symbol of male supremacy. "I went to women's lib meetings for awhile," one MTF stated in 1971, "and was really getting into it until some woman wearing an army uniform walked up to me and said I should take off my false eyelashes and not expose my breasts so much." According to some observers, the difference in style reflected an underlying difference in politics. In a 1973 study sociologist Thomas Kando found that MTFs had more stereotypically feminine attitudes than nontranssexual women. He called them "reactionary," the "Uncle Toms of the sexual revolution." Other observers disagreed. In 1976 sociologist Deborah Feinbloom noted that MTFs changed with the times. "We now see young clients," she wrote, "who wear pants, boots, and fairly unisex type clothing. They define themselves as feminists, some as heterosexual, some as homosexual." In the 1980s anthropologist Anne Bolin critiqued Kando directly. She conducted a parallel study and came up with different conclusions. The MTFs she studied tended to endorse feminism and reject "hyper-femininity."[10] The historical records suggest that transsexuals have, from the 1950s on, disagreed openly among themselves about "women's place." Some MTFs and FTMs did indeed express antifeminist views, but others embraced feminism and rejected gender stereotypes.[11] It was the latter group, the feminists, who came into conflict with others in the women's movement.

The clash broke into open battles in the 1970s. The tensions surrounding transsexuals in the women's movement surfaced in 1971, and by 1972, TAO noted, "the women's movement began to polarize around the issue."[12] In 1973 the San Francisco Daughters of Bilitis (DOB), the lesbian rights organization, split over the issue and ultimately expelled MTF Beth Elliott, who had served as the group's vice-president, on the grounds that she did not qualify as a woman. Later the same year, around twelve hundred women attending the West Coast Lesbian Conference in Los Angeles divided over whether Elliott, a singer and guitarist, should perform onstage. Some tried to shout her off the stage, and others rose in her defense. The next day radical feminist Robin Morgan denounced Elliott from the podium. During her keynote address, Morgan accused "transvestite or transsexual males" in the women's movement of "leeching off women." She refrained from naming Elliott but referred to the expulsion from DOB and hyperbolically labeled her "an opportunist, an infiltrator, and a destroyer—with the mentality of a rapist."[13] The debate over transsexuals came up sporadically in other local feminist communities. It hit the feminist press again in 1977, when some lesbian-feminists protested the employment of Sandy Stone, an MTF, at Olivia Records, a prominent lesbian-feminist recording company.[14]

The animosity reached its peak with Janice Raymond's 1979 book, *The Transsexual Empire,* an extended antitranssexual diatribe from a feminist standpoint. Raymond acknowledged that lesbian-feminist MTFs did not adhere to gender stereotypes of women. But, according to Raymond, they exercised masculine invasiveness. "The transsexually constructed lesbian-feminist," she wrote, "not only colonizes female bodies but appropriates a 'feminist' soul." Following Morgan, she used the loaded language of "rape." MTFs, she wrote, "rape women's bodies by reducing the real female form to an artifact, appropriating this body for themselves." Through both nature and nurture, she suggested, MTFs qualified as male and men.[15] Raymond had little to no interest in building coalitions of feminist allies; she drew a line that excluded MTFs, regardless of their political views or actions, from the women's movement. In classic sectarian fashion, she tried to purge the movement of those she claimed tainted it, and attacked her allies instead of her enemies.

Raymond noted that other feminists had publicly disagreed with her exclusionary approach toward transsexuals, and in so doing she touched on the more profound challenge that transsexuals posed to her vision of feminism: how to define sex and gender. "If feminists cannot agree on the boundaries of what constitutes femaleness," Raymond worried, "then what can we hope to agree on?" She opposed "the leveling of genuine boundaries."[16] Like the doctors who opposed sex-change surgery and the judges who rejected the petitions of transsexuals, Raymond refused to redefine sex. For Raymond, biological sex was self-evident, or at least determined by chromosomes, and one's biological sex and one's history as a girl or boy determined whether or not one qualified socially as a woman. Gender identity and altered bodies could not, in Raymond's view, make someone born with a male body and reared as a boy qualify as a woman.

As the early transsexual organizations foundered, transsexual feminists, under fire, retreated also from the women's movement. As they departed, they spelled out their own definition of gender. In a 1975 article titled "The Transsexual/Lesbian Misunderstanding," Margo, an MTF, posed a counterdefinition. "Male-to-female transsexuals *are women*," she wrote, "if they are living as such." She questioned the boundaries of sex. "*Not* everyone," she noted, "is so clearly female or male, even on a purely physical level." And in any case, "physical sex" did "not necessarily determine gender identity." People changed both "physical sex and social identity, in order to live in accordance with their inner sense of self." Margo challenged feminists to accept "the truly radical" answer to the question of what makes women women. She called for self-determined gender. "We are women," she said, "because we have female gender identities, regardless of either our genitals or our adherence or nonadherence to sex roles; in short, we are women because we *feel* ourselves to be women in our own terms."[17]

The tentative coalitions of feminists and transgendered activists fractured, and the potential for a joint movement challenging the dominant norms of sex, gender, and sexuality did not reappear until the 1990s. Even then the battles continued. From 1991 on, there were bitter confrontations at the Michigan Womyn's Music Festival (MWMF), an annual lesbian-feminist event, attended by several thousand women. After a festival security guard expelled a transsexual woman in 1991, the MWMF instituted a formal policy, announcing that only "womyn-born-womyn," or those born with female bodies, could attend the women-only event. Year after year a handful of transsexual women and their allies came to the festival, and each year the festival organizers, with vocal backing from their supporters, announced policies to exclude them. "The Festival is womyn's space," wrote Lisa Vogel, one of the MWMF producers, in 1999. "We also define that further as . . .

a place for people who were born and have lived their entire life experience as female."[18] In contrast, the transsexual activists, like Margo in 1975, called for self-definition and rejected the biological framework in which the sex assigned at birth determined who counted as a woman. By the end of the 1990s the transsexual activists had gained more allies at the MWMF, and despite the standing policy, the festival organizers no longer attempted to expel them.[19] But the boundaries of sex and gender—who qualified as a woman and who qualified as a man—still divided the women's movement.

*T*he doctors, too, came under attack. From the left, feminists and gay liberationists challenged the doctors' vision of sex, gender, and sexuality and disparaged the liberal doctors for failing to take more radical stands. From the right, other doctors disputed the merits of sex-reassignment surgery and denounced the liberal doctors for their endorsement of unorthodox medical practice. Confronting a two-flanked attack, the doctors and researchers lost their earlier optimism. They continued to work through HBIGDA, but they could not control either the theories of sex and gender or the practice of medicine.

The rise, or revitalization, of feminist ideologies launched a new phase in the reconceptualization of sex. In the 1970s a growing number of feminist scholars, with varying visions of feminism, took up the task of studying sex, gender, and sexuality. For the most part, feminists emphasized the social construction of gender and separated it from sex. They not only severed masculine and feminine behavior from their traditional moorings in biological sex but also questioned their utility. One study asked: "Are sex roles necessary—for individuals? for a society? Why?"[20] Some of the feminist scholars drew directly on the work of John Money, Robert Stoller, and Richard Green and on the understandings of gender formulated in studies of transsexuality.

In *Gender: An Ethnomethodological Approach,* published in 1978, Suzanne Kessler and Wendy McKenna accepted and built on the mid-twentieth-century research that focused on the construction of gender, but they disparaged the way the doctors and scientists perpetuated gender stereotypes and wrote them into science. They focused on "gender attribution," on how people engage in the "everyday process" of distinguishing women from men. On the street, Kessler and McKenna argued, people do not see chromosomes, hormones, reproductive capacities, and genitals as they routinely assign a sex to any passerby. People, they said, make gender attributions from a host of other socially constructed signs, based primarily on appearance and behavior. Kessler and McKenna showed how transsexuals' deliberate management of gender could "illuminate . . . the day-to-day social construction of gender by all persons." How does anyone appear as a woman or a man? Transsexuals, who worked more consciously to convince viewers of their preferred gender status, served as a case study for a universal issue. Kessler and McKenna reviewed the earlier literature and took it one step further. They not only distinguished gender from biological sex, as did Money, Stoller, and others; they also claimed that the social construction of gender led to the binary view of biological sex. Biology was not "the ultimate truth" of gender. "Scientists," they wrote, "construct dimorphism where there is continuity. Hormones, behavior, physical characteristics, developmental processes, chromosomes, psychological qualities have all been fitted into gender dichotomous categories." Science thus "justifies . . . the already existing knowledge that a person is either a woman or a man." Kessler and McKenna thus asserted the primacy of gender in defining the very categories of female and male, and in a modified form they returned, without seeming to know it, to an early twentieth-century model of biological sex as a continuum.[21]

In the 1970s and 1980s most feminists did not pay such close attention to the work of the researchers who studied transsexuality, and most accepted the categories of female and male as self-evident. But feminists increasingly borrowed the language of gender and distinguished gender from biological sex and also from sexual desire. The predominant feminist vision downplayed biological sex differences and depicted the behaviors and attitudes associated with gender as damaging stereotypes that subordinated women. In the mid-1970s, however, some "cultural feminists," to use Alice Echols' label, backed away from the model that cast gender as socially constructed. They suggested or stated that certain traits associated with gender reflected biological sex differences. They tended to valorize women (and "women's culture") as inherently nurturant, creative, and cooperative, and to discount men as inherently violent, destructive, and invasive.[22]

In *The Transsexual Empire,* Janice Raymond, like many cultural feminists, vacillated between the two visions (gender as socially constructed and gender as reflecting biological sex differences) and tried to combine them. She hit as hard at the doctors as she did at transsexuals. In her critique of doctors, Raymond emphasized the social-constructionist half of her vision even while she accused the doctors of noxious male behavior, trying "to wrest from women the power inherent in female biology." Through transsexual surgery, Raymond argued, male doctors created stereotypically feminine women to "create their ultimate man-made woman." In the gender-identity clinics, doctors and scientists preserved their patriarchal power and reinforced and re-created gender stereotypes. Raymond dealt at greatest length with the writings of John Money. In Raymond's view, he gave too much credence to biological influences in the development of gender. That is, he did not sever gender from biological sex to the same extent feminists did. At the same time, Raymond found, Money gave too much power to "socialization" in creating an immutable gender identity. For Raymond, socialization did not create a permanent structure of gender; the women's movement could and did challenge the prevailing version of gender despite the socialization women had undergone in their youth. "One of the primary tenets of the women's movement," Raymond wrote, "has been that so-called gender identity differences are not natural or immutable. And, as such, they are amenable to change." (Here Raymond seems to have confused gender identity, the psychological sense of a sexed self, with gender roles, the social norms for men's and women's behavior. The women's movement rarely questioned women's gender identity—their sense that they were women—but did question the naturalness and the immutability of the stereotyped gender roles that routinely constrained women.) While Money called for "flexibility within the range of stereotypes," Raymond called for their elimination.[23]

Raymond's *Transsexual Empire* represented a broader critique of gender-identity clinics undertaken by feminists, gays, and their allies.

More generally, the feminist and gay liberation movements put the doctors and scientists on the defensive. They challenged the doctors' self-image as liberal mavericks and portrayed them instead as conservatives who undermined "the movement to eradicate sex-role stereotyping and oppression."[24] The doctors at UCLA came under the greatest fire, especially George Rekers, who had taken over the childhood gender program earlier run by Richard Green. The UCLA program aimed to prevent transsexuality and homosexuality by training feminine boys to behave in masculine ways. Rekers took a more heavy-handed, conservative approach than Green, insisting on behavior modification and stigmatizing homosexuality in ways that Green renounced.[25] In 1975 a group called Coalition against the Dehumanization to Children demanded that the program end. The "so-called 'normal masculine role behavior,'" its statement read, "is nothing more than the outdated stereotype of the dominant, competitive, violence-prone males, who are oppressors of women, gays and all peoples." In an exposé of the UCLA program published in *Rolling Stone,* science writer David M. Rorvik acknowledged the "liberal lip service" the doctors paid to social change, but then asked: "How will society ever change if accommodating psycho-technologists keep changing *us* to conform to society?" He questioned a program that "cleansed" boys of "offending feminine traits."[26] The new critique condemned the doctors and scientists who accepted and reinforced traditional norms of gender and sexuality.

The critique of gender-identity clinics arose as part of a wider cultural challenge to the medical profession. In the early 1970s various critics questioned the authority of doctors and protested the quality of medical care in the United States. To the radical critics, psychiatrists in particular helped "label as 'deviant' people who have 'the right to be different.'"[27] As part of that larger challenge, the gay liberation movement cast homosexuality as valuable variation, not as mental illness, and condemned the doctors who portrayed homosexuality as a disease and attempted to cure or eliminate it. In 1978 another critique of the UCLA program called it "the most insidious attempt to stamp out the development of gay identity in young children."[28] Meanwhile, the more liberal doctors like Richard Green defensively distanced themselves both from the more conservative doctors like Rekers and from their own earlier adherence to more rigid gender and sexual stereotypes.[29]

Clearly, the liberal vision had not wholly prevailed. The liberal doctors and scientists were no longer the cutting-edge theorists of sex, gender, and sexuality. Others either had taken their work as a springboard from which to launch a more radical critique of social and scientific norms or had used the doctors' and researchers' words against them to illustrate the underlying sexist or antigay assumptions. From inside the medical profession, too, the doctors found themselves embattled. The founding of the university-based clinics had inspired sporadic opposition among some doctors who considered sex-change surgery beyond the pale of acceptable medicine. The psychoanalysts in particular renewed their attack.

In the late 1960s and afterward, they objected once again to transsexual surgery. In 1967, for example, psychiatrist Joost A. M. Meerloo presented transsexuals as "borderline psychotics" with "a deep-seated depression and a psychotic denial of self" and asked: "Do we have to collaborate with the sexual delusions of our patients?" In 1969 Charles W. Socarides fired another volley in his longstanding opposition to transsexual surgery. He rejected any redefinition of sex: all humans were either male or female, "determined genetically at the moment of conception." For Socarides, surgery involved "mutilative and potentially harmful procedures" that would "add to the deep conflicts already present."[30]

From the late 1960s on, rumors repeatedly surfaced of trouble within the Johns Hopkins Gender Identity Clinic. By 1967 Robert Stoller had heard of "a battle raging between the Department of Psychiatry and some members of the team that does the transformation procedures." By the mid-1970s the dissent had taken public form. Jon K. Meyer, a psychoanalyst at Hopkins, questioned the long-term benefits of surgery. In a 1974 article coauthored with John E. Hoopes, Meyer wrote: "Most of the patients continue to be emotionally and socially much the same as they were in the preoperative phase." Surgery, they concluded, "seems to temporarily palliate an unfortunate emotional state, rather than really cure the problem." Other doctors followed Meyer and Hoopes's lead. Robert Stoller reiterated his long-standing skepticism about transsexual surgery. Like Meyer, he wondered about the long-term benefits to patients, and he criticized his colleagues for their gung-ho attitude toward surgery. At a 1975 symposium at the American Medical Association, Stoller went on the offensive. "The level of discourse on transsexualism stinks," he said. "It's a scandal." At the same symposium, Lionel Ovesey, a psychiatrist at Columbia, agreed "wholeheartedly with Dr. Stoller's assessment." A year and a half later, a third panelist at the 1975 symposium, Charles Ihlenfeld, Harry Benjamin's former partner, decided to stop treating transsexuals. "We are trying to treat superficially," he said, "something that is much deeper."[31]

Much of the criticism focused on follow-up studies or the lack thereof. Although the follow-up studies that existed indicated that only a tiny minority of patients regretted their surgeries, they did not offer enough convincing data for the skeptics. In 1977 Jon Meyer presented his own follow-up study to the American Psychiatric Association. Two years later, with coauthor Donna J. Reter, he published his findings in the *Archives of General Psychiatry*. Using patients who had sought surgery at the Johns Hopkins Gender Identity Clinic, Meyer and Reter compared those who had undergone surgery with those who had not. As in earlier follow-up studies, they did not find that patients regretted sex reassignment, although one FTM regretted phalloplasty and its complications. They also learned that most of the unoperated patients either managed to obtain surgery after the follow-up study began or continued to seek it. Their study thus indicated an ongoing desire for surgery and a lack of regret afterward. But what Meyer and Reter found most striking was the "objective" measurement of "adjustment." The group of patients who had had surgery before the study began did not score any higher than those who remained unoperated at the end of the study. To assess adjustment objectively, Meyer and Reter assigned each subject a score. They added points for improvements in job level and "gender-appropriate" marriage or cohabitation, by which they referred to an MTF who "live[d] with, or marrie[d], a man as a female" or by implication an FTM who lived with or married a woman as a male, and they subtracted points for arrests or jail sentences, psychiatric treatment, decline in job level, and "nongender-appropriate" cohabitation or marriage. The scoring suggested that Meyer and Reter themselves valued upward mobility, heterosexuality, and patients who avoided asking for psychiatric help. But that was not the point they hoped to make. "Sex reassignment surgery," they concluded, "confers no objective advantage in terms of social rehabilitation." They conceded, however, that it remained "subjectively satisfying" to patients who had gone through an organized gender-identity program.[32]

With the Meyer and Reter study, the Johns Hopkins Gender Identity Clinic imploded. In October 1979 Meyer called a press conference to publicize his study and announced at the same time that Hopkins would no longer perform sex-reassignment surgery. Meyer and Money, who had helped found the clinic, had a history of longstanding mutual hostility, both "personal and professional." Meyer held his press conference when Money was out of the country. The *New York Times* headline announced: "Benefits of Transsexual Surgery Disputed as Leading Hospital Halts the Procedure."[33] The medical center had other reasons for terminating its transsexual surgery program. The surgeons involved had taken jobs elsewhere, and some of its officials had long found the program embarrassing. The hospital had decided at least six months earlier to change its policies permitting sex-reassignment surgery, but it had made no public announcement. Meyer's press conference, though, seemed to suggest that his study had led to the policy change.

Meyer took the opportunity to publicize his objections to transsexual operations. "My personal feeling," he told reporters, "is that surgery is not a proper treatment for a psychiatric disorder, and it's clear to me that these patients have severe psychological problems that don't go away following surgery." He referred explicitly to "one case," probably that of Reed Erickson, "in which a woman required hospitalization for drug dependency and suicidal intentions after being changed to a man." (During his psychotic episode Erickson had stayed for ten days in Johns Hopkins' psychiatric clinic, treated for "psychosis with drug intoxication.")[34] Other researchers came forward immediately to criticize Meyer's study and defend transsexual surgery, at least when performed under strict guidelines in major medical centers.[35]

Nonetheless, the doctors who endorsed transsexual surgery came under renewed public scrutiny. *Psychology Today,* for example, published a lengthy article by Richard M. Restak, a neurologist trained in psychiatry, titled "The Sex-Change Conspiracy." The author cited Meyer's study (ignoring Reter's coauthorship) and concluded: "Unless reliable research to the contrary appears . . . it seems clear that the surgery is a drastic nonsolution to the problem and should be sharply restricted." The article also noted another study, published in the same issue of the *Archives of General Psychiatry* in which Meyer and Reter's piece appeared, that claimed that psychotherapy had relieved three transsexuals of their desires for surgery. "Psychological cures" now seemed possible. In a seesaw version of disciplinary ascendancy, as psychologists and psychiatrists rose, surgeons fell into disrepute. In an obvious reference to lobotomy, Restak compared transsexual surgery to the discredited "crude 'ice-pick' psychosurgical operations" of the 1940s and 1950s and noted the economic motives of the surgeons who performed transsexual operations. He also wondered in print about their mental state. "Is there something," he asked, "in the personality and motivations of those who perform these operations that disposes them to go along with the patient's desire, despite the problems it raises?" In *Psychology Today,* it looked as if the surgeons, too, could benefit from therapy.[36]

The Johns Hopkins clinic had never treated many transsexuals, and Stanford, which sponsored the largest such program, continued to offer sex-reassignment surgery. Still, the demise of the Hopkins program, and the publicity surrounding its fall, had an impact. It led to the termination of "a number of small transsexual clinics," and it may have halted the entry of other university medical centers into transsexual surgery. It also provided ammunition for insurance companies that hoped to avoid offering coverage for sex-change operations. "Insurance carriers and state legislators," one surgeon complained, were "just beginning to recognize that these troubled people have a legitimate problem." Now they were "using this announcement to justify considering transsexuals freaks and frauds again."[37] The barrage of negative publicity also diminished the cultural clout of the doctors who endorsed transsexual surgery. As some supporters of surgery noted, "We sense a growing fear of transsexualism which has found a voice in the public press."[38]

More generally, the doctors who supported surgery watched their influence wane in the 1980s. In the 1970s their expert testimony had figured prominently in the decisions of a few judges who ruled in favor of transsexuals. In the 1980s, as liberalism more generally went into decline, the liberal doctors had less impact on the courts. In 1987, for example, the Ohio Probate Court refused to allow a postoperative MTF to change the sex on her birth certificate or secure a license to marry a man. If she was born with male "physical characteristics" and still had "male chromosomes," she counted legally as male. The liberals' definition of legal sex, in which gender identity and altered genitals trumped both chromosomes and the genitals seen at birth, did not persuade the judge, even though a New Jersey court, in *M. T. v. J. T.* (1976), had provided such a precedent. The judge directly rejected the testimony of a local doctor as well as the "very liberal posture" of the New Jersey court.[39] Several federal courts also rejected the liberal doctors' vision with decisions that refused to protect transsexuals from employment discrimination. Richard Green served as an expert witness in one precedent-setting case, *Ulane v. Eastern Airlines,* but the U.S. Court of Appeals reversed the lower court decision that had relied on his and other doctors' testimony and their definition of sex. The liberal influence in the courts dwindled in the 1980s and did not expand again until the 1990s.[40]

The new developments clearly grew out of the old, but to a certain extent they also ended an era. The rise of feminism and gay liberation changed the terms of the debates on sex, gender, and sexuality, and the demise of the program at Johns Hopkins demonstrated the fragility of the university-based research clinics that had for a decade dominated the medical practice of transsexual surgery. Other trends accelerated the shift away from the cohorts of doctors, activists, and journalists who had addressed transsexuality in the 1950s and 1960s and toward new groups of doctors and activists and new forms of mass media.

No trend had greater impact than the privatization of medical treatment. In the 1970s and afterward, a number of doctors in private practice discovered that transsexual surgery could provide a sizable income. After the Johns Hopkins clinic and other such university-based programs had legitimated transsexual surgery, more private psychologists, psychiatrists, and physicians began to treat transsexual patients. By the end of the decade transsexuality had grown, according to one report, to "a $10-million-a-year business," and private doctors constituted the fastest-growing sector on the supply side of the market.[41] While Richard Green, John Money, and others fended off their critics, private practitioners used their skills to attract a national niche market to new local centers for sex-change surgery.

In San Francisco and Los Angeles, Dr. John Ronald Brown pioneered the trend. From the late 1960s on, he offered cut-rate surgery to MTFs (and at least one FTM) who did not have the time, money, or luck to push their way into the university-based gender-identity programs or find surgeons outside the United States. Brown worked with and hired MTFs who helped him with his practice. Angela Douglas, on whom Brown operated in 1977, saw him as a friend of transsexuals who "fed, housed, paid and helped hundreds, and gave free or nearly free surgery to at least two hundred of us." She paid about six hundred dollars, she said, for surgery that would have cost ten times as much elsewhere.[42] Brown claimed to have developed techniques that preserved sexual feeling by using "the glans penis . . . to create the clitoris." In the years before the legalization of abortion, some doctors and midwives had profitable underground practices, of varying quality, for desperate women who wanted to end their pregnancies. In a similar vein, Brown offered transsexual surgery on demand to people desperate to change their sex. He admitted that "he operated on anyone who came along, no questions asked, and the only qualification was that they have the money."[43]

Brown sometimes presented himself as the champion of transsexuals, but he also won a well-earned reputation as the back-alley butcher of transsexual surgery. Some MTFs appreciated his work; others expressed horror. Donna Colvin, a San Francisco MTF who worked for Brown, remembered him as a drug-dependent mercenary. Brown, she recalled, shot up Valium before performing surgery. He performed operations under unsanitary conditions on kitchen tables and in hotel rooms. He purposely damaged the vagina of an MTF who angered him, and he left an FTM with raw gaping wounds after a botched mastectomy. He let his business partner, Andrew James Spence, who was not a doctor, perform surgery. By the end of the 1970s, the San Francisco press had reported on the death of one of his patients and on lawsuits filed by another. In 1977 Brown lost his license to practice medicine in California. Over the next few years he lost his license repeatedly—in Hawaii, Alaska, and St. Lucia—and eventually started anew in Tijuana, where he performed cosmetic surgeries as well as transsexual operations. His career ended in 1998 after the death of a seventy-nine-year-old man who had hired Brown to amputate his leg to satisfy a sexual fetish. Before he landed in prison, convicted of murder, Brown had performed, by his own count, six hundred MTF surgeries.[44]

By the late 1970s reputable doctors had followed Brown's lead. In the 1970s Stanley Biber turned the tiny town of Trinidad, Colorado, into the "Sex-Change Surgery 'Capital'" of the United States, much as Georges Burou had created an international center for MTF surgery in Casablanca in the 1960s. By 1976 he had performed more than 100 sex-change operations at Mount San Rafael Hospital. Most of his patients, who included a few FTMs as well as MTFs, came from out of state. "There's an underground network," Biber told a reporter, "and the word's just gotten around that we have the facilities here to do the surgery [and] we don't rip anybody off." For a while Biber almost cornered the market. In the 1980s, according to one source, "about two-thirds of the nation's sex-change surgeries were done at Mount San Rafael." By the end of the 1990s Biber, still in business, had performed 3,800 sex-change operations. Eugene Schrang, another surgeon who specializes in transsexual surgery, acknowledged that Biber "probably has done more operations than anyone else in the field."[45] But by the end of the century other doctors had replaced Biber as the surgeon most recommended by transsexuals themselves. In the 1990s Toby Meltzer, in Portland, Oregon, won praise from both FTMs and MTFs for his technical skills and caring manner. Schrang, who works in

Neenah, Wisconsin, had earned a reputation for crafting "gorgeous" genitals for MTFs.[46]

HBIGDA recognized the rise of private practitioners and tried to guide their professional behavior. Under its original standards of care, private endocrinologists and surgeons could not offer treatment on demand. Psychologists and psychiatrists (and, in later versions, other clinicians) were to recommend medical treatment, and they were to have seen their clients for several months before making such recommendations. MTFs were to live as women and FTMs as men for at least a year before they could undergo surgery. If they adhered to these guidelines, private practitioners could protect their professional standing and distinguish themselves from "chop shop" doctors like John Brown.

The privatization of transsexual surgery opened the gates, at least slightly, allowing more transsexuals to find doctors willing to offer surgical treatment. Those who had the money could usually find medical treatment in the United States, and they had a wider range of options. In the medical market, the consumers no longer had to settle for any surgeon they could find. If they had the funds, they could choose from among a handful of specialists.

Some of the private psychologists and psychiatrists recommended surgery for individuals who would not have made it through the more highly selective university research and treatment programs. Louis G. Sullivan, for example, identified openly as a gay FTM, who wanted to have sex as a man with men. He befriended drag queens, frequented gay male bars, dressed part-time as a man, and performed oral sex on gay men. Because he failed to fit the classic transsexual model, in which FTMs had sex with women, he found medical treatment only through private practitioners. In 1979 his therapist, a member of HBIGDA, referred him to a physician who began testosterone injections, and in 1980 he found a surgeon who performed a bilateral mastectomy. In the same year the Gender Dysphoria Program at Stanford rejected him for phalloplasty because his personal history did not fit the image, as the surgeon's administrative assistant explained, "of persons who, in our program, have made successful adjustments with gender reorientation." In the 1980s transsexuals turned increasingly to private practitioners. "More transsexuals who presented atypical histories or desires," historian Susan Stryker notes, "were able to get what they wanted for themselves through the personal relationships they established with sympathetic individual psychotherapists."[47] The original cohort of doctors who had pushed for sex-change surgery no longer controlled the field.

Just as a new group of doctors entered the field, so a new group of activists filled the vacuum left by the decline of the early advocacy organizations. In the mid-1970s a few transsexuals began to push locally for changes in public policy. In Minneapolis, Diana Slyter worked with gay activists to have transsexuals included in an antidiscrimination civil rights ordinance, passed in 1974, and a few years later, Margaret Deirdre O'Hartigan successfully sued the state of Minnesota to have it pay for her sex-reassignment surgery. In California, Joanna Clark lobbied successfully for a state law to allow transsexuals to change the name and sex on their birth certificates. The bill went into effect on January 1, 1978. Clark also helped defeat a bill in the California state senate that would have prohibited the use of public (Medi-Cal) funds to pay for sex-reassignment surgery. By the end of the 1970s Clark had set her sights at the federal level. She began to campaign, this time without success, to add "sexual orientation" and "sexual status" to Title VII of the Civil Rights Act of 1964. The change would have expanded federal guidelines prohibiting employment discrimination to include gays and transsexuals.[48]

In this new phase of activism, FTMs emerged from the shadows of transsexuality. In the early 1970s the doctors, especially those at Stanford, began to pay more attention to FTMs and to perform more FTM surgeries. After an interdisciplinary symposium on transsexualism, held at Stanford in 1973, one participant noted it was "the first time in a major conference" that "a significant amount of time was given to the female transexual."[49] Perhaps the feminist movement had its impact here as well. The neglect of female-to-male transsexuals no longer seemed as tenable in a world in which women demanded that doctors attend to the medical needs of the female body as well as the male. In any case, by the early to mid-1970s, a few FTMs began to work more publicly with professional caregivers, and the mainstream media began to take note of FTMs. In 1973, for example, *Good Housekeeping* magazine published an article titled "My Daughter Changed Sex," and in 1974, on NBC's *Tomorrow* talk show, Tom Snyder interviewed Norman Fisk and Richard Green and also Lee and Scott, two FTMs who had undergone surgery at Stanford. The following year, *Cosmopolitan* magazine featured Lee and Scott in an article titled "Women Who Dare to Become Men." Lee worked one day a week as a peer counselor at the Stanford clinic, and he and his wife had turned their home "into a halfway house for some thirty transsexual patients in the final stages of gender change."[50] The publicity continued as a handful of other FTMs went public with their surgery. In 1976 Steve Dain, a female-to-male high school teacher, made front-page news in the San Francisco Bay area. After his surgery at Stanford he decided not to hide, relocate, or change his job. The press showed special interest in his story after the school superintendent had him arrested when he came back to work as a man. (Eventually Dain sued and won.) The next year Mario Martino published his autobiography, *Emergence,* the first book-length account of the life of an FTM transsexual.[51]

As FTMs came into the public eye, a few began to assert their presence in activist circles. One of the first was Jude Patton, who had undergone surgery at Stanford in the early 1970s. In February 1976 Patton began to edit *Renaissance Newsletter,* a publication he started for transsexuals, and later that year he joined three other transsexuals, including Joanna Clark, to found Renaissance: Gender Identity Services, in Santa Ana, California, an organization that engaged in advocacy, community education, and medical referrals. While Clark focused her efforts on lobbying, Patton lectured extensively to college students and medical professionals. In 1977 alone he reported 160 speaking engagements.[52] He also worked with HBIGDA as a consumer advocate in the professionals' organization. In its first years he served as the first and only transsexual member of its board. Eventually, in the 1980s, Patton and Clark started J2CP Information Services (named for themselves, the two J's—Jude and Joanna—and their last names Clark and Patton), an organization that inherited the educational work of the Janus Information Facility, which had taken over the job from the Erickson Educational Foundation.

In the 1970s and 1980s transgendered people formed local peer support groups in cities across the nation, and at the same time private psychotherapists and social workers offered "gender identity services" in major cities, including San Francisco, Seattle, Chicago, and Boston. But almost all the groups and services still catered primarily to MTFs. In 1976, in his private journals, Louis Sullivan noted, "there's just so much I can't say in a M-F group."[53] At the end of the 1970s Sullivan started to work at the Janus Information Facility as its first FTM peer counselor. In 1980 Sullivan published a booklet, *Information for the Female to Male Crossdresser and Transsexual,* distributed by JIF, which became the classic guide, still used today, on how to live as a man. Sullivan cultivated connections with other FTMs and soon found himself at the center of new FTM networks, locally in the San Francisco Bay area and, through correspondence, nationally and internationally as well. In 1986 Sullivan helped organize a new local support group called FTM, which held "get-togethers" in the Bay area, where FTMs could "meet and learn from others who understand." In 1987 he began to edit a newsletter, also titled *FTM.* After Sullivan died of AIDS in 1991, Jamison Green took over the newsletter and helped build the group into FTM International, the largest FTM organization in the United States and perhaps the world.[54]

The rising visibility of FTMs provided the social setting in which more transgendered FTMs decided to pursue transsexual surgery. Once they could read about, see, meet, and talk to postoperative FTMs, surgery came to seem a more realistic option and a more attractive goal. Louis Sullivan, for example, pursued surgery seriously only after he read about and then corresponded with Steve Dain, and Sullivan in turn worked with researchers to provide "some kind of documentation" of his life as a gay man so that other gay FTMs would not experience his own earlier sense of isolation.[55] In the 1950s and 1960s the doctors who studied transsexuality routinely observed that MTFs greatly outnumbered FTMs, but by the early 1980s they noticed that the ratio had shifted. More and more FTMs showed up at the doctors' doors requesting medical treatment. In Cleveland, at the Case Western Reserve University Gender Identity Clinic, psychoanalyst Leslie Lothstein, who wrote the first scholarly book on FTMs, noted "a dramatic change in our intake, with women [FTMs] accounting for approximately half of the sex change applicants." "Women," he concluded, "are viewing sex change as a viable option."[56]

In the 1970s and afterward, mainstream newspapers and magazines continued to feature stories on transsexuals, and they tended to focus, as they had earlier, on a handful of "stars," generally white, middle- or upper-class MTFs who had some other claim to celebrity status. In the 1970s the transsexual "stars" who attracted the most mainstream media notice were the British author Jan Morris and the American tennis player Renée Richards. In the 1950s Morris, then known as James, had won acclaim as the journalist who had joined and reported on the first British expedition to ascend Mt. Everest. After her sex-change surgery she wrote a lyrical autobiography, *Conundrum,* published in 1974, that won positive reviews in *Time, Newsweek, Harper's,* and other mainstream publications. Richards gained center stage when she fought for and won the right to play professional tennis as a woman. To a certain extent, Morris and Richards replaced Christine Jorgensen as the most touted transsexuals of their day. Richards received sackfuls of mail, "probably forty thousand letters," including letters "from blacks, convicts, Chicanos, hippies, homosexuals, people with physical handicaps and, of course, transsexuals." The vast majority of letter writers, she reported, asked her "to stand up for your rights and, in so doing, stand up for the rights of the world's downtrodden."[57] Once again, the popular culture publicized transsexuality, and once again, readers responded.

Transsexuality still sold, and in the 1970s additional mass-media industries started to cash in. From 1970 on, transsexual characters, especially MTFs, began to appear in feature-length films. In the 1960s "sexploitation" films made nudity, sexual situations, and simulated sex acts routine Hollywood fare.[58] As explicit sex shifted from the pornographic margins to the center of movie production, transsexuality on the screen simultaneously moved from taboo to acceptable. After *The Christine Jorgensen Story* and *Myra Breckinridge* debuted in 1970, transsexuality appeared sporadically in other movies. In 1972 a British film, *I Want What I Want,* drawn from a British novel of the same name, told the story of an MTF, played by Anne Heywood, who longed to change sex. The film avoided the mawkish tedium of *The Christine Jorgensen Story* and the arch satire of *Myra Breckinridge*.[59] In 1975 *Dog Day Afternoon*, based on a true story, won more mainstream attention, including an Academy Award for best original screenplay. Al Pacino starred as an anxious bank robber who stole in order to fund the surgery of his MTF lover.

In the 1980s a handful of other films featured transsexuality. Lee Grant directed and narrated the documentary film *What Sex Am I?* (1984), which provided a sympathetic view of transvestites and transsexuals; and Vanessa Redgrave starred in *Second Serve* (1986), a film based on the autobiography of Renée Richards. A few other mainstream films, such as *Come Back to the Five and Dime, Jimmy Dean Jimmy Dean* (1982), *The World According to Garp* (1982), and *Kiss of the Spider Woman* (1985), had transsexual subthemes. But it was not until the 1990s that transsexual and other transgendered characters appeared repeatedly on the big screen as major box-office draws. From *Paris Is Burning* (1990) to *Boys Don't Cry* (1999), various films appealed successfully to the growing public fascination with gender transgression.

In the 1970s and 1980s transsexuals found another forum for public outreach. In the 1950s television had for the most part barred Christine Jorgensen, whose story lay beyond the pale of family entertainment. From the 1960s on, though, radio and television talk shows had occasionally used transsexuals, especially Jorgensen, to bring in listeners and viewers. In the 1970s television producers took a new and broader interest. In 1975 the CBS drama series *Medical Center* ran a two-part episode on "a troubled doctor who suffered in his need for the sex reassignment operation." In the same year, *NBC News* included segments on transsexuality in its reports on science.[60] The rise of tabloid talk shows, with audience interaction, changed both the quantity and quality of transsexuals' television appearances. The early tabloid shows, especially Phil Donahue's, focused on activists and other public figures. In 1976, for example, Jude Patton and Deborah Hartin appeared on *Donahue,* and in 1977 Steve Dain and Christine Jorgensen appeared in a show with Geraldo Rivera.[61]

In the 1980s and 1990s the tabloid television genre descended the cultural ladder with new shows geared to younger, rowdier, less-educated audiences. The new shows showed less concern for middle-class proprieties and more interest in the outrageous. This new breed of shows, one commentator noticed, "had an almost inexhaustible appetite for portraying and discussing the sexually ambiguous." They no longer needed the discourse of science to legitimate public discussion of transsexuality. They elevated "personal experience" and gave transsexuals "a chance to break the monopoly on 'truth'" held by scientific authorities. Within the limits of an orchestrated program, transsexuals could speak in their own voices. They were the experts on themselves. They spoke on national television, and they had at least a passing chance at bringing their own stories, for a minute or two, to the millions of viewers who watched them.[62]

In a sample of more than 160 tabloid shows on sexual nonconformity, sociologist Joshua Gamson included the transcripts of 30 shows specifically focused on transsexuals and counted 111 self-identified transsexuals among the talk show guests. The 30 shows, mostly from the 1990s, avoided political issues and instead centered most often on family conflicts or confessional testimonies. But sometimes they also raised the larger question of what constitutes female and male. On the talk show *Rolonda,* an FTM asked: "What makes a man a man and what makes a woman a woman? . . . We need to answer those things, all of us." Even Jerry Springer, the talk show host most reviled for pandering to the baser tastes of his audience, removed himself from the fray long enough to ponder the issues on the air. "Perhaps we'd like to think there are only two classifications: male and female," he said. "But the reality is . . . we are all simply degrees of one or the other: either mostly male or mostly female, mostly man, mostly woman." The talk shows avoided the finer points of academic theory, but they provided, as Gamson writes, "ground-level versions" of theories that questioned the boundaries of sex and emphasized the social construction of gender.[63]

*A*s new doctors, new activists, and new media presentations entered the field, the older generation—Christine Jorgensen, Harry Benjamin, and the other pioneers of American transsexuality—stepped to the sidelines. In the 1970s and 1980s they took on the role of elders who passed the torch to a younger generation. They could remember the first American surgeons who had performed sex-reassignment surgery, they could recollect their own earlier advocacy on behalf of transsexuals, and they could hear in the movies and tabloid talk shows the echoes of the sensational stories in the newspapers and magazines of the 1950s.

Harry Benjamin finally retired in the mid-1970s, and over the next decade he continued to meet with physicians and therapists who came to learn from him about his work with transsexuals. He worried, as Zelda Suplee remembered, that "he would be forgotten." She "maneuvered," as she put it, to have the Fourth International Gender Symposium on Gender Identity, held at Stanford in 1975, dedicated to him and a few years later to have the professional organization—the Harry Benjamin International Gender Dysphoria Association—named permanently in his honor.[64] For years Benjamin had injected himself with testosterone in an attempt to enhance his vitality. But testosterone could not stop the advance of age. In the 1980s Benjamin's vision deteriorated, and he became increasingly housebound. On August 24, 1986, he died in his sleep at the age of 101. He was survived by his wife, Gretchen. A few months later his friends and colleagues gathered in New York to pay him tribute. John Money recalled Benjamin's "lonely advocacy of a group of patients generally despised and ridiculed by the medical establishment," and Richard Green spoke of Benjamin's "compassion" and "his heroism in the face of scorn." "He treated me with respect," Renée Richards remembered, "as an equal, as a patient, as someone in need." Over a phone line, Christine Jorgensen, too, addressed the assemblage. "I could recommend Harry Benjamin," she remembered, "to all those thousands of people who contacted me . . . he was absolutely a godsend for me . . . an absolute gem."[65]

Like Benjamin, Jorgensen had gone into semiretirement in the 1970s, but she maintained a public presence through the decade. In the mid-1970s a story in the *New York Times Magazine* counted her—along with Dick Gregory, Ralph Nader, and Gloria Steinem—among the "superstars" invited to speak at public lecture series. She could have been, the report stated, "what the business crudely classifies as a 'freak show.'" But Jorgensen still had her charm, and the "audiences drawn by curiosity" became "convinced of her sincerity" and often gave her standing ovations.[66] In her lectures and interviews Jorgensen took the opportunity to advise youth on the social movements of her day. In the early 1970s she distanced herself from the women's movement. "I don't know very many women who aren't liberated," she said. "Men need liberation, too." But by the late 1970s and early 1980s she had taken to reading feminist literature and expressed greater sympathy for the feminist cause. She told a reporter she would "not tolerate male chauvinism," and she shied away from the stereotypes of gender. "It's hard to say," she said, "what a woman or man should be today . . . It's okay if a woman wants to stay home and be a housewife, but I feel she's really narrowing her life down."[67] In the late 1970s she also spoke out publicly for homosexual rights, and joined the Coalition for Human Rights in southern California to combat singer Anita Bryant's anti-homosexual campaign. She positioned herself as a moderate. "Don't be way out and weird," she warned activists. "Anyone who wants to be one of those is hindering the movement." In the early 1980s she got involved "with fund raising for AIDS."[68] Mostly, though, she continued to see herself as a spokesperson for transsexuals, and she continued to point out the lines dividing sex, gender, and sexuality. In the late 1970s she said she preferred the word *transgender* to *transsexual*. "Gender is different," she said, "than sexual preference. It doesn't have to do with bed partners, it has to do with identity." She befriended the MTF activist Joanna Clark and in the early 1980s spoke out publicly with Clark on behalf of transsexual rights.[69]

At home, out of the public eye, Jorgensen worked on her autobiographical writings, doted on her dogs, and, defying gender stereotype, puttered with the electrical wiring and plumbing, using household skills she had learned from her father. Friends, who knew her as "Chris," admired her warmth and her sense of humor. With her closest friends, though, she "like[d] to give orders," and she could get opinionated and argumentative, most notably after drinking. By her own admission, she drank copiously, especially whiskey and vodka, a sign perhaps that the pain in her life had taken its toll. "I play hard," she said in the mid-1980s, "I drink hard, I smoke hard. I do everything almost to excess." She liked to throw and attend parties, go out to res-

taurants and theaters, and regale her friends with stories about her famous acquaintances.[70]

And she plotted entrepreneurial ventures to supplement her dwindling income. She wanted to rerelease the movie version of her life, and
she sued United Artists, and lost, when the company downgraded the
film to late-night television reruns.[71] She planned to update her autobiography with a second, franker volume, and she also hoped to publish a
cookbook of Scandinavian recipes. She made plans to write a novel
based in Denmark during World War II and to market a line of "Tur-
bans by Christine."[72] In the late 1970s and early 1980s she briefly revived her nightclub act, which she opened with the song "I Enjoy Being a Girl" and closed with a Wonder Woman skit. (When Warner
Communications demanded she cease using the trademarked Wonder
Woman property, she changed the costume slightly and reveled in the
publicity.)[73] In the mid-1980s she returned to Denmark to appear in a
documentary film, *Paradise Is Not for Sale*, on transsexuality. She also
hoped to write a book on the "history of gender crossdressing," conduct an in-depth videotaped interview, "An Evening with Christine,"
and launch a musical version of her life story, in which she imagined a
song titled "What Is a Man, What Is a Woman," and also a comedy
number with the unlikely title "Sex and Gender."[74]

In 1986 Jorgensen discovered she had bladder cancer. As her condition deteriorated, she spent her days mostly at home in southern California. To the end, she loved publicity. "Let's hope I die," she report-
edly said, "on a slow news day." She died on May 3, 1989, at the age of
sixty-two. The newspapers and news magazines paid their final homage
with obituaries recounting her unusual life. The *New York Times*
printed a straightforward account, but *U.S. News & World Report*
chose to editorialize that "her life was filled with sadness." Jorgensen
would not have seen it that way. She had had her share of hardship, but
she had also led a life with friends, triumphs, and accomplishments, and
she had disliked it when other transsexuals portrayed themselves as
tragic victims who "can't expect to be happy in life." Jorgensen had always preferred to celebrate her life; in fact she had "asked that friends
and relatives remember her at a lavish party" in lieu of a funeral. Brenda
Lana Smith, a former Danish consul from Bermuda and an MTF who

lived with Jorgensen in her last months, threw the party Jorgensen had requested, "the bumper send-off," Smith remembered, "she'd be proud of and deserved." Around a hundred and fifty guests attended, including Richard Green, Jude Patton, and the actor John Hansen, who had played Jorgensen in the movie version of her life.[75]

*N*either Benjamin nor Jorgensen lived to see the transgender movement that emerged in force in the 1990s. Transsexual activists joined in coalitions with crossdressers, intersexed people, and others who crossed the boundaries of sex and gender. They formed new organizations ranging from the defiantly radical groups Transgender Nation and Transexual Menace to the concertedly professional American Educational Gender Information Service (AEGIS), which took over the informational services of J2CP in the early 1990s. The new activists pressured HBIGDA to revise its standards of care and include transsexuals in its deliberations, and they convinced major gay rights groups, such as the National Gay and Lesbian Task Force, to include the rights of transgendered people in their political efforts. They protested the violence and brutality—the shockingly regular assaults on and murders of transgendered people—and sought to include the rights of transsexuals and other transgendered people in antidiscrimination legislation. They put out an array of magazines and newsletters—*TransSisters: The Journal of Transsexual Feminism, TNT* or *Transsexual News Telegraph, Gender Euphoria,* the Canadian *gendertrash*—to build community and convey information. They held conferences that called for free expression of gender variance, and they used the Internet to organize and invite people otherwise isolated to seek information, join public protests, and enter freely into conversations with their peers from the privacy of their homes. The Internet opened new opportunities for global communication, international organization, and transnational protest.[76] In the year 2000 the roster of prominent organizations included the International Foundation for Gender Education (www.ifge.org), American Boyz (www.amboyz.org), FTM International (www.ftm-intl.org), Gender PAC (www.gpac.org), and It's Time, America! (www.tgender.net/ita).

The new movement also took up the longstanding task of redefining sex, gender, and sexuality. Sandy Stone helped launch a new transgender scholarship with her 1991 essay, "The *Empire* Strikes Back: A Posttranssexual Manifesto." Stone called for transsexuals to live openly as transsexuals, to refrain from hiding their pasts and subsuming their histories under the doctors' standard version of the transsexual life story. She challenged the "binary, oppositional mode of gender identification," and she pointed to the "myriad of alterities," the diversity and complexity of identities and desires.[77] A host of new books and articles by transsexuals soon followed, not only autobiographies, but also political and scholarly studies.

The definition of sex was (and is) still up for grabs, and transsexual activists and scholars appropriated and revised the definitions constructed over the course of the twentieth century. The new transsexual theorists disagreed openly with one another (and with the many transsexuals and nontranssexuals less concerned with theories of sex and gender). But as a group they tended to start with premises that early twentieth-century theorists had only begun to outline: that sex, gender, and sexuality represent analytically distinct categories, that the sex of the body does not determine either gender or sexual identity, that doctors can alter characteristics of bodily sex. Some disputed binary definitions of biological sex by adopting a newer version of the early twentieth-century concept of a spectrum of sexes, a vision of multiple sexes "from very male to very female, with countless variations in between." Others focused on gender identities, not rigid identities, but "identities in progress . . . distinct from the material body." Some saw in transsexuals an evolving core sense of self and others a postmodern "fluidity . . . a limitless number of genders, for any length of time, at any rate of change." Many combined the feminists' critique of the constraints of rigid gender dichotomies and the gay liberationists' goal of freedom of expression, and rendered healthy the variations that doctors had routinely cast as illness and disorder. "Transgender and transsexual," Jason Cromwell wrote, "are genders that exist outside the binary of two." And they distinguished the practice of transsexuality from the medical discourse that grouped case histories into categories for diagnosis and treatment. "Transsexuality," Susan Stryker noted, "is simultaneously an elaborately articulated medico-juridical discourse imposed on particular forms of deviant subjectivity, and a radical practice that promises to explode the dominant constructions of self and society."[78]

$\mathcal{T}$he rise of the transgender movement capped the century in which sex change first became a medical specialty and transsexuals first emerged as a visible social group. From the early twentieth-century experiments on changing the sex of animals to the liberationist movement of the 1990s, the topic of sex change had served as a key site for the definition and redefinition of sex in popular culture, science, medicine, law, and daily life. In a century when others had challenged the social categories and hierarchies of class, race, and gender, the people who hoped to change their sex had brought into question another fundamental category—biological sex itself—commonly understood as obvious and unchangeable. In the modern push for self-expression, they had taken the meanings of self-transformation and social mobility to a new level, and from the margins of society, they had grappled with the everyday ways in which unconventional individuals confounded and provoked the mainstream. In the process, they had engaged with doctors, scientists, reporters, lawyers, judges, feminists, and gay liberationists, among others. Together, these various groups had debated big questions of medical ethics, nature and nurture, self and society, and the scope of human rights. None of them could fix the definition of sex, which remains a topic of debate in medical journals, courtrooms, and television talk shows, and none of them could settle the question of the interconnections among sex, gender, and sexuality. Still, by the end of the twentieth century, the transgender activists could hope at least for a future in which the variations of sex and gender might no longer elicit stigma, ridicule, harassment, or assault.

The activists of the 1990s looked to the past as well as to the future. In 1993 some MTFs gathered to celebrate the fortieth anniversary of Christine Jorgensen's celebrity. Riki Ann Wilchins drew the connection between Jorgensen's lonely stand and the sense of community that had since evolved. "Community," she said, "is what we build here today, by coming together to claim our own, our history, and our Christine."

Jorgensen, she remembered, stood "all alone in God's own light in a way none of us have had to since, [and] made all of this and all of us possible."[79]

It seems only fitting that Jorgensen should be remembered by those who came after her. In the 1950s she shook the foundations of sex, gender, and sexuality. In a decade stereotyped as complacent, she inspired public and private debates on who qualified as female and male. She inaugurated a new era in which American doctors and journalists routinely used sex change to highlight the promise and pitfalls of science, to reconceive sex, and to distinguish sex from gender and sexuality. In the 1960s Jorgensen called herself "a minority of one."[80] She was not, she knew, alone, but she held the microphone and took the spotlight that singled her out as the sole stand-in and willing advocate for a larger group of people.

In all of this, Jorgensen could have been the exception that proved the rule, but instead she became the exception that undermined the rules. It could have been said, for example, that we are all distinctly male or female except for a few people like Christine Jorgensen; instead, transsexuals, doctors, and journalists argued repeatedly that no one is one hundred percent male or one hundred percent female. It could have been argued that sex cannot be changed; instead, various observers reconceived sex as the sum of constituent parts, some of which could be altered and some of which could not. It could have been claimed that gender is part of biological sex, except in the case of a handful of people including Jorgensen; instead, researchers debated the sources of gender and saw in transsexuality "an opportunity to study the whole problem of how human beings normally get their sense of being a male or a female."[81] It could have been stated (and sometimes it was) that Jorgensen was a gay crossdresser; instead, a prevailing view gradually emerged that transsexuality differed from homosexuality and transvestism. In sum, in the context of her day, with the concepts of sex, gender, and sexuality already in flux, Jorgensen showed her public how sex changed, a process that continues today.

ABBREVIATIONS

CJP	Christine Jorgensen Papers, Royal Danish Library, Copenhagen
GLBTHS	Gay, Lesbian, Bisexual, Transgender Historical Society of Northern California, San Francisco
HBC	Harry Benjamin Collection, KI
KI	The Kinsey Institute for Research in Sex, Gender, and Reproduction, Indiana University, Bloomington
LLC	Louise Lawrence Collection, KI
NYAM	New York Academy of Medicine, New York
ONE	ONE Institute and Archives: The International Gay and Lesbian Heritage Research Center, University of Southern California, Los Angeles
RSP	Robert J. Stoller Papers, Special Collections, University of California at Los Angeles
VPC	Virginia Prince Collection, Special Collections, Oviatt Library, California State University at Northridge

NOTES

INTRODUCTION

1. "Ex-GI Becomes Blonde Beauty," *New York Daily News*, December 1, 1952, 1; "Christine and the News," *Newsweek*, December 15, 1952, 64.

2. See, for example, John D'Emilio and Estelle B. Freedman, *Intimate Matters: A History of Sexuality in America*, 2d ed. (Chicago: University of Chicago Press, 1997); Paul Robinson, *The Modernization of Sex*, 2d ed. (Ithaca: Cornell University Press, 1989); Sharon R. Ullman, *Sex Seen: The Emergence of Modern Sexuality in America* (Berkeley: University of California Press, 1997); Jonathan Ned Katz, *The Invention of Heterosexuality* (New York: Dutton, 1995).

3. Magnus Hirschfeld, *Transvestites: The Erotic Drive to Cross Dress*, trans. Michael A. Lombardi-Nash (1910; reprint, Buffalo: Prometheus, 1991), 219, 226; Gregorio Marañon, *The Evolution of Sex and Intersexual Conditions* (London: George Allen and Unwin, 1932), 24.

4. Margaret Mead, *Male and Female: A Study of the Sexes in a Changing World* (New York: William Morrow, 1949); Alfred C. Kinsey, *Sexual Behavior in the Human Male* (Philadelphia: W. B. Saunders, 1948).

5. For some early examples, see Suzanne Kessler and Wendy McKenna, *Gender: An Ethnomethodological Approach* (New York: Wiley, 1978); Michel Foucault, *The History of Sexuality*, trans. Robert Hurley, vol. 1 (New York: Pantheon, 1978); Jeffrey Weeks, *Sex, Politics and Society: The Regulation of Sexuality since 1800* (London: Longman, 1981); Sherry B. Ortner and Harriet Whitehead, eds., *Sexual Meanings: The Cultural Construction of Gender and Sexuality* (Cambridge: Cambridge University Press, 1981); Gayle Rubin, "Thinking Sex: Notes for a Radical Theory of the Politics of Sexuality," in *Pleasure and Danger: Exploring Female Sexuality*, ed. Carole S. Vance (Boston: Routledge, 1984), 267–319. For important recent formulations, see, for example, Judith Butler, *Gender Trouble: Feminism and the Subversion of Identity* (New York: Routledge, 1990); Anne Fausto-Sterling, *Sexing the Body: Gender Politics and the Construction of Sexuality* (New York: Basic Books, 2000).

6. See Richard Green, "Mythological, Historical, and Cross-Cultural Aspects of Transsexualism," in *Transsexualism and Sex Reassignment*, ed. Richard Green and John Money (Baltimore: Johns Hopkins Press, 1969), 13–22; Vern L. Bullough, "Trans-

sexualism in History," *Archives of Sexual Behavior* 4:5 (1975), 561–571; Leslie Feinberg, *Transgender Warriors: Making History from Joan of Arc to RuPaul* (Boston: Beacon, 1996); Jason Cromwell, "Passing Women and Female-bodied Men: (Re)claiming FTM History," in *Reclaiming Gender: Transsexual Grammars at the Fin de Siècle,* ed. Kate More and Stephen Whittle (London: Cassell, 1999), 34–61.

7. A. Bakker, P. J. M. van Kesteren, L. J. G. Gooren, and P. D. Bezemer, "The Prevalence of Transsexualism in the Netherlands," *Acta Psychiatrica Scandinavica* 87 (1993), 237–238; John Cloud, "Trans across America," *Time,* July 20, 1998, 48.

8. See, for example, Gayle Rubin, "Of Catamites and Kings: Reflections on Butch, Gender, and Boundaries," in *The Persistent Desire: A Femme-Butch Reader,* ed. Joan Nestle (Boston: Alyson, 1992), 466–482.

9. Robert Salladay, "Conservatives Gear to Fight 'Drag Queen Bill,' Critical Vote on Gender Discrimination," *San Francisco Chronicle,* July 3, 2001, read online at www. sfgate.com.

10. Sander L. Gilman, *Making the Body Beautiful: A Cultural History of Aesthetic Surgery* (Princeton: Princeton University Press, 1999), 269; Bernice Hausman, *Changing Sex: Transsexualism, Technology, and the Idea of Gender* (Durham, N.C.: Duke University Press, 1995), 138; Dwight B. Billings and Thomas Urban, "The Socio-Medical Construction of Transsexualism: An Interpretation and Critique," *Social Problems* 29:3 (February 1982), 272.

11. Martine Rothblatt, *The Apartheid of Sex: A Manifesto on the Freedom of Gender* (New York: Crown, 1995), 18. To be fair to Rothblatt, she is writing here of transgender activists, among whom she includes transsexuals.

12. See, for example, Homi K. Bhabha, *The Location of Culture* (London: Routledge, 1994). For overviews of this literature, see Pnina Werbner and Tariq Madood, eds., *Debating Cultural Hybridity: Multicultural Identities and the Politics of Anti-Racism* (London: Zed, 1997); Susan Stanford Friedman, *Mappings: Feminism and the Cultural Geographies of Encounter* (Princeton: Princeton University Press, 1998), 82–93.

13. Julia Epstein and Kristina Straub, "Introduction: The Guarded Body," in *Body Guards: The Cultural Politics of Gender Ambiguity,* ed. Julia Epstein and Kristina Straub (New York: Routledge, 1991), 4. For an extended critique of gender theory that ignores the everyday lives of transgendered people, see Ki Namaste, "'Tragic Misreadings': Queer Theory's Erasure of Transgender Subjectivity," in *Queer Studies: A Lesbian, Gay, Bisexual, and Transgender Anthology,* ed. Brett Beemyn and Mickey Eliason (New York: New York University Press, 1996), 183–203.

14. Hausman, *Changing Sex,* 140.

1. SEX CHANGE

1. "Girl into Man," *Your Body,* May 1937, 605.

2. N. S. Yawger, "Transvestism and Other Cross-Sex Manifestations," *Journal of Nervous and Mental Disease* 92 (July–December 1940), 41.

3. This, in abbreviated form, is the common historical narrative found in the recent scientific and social-scientific literature. It appears repeatedly with minor variations and occasional acknowledgment of sporadic earlier cases of sex-reassignment surgery. See, for example, Bernice L. Hausman, *Changing Sex: Transsexualism, Technology, and the Idea of*

Gender (Durham: Duke University Press, 1995); Vern L. Bullough and Bonnie Bullough, *Cross Dressing, Sex, and Gender* (Philadelphia: University of Pennsylvania Press, 1993), 254–256.

4. On "passing," see Jonathan Katz, *Gay American History: Lesbians and Gay Men in the U.S.A.* (New York: Avon, 1976), 317–422; San Francisco Lesbian and Gay History Project, "'She Even Chewed Tobacco': A Pictorial Narrative of Passing Women in America," in *Hidden from History: Reclaiming the Gay and Lesbian Past,* ed. Martin Bauml Duberman, Martha Vicinus, and George Chauncey Jr. (New York: New American Library, 1989), 183–194; Louis Sullivan, *From Female to Male: The Life of Jack Bee Garland* (Boston: Alyson, 1990).

5. Eugen Steinach, *Sex and Life: Forty Years of Biological and Medical Experiments* (New York: Viking, 1940), 66; see also Harry Benjamin, "Eugen Steinach, 1861–1944: A Life of Research," *Scientific Monthly* 61 (1945), 427–442; *Sexual Anomalies and Perversions: A Summary of the Work of the Late Dr. Magnus Hirschfeld, Compiled as a Humble Memorial by His Pupils* (London: Francis Aldor, 1944), 172–177; Sigmund Freud, "Three Contributions to the Theory of Sex," in *The Basic Writings of Sigmund Freud,* ed. A. A. Brill (New York: Modern Library, 1938), 610. For some precursors to Steinach, see John Money, "The Genealogical Descent of Sexual Psychoneuroendocrinology from Sex and Health Theory: The Eighteenth to the Twentieth Centuries," *Psychoneuroendocrinology* 8:4 (1983), 391–393. For a general history of sex hormones, see Nelly Oudshoorn, *Beyond the Natural Body: An Archeology of Sex Hormones* (London: Routledge, 1994). For more on Steinach and his critics, see Anne Fausto-Sterling, *Sexing the Body: Gender Politics and the Construction of Sexuality* (New York: Basic Books, 2000), 158–169.

6. Steinach, *Sex and Life,* 74–79; Max Thorek, *The Human Testis* (Philadelphia: J. B. Lippincott, 1924), 267–268, 317–325. On early ovarian transplantation, see F. H. Martin, "Transplantation of Ovaries," *Surgery, Gynecology, and Obstetrics* 7 (1908), 7. The transplantations declined as scientists developed hormonal extracts and synthetic hormones in the 1920s and 1930s.

7. Earl Lind, *Autobiography of an Androgyne* (New York: Medico-Legal Journal, 1918), 196; see also p. xi.

8. J. Allen Gilbert, "Homo-Sexuality and Its Treatment," *Journal of Nervous and Mental Disease* 52:4 (October 1920), 302, 321. In Gilbert's article, Hart is referred to as "H." Jonathan Katz's sleuthing uncovered Hart's identity. See Katz, *Gay American History,* 419.

9. Max Marcuse, "Ein Fall von Geschlechtsumwandlungstrieb," *Zeitschrift für Psychotherapie und Medizinische Psychologie* 6 (1916), 176–193; Harry Benjamin, *The Transsexual Phenomenon* (New York: Julian, 1966), 252. On the early German surgeries, see Richard Mühsam, "Chirurgische Eingriffe bei Anomalien des Sexuallebens," *Die Therapie der Gegenwart* 67 (October 1926), 452–453, 455; see also Friedemann Pfäfflin, "Sex Reassignment, Harry Benjamin, and Some European Roots," presidential address, Fifteenth Harry Benjamin International Gender Dysphoria Symposium, Vancouver, 1997.

10. Magnus Hirschfeld, *Transvestites: The Erotic Drive to Cross Dress,* trans. Michael A. Lombardi-Nash (1910; reprint, Buffalo: Prometheus, 1991), 235.

11. Magnus Hirschfeld, "Die Intersexuelle Konstitution," *Jahrbuch für Sexuelle Zwischenstufen* 23 (1923), 15.

12. *Sexual Anomalies and Perversions,* 179, 218; see also 183. For a good recent overview of Hirschfeld's work, see James D. Steakley, *"Per Scientiam ad Justitiam:* Magnus Hirschfeld and the Sexual Politics of Innate Homosexuality," in *Science and Homosexualities,* ed. Vernon A. Rosario (New York: Routledge, 1997), 133–154; on Hirschfeld and Steinach, see Chandak Sengoopta, "Glandular Politics: Experimental Biology, Clinical Medicine, and Homosexual Emancipation in Fin-de-Siècle Central Europe," *Isis* 89:3 (September 1998), 445–473; for a request "to remove the testicle and replace it by a female ovary," see K. S. to Magnus Hirschfeld, October 5, 1920, Hirschfeld Scrapbook, 72, KI.

13. For the most detailed accounts of Richter, see Ellen Baekgaard's recollections in Preben Hertoft and Teit Ritzau, *Paradiset er ikke til salg: Trangen til at vaere begge koen* (Paradise is not for sale: The desire to be both sexes) ([no city] Denmark: Lindhardt og Ringhof, 1984), 79–81. See also Pierre Najac's firsthand account of Richter's last surgery in Janine Merlet, *Vénus et Mercure* (Paris: Editions de la Vie Moderne, 1931), 182–185; Felix Abraham, "Genitalumwandlung an Zwei Männlichen Transvestiten," *Zeitschrift für Sexualwissenschaft und Sexualpolitik* 18:4 (September 10, 1931), 224. According to Ellen Baekgaard, Dorchen Richter feared the Nazis and tried to leave Germany in 1933. What became of her is unknown.

14. Abraham, "Genitalumwandlung an Zwei Männlichen Transvestiten," 223–226; Ludwig L. Lenz, *Memoirs of a Sexologist: Discretion and Indiscretion* (New York: Cadillac, 1954), 463.

15. Niels Hoyer, ed., *Man into Woman: An Authentic Record of a Change of Sex* (New York: E. P. Dutton, 1933), 284. The original Danish edition, *Fra mand til kvinde,* was published in 1931; the German translation, *Ein Mensch Wechselt Sein Geschlecht,* was published in 1932. On Elbe's death and the involvement of Hirschfeld and the Institute for Sexual Science, see Hertoft and Ritzau, *Paradiset er ikke til salg,* 82–83. For another account of male-to-female surgery in Germany in 1931, see the articles on Herta Wind in "Legal Fight over Sex Change Book," *Daily Telegram,* January 5, 1955, Changelings folder, ONE; "His Two Sons Began to Call Him 'Auntie'" [n.p., c. 1950s], Christine Jorgensen Scrapbook, LLC.

16. C. V. C. to Harry Benjamin, June 1, 1956, C. V. C folder, box 8, Series IIC, HBC. For a slightly different version, see "Conversation with C. V. C.," October 12, 1955, Autobiography/Letters box, CJP.

17. Several of the doctors involved in early sex-change research were of Jewish descent. Steinach, Marcuse, and Hirschfeld all went into exile when the Nazis came to power.

18. See especially Hausman, *Changing Sex.*

19. See J. J. Hage, J. J. A. M. Bloem, and H. M. Suliman, "Review of the Literature on the Techniques for Phalloplasty with Emphasis on the Applicability in Female-to-Male Transsexuals," *Journal of Urology* 150 (October 1993), 1093–98.

20. See Thomas Laqueur, *Making Sex: Body and Gender from the Greeks to Freud* (Cambridge, Mass.: Harvard University Press, 1990); Londa Shiebinger, *The Mind Has No Sex? Women in the Origins of Modern Science* (Cambridge, Mass.: Harvard University

Press, 1989); Cynthia Eagle Russett, *Sexual Science: The Victorian Construction of Womanhood* (Cambridge, Mass.: Harvard University Press, 1989).

21. Rosalind Rosenberg, *Beyond Separate Spheres: Intellectual Roots of Modern Feminism* (New Haven: Yale University Press, 1982); Russett, *Sexual Science,* chap. 6.

22. On the prevalence of this vision, see Chandak Sengoopta, *Otto Weininger: Sex, Science, and Self in Imperial Vienna* (Chicago: University of Chicago Press, 2000), 47.

23. Charles Darwin, *The Variation of Animals and Plants under Domestication,* vol. 2 (London: John Murray, 1868), 52. Darwin was not the only nineteenth-century scientist who posited a "concept of latent hermaphroditism." See Ornella Moscucci, *The Science of Woman: Gynaecology and Gender in England, 1800–1929* (Cambridge: Cambridge University Press, 1990), 17–20.

24. Gregorio Marañon, *The Evolution of Sex and Intersexual Conditions* (London: George Allen and Unwin, 1932), 247.

25. See Rosenberg, *Beyond Separate Spheres,* 104–105.

26. Marañon, *Evolution of Sex,* 17.

27. Nancy A. Harrowitz and Barbara Hyams, eds., *Jews and Gender: Responses to Otto Weininger* (Philadelphia: Temple University Press, 1995). The quotation is from the essay by Gerald Stieg, "Kafka and Weininger," 195.

28. Otto Weininger, *Sex and Character* (London: William Heinemann, [1903]), 7–8.

29. Ibid., 33. See also Sengoota, *Otto Weininger,* chap. 4.

30. Weininger, *Sex and Character,* 195, 320–321. Marañon also used the theory of bisexuality to comment on the "retarded development of the woman"; *Evolution of Sex,* 66.

31. Freud, "Three Contributions," 559. On Fliess and Freud, see Jeffrey Moussaief Masson, ed., *The Complete Letters of Sigmund Freud to Wilhelm Fliess, 1887–1904* (Cambridge, Mass.: Harvard University Press, 1985), 463–468; Hannelore Rodlauer, "Fragments from Weininger's Education (1895–1902)," in Harrowitz and Hyams, *Jews and Gender,* 50–51. For mention of other late nineteenth-century scientists who endorsed formulations of bisexuality, see Sandor Rado, "A Critical Examination of the Concept of Bisexuality," in Rado, *Psychoanalysis of Behavior: Collected Papers* (New York: Grune and Stratton, 1956), 140.

32. Magnus Hirschfeld, *Transvestites: The Erotic Drive to Cross Dress* (1910; reprint, Buffalo: Prometheus, 1991), 229.

33. Freud, "Three Contributions," 558.

34. Magnus Hirschfeld, "Die Objektive Diagnose der Homosexualität," *Jahrbuch für Sexuelle Zwischenstufen* 1 (1899), 4–35. See also Sengoopta, "Glandular Politics," 454.

35. Hirschfeld, *Transvestites,* 219; Magnus Hirschfeld, "Die Intersexuelle Konstitution," *Jahrbuch für Sexuelle Zwischenstufen* 23 (1923), 3; James D. Steakley, *"Per Scientiam ad Justitiam,"* 143.

36. Havelock Ellis, "Sexo-Aesthetic Inversion," *Alienist and Neurologist* 34 (1913), 273, 279.

37. Alice Domurat Dreger, *Hermaphrodites and the Medical Invention of Sex* (Cambridge, Mass.: Harvard University Press, 1998).

38. On chromosomes and sex determination, see Ernst Mayr, *The Growth of Biological Thought: Diversity, Evolution, and Inheritance* (Cambridge, Mass.: Harvard University

Press, 1982), 750–752; Stephen G. Brush, "Nettie M. Stevens and the Discovery of Sex Determination by Chromosomes," in *History of Women in the Sciences: Readings from Isis,* ed. Sally Gregory Kohlstedt (Chicago: University of Chicago Press, 1999), 337–346. On hormones, see Diana Long Hall, "Biology, Sex Hormones, and Sexism in the 1920s," in *Women and Philosophy: Toward a Theory of Liberation,* ed. Carol C. Gould and Marx W. Wartofsky (New York: Putnam's, 1973), 81–96. For a contemporary example, see Emil Novak and J. Herman Long, "Ovarian Tumors Associated with Secondary Sex Changes," *Journal of the American Medical Association* 101 (1935), 1060: "the primary sex differentiating force originates from the zygote . . . In the higher forms, however, this can be modified or overridden by the endocrine influence."

39. Eugen Steinach, *Sex and Life* (New York: Viking, 1940), 7, 67.

40. Thorek, *The Human Testis,* 281.

41. Oudshoorn, *Beyond the Natural Body,* 29. I have relied here on Oudshoorn's fine account of the history of endocrinology. But Oudshoorn does not acknowledge the earlier formulations of the theory of human bisexuality in the works of Hirschfeld, Weininger, and others.

42. See, for example, Thorek, *The Human Testis,* 247, 254; Robert T. Frank, *The Female Sex Hormone* (Springfield, Ill.: Charles C. Thomas, 1929), 7, 8, 115; Hugh Hampton Young, *Genital Abnormalities, Hermaphroditism, and Related Adrenal Diseases* (Baltimore: Williams and Wilkins, 1937), 35.

43. Stephanie Kenan, "Who Counts When You're Counting Homosexuals? Hormones and Homosexuality in Mid-Twentieth-Century America," in Rosario, *Science and Homosexualities,* 197–218.

44. George W. Henry, *Sex Variants: A Study of Homosexual Patterns* (New York: Paul B. Hoeber, 1948), 1026. The study was originally published in two volumes in 1941 under the title *All the Sexes.*

45. On Henry's work, see Jennifer Terry, *An American Obsession: Science, Medicine, and the Place of Homosexuality in Modern Society* (Chicago: University of Chicago Press, 1999), chap. 6.

46. Quoted in Beth Bailey, *From Front Porch to Back Seat: Courtship in Twentieth-Century America* (Baltimore: Johns Hopkins University Press, 1988), 102.

47. Rohama Lee, "A Case of Sex Mutation," *Sexology* 8:11 (March 1942), 27. See also Elba L. Downey, "Are We All Double-Sexed?" part 2, *Sexology* 9:6 (December 1942), 429–431; "We Are Both Sexes," *Sexology* 12:5 (December 1945), 303.

48. See Terry, *An American Obsession,* chap. 5.

49. Margaret Mead, *Sex and Temperament in Three Different Societies* (New York: Morrow, 1935), 319, 321.

50. Lewis M. Terman and Catharine Cox Miles, *Sex and Personality: Studies in Masculinity and Femininity* (New York: McGraw-Hill, 1936), vi, 3.

51. Alfred C. Kinsey, Wardell B. Pomeroy, and Clyde E. Martin, *Sexual Behavior in the Human Male* (Philadelphia: W. B. Saunders, 1948), 639.

52. S. W. to Alfred C. Kinsey, December 14, 1947, Correspondence file S. W., KI.

53. C. V. C. to Mr. and Mrs. George Jorgensen, n.d. [c. December 1952], Letters box, CJP; "Conversation with C. V. C.," October 12, 1955, with Irmis Johnson's notes for Jorgensen autobiography, Autobiography/Letters box, CJP. On Benjamin's recollec-

tion, see [Harry Benjamin,] handwritten comments on Jorgensen's autobiography, First Half of Book folder, Letters box, CJP.

54. Hoyer, *Man into Woman,* 178, viii, xi–xii. See Young, *Genital Abnormalities,* 200–201.

55. "A Man Becomes a Woman," *Sexology* 1:4 (December 1933), 252, 253, 254. For a shorter review of *Man into Woman,* see the same issue of *Sexology,* p. 268.

56. "When Science Changed a Man into a Woman!" n.p., n.d. [c. 1934], "Order Book" Scrapbook, box 1/1 Scrapbooks, VPC.

57. Thanks to Susan Stryker for pointing out this connection. See Mark Richard Siegel, *Hugo Gernsback, Father of Modern Science Fiction* (San Bernardino: Borgo, 1988).

58. "Man in Woman's Body," *Your Body* 4:1 (September 1937), 15.

59. J. P. Harbuck, "Sex Repeal! Science Solves the Riddle of Man-Women Wonders," *True,* September 1939, 50–55, 119–120, box 1/4 Clippings, VPC. For contemporary scientific accounts on ovarian and adrenal tumors, see Novak and Long, "Ovarian Tumors," 1057–63; Young, *Genital Abnormalities,* chaps. 8, 10.

60. "Boy Prisoner Slowly Changing into a Girl," n.p., n.d. [c. 1936], "Order Book" Scrapbook, box 1/1 Scrapbooks, VPC.

61. "When Science Changed a Man into a Woman!" 2.

62. "['Bad-Old'?] Days of Newly-Made Man" (headline partially cut off), *New York Daily Mirror,* n.d. [c. 1936], "Order Book" Scrapbook, box 1/1 Scrapbooks, VPC.

63. "Ex-Girl; Now a Hubby, Arrives, Tells about It," *New York Daily News,* December 11, 1955, 5, Sex Conversions folder, Clippings/Letters box, CJP.

64. See Brett Riley, "Are Sexual Changes Possible?" n.p., n.d. [c. late 1930s or 1940s], box 1/4 Clippings, VPC.

65. "['Bad-Old'?] Days of Newly-Made Man"; "Boy Ex-Girl 'Corsetiere,'" *New York Daily Mirror,* n.d. [c. 1936]; "Former Girl Athlete Arrives, Now a Man," n.p., n.d. [c. 1936]; "Once Girl, He Talks of Loves," *New York Daily Mirror,* n.d. [c. 1936], all in "Order Book" Scrapbook, box 1/1 Scrapbooks, VPC.

66. Joseph McCabe, *Women Who Become Men: The Development of Unusual Variations, Including Hermaphrodites, Pseudo-Hermaphrodites, and Virgin Birth* (Girard, Kans.: Haldeman-Julius Publications, 1938), 29.

67. "Women into Men by Surgery?" *Sexology* 3:12 (August 1936), 775; Jacob Hubler, "Science Turns Girl into Boy," *Sexology* 2:3 (November 1934), 158.

68. Teresa de Lauretis, *The Practice of Love: Lesbian Sexuality and Perverse Desire* (Bloomington: Indiana University Press, 1994), xix. Especially in gay and lesbian studies, historians have begun to explore how, when, and in what shifting forms specific sexual identities appeared in the modern era. For recent examples in U.S. history, see Lisa Duggan, "The Trials of Alice Mitchell: Sensationalism, Sexology, and the Lesbian Subject in Turn-of-the-Century America," *Signs: Journal of Women in Culture and Society* 18:4 (Summer 1993), 791–814; Elizabeth Lapovsky Kennedy and Madeline D. Davis, *Boots of Leather, Slippers of Gold: The History of a Lesbian Community* (New York: Routledge, 1993); George Chauncey, *Gay New York: Gender, Urban Culture, and the Making of the Gay Male World, 1890–1940* (New York: Basic Books, 1994); Katie Gilmartin, "'We Weren't Bar People': Middle-Class Lesbian Identities and Cultural

Spaces," *GLQ: A Journal of Lesbian and Gay Studies* 3:1 (1996), 1–51; Estelle B. Freedman, "'The Burning of Letters Continues': Elusive Identities and the Historical Construction of Sexuality," *Journal of Women's History* 9:4 (Winter 1998), 181–200.

69. On the impact of reading on other forms of sexual identity, see Regina Kunzel, "Pulp Fictions and Problem Girls: Reading and Rewriting Single Pregnancy in the Postwar United States," *American Historical Review* 100:5 (December 1995), 1480; Duggan, "The Trials of Alice Mitchell"; Helen Lefkowitz Horowitz, "'Nous Autres': Reading, Passion, and the Creation of M. Carey Thomas," *Journal of American History* 79:1 (June 1992), 68–95.

70. Letter to the editor, "Dissatisfaction with Sex," *Sexology* 1:12 (August 1934), 810; letter to the editor, "Changing Sex," *Sexology* 5:4 (December 1937), 265.

71. "They Want to Change Sexes," *Sexology* 5:1 (September 1937), 32.

72. For additional early accounts in which those who sought sex-change surgery described their own conditions, see Yawger, "Transvestism," 45; Henry, *Sex Variants,* 429–435, 489–496, 534–542; D. M. Olkon and Irene Case Sherman, "Eonism with Added Outstanding Psychopathic Features," *Journal of Nervous and Mental Disease* 99 (January–June 1944), 160–161.

73. Pauli Murray, handwritten notes, "Interview with Dr. ___," December 16 [1937], and "Questions Prepared," December 17, 1937, both in folder 71, box 4, Series I, Pauli Murray Papers, Arthur and Elizabeth Schlesinger Library on the History of Women, Radcliffe Institute for Advanced Study, Harvard University.

74. Pauli Murray, "Summary of Symptoms of Upset," March 8, 1940, and "Memorandum on P. M.," July 13, 1942, both in ibid. Anyone familiar with U.S. women's or African-American history will recognize the name Pauli Murray. She went on to lead an astonishingly accomplished life as a lawyer, civil rights activist, feminist, author, poet, and Episcopal priest. Thanks to Dayo Gore for directing me to these records and to Stacy Braukman for crucial research assistance.

75. "Dissatisfaction with Sex," 810; "Changing Sex," 265.

76. See, for example, "Woman into Man," *Sexology* 10:8 (March 1944), 484–485; David O. Cauldwell, "A Man Becomes a Woman," *Sexology* 13:2 (September 1946), 73–79, and 13:3 (October 1946), 149–152; letter to the editor, "Homosexuality," *Sexology* 9:6 (November 1942), 390, 392; letter to the editor, "'Man into Woman'?" *Sexology* 13:1 (August 1946), 59–60; letter to the editor, "Man into Woman," *Sexology* 13:5 (December 1946), 312; letter to the editor, "Desire to Be of the Opposite Sex," *Sexology* 15:1 (August 1948), 53.

77. Young, *Genital Abnormalities,* 309.

78. "Case History of S. W.," 7, 9, S. W. folder, box 8, Series IIC, HBC.

79. S. W. to Alfred C. Kinsey, November 2, 1945, ibid.

80. Henry, *Sex Variants,* 425–438, 487–498, 534–546. For an exception, a Chicago surgeon who knew of and endorsed the sex-change surgeries in Germany, see Thorek, *The Human Testis,* 261.

81. Olkon and Sherman, "Eonism," 166; S. W. to Alfred C. Kinsey, November 2 and October 20, 1945, S. W. folder, box 8, Series IIC, HBC.

82. "'Man' Asks Legal Right to Assume Woman Status," *Los Angeles Examiner,* July 3, 1941, TV Barbara Richards Envelope, no. 82, KI; Barbara Ann Richards, as told to Bart Lytton, "Nature Betrayed My Body," *Sensation,* November 1941, 88, box 1/4 Clip-

pings, VPC. On the endocrinologist, see "Young Bride Won't Leave Mate Who's Victim of Sex Change," *Oakland Tribune,* July 4, 1941, "Photo and Return" Scrapbook, LLC.

83. "Nature Betrayed My Body," 88; "Prank by Mother Nature Turns Los Angeles Salesman into Woman," *Los Angeles Times,* July 3, 1941, TV Barbara Richards Envelope, KI; Lorraine Wilcox Richards, "My Husband Is a Woman" [n.p., c. 1941], Blue Notebook, box 1/1 Scrapbooks, VPC.

84. "Nature Betrayed My Body," 88.

85. "Edward Changes Name to Barbara," *Los Angeles Herald Express,* October 10, 1941; Myron Weiss, "The Husband Who Changed into a Woman," *Spot,* January 1942, both in TV Barbara Richards Envelope, KI.

86. On Lauren Wilcox, see Louise Lawrence, autobiography, typescript, 71–72, Large Box; Louise Lawrence, 1944 diary, entries for May 28, June 2, and June 28; Louise Lawrence to Alfred C. Kinsey, September 21, 1950, Alfred C. Kinsey folder, all in LLC. See also Karl M. Bowman and Bernice Engle, "Medicolegal Aspects of Transvestism," *American Journal of Psychiatry* 113:7 (January 1957), 587.

87. A. O. to Barbara Richards, May 30, 1942, TV Barbara Richards Envelope, KI.

88. S. W. to Alfred C. Kinsey, February 13, 1948, S. W. folder, box 8, Series IIC, HBC; D. O. Cauldwell, *Questions and Answers on the Sex Life and Sexual Problems of Trans-Sexuals* (Girard, Kans.: Haldeman-Julius Publications, 1950), 5–6.

89. Gene St. Ledges, "Can Science Switch Sexes?" *Whisper,* January 1950; "Would You Change Your Sex?" *Glance,* March 1950, both in box 1/1 Scrapbooks, VPC.

90. Jim Kepner, "Excavating Lesbian and Gay History," *ONE/IGLA Bulletin* 2 (Spring/Summer 1996), 9.

91. For biographical information on Cauldwell, see D. O. Cauldwell, *Sex Transmutation—Can One's Sex Be Changed?* (Girard, Kans.: Haldeman-Julius Publications, 1951), 29.

92. For one reader's response to his "facetious" tone, see Louise Lawrence to Harry Benjamin, February 13, 1950, TRNSV notebook, LLC.

93. D. O. Cauldwell, "Psychopathia Transexualis," *Sexology* 16:5 (December 1949), 276, 278.

94. Ibid., 280, 274.

95. Cauldwell, *Questions and Answers,* 3.

96. Cauldwell, *Sex Transmutation,* 3.

97. Cauldwell, *Questions and Answers,* front cover, 11.

98. Cauldwell, *Sex Transmutation,* 11, 19, 21.

99. Cauldwell, *Questions and Answers,* 13, 24; idem, *Sex Transmutation,* 28.

100. Because Jews predominated in the German tradition of sexology, and because of his surname and his network of friends and colleagues, people frequently assumed that Benjamin, too, was Jewish. But only his paternal grandfather was Jewish. Along with his brother and sister, he was reared as a Lutheran. As an adult, he was not religious.

101. Morris Fishbein, *The Facts about Rejuvenation* (Girard, Kans.: Haldeman-Julius Publications, n.d. [c. 1930]), 16. This pamphlet (number 648 in the Haldeman-Julius Little Blue Book series) mocks the claims to rejuvenation and criticizes Steinach and Benjamin.

102. Harry Benjamin to R. E. L. Masters, December 29, 1961, R. E. L. Masters folder, box 6, Series IIC, HBC.

103. On the Steinach film and the World League conference, see documents on Steinach and Benjamin on the website of the Magnus Hirschfeld Archive for Sexology, www2.hu-berlin.de/sexology/GESUND/ARCHIV/PIONEE.HTM. On the platform of the World League for Sexual Reform, see [Harry Benjamin,] "Principal Points of the League's Platform," typewritten page, 1932, folder 1, box 1, Series IIC, Havelock Ellis Collection, KI.

104. Tom Buckley, "Transsexuality Expert, 90, Recalls 'Maverick' Career," *New York Times,* January 11, 1975; Harry Benjamin to Alfred C. Kinsey, May 29, 1944, Correspondence file Harry Benjamin, KI. For biographical information, see Harry Benjamin, "Reminiscences," *Journal of Sex Research* 6:1 (February 1970), 3–9; "Memorial for Harry Benjamin," *Archives of Sexual Behavior* 17:5 (October 1988), 3–31; "Harry Benjamin, M.D.," one-page typescript, John Marquardt folder, box 6, Series IIC, HBC. On Benjamin's early public defense of prostitution and homosexuality, see, for example, Harry Benjamin, "An Echo of and an Addendum to 'For the Sake of Morality,'" *Medical Journal and Record,* August 5, 1931, 118–120; see also Erin G. Carlston, "'A Finer Differentiation': Female Homosexuality and the American Medical Community, 1926–1940," in Rosario, *Science and Homosexualities,* 185–186.

105. Henry, *Sex Variants,* 495. Henry gave Spengler the pseudonym "Rudolph von H." and did not mention that Harry Benjamin was Spengler's physician, but other corroborating sources use the actual name Spengler and provide enough overlapping biographical data to corroborate that "Rudolph von H." was indeed Spengler and that Benjamin served as physician. See Leah Cahan Schaefer and Connie Christine Wheeler, "Harry Benjamin's First Ten Cases (1938–1953): A Clinical Historical Note," *Archives of Sexual Behavior* 24:1 (February 1995), 77–78; Harry Benjamin, "Introduction," in Richard Green and John Money, *Transsexualism and Sex Reassignment* (Baltimore: Johns Hopkins Press, 1969), 1–2. On "progynon," see Frank, *Female Sex Hormone,* 144.

106. Medical Report on V. B., July 19, 1948, pp. 1–3; V. B. to Harry Benjamin, May 19, 1949, both in V. B. folder, box 3, Series IIC, HBC. On the mayhem statute see Robert Veit Sherwin, "The Legal Problem in Transvestism," *American Journal of Psychotherapy* 8:2 (April 1954), 243–244.

107. Harry Benjamin to V. B., May 31, 1949; Harry Benjamin to Edmund G. Brown, November 22, 1949; both in V. B. folder, box 3, Series IIC, HBC.

108. Berdeen Frankel Meyer, "Case Summary and Closing Note," October 2, 1950, 8, ibid. For more on Kinsey's involvement, see Joanne Meyerowitz, "Sex Research at the Borders of Gender: Transvestites, Transsexuals, and Alfred C. Kinsey," *Bulletin of the History of Medicine* 75:1 (Spring 2001), 72–90.

109. Leo L. Stanley, *Men at Their Worst* (New York: D. Appleton-Century, 1940), 203; "'It' Girl," *The Billboard* [c. 1941], Scrapbook "Photo and Return," p. 18, LLC. On Lauren Wilcox's surgery, see Louise Lawrence, 1944 diary, entries for May 28, June 2, and June 28, LLC; Bowman and Engle, "Medicolegal Aspects of Transvestism," 587.

110. C. V. C. to Harry Benjamin, August 9, 1956, C. V. C. folder, box 8, Series IIC, HBC; H. H. Huelke, "Ein Transvestit (Der Fall Hinrich B.)," *Kriminalistik* 3 (1949), 92. (The Nazis, according to C. V. C., made male-to-female transsexuals take one of three gender-ambiguous names—Christel, Toni, and Friedel.) On Switzerland, see Eugene de Savitsch, *Homosexuality, Transvestism, and Change of Sex* (Springfield, Ill.:

Charles C. Thomas, 1958), chaps. 10, 11. On Dillon in England, see Liz Hodgkinson, *Michael, Née Laura* (London: Columbus, 1989), chaps. 4, 5.

111. Henry, *Sex Variants,* 540–541.

112. "Ordinary lives today," Arjun Appadurai writes, "are more often powered not by the givenness of things but by the possibilities that the media (either directly or indirectly) suggest are available"; *Modernity at Large: Cultural Dimensions of Globalization* (Minneapolis: University of Minnesota Press, 1996), 55.

2. "EX-GI BECOMES BLONDE BEAUTY"

1. "What's a Woman? City Bureau Baffled by Chris Jorgensen," *New York Daily News,* March 31, 1959, 3; Christine Jorgensen, *Christine Jorgensen: A Personal Autobiography* (New York: Paul S. Eriksson, 1967), 289; "Bars Marriage Permit," *New York Times,* April 4, 1959, 20; "Bar Wedding for Christine," *New York Mirror,* April 4, 1959, 1.

2. Radio interview with Christine Jorgensen, conducted by Doris Abramson and Haskell Coplin, 1968, audiotape in possession of author.

3. "Christine Jorgensen," *True Confessions,* September 1954, 36.

4. Jorgensen, *Christine Jorgensen, 7.*

5. Interview with Christine Jorgensen, conducted by Mike Wallace, 1959, audiotape in possession of author.

6. Jorgensen, *Christine Jorgensen, 20, 24;* "Notes—Conversation w Christine re Revise," November 3, 1955, Autobiography/Letters box, CJP.

7. Jorgensen, *Christine Jorgensen, 33, 43, 58, 60.*

8. Handwritten notes, 1945–1946, pocket notebook, Photos and Books box, CJP.

9. Jorgensen, *Christine Jorgensen, 74, 75.*

10. Ibid., 75; Paul de Kruif, *The Male Hormone* (1945; reprint, Garden City, N.Y.: Garden City Publishing, 1947).

11. Jorgensen, *Christine Jorgensen, 79, 81.*

12. George Jorgensen to Genevieve and Joe Angelo, July 20, 1950, Very Important Letters folder, Letters box, CJP. The Angelos befriended Jorgensen before the trip to Denmark. In the letter Jorgensen tells of meeting the endocrinologist Christian Hamburger in Copenhagen: "He wants me to stop the tablets you sent to me and then check the return to normal."

13. "Chapter ___" [c. 1950s], ms. draft, Jorgensen's handwriting, Autobiography/ Letters box, CJP; Christian Hamburger, Georg Stürup, and E. Dahl-Iversen, "Transvestism: Hormonal, Psychiatric, and Surgical Treatment," *Journal of the American Medical Association* 152:5 (May 1953), 393.

14. Christian Hamburger and Mogens Sprechler, "The Influence of Steroid Hormones on the Hormonal Activity of the Adenohypophysis in Man," *Acta Endocrinologica* 7 (1951), 170.

15. "Notes Re Awareness of Homosexuality," September 16, 1955; "Notes—Chris Jorgensen, Dec. 24" [c. 1952], both in Autobiography/Letters box, CJP.

16. Jerry Parker, "Remembering Christine Jorgensen," *Courier-Journal,* October 21, 1979, Christine Jorgensen vertical file, KI.

17. Jorgensen, *Christine Jorgensen, 38.*

18. Parker, "Remembering Christine Jorgensen."

19. Hamburger, Stürup, and Dahl-Iversen, "Transvestism," 393. For a gay man's story, see, for example, Martin Duberman, *Cures: A Gay Man's Odyssey* (New York: Dutton, 1991).

20. The letter, written in the summer of 1950, is quoted in Jorgensen, *Christine Jorgensen*, 100.

21. R. E. Berry, "Most Happy at Change, Hopes Some Day to Wed," *New York Journal-American*, December 1, 1952, 6; "Notes—Chris Jorgensen."

22. Jorgensen, *Christine Jorgensen*, 102.

23. Hamburger and Sprechler, "The Influence of Steroid Hormones," 173; George Jorgensen to Genevieve and Joe Angelo, January 2, 1951, Very Important Letters folder, Letters box, CJP.

24. "Letter Written by George Jorgensen, Jr." [c. 1950 or 1951], Autobiography/ Letters box, CJP.

25. "Notes Dr. George Stürup," January 14 [c. 1953], 3, 4, Autobiography/Letters box, CJP.

26. Alvin Davis, "The Truth about 'Christine' Jorgensen," *New York Post*, April 6 and April 9, 1953, Christine Jorgensen Scrapbook, LLC.

27. Georg K. Stürup, "Legal Problems Related to Transsexualism and Sex Reassignment in Denmark," in *Transsexualism and Sex Reassignment*, ed. Richard Green and John Money (Baltimore: Johns Hopkins Press, 1969), 456.

28. Hamburger, Stürup, and Dahl-Iversen, "Transvestism," 394; "Notes—Chris Jorgensen."

29. "Letter Informing Parents," *New York Daily News*, December 1, 1952, 10. A slightly edited version of the letter appears in Jorgensen's autobiography.

30. Hamburger, Stürup, and Dahl-Iversen, "Transvestism," 394.

31. "Ex-GI Becomes Blonde Beauty," *New York Daily News*, December 1, 1952, 3.

32. "The Great Transformation," *Time*, December 14, 1952, 58; "Christine and the News," *Newsweek*, December 15, 1952, 64; Jorgensen, *Christine Jorgensen*, 322, 185; Dallas Denny, "Black Telephones, White Refrigerators: Rethinking Christine Jorgensen," in *Current Concepts in Transgender Identity*, ed. Dallas Denny (New York: Garland, 1998), 41–42; interview with Vern Bullough, conducted by author, July 17, 1996.

33. "Stage Bids for Christine; Ex-GI Coy, Locks Her Door," *New York Post*, December 2, 1952, 3.

34. Leon Racht, "Weeping Mother Always Believed Child Was Boy," *New York Journal-American*, December 1, 1952, 6; "VA Data Shows Girl Was 'Normal' Male," *New York Journal-American*, December 1, 1952, 6; "Christine Jorgensen May Make Movie; Said Undecided over Hollywood Offer," *Stars and Stripes*, December 11, 1952, Christine Jorgensen Scrapbook, LLC.

35. "Bronx Vet Made into a Girl Glad Long Ordeal Is Over," *New York Post*, December 1, 1952, 5; "Christine: 'I Wish Nobody Knew,'" *New York Post*, December 5, 1952, 4; "Beautiful Christine Dazzles Newsmen," *New York Journal-American*, December 11, 1952, 3.

36. "Stage Bids for Christine"; Paul Ifverson, "'I Could Have Gone for the He-She Girl,' Says Reporter," *New York Daily News*, December 3, 1953, 3; "Beautiful Christine Dazzles Newsmen."

37. "Christine: 'I Wish Nobody Knew.'"

38. "GI from Texas Just a Friend, Says Christine," *New York Daily News,* December 6, 1952, 7. See also "'Chris My Girl Friend,' Says GI," *San Mateo Times,* December 5, 1952, Christine Jorgensen Scrapbook, LLC; "Woman Who Was Man Admits She Hopes to Marry," *Chicago Tribune,* December 6, 1952, "Christine" Chicago Scrapbook, private collection of Joseph Agnew.

39. "Catholic Paper Hits Christine Publicity," *New York Journal-American,* December 12, 1952, 10.

40. "How AW Got and Prepared Christine Story," *Editor and Publisher,* March 28, 1953, 62; contract with Hearst Corporation, December 22, 1952, 6, Contracts folder, Autobiography/Letters box, CJP. In her autobiography Jorgensen claimed she received $20,000 for the *American Weekly* series; other reports claimed she earned $30,000. See Jorgensen, *Christine Jorgensen,* 137; "Homecoming," *Time,* February 23, 1953, 28. The actual contract offers $25,000 plus royalties from syndication.

41. "Christine Back Home as a Beautiful Woman," *New York Journal-American,* February 12, 1953, 1.

42. "Sleek Christine Exudes Charm in U.S.," *Stars and Stripes,* February 13, 1953; "'Glad as Any U.S. Woman to Be Back," *Los Angeles Examiner,* February 13, 1953; "Christine Home Again; Gets Big NY Welcome," *San Francisco Examiner,* February 13, 1953, all in Christine Jorgensen Scrapbook, LLC.

43. "Christine Back Home"; Joseph Famm, "Chris Back Home, Perfect Little Lady," *New York Daily Mirror,* February 13, 1953, 3.

44. Josephine Di Lorenzo and Joseph Martin, "Christine Flies In; She's No Soprano," *New York Daily News,* February 13, 1953, 3.

45. Advertisement for "The Story of My Life," *New York Daily Mirror,* February 13, 1953, 19; Christine Jorgensen, "The Story of My Life," *American Weekly,* February 15, 1953, 5. On stories of individual achievement in postwar mass-circulation magazines, see Joanne Meyerowitz, "Beyond the Feminine Mystique: A Reassessment of Postwar Mass Culture, 1946–1958," *Journal of American History* 79:4 (March 1993), 1455–82.

46. The concept of a woman "trapped" in a male body is a modernized version of the older "female soul in a male body," which Karl Ulrichs employed in the nineteenth century. On Ulrichs, see Gert Hekma, "'A Female Soul in a Male Body': Sexual Inversion as Gender Inversion in Nineteenth-Century Sexology," in *Third Sex, Third Gender: Beyond Sexual Dimorphism in Culture and History,* ed. Gilbert Herdt (New York: Zone, 1996), 213–239.

47. Jorgensen, "The Story of My Life," February 22, 1953, 4, 6; March 8, 1953, 8, 9.

48. Jorgensen, *Christine Jorgensen,* 176, 188. On circulation boosts, see "How AW Got and Prepared Christine Story"; "Is Crime News Losing Its Circulation Power?" *Editor and Publisher,* June 5, 1954, 60.

49. See Joanne Meyerowitz, "Sex, Gender, and the Cold War Language of Reform," in *Rethinking Cold War Culture,* ed. Peter Kuznick and James Gilbert (Washington, D.C.: Smithsonian Institution Press, 2001), 106–123.

50. Advertisement for "The Story of My Life."

51. Jorgensen, "The Story of My Life," March 1, 1953, 17.

52. On women during and after the war, see, for example, Susan M. Hartmann, *The Home Front and Beyond: American Women in the 1940s* (Boston: Twayne, 1982). On postwar contests over women's gender roles, see, for example, William H. Chafe, *The*

Paradox of Change: American Women in the Twentieth Century (New York: Oxford University Press, 1991). On wartime and postwar concerns about masculinity, see Edward A. Strecker, *Their Mothers' Sons: The Psychiatrist Examines an American Problem* (New York: J. B. Lippincott, 1946); Barbara Ehrenreich, *The Hearts of Men: American Dreams and the Flight from Commitment* (Garden City, N.Y.: Doubleday/Anchor, 1983), chaps. 3, 4; Beth L. Bailey, *From Front Porch to Back Seat: Courtship in Twentieth-Century America* (Baltimore: Johns Hopkins University Press, 1988), 103–108.

53. On the increased interest in impersonation, see E. Carlton Winford, *Femme Mimics* (Dallas: Winford, 1954), 19: "World War II was a turning point in the art of female impersonation . . . From 1950 to 1954 the number of entertainment places featuring female impersonators doubled."

54. Jorgensen, "The Story of My Life," February 22, 1953, 5. On the increasing visibility of homosexuality and the intensified homophobic reaction, see John D'Emilio, *Sexual Politics, Sexual Communities: The Making of a Homosexual Minority in the United States, 1940–1970* (Chicago: University of Chicago Press, 1983); Allan Bérubé, *Coming Out under Fire* (New York: Free Press, 1990).

55. Alton Blakeslee, "Thousands Do Not Know True Sex," *New York Daily News*, December 7, 1952, 6; "Stage Bids for Christine"; Jack Geiger, "Sex Surgery Specialist Reports Hundreds of Boy-Girl Operations" [n.p., c. December 2, 1952], Christine Jorgensen Scrapbook, LLC; "Doctor Tells of Five Sex Operations," *New York Daily News*, December 18, 1952, 4; "The Great Transformation," *Time*, December 15, 1952, 59.

56. G. B. Lal, "MD's and Public to Eagerly Follow Christine's Life," *New York Journal-American*, December 7, 1952, 18-L.

57. Louise Lawrence to Harry Benjamin, December 9, 1952, TRNSV notebook, LLC; I. O. to Christine Jorgensen, January 22, 1953; L. N. to Christine Jorgensen, March 20, 1953, both in Sex Change—Other than CJ folder, Letters box, CJP.

58. Jorgensen, *Christine Jorgensen*, 178; "Copy of the Winchell Broadcast" [c. February 1953], Letters box, CJP; Jorgensen, "The Story of My Life," March 8, 1953, 11; idem, *Christine Jorgensen*, 173.

59. "Is Christine Really a Man after All?" *San Francisco Chronicle*, February 16, 1953; "Christine Discounted as 100 Pct. Woman by Her Copenhagen Doctor," *San Francisco Call-Bulletin*, February 18, 1953, both in Christine Jorgensen Scrapbook, LLC.

60. Harry E. Maule, Random House, to Christine Jorgensen, February 17, 1953, Contracts folder, Autobiography/Letters box, CJP; "Christine's Story, in American Weekly, Not to Be Random House Book," text of broadcast, Dorothy and Dick Kollmar Show, WOR, New York, March 9, 1953, 1953 folder, Clippings/Letters box, CJP.

61. "AMA Studies Christine—Some U.S. Doctors Say She's Not a Woman Still," *San Francisco Chronicle*, March 11, 1953, Christine Jorgensen Scrapbook, LLC.

62. Davis, "The Truth about 'Christine' Jorgensen," April 6, 1953.

63. "The Case of Christine," *Time*, April 20, 1953, 82; "Boy or Girl?" *Newsweek*, May 4, 1953, 91; Hamburger, Stürup, and Dahl-Iversen, "Transvestism," 396; Robert King, "Christine Jorgensen: Is She *Still* a Man?" *Modern Romances*, August 1953, 40–41, 95–96, Christine Jorgensen folder, ONE; Alvin Davis, "'Christine' Jorgensen is NOT a Woman," *Cavalier*, October 1953, 2–5, 62–64.

64. Jorgensen, *Christine Jorgensen*, 207, 209.

65. Louise Lawrence to Harry Benjamin, April 22, 1953, TRNSV notebook, LLC.

66. For a different interpretation of the media's treatment of Jorgensen, see David Harley Serlin, "Christine Jorgensen and the Cold War Closet," *Radical History Review* 62 (Spring 1995), 136–165.

67. See Jorgensen, *Christine Jorgensen*, 193–200.

68. "Christine Hires Agent for Full-Time Stage Career," *San Francisco Examiner,* April 30, 1953; "2000 in L.A. Greet Christine," *Los Angeles Herald and Express,* May 7, 1953, both in Christine Jorgensen Scrapbook, LLC.

69. "Chris Really Arrives," *Los Angeles Mirror,* May 7, 1944, Christine Jorgensen Scrapbook, LLC.

70. Script of Jorgensen/Bell nightclub act [c. 1953], Clippings/Letters box, CJP.

71. For an account of the show, see Roy Ald, "As I See Christine," *True Confessions,* September 1954, 64.

72. Jorgensen, *Christine Jorgensen*, 229.

73. Hy Gardner, "Coast to Coast," *New York Herald Tribune,* January 6, 1954, unlabeled scrapbook, LLC; Lee Mortimer, "Latin Quarter Revue Adds Christine," *New York Daily Mirror,* January 6, 1954, Christine Jorgensen Scrapbook, LLC; Martin J. de la Rosa to author, November 27, 1995.

74. "Blick vs. Christine," *Washington News,* September 9, 1953, Transexualism vertical file, KI. For Jorgensen's account of these events, see Jorgensen, *Christine Jorgensen,* 231–252.

75. "The Men in Christine's Life," *Pose* [c. October 1953], box 2/4 Clippings, VPC; "Christine Jorgensen thru a Keyhole," *Whisper* [n.d.], 16, box 1/1 Scrapbook, VPC; Lowell Crane, "The Hush-Hush Romance of Christine Jorgensen and Vanderbilt Stepson," *Confidential,* November 1954, "Christine" Chicago Scrapbook; Richard Donaldson, "Jimmy Donahue's Private Peek," *Confidential,* September 1955, 42, Christine Jorgensen vertical file, KI; Jorgensen, *Christine Jorgensen,* 256; Wolfgang Smutts, "Disillusioned Christine to Become Man Again" [n.p., n.d.], 8, "Christine" Chicago Scrapbook.

76. All the jokes quoted in this paragraph come from newspaper clippings in the Christine Jorgensen Scrapbook, LLC. Most are undated clippings (c. 1953 and 1954) from unknown sources. They include articles from *Laff* magazine (May 1953) and from *Stars and Stripes* (c. July 1953) and undated clippings from New York columnists Walter Winchell and Earl Wilson and San Francisco columnist Herb Caen. See pages 42, 44, 54, 58, 70 of the Christine Jorgensen Scrapbook, LLC.

77. Whitey Roberts' private files of jokes were found in Hollywood in the library of the Magic Castle, a private club for magicians. Thanks to Nancy Stoller for sharing the list of jokes on Jorgensen and sex change. For an analysis of Roberts' jokes on homosexuality, see Nancy E. Stoller and Peter M. Nardi, "'Fruits,' 'Fags,' and 'Dykes': Nance Jokes from the '50s and '60s," paper presented at the American Sociological Association, August 1997.

78. "'House of Oddities' and Fake Christine Banned from Fair," newspaper clipping [n.p., c. September 1953], Letters box, CJP.

79. The chocolate bar is pasted into the Christine Jorgensen Scrapbook, LLC; "Flash! Another Man to Be Feminized into Danish Pastry!" [Los Angeles?] *Daily Mirror,* May 10, 1954, Changelings folder, ONE.

80. Jorgensen, interview by Abramson and Coplin.

81. Christine Jorgensen, "It's a Change," 1956, Night Club Act folder, Clippings/ Letters box, CJP.

82. Sally Quinn, "Christine: Explaining Transsexualism," *Washington Post,* July 8, 1970, B3.

83. "Christine Jorgensen," *True Confessions,* September 1954, 36; Christine Jorgensen, interview by Mike Wallace, 1959, audiotape in author's possession.

84. Jorgensen, "The Story of My Life," February 15, 1953, 5; March 15, 1953, 15; *Christine Jorgensen Reveals,* record album [c. 1957], KI.

85. Jorgensen, interview by Mike Wallace, 1959; Bruce Laffey, *Beatrice Lillie: The Funniest Woman in the World* (New York: Wynwood, 1989), 179; Jorgensen, interview by Abramson and Coplin.

86. William Calhoun to Christine Jorgensen, October 6, 1954, Documentation for CJ: A Personal Autobiog folder, Clippings/Letters box, CJP.

87. Information on Jorgensen's vagina comes from a telephone interview with Jeannie Youngson by author, January 7, 1996, and from a telephone interview with Terry Schreiber by author, January 6, 1996. On her reconstructive surgeries, see John Heidenry, *What Wild Ecstasy: The Rise and Fall of the Sexual Revolution* (New York: Simon and Schuster, 1997), 100; "Christine Jorgensen Hits 55," *Toronto Star,* June 21, 1981, Ephemera, Subject: Transsexualism, International Gay Information Center Collection, New York Public Library. The information on Lawrence Tierney comes from the interview with Youngson.

88. "Christine Jorgensen Hits 55"; David Galligan, "Christine Jorgensen: A Silver Jubilee (of Sorts)," *Advocate,* December 27, 1978, 51.

89. Charles V. Yates to Christine Jorgensen, September 3, 1954, Yates folder; Christine Jorgensen to Bill Pinson, August 5, 1955, 1953 folder, both in Clippings/Letters box, CJP; Christine Jorgensen to Alfred C. Kinsey, September 11, 1955, Correspondence file Christine Jorgensen, KI.

90. Jorgensen, interview by Mike Wallace, 1959.

91. "In Christine's Footsteps," *Time,* March 8, 1954, 63; Charlotte McLeod, "I Changed My Sex," *Sir!* February 1955, 12.

92. Charlotte McLeod as told to Mark Shuler, "I Wanna Get Married" [n.p., c. 1954], 19, box 4/4 Clippings, VPC.

93. For a variety of clippings on McLeod, see Christine Jorgensen Scrapbook, 101–104, LLC. McLeod reappeared briefly in November 1959, when she got married in Miami. On her marriage see, for example, Joy Reese Shaw, "Her Own Story: Once G.I., Now a Bride," *Miami Herald,* November 13, 1959, 20; "Ex-GI Has Surgery Becomes a Bride," *San Francisco Chronicle,* November 14, 1959, Transexualism vertical file, KI. Later in life McLeod married again and raised children (her husband's from a previous marriage) in a home outside Los Angeles. She eventually moved back to Tennessee to care for her mother and made a living caring for the elderly. See interview with Aleshia Brevard Crenshaw by Susan Stryker, August 28, 1997, 43–47, transcript, GLBTHS.

94. McLeod, "I Changed My Sex," 12; McLeod, "I Wanna Get Married," 19.

95. McLeod, "I Changed My Sex," 12.

96. "Father in Britain Changed to Woman," *San Francisco News,* March 6, 1954, Christine Jorgensen Scrapbook, LLC; for other stories on Cowell, from both U.S. and British newspapers, see Christine Jorgensen Scrapbook, 106–120, LLC.

97. "California Millionaire Plans Sex Change to Woman," *Los Angeles Herald and Express,* May 4, 1954, box 1/1 Manuscripts, Correspondence, Photos, VPC; "Bunny like Christine? Heavens, No, My Dear!" *Los Angeles Mirror,* May 14, 1954, Bunny Breckinridge folder, ONE; "The She-He Millionaire," *Private Lives,* May 1955, 32–35, Transexualism vertical file 2, KI; "Odd Millionaire Who Wants to Be a Woman Jailed in Raid on San Francisco Waterfront Bar," *Keyhole* [c. May or June 1955], Bunny Breckinridge folder, ONE. Breckinridge tried to arrange surgery first in Denmark and later in Mexico. He maintained a public presence in the 1950s as an actor in B-grade films, now cult classics, made by director (and crossdresser) Edward D. Wood Jr. On the connection with Wood see Rudolph Grey, *Nightmare of Ecstasy: The Life and Art of Edward D. Wood, Jr.* (Portland, Ore.: Feral House, 1994); and the film *Ed Wood* (1994), directed by Tim Burton, in which actor Bill Murray plays Breckinridge.

98. On Rees, see Tamara Reese [*sic*], *"Reborn": A Factual Life Story of a Transition from Male to Female* (n.p., 1955), KI; and clippings on Rees in Christine Jorgensen Scrapbook, 123–132, LLC.

99. Joseph Martin and Henry Lee, "Tamara Would Start a New Life Where Nobody Knows of the Old," *New York Sunday News* [c. November 7, 1954]; "'Of Course I Can Marry,' Says Ex GI, Now Woman," *Sacramento Bee,* November 15, 1954, both in Christine Jorgensen Scrapbook, LLC.

100. Reese, *"Reborn,"* 15, 17.

101. Advertisement for "Hollywood Burlesk," *San Diego Union,* August 13, 1955, Transexualism vertical file 2, KI; on Rees's act, see "The Paratrooper Who Turned Stripper" [n.p., n.d.], Blue Notebook, box 1/1 Scrapbook, VPC.

102. Jack Mitchell, "What's Behind . . . The Strange Marriage of Christine No. 2?" *Top Secret,* February 1956, 12, 14, Blue Notebook, box 1/1 Scrapbook, VPC. On her split with her first husband, see *San Francisco Call-Bulletin,* November 21, 1955, Christine Jorgensen Scrapbook, LLC. Eventually Rees retreated from the public arena, married again, and adopted children. Both Walter Alvarez and Harry Benjamin recommended her—and gave her name, address, and phone number—to other transsexuals who wanted guidance. On her later life see, for example, Ralph R. Greenson, "On Homosexuality and Gender Identity," *International Journal of Psycho-Analysis* 45 (1964), 218; Walter C. Alvarez to Harry Benjamin, January 9, 1970, Walter C. Alvarez folder, box 3, Series IIC, HBC.

103. See advertisement for Bourbon's albums, Transexualism vertical file, KI. On Bourbon, see Don Romesburg, "Ray Bourbon: A Queer Sort of Biography" (M.A. thesis, University of Colorado, 2000), especially chap. 4.

104. Advertisement with medical report, *Los Angeles Examiner,* July 28, 1956, Rae Bourbon folder, ONE; advertisement for "She Lost It in Juarez," box 2/4 Clippings, VPC; "Sex-Switch Man Insists 'I'm a Woman,'" *Los Angeles Mirror,* July 31, 1956, Rae Bourbon folder, ONE.

105. Interview with Carmelita Nass, conducted by Bob Davis, October 28, 1996, 28, transcript, GLBTHS. On Bourbon's later life, see "Death in Prison for the Queen of Them All?" *Advocate,* November 11, 1970, 7, 10, 11. Bourbon spent his final years in prison in Texas convicted of murder.

106. In addition to the cases mentioned here, the American press reported male-to-female sex changes of people from other nations, including the surgeries of Martha (Jorge) Olmos Ramiro of Mexico, Jeanette (Jean) Jiousselot of France, and Frank Little

of Scotland. See, for example, "3 Mexican Interns Change Sex of Man," *Los Angeles Examiner*, May 6, 1954, box 1/1 Scrapbook, VPC; "Father of 2 Decides He's a Woman," *New York World-Telegram and Sun*, February 4, 1957, Transexualism vertical file 2, KI; "Scientist, 40, Father of 3, Changing Sex," *Los Angeles Times*, November 25, 1957, Transsexual Clippings folder, ONE.

107. "Male Shake Dancer Plans to Change Sex, Wed GI in Europe," *Jet*, June 18, 1953, 24–25.

108. "Why the Sex-Change Surgeons Would Rather Switch than Fight It," *Confidential* [c. 1966], box 3/4 Clippings, VPC.

109. Bill Jones, "Impersonator to Take Psychiatric Treatment," *Denver Rocky Mountain News*, November 22, 1958, box 2/3 Transvestia, file 4, VPC. See also clippings in John Murphy Goodshot folder, ONE.

110. Omar Garrison, "Strange Case: One Body—Two Sexes," *Los Angeles Mirror*, January 12–15, 1953, box 1/1 Scrapbook, VPC; "Are They Men or Women?" [n.p., c. 1953], box 1/4 Clippings, VPC. See also "Vice Versa," *Women in Crime*, May 1953, "Christine" Chicago Scrapbook.

111. "She Switched Sexes," *Brief*, August 1954, 43, Transexualism vertical file 2, KI. On Forbes-Semphill see, for example, "The Sex Change," *Man's Day* [c. 1953], box 1/1 Scrapbook, VPC; on Dillon, see "A Change of Heir," *Time*, May 26, 1958, 34. Other brief reports announced the surgical sex change in Persia of Farideh Najafi, who wanted "to join the Shah's Army," the proposed surgery of an unnamed Trinidadian, and the legal (but not surgical) change of British schoolteacher Donald Bury, formerly Olive. See, for example, "Girl Who's Turning into a Man," *Scoop*, January 1954, Transexualism vertical file 2, KI; "Sex Change to Make Trinidad Woman a Man," *Jet*, April 1, 1954, 18; "Miss Olive Is Mister," *Newsweek*, April 16, 1956, 105.

112. "Man into Woman," *True Confessions* [c. March 1953], box 1/1 Scrapbooks, VPC; "I Was Forced into 'Manhood,'" *HE*, January 1954, Transexualism vertical file 2, KI; George Jackson, "Why I Want to Change My Sex," *Sir!* Winter 1954, 16, 17, 66, 67; Juan Morales, "Sex Surgery While You Wait!" *Whisper*, April 1955, Transexualism vertical file 2, KI; A. Smith-Henderson, "The Weird Psychology of Sex Changes," *Hit Annual*, Winter 1957, Transsexuals folder, ONE.

113. "Feathered Christine Causes Amazement among Farm Flock," *Keyhole*, March 2, 1955, Changelings folder, ONE; "New Sex Switches," *People Today*, May 5, 1954, 15, Transexualism vertical file, KI.

114. Memo, Peter Rachtman to Warren Bayless, September 14, 1967, Christine Jorgensen—Bayless correspondence folder, Letters box, CJP.

115. On the competition among mass media, see James L. Baughman, *The Republic of Mass Culture: Journalism, Filmmaking, and Broadcasting in America since 1941* (Baltimore: Johns Hopkins University Press, 1992).

116. Advertisement for Bourbon's albums, Transexualism vertical file, KI.

117. "Christine Jorgensen Reveals."

118. Aline Mosby, "Make Movie on Christine!" [n.p., c. 1953], box 3/4 Clippings, VPC; "Glen or Glenda?" advertising poster, box 1/1 Manuscripts, VPC; "Christine Jorgensen Reveals." On Jorgensen's rejection of the film role, see Grey, *Nightmare of Ecstasy*, 39, 122. For the various titles under which the picture was released, see the cover of the videotape version, *Glen or Glenda?* Rhino Home Video.

119. "How Charles Became Charlotte!" *Picture Scope,* July 1954, Transexualism vertical file, KI.

120. Jordan Park, *Half* (n.p.: Lion Books [c. 1953]); Mark Shane, *Sex Gantlet to Murder* (Fresno: Fabian, 1955); idem, *The Lady Was a Man* (Fresno: Fabian, 1958). On the popular association of male-to-female transsexuals with psychopathic violence, see Marjorie Garber, *Vested Interests: Cross-Dressing and Cultural Anxiety* (New York: Harper-Collins, 1993), 115–116.

121. Neils Hoyer, ed., *Man into Woman* (New York: Popular Library, 1953); Roberta Cowell, *Roberta Cowell's Story* (London: William Heinemann, 1954); Reese, *"Reborn"*; Eugene de Savitsch, *Homosexuality, Transvestism, and Change of Sex* (Springfield, Ill.: Charles C. Thomas, 1958).

122. Letter from Otto Grossman, *New York Post* [c. April 1953]; letter from Marie L. Coleman, *New York Post* [c. April 1953]. These and other letters to the *Post* are in the Christine Jorgensen Scrapbook, 57, LLC. See also the letters in response to a story on Charlotte McLeod: *Sir!* March 1955, 6, Transexualism vertical file 2, KI. For other responses, see Jimmy Jemail, "The Inquiring Fotographer," *New York Daily News,* December 5, 1952, 11.

123. Paul Robinson to Estelle Freedman, email message, October 23, 1995; Paul Robinson to author, email message, September 17, 1999.

124. Lal, "MD's and Public"; Shailer Upton Lawton, "Men and Women," *True Confessions,* May 1953, 124; "Christine Jorgensen Reveals."

125. McLeod, "I Changed My Sex," 10; "Bunny like Christine?"; Reese, *"Reborn,"* 56.

126. Jorgensen, *Christine Jorgensen,* 189.

127. These collections have proven invaluable in my research. In addition to Louise Lawrence's scrapbook at the Kinsey Institute, see the various scrapbooks and clipping collections in the Virginia Prince Collection. Special thanks to Joseph Agnew for lending me the "Christine" scrapbook from Chicago in his private collection. On "The Obligatory Transsexual File," see Sandy Stone, "The Empire Strikes Back: A Posttranssexual Manifesto," in *Body Guards: The Cultural Politics of Gender Ambiguity,* ed. Julia Epstein and Kristina Straub (New York: Routledge, 1991), 285.

128. P. T. to Christine Jorgensen, January 20, 1955, unlabeled folder, Letters box, CJP.

129. Jorgensen, *Christine Jorgensen,* 217.

130. D. R. to Christine Jorgensen, May 6, 1953, Sex Change—Other than CJ folder; anonymous to Christine Jorgensen [c. 1953], Christine folder; M. C. to Christine Jorgensen, February 1953, Sex Change—Other than CJ folder; R. L. to Christine Jorgensen, September 2, 1969, Sex Change—Other than CJ folder, all in Letters box, CJP.

131. "Betty," "Gracie," and "Joan" to Christine Jorgensen, December 10, 1952, loose; L. M. to Christine Jorgensen, March 17, 1953, Sex Change—Other than CJ folder; B. S. to Christine Jorgensen, May 13, 1954, unlabeled folder, all in Letters box, CJP.

132. R. E. L. Masters, *Sex-Driven People: An Autobiographical Approach to the Problem of the Sex-Dominated Personality* (Los Angeles: Sherbourne, 1966), 232.

133. S. W. to Alfred C. Kinsey, December 8, 1952, Correspondence file S. W., KI; Harry Benjamin, July 2, 1954, S. W. folder, box 8, Series IIC, HBC; A. S. probably to Harry Benjamin, first page missing [c. March 1954], A. D. folder, box 4, ibid.; Louise Lawrence to Harry Benjamin, April 6, 1953, TRNSV notebook, LLC.

134. Benjamin, *The Transsexual Phenonomenon,* 245–246; S. G. to Christine Jorgensen, June 3, 1953, Sex Change—Other than CJ folder; L. T. to Christine Jorgensen, April 7, 1953, unlabeled folder, both in Letters box, CJP; Mario Martino with harriet, *Emergence: A Transsexual Autobiography* (New York: Crown, 1977), 40. For additional accounts of female-to-males' responses to Jorgensen, see Holly Devor, *FTM: Female-to-Male Transsexuals in Society* (Bloomington: Indiana University Press, 1997), 354–355. For a lengthier discussion of the ongoing marking of transsexuality as male-to-female, see Garber, *Vested Interests,* chap. 4.

135. Jorgensen, *Christine Jorgensen,* 79.

136. Stacy Crawford, as told to Mona Joslin Cross, *The Eve Principle: The Story of a Truly Unique Transsexual* (New York: Vantage, 1984), 33.

137. Mr. Mayer to Christine Jorgensen, April 9, 1953, Sex Change—Other than CJ folder; Morton Singer to Christine Jorgensen, March 10, 1953, Very Important Letters folder; Evelyn West to Christine Jorgensen, December 15, 1952, Sex Change—Other than CJ folder, all in Letters box, CJP.

138. Beatrice James to Christine Jorgensen, March 24, 1952, Sex Change—Other than CJ folder; "The Truth" to Christine Jorgensen [c. September 1953], unlabeled folder; James Schlang to Christine Jorgensen, April 10, 1953, loose, all in Letters box, CJP.

139. "Christine Jorgensen Reveals."

140. H. S. to Christine Jorgensen [c. 1953], Christine folder; Crystal Knowland to Christine Jorgensen, March 14, 1953, loose; Ralph Kelley to Christine Jorgensen, December 7, 1952, loose, all in Letters box, CJP.

141. J. M. to Christine Jorgensen, April 19, 1953, Sex Change—Other than CJ folder; Nell George to Christine Jorgensen, March 15, 1953, loose, both in Letters box, CJP.

142. Barbara Williams to George and Florence Jorgensen, December 1, 1952; Jim McCurdy to Christine Jorgensen, March 1, 1953; loose, both in Letters box, CJP.

3. FROM SEX TO GENDER

1. *Christine Jorgensen Reveals,* record album [c. 1957], available at KI. See also interview with Christine Jorgensen, conducted by Mike Wallace, 1959, audiotape in author's possession; telephone interview with Jo Smith, conducted by author, January 10, 1996.

2. Alton Blakeslee, "Thousands Do Not Know True Sex," *New York Daily News,* December 7, 1952, 6; G. B. Lal, "MD's and Public to Eagerly Follow Christine's Life," *New York Journal-American,* December 7, 1952, L-18.

3. Shailer Upton Lawton, "Men and Women: Amazing Truths about Sex Glands," *True Story,* May 1953, 55, 124, 125.

4. Christine Jorgensen, "The Story of My Life," *American Weekly,* March 8, 1953, 11; Christian Hamburger, Georg K. Stürup, and E. Dahl-Iversen, "Transvestism: Hormonal,

Psychiatric, and Surgical Treatment," *Journal of the American Medical Association* 152 (May 1953), 392.

5. Harry Benjamin to Alfred C. Kinsey, April 16, 1953, Correspondence file Harry Benjamin, KI.

6. Harry Benjamin to Christian Hamburger, May 13, 1953, TRNSV notebook, LLC; Harry Benjamin, "Transvestism and Transsexualism," *International Journal of Sexology* 7:1 (1953), 12.

7. See, for example, Murray L. Barr and G. Edgar Hobbs, "Chromosomal Sex in Transvestites," *Lancet,* May 20, 1954, 1100–10.

8. Benjamin, "Transvestism and Transsexualism," 13; Harry Benjamin to Alfred C. Kinsey, June 5, 1953, Correspondence file Harry Benjamin, KI.

9. Hamburger, Stürup, and Dahl-Iversen, "Transvestism," 392–393; Benjamin, "Transvestism and Transsexualism," 13.

10. Hamburger, Stürup, and Dahl-Iversen, "Transvestism," 396; Benjamin, "Transvestism and Transsexualism," 14.

11. J. Allen Gilbert, "Homo-Sexuality and Its Treatment," *Journal of Nervous and Mental Disease* 52:4 (October 1920), 321; D. M. Olkon and Irene Case Sherman, "Eonism with Added Outstanding Psychopathic Features," *Journal of Nervous and Mental Disease* 99 (January–June 1944), 166.

12. Otto Fenichel, *The Psychoanalytic Theory of Neurosis* (New York: W. W. Norton, 1945), 344–345; idem, "The Psychology of Transvestism," in *The Collected Papers of Otto Fenichel* (New York: W. W. Norton, 1953), 179. The essay was first published in 1930.

13. Sandor Rado, "A Critical Examination of the Concept of Bisexuality," in Rado, *Psychoanalysis of Behavior: Collected Papers* (New York: Grune and Stratton, 1956), 142–145. For another repudiation of biological bisexuality, see Alfred C. Kinsey, Wardell B. Pomeroy, and Clyde E. Martin, *Sexual Behavior in the Human Male* (Philadelphia: W. B. Saunders, 1948), 658–659.

14. Paul Starr, *The Social Transformation of American Medicine* (New York: Basic Books, 1982), 337. See also Nathan G. Hale Jr., *The Rise and Crisis of Psychoanalysis in the United States: Freud and the Americans, 1917–1985* (New York: Oxford University Press, 1995), 187–210; Gerald N. Grob, "Psychiatry's Holy Grail: The Search for the Mechanisms of Mental Diseases," *Bulletin of the History of Medicine* 72 (1998), 211–212.

15. D. O. Cauldwell, "Psychopathia Transexualis," *Sexology* 16:5 (December 1949), 274–280.

16. George H. Wiedeman, "Transvestism," *Journal of the American Medical Association* 152:12 (July 18, 1953), 1167; Mortimer Ostow, "Transvestism," ibid., 152:16 (August 15, 1953), 1553.

17. Harry Benjamin, "Transsexualism and Transvestism as Psycho-Somatic and Somato-Psychic Syndromes," *American Journal of Psychotherapy* 8 (April 1954), 222, 225, 226; Emil A. Gutheil, "The Psychologic Background of Transsexualism and Transvestism," ibid., 233, 236, 238.

18. On the growing influence in the United States of psychogenic theories of homosexuality, see Jennifer Terry, *An American Obsession: Science, Medicine, and Homosexuality in Modern Society* (Chicago: University of Chicago Press, 1999), 290–296.

19. See, for example, Joel Braslow, *Mental Ills and Bodily Cures: Psychiatric Treatment in the First Half of the Twentieth Century* (Berkeley: University of California Press, 1997).

20. Frederic G. Worden and James T. Marsh, "Psychological Factors in Men Seeking Sex Transformation: A Preliminary Report," *Journal of the American Medical Association* 157:15 (April 9, 1955), 1292, 1293, 1294, 1297, 1298.

21. Harry Benjamin, "Sex Transformation," *Journal of the American Medical Association* 158:3 (May 21, 1955), 217; Harry Benjamin to Alfred C. Kinsey, May 2 and May 23, 1955, Correspondence file Harry Benjamin, KI.

22. Christine Jorgensen, "The Story of My Life," *American Weekly*, February 15, 1953, 7; Alvin Davis, "The Truth about 'Christine' Jorgensen," *New York Post*, April 6, 7, and 9, 1953, Christine Jorgensen Scrapbook, LLC; "Altered Ego," *Time*, April 18, 1955, 91.

23. For other European doctors who supported sex-change surgery in the 1950s, see Per Anchersen, "Problems of Transvestism," *Acta Psychiatrica et Neurologica Scandinavica* 106 (1956), 249–256; Sir Harold Gillies and D. Ralph Millard Jr., *The Principles and Art of Plastic Surgery* (Boston: Little, Brown, 1957), 370–371, 383–388. For a list of prominent opponents in the 1950s, see N[areyz] Lukianowicz, "Survey of Various Aspects of Transvestism in the Light of Our Present Knowledge," *Journal of Nervous and Mental Disease* 128:1 (January 1959), 59–60; see also John B. Randell, "Transvestitism and Trans-Sexualism: A Study of 50 Cases," *British Medical Journal*, December 26, 1959, 1448–52.

24. Walter C. Alvarez, "How Surgery Helps Clear Up Sex Mixups," *Chicago Sun-Times*, May 23, 1955, 44; Eugene de Savitsch, *Homosexuality, Transvestism, and Change of Sex* (Springfield, Ill.: Charles C. Thomas, 1958), 95.

25. Karl M. Bowman and Bernice Engle, "Medicolegal Aspects of Transvestism," *American Journal of Psychiatry* 113:7 (January 1957), 583.

26. Ibid., 586, 587, 588.

27. Karl Heinrich Ulrichs, *The Riddle of "Man-Manly" Love: The Pioneering Work on Male Homosexuality*, vol. 1 (Buffalo: Prometheus, 1994), 58. See Gert Hekma, "'A Female Soul in a Male Body': Sexual Inversion as Gender Inversion in Nineteenth-Century Sexology," in *Third Sex, Third Gender: Beyond Sexual Dimorphism in Culture and History*, ed. Gilbert Herdt (New York: Zone, 1996), 213–239.

28. D. O. Cauldwell, *Questions and Answers on the Sex Life and Sexual Problems of Trans-Sexuals* (Girard, Kans.: Haldeman-Julius Publications, 1950), front cover; Hamburger, Stürup, and Dahl-Iversen, "Transvestism," 391, 396; Benjamin, "Transvestism and Transsexualism," 13.

29. John I. Brewer and Harry Culver, "True Hermaphroditism," *Journal of the American Medical Association* 148:6 (February 9, 1952), 433, 435. For an excellent account of the emergence of this position, see Bernice Hausman, *Changing Sex: Transsexualism, Technology, and the Idea of Gender* (Durham, N.C.: Duke University Press, 1995), chap. 3.

30. Michael Dillon, *Self: A Study in Ethics and Endocrinology* (London: William Heinemann, 1946), 53.

31. Hamburger, Stürup, and Dahl-Iversen, "Transvestism," 394; Benjamin, "Transsexualism and Transvestism as Syndromes," 229.

NOTES TO PAGES 113–118

311

32. Quoted in Gobind Behari Lal, "'7 Sexes' Doctrine Launched," *Los Angeles Examiner,* September 29, 1960, sec. 4, p. 12.

33. Brewer and Culver, "True Hermaphroditism," 434. On the connections with Mead and others who studied "sex roles," see John L. Hampson and Joan G. Hampson, "The Ontogenesis of Sexual Behavior in Man," in *Sex and Internal Secretions,* ed. William C. Young, vol. 2 (Baltimore: Williams and Wilkins, 1961), 1418.

34. John Money, "Hermaphroditism, Gender, and Precocity in Hyperadrenocorticism: Psychologic Findings," *Bulletin of the Johns Hopkins Hospital* 96 (June 1955), 254, 258. See, for example, John Money, Joan G. Hampson, and John L. Hampson, "Imprinting and the Establishment of Gender Role," *American Medical Association Archives of Neurology and Psychiatry* 77 (March 1957), 333–336.

35. Alfred C. Kinsey, Wardell B. Pomeroy, Clyde E. Martin, and Paul H. Gebhard, *Sexual Behavior in the Human Female* (Philadelphia: W. B. Saunders, 1953), 643–644.

36. Money, Hampson, and Hampson, "Imprinting," 335; Money, "Hermaphroditism, Gender, and Precocity," 258. The articles had implications for medical treatment. They implied that infants, who had not yet learned a gender, could be assigned to either sex without psychological damage but that adults should be treated only in accord with their established gender. These findings reinforced the already prevalent practice of performing surgery on intersexed infants to force them to approximate maleness or femaleness, but they made genetic sex irrelevant in deciding which sex to approximate. They also led to the now notorious case of David Reimer, a toddler for whom John Money recommended a disastrous sex reassignment (from boy to girl) after a botched circumcision destroyed the boy's penis. On Reimer, see John Colapinto, *As Nature Made Him: The Boy Who Was Raised as a Girl* (New York: HarperCollins, 2000).

37. Ralph R. Greenson, "On Homosexuality and Gender Identity," *International Journal of Psycho-Analysis* 45 (1964), 217; Robert J. Stoller, "A Contribution to the Study of Gender Identity," *International Journal of Psycho-Analysis* 45 (1964), 220.

38. Ibid., 221, 223, 225. The other case study presented, Stoller later discovered, was a male-to-female transsexual who had convinced Stoller and his colleagues that she had an intersexed condition.

39. Robert J. Stoller to Charles W. Socarides, October 14, 1968, General, Q–Z, 1968–1969 folder, box 37, RSP.

40. Robert J. Stoller, *Sex and Gender: On the Development of Masculinity and Femininity* (New York: Science House, 1968), 102, 216, 205.

41. Ibid., 2, 29, 66, 74, 83.

42. John Money and Clay Primrose, "Sexual Dimorphism and Dissociation in the Psychology of Male Transsexuals," *Journal of Nervous and Mental Disease* 147:5 (1968), 481; see also John Money and John G. Brennan, "Sexual Dimorphism in the Psychology of Female Transsexuals," *Journal of Nervous and Mental Disease* 147:5 (1968), 497.

43. Harry Benjamin, "Nature and Management of Transsexualism," *Western Journal of Surgery, Obstetrics and Gynecology* 72 (March–April 1964), 106, 107.

44. Harry Benjamin, "Clinical Aspects of Transsexualism in the Male and Female," *American Journal of Psychotherapy* 18:3 (July 1964), 462.

45. Harry Benjamin, *The Transsexual Phenomenon* (New York: Julian, 1966), 4, 5, 8, 9, 18, 46, 47, 163.

46. For examples of psychoanalytic case studies, see Nahman H. Greenberg, Alan K. Rosenwald, and Paul E. Nielson, "A Study in Transsexualism," *Psychiatric Quarterly* 34 (1960), 203–235; Nikolas Golosow and Elliott L. Weitzman, "Psychosexual and Ego Regression in the Male Transsexual," *Journal of Nervous and Mental Disease* 149:4 (1969), 328–336.

47. Ira B. Pauly, "Male Psychosexual Inversion: Transsexualism," *Archives of General Psychiatry* 13 (August 1965), 175; Leslie M. Lothstein, "Theories of Transsexualism," in *Sexuality and Medicine,* ed. Earl E. Shelp, vol. 1: *Conceptual Roots* (Dordrecht: D. Reidel, 1987), 69.

48. There was some association in the literature between Klinefelter's Syndrome (XXY chromosomes) and crossgender identification, but the vast majority of transsexuals tested had normal chromosome patterns. On the failure to find biological correlates, see J. Housden, "An Examination of the Biologic Etiology of Transvestism," *International Journal of Social Psychiatry* 11:4 (Autumn 1965), 301–305; Pauly, "Male Psychosexual Inversion," 173; Jan Wålinder, "Transsexuals: Physical Characteristics, Parental Age, and Birth Order," in *Transsexualism and Sex Reassignment,* ed. Richard Green and John Money (Baltimore: Johns Hopkins Press, 1969), 221–231. On the association with Klinefelter's Syndrome, see Stoller, *Sex and Gender,* 82–83.

49. Benjamin, *Transsexual Phenomenon,* 53; see also 152.

50. Pauly, "Male Psychosexual Inversion," 178; Benjamin, *Transsexual Phenomenon,* 113.

51. Robert Veit Sherwin, "The Legal Problem in Transvestism," *American Journal of Psychotherapy* 8:2 (April 1954), 244; Rollin M. Perkins to Willard E. Goodwin, July 9, 1954, Male Transsexualism section, box 9, RSP.

52. "Homosexual Transvestite," *Sexology* 22:6 (January 1956), 390. See also D. O. Cauldwell, "Is 'Sex Change' Ethical?" *Sexology* 22:2 (September 1955), 108–112; "Lesbian's Strange Desires," *Sexology* 22:6 (January 1956), 401.

53. Stanley Mosk to Robert J. Stoller, December 4, 1962, Male Transsexualism section, box 9, RSP. Mosk was apparently unaware of the earlier correspondence between Harry Benjamin and Edmund G. Brown.

54. Richard P. Bergen, "Transvestism Surgery," *Journal of the American Medical Association* 182:8 (November 24, 1962), 150.

55. See Richard Green, Robert J. Stoller, and Craig MacAndrew, "Attitudes toward Sex Transformation Procedures," *Archives of General Psychiatry* 15 (August 1966), 179.

56. Richard Green, "Change-of-Sex," *Medical Aspects of Human Sexuality* 3:10 (October 1969), 112.

57. See Elmer Belt to Harry Benjamin, June 23, 1958, Elmer Belt folder, box 3, Series IIC, HBC.

58. Robert J. Stoller to David L. Hoffberg, September 5, 1968, General, H–P, 1968–1969 folder, box 37, RSP.

59. "Four Doctors Accused in Sex-Shift Surgery" [Rochester newspaper], June 23, 1962, box 1/4 Clippings, VPC; "Doctors Sued for Sex Surgery; Man Says He's Not a 'Freak'" [n.p.], June 23, 1962, Transexualism vertical file 2, KI. On the lack of other such suits in the United States and on settling out of court, see Green, "Change-of-Sex," 106. On doctors' concerns about the suit, see Harry Benjamin to Elmer Belt, June 29,

1962; Belt to Benjamin, July 2, 1962, both in Elmer Belt, 1962–1965 folder, box 3, Series IIC, HBC.

60. Eugene de Savitsch, *Homosexuality, Transvestism, and Change of Sex* (Springfield, Ill.: Charles C. Thomas, 1958), 90; Harry Benjamin to Wardell B. Pomeroy, February 28, 1963, Correspondence file Harry Benjamin, KI; Wardell B. Pomeroy to Walter Alvarez, August 16, 1963, Correspondence file Walter Alvarez, KI.

61. Green, Stoller, and MacAndrew, "Attitudes toward Sex Transformation Procedures."

62. Richard Green, "Physician Emotionalism in the Treatment of the Transsexual," *Transactions of the New York Academy of Sciences,* 2d ser., 29 (1967), 441.

63. Ira B. Pauly, "The Current Status of the Change of Sex Operation," *Journal of Nervous and Mental Disease* 147:5 (1968), 467.

64. Benjamin, *Transsexual Phenomenon,* 123, 135.

65. Pauly, "Male Psychosexual Inversion," 177; Howard J. Baker and Richard Green, "Treatment of Transsexualism," *Current Psychiatric Therapies* 10 (1970), 96.

66. Pauly, "Adult Manifestations of Female Transsexualism," 79–80; Donald W. Hastings to Robert J. Stoller, March 23, 1965, Ethics of Sex Transformation folder, box 30, RSP.

67. Ira B. Pauly, "The Current Status of the Change of Sex Operation," 4, paper presented at the Fourth World Congress of Psychiatry, Madrid, September 1966, KI Library; Robert J. Stoller, "'It's Only a Phase': Femininity in Boys," *Journal of the American Medical Association* 201:5 (July 31, 1967), 314–315; Mari Jo Buhle, *Feminism and Its Discontents: A Century of Struggle with Psychoanalysis* (Cambridge, Mass.: Harvard University Press, 1998), 188.

68. Richard Green and John Money, "Incongruous Gender Role: Nongenital Manifestations in Prepubertal Boys," *Journal of Nervous and Mental Disease* 131 (1960), 167.

69. "The Department of Psychiatry wishes to announce the formation of a Gender Identity Research Clinic," typewritten statement [c. 1962], Gender Clinic Meetings, 1962–1970 folder, box 16, RSP.

70. Robert J. Stoller, "Memorandum," November 15, 1962; idem, "Memorandum," November 27, 1962, Gender Clinic Meetings, 1962–1970 folder; "Gender Identity Research Clinic: Annual Report, July 1, 1963–June 30, 1964," Research Meetings, 1964–1965 folder, all in box 16, RSP.

71. Robert J. Stoller to Paul H. Gebhard, November 3, 1964, Correspondence file Robert Stoller, KI; Robert J. Stoller, "The Treatment of Transvestism and Transsexualism," in *Current Psychiatric Therapies,* ed. Jules H. Masserman, vol. 6 (New York: Grune and Stratton, 1966), 102.

72. On other clinics and their contemporary operations, see Phyllis Burke, *Gender Shock: Exploding the Myths of Male and Female* (New York: Doubleday/Anchor, 1996).

73. Daniel G. Brown, "Psychosexual Disturbances: Transvestism and Sex-Role Inversion," *Marriage and Family Living* 22:3 (August 1960), 224.

74. Green, "Change-of-Sex," 113.

75. There was at least one exception. Gobind Behari Lal, a retired science journalist and a friend of Benjamin's, used the theory of bisexuality to reject both the "separateness

of man and woman" and "the overlordship of man over woman." Benjamin published Lal's comments in an appendix to *The Transsexual Phenomenon* (167).

4. A "FIERCE AND DEMANDING" DRIVE

1. Robert S. Redmount, "A Case of a Female Transvestite with Marital and Criminal Complications," *Journal of Clinical and Experimental Psychopathology* 14:2 (June 1953), 95; K. G. autobiography, April 1964, no. 33 Diary Room, KI.

2. T. Sorensen and P. Hertoft, "Sexmodifying Operations on Transsexuals in Denmark in the Period 1950–1977," *Acta Psychiatrica Scandinavica* (January 1980), 62–63.

3. Christian Hamburger, "The Desire for Change of Sex as Shown by Personal Letters from 465 Men and Women," *Acta Endocrinologica* 14:4 (1953), 363, 375.

4. Christian Hamburger to E. M., January 9, 1953, D. M. folder, box 6, Series IIC, HBC.

5. C. W. to Harry Benjamin, January 21, 1954; Benjamin to C. W., January 25, 1954, both in C. W. folder, box 8, Series IIC, HBC; Christian Hamburger to A. S., February 17, 1954, A. D. folder, box 4, ibid.

6. For examples of referrals, see Henrietta Thomas, "Harry Benjamin, M. D.: A Remembrance," *Chrysalis Quarterly* 1:5 (1993), 16; H. W. to Harry Benjamin, January 8, 1956, P. W. folder, box 8, Series IIC, HBC; B. S. to Harry Benjamin, June 11, 1954, B. S. folder, box 7, ibid.; Robert J. Stoller to D. B., November 14, 1968, General, A–G, 1968–1969 folder, box 37, RSP.

7. Margo Howard-Howard with Abbe Michaels, *I Was a White Slave in Harlem* (New York: Four Walls Eight Windows, 1988), 78; Renée Richards with John Ames, *Second Serve: The Renée Richards Story* (New York: Stein and Day, 1983), 164; Jan Morris, *Conundrum* (New York: New American Library, 1975), 51.

8. Ira B. Pauly, "Adult Manifestations of Female Transsexualism," in *Transsexualism and Sex Reassignment,* ed. Richard Green and John Money (Baltimore: Johns Hopkins Press, 1969), 73.

9. John E. Hoopes, Norman J. Knorr, and Sanford R. Wolf, "Transsexualism: Considerations Regarding Sexual Reassignment," *Journal of Nervous and Mental Disease* 147:5 (1968), 513; Mario Martino with harriet, *Emergence: A Transsexual Autobiography* (New York: Crown, 1977), 242. On Mexican Americans see, for example, Pauly, "Adult Manifestations of Female Transsexualism," 73.

10. Harry Benjamin to Christine Jorgensen, February 16, 1953, Documentation for CJ: A Personal Autobiog folder, box Clippings/Letters, CJP; R. W. to Harry Benjamin, March 19, 1956, R. W. folder, box 8, Series IIC, HBC; C. S. to Harry Benjamin [c. September 19, 1954], C. S. folder, box 7, ibid.

11. H. W. to Harry Benjamin [c. May 15, 1956], P. W. folder, box 8, Series IIC, HBC; P. K. to Harry Benjamin, September 23, 1968, P. K. folder, box 5, ibid. See also Gloria Marmar Warner and Marion Lahn, "A Case of Female Transsexualism," *Psychiatric Quarterly* 44 (1970), 478; S. W. to Harry Benjamin, July 2, 1954, S. W. folder, box 8, Series IIC, HBC; Pauly, "Adult Manifestations of Female Transsexualism," 59–87.

12. C. E., Life History [c. 1953], C. E. folder, box 4, Series IIC, HBC.

13. R. E. L. Masters, *Sex-Driven People: An Autobiographical Approach to the Problem of the Sex-Dominated Personality* (Los Angeles: Sherbourne, 1966), 224; Robert S.

McCully, "An Interpretation of Projective Findings in a Case of Female Transsexualism," *Journal of Projective Techniques and Personality Assessment* 27 (1963), 436.

14. Warner and Lahn, "A Case of Female Transsexualism," 478; Robert J. Stoller, *Sex and Gender: On the Development of Masculinity and Femininity* (New York: Science House, 1968), 200.

15. Redmount, "A Case of a Female Transvestite," 95, 97; Harry Benjamin, *The Transsexual Phenomenon* (New York: Julian, 1966), 251; B. S. to Harry Benjamin, January 31, 1957, B. S. folder, box 7, Series IIC, HBC.

16. Interview with Regina Elizabeth McQuade by Susan Stryker, July 17, 1997, 1, transcript, GLBTHS.

17. H. W. to Harry Benjamin [c. May 15, 1956], P. W. folder, box 8; C. E. to Harry Benjamin, December 3, 1953, C. E. folder, box 4; both in Series IIC, HBC; Benjamin, *The Transsexual Phenomenon,* 138.

18. T. J. M. to Robert J. Stoller, November 1965, Female Transsexualism section, box 9, RSP; Benjamin, *The Transsexual Phenomenon,* 242.

19. Harry Benjamin, handwritten note on R. W., April 5 [1956], R. W. folder, box 8, Series IIC, HBC; Redmount, "A Case of a Female Transvestite," 96.

20. Jane C. Doe (pseud.), "Autobiography of a Transsexual," *Diseases of the Nervous System,* April 1967, 251, 252.

21. On the emerging sense of community, see Chapters 5 and 6.

22. T. J. M. to Robert J. Stoller, November 1965.

23. R. W. B. to Harry Benjamin, March 27, 1967, R. W. B. folder, box 3, Series IIC, HBC; P. K. to Harry Benjamin, September 23, 1968, P. K. folder, box 5, ibid.

24. Lynne Layton, *Who's That Girl? Who's That Boy? Clinical Practice Meets Postmodern Gender Theory* (Northvale, N.J.: Jason Aronson, 1998), 11, 25; Jay Prosser, *Second Skins: The Body Narratives of Transsexuality* (New York: Columbia University Press, 1998), 158. Prosser argues, "it is the life-plot [of gender inversion] rather than actual somatic sex change that symptomizes the transsexual."

25. S. W. to Harry Benjamin, August 19, 1954, S. W. folder, box 8, Series IIC, HBC; L. C. to Harry Benjamin and Virginia Allen, April 10, 1971, L. C. folder, box 4, ibid.; Stoller, *Sex and Gender,* 200; Masters, *Sex-Driven People,* 248.

26. Pauly, "Adult Manifestations of Female Transsexualism," 76, 77. See also Karl M. Bowman and Bernice Engle, "Medicolegal Aspects of Transvestism," *American Journal of Psychiatry* 113:7 (January 1957), 587.

27. C. E. to Harry Benjamin, November 30 [1953], C. E. folder, box 4, Series IIC, HBC; see also Masters, *Sex-Driven People,* 244.

28. Ira B. Pauly, "Male Psychosexual Inversion: Transsexualism," *Archives of General Psychiatry* 13:2 (August 1965), 176; Nahman H. Greenberg, Alan K. Rosenwald, and Paul E. Nielson, "A Study in Transsexualism," *Psychiatric Quarterly* 34 (1960), 220; A. S. to Harry Benjamin, June 16, 1954, A. D. folder, box 4, Series IIC, HBC.

29. G. S. to Harry Benjamin, March 12, 1954, J. S. folder, box 7, Series IIC, HBC; R. B. to Harry Benjamin, October 24, 1953, R. B. folder, box 3, ibid.; Doe, "Autobiography," 251, 254.

30. J. F. to Harry Benjamin, December 26, 1969, J. F. folder, box 4, Series IIC, HBC.

31. G. S. to Harry Benjamin, April 25, 1954, J. S. folder, box 7, Series IIC, HBC; M. G. to Harry Benjamin, March 12, 1969, M. G. folder, box 4, ibid.; H. W. to Harry Benjamin [c. May 15, 1956], P. W. folder, box 8, ibid.

32. T. J. M. to Robert J. Stoller, November 1965; Hoopes, Knorr, and Wolf, "Transsexualism," 515; C. W. to Harry Benjamin, January 21, 1954.

33. Dean St. Dennis, "Boy Who Doesn't Want to Be One," *San Francisco Chronicle,* December 31, 1962, folder 33, box 15, Series IIIB, HBC.

34. Harry Benjamin to Elmer Belt, January 3, 1955, Correspondence file Harry Benjamin, KI; Robert J. Stoller to J. W., November 22, 1965, General, Q–Z, 1965–1966 folder, box 37, RSP.

35. Milton T. Edgerton, Norman J. Knorr, and James R. Callison, "The Surgical Treatment of Transsexual Patients," *Plastic and Reconstructive Surgery* 45:1 (January 1970), 38, 41.

36. S. W. to Alfred C. Kinsey, December 1, 1952, Correspondence file S. W., KI.

37. S. W. to Harry Benjamin, July 2, 1954, S. W. folder, box 8, Series IIC, HBC; S. W. to Alfred C. Kinsey, March 11, 1953, Correspondence file S. W., KI.

38. S. W. to Harry Benjamin, August 19, 1954; note by Harry Benjamin, February 1958, both in S. W. folder, box 8, Series IIC, HBC.

39. D. M. to Harry Benjamin, December 29, 1954, D. M. folder, box 6, Series IIC, HBC.

40. "Why More Men Want to Change Their Sex" [n.p., c. 1955], 33, Blue Notebook, box 1/1 Scrapbook, VPC. On the FTM's surgery in his sister's kitchen, see D. B. M. to Harry Benjamin, October 26, 1965, D. M. folder, box 6, Series IIC, HBC.

41. T. J. M. to Robert J. Stoller, November 1965.

42. C. E., Life History [c. 1953], C. E. folder, box 4, Series IIC, HBC; "Transsexual," *Sexology* 31:6 (January 1965), 395; M. O. to Harry Benjamin, October 13, 1968, M. O. folder, box 6, Series IIC, HBC.

43. Benjamin, *The Transsexual Phenomenon,* 96. For recent accounts of the effects of hormones, see Rosemary Basson and Jerilynn C. Prior, "Hormonal Therapy of Gender Dysphoria: The Male-to-Female Transsexual," in *Current Concepts in Transgender Identity,* ed. Dallas Denny (New York: Garland, 1998), 277–296; Jerilynn C. Prior and Stacy Elliott, "Hormonal Therapy of Gender Dysphoria: The Female-to-Male Transsexual," in Denny, *Current Concepts,* 297–313.

44. Grace to Nancy, no. 13 [c. 1958], Grace–Nancy notebook; Louise Lawrence to B. S., June 7, 1954, Alfred C. Kinsey folder, LLC; Louise Lawrence to Harry Benjamin, April 24, 1953, TRNSV notebook, LLC.

45. T. J. M. to Robert J. Stoller, November 1965.

46. Pauly, "Male Psychosexual Inversion," 177.

47. C. E. to Harry Benjamin, October 5, 1953, C. E. folder, box 4, Series IIC, HBC. See also C. E. to Benjamin, December 3, 1953, ibid.; Louise Lawrence to Benjamin, December 29, 1953, TRNSV notebook, LLC; Bowman and Engle, "Medicolegal Aspects of Transvestism," 587.

48. Mary Smith, "They Said I Was Courageous!" manuscript, A. D. folder, box 4, Series IIC, HBC. See also "Mary Smith," "Females in Male Bodies," *Sexology* 25:7 (February 1959), 428–433. The version in *Sexology* omits details of the operation and its success, presumably in an attempt to keep readers from copycat surgery. On Elmer Belt, see A. D. to Harry Benjamin, September 21, 1954, and February 13, 1955, A. D. folder, box 4, Series IIC, HBC.

49. Elmer Belt to Harry Benjamin, August 15, 1960, Elmer Belt, 1959–1962 folder; Belt to Benjamin, October 16, 1962, Elmer Belt, 1962–1965 folder, both in box 3, Series IIC, HBC.

50. On Belt's surgical technique, see Elmer Belt to Alfonso de la Pena, April 25, 1960, Elmer Belt, 1959–1962 folder, box 3, Series IIC, HBC. On his decision to quit, see Elmer Belt to Harry Benjamin, October 16, 1962, Elmer Belt, 1962–1965 folder, box 3, ibid. On Barbara Richards Wilcox, see Leah Cahan Schaefer and Connie Christine Wheeler, "Harry Benjamin's First Ten Cases (1938–1953): A Clinical Historical Note," *Archives of Sexual Behavior* 24:1 (February 1995), 80. Schaefer and Wheeler call Wilcox "Carol."

51. R. J. to Harry Benjamin, April 27, 1955, R. J. folder, box 5, Series IIC, HBC; Benjamin, *The Transsexual Phenomenon,* 118.

52. Robert J. Stoller to D. B., November 14, 1968, General, A–G, 1968–1969 folder, box 37, RSP; Harry Benjamin to J. E., October 29, 1965, Correspondence file Harry Benjamin, KI. See also Richard Green to Henry Work, April 24, 1969, Richard Green section, box 3, RSP.

53. For a brief history, see Edgerton, Knorr, and Callison, "Surgical Treatment." See also James Fairchild Baldwin, "The Formation of an Artificial Vagina by Intestinal Transplantation," *Annals of Surgery* 40 (1904), 398–403; Howard W. Jones, "Operative Treatment of the Male Transsexual," in Green and Money, *Transsexualism and Sex Reassignment,* 313–317; Benjamin, *The Transsexual Phenomenon,* 102–104.

54. Patricia Morgan, as told to Paul Hoffman, *The Man-Maid Doll* (Secaucus, N.J.: Lyle Stuart [c. 1973]), 60, 63.

55. Jones, "Operative Treatment," 316; Elmer Belt to B. O., September 5, 1956, B. O. folder, box 6, Series IIC, HBC; Else K. La Roe, *Woman Surgeon: The Autobiography of Else K. La Roe, M.D.* (New York: Dial, 1957), 359. On Else La Roe and breast implants, see Watson Crews Jr., "The Full Facts about Sex Change," *New York Sunday News,* March 22, 1964, 26. For an early fictional account, in which a doctor changed (and then rechanged) the sexes of a married couple, see I. S. (Isadore Schneider), *Doctor Transit* (New York: Boni and Liveright, 1925).

56. Pauly, "Male Psychosexual Inversion," 179; Benjamin, *The Transsexual Phenomenon,* 119, 147; Edgerton, Knorr, and Callison, "Surgical Treatment," 39.

57. See, for example, Richard Green, "Change-of-Sex," *Medical Aspects of Human Sexuality* 3:10 (October 1969), 101.

58. Harry Benjamin to L. M., May 20, 1954, L. M. folder, box 6, Series IIC, HBC; Robert J. Stoller to Harry Guntrip, March 4, 1969, General, A–G, 1968–1969 folder, box 37, RSP; memorandum from Richard Green to Dr. Baker et al., February 7, 1970, Gender Clinic Meetings, 1962–1970 folder, box 16, RSP.

59. On butch-femme working-class culture, see Elizabeth Lapovsky Kennedy and Madeline Davis, *Boots of Leather, Slippers of Gold: The History of a Lesbian Community* (New York: Routledge, 1993). On the declining vogue of "fairies," see George Chauncey, *Gay New York: Gender, Urban Culture, and the Making of the Gay Male World, 1890–1940* (New York: Basic Books, 1994), 358.

60. Benjamin, *The Transsexual Phenomenon,* 156.

61. Warner and Lahn, "A Case of Female Transsexualism," 478–480.

62. John Money and John G. Brennan, "Sexual Dimorphism in the Psychology of Female Transsexuals," *Journal of Nervous and Mental Disease* 147:5 (1968), 495–496.

63. Sir Harold Gillies, "Congenital Absence of the Penis," *British Journal of Plastic Surgery* 1 (1948), 8–28; see also John E. Hoopes, "Operative Treatment of the Female Transsexual," in Green and Money, *Transsexualism and Sex Reassignment*, 335–352; Edgerton, Knorr, and Callison, "Surgical Treatment," 40.

64. See Liz Hodgkinson, *Michael, Née Laura* (London: Columbus Books, 1989), chaps. 4, 5.

65. S. G. to Harry Benjamin, November 8 and 18, 1963, S. G. folder, box 4, Series IIC, HBC.

66. Martino, *Emergence*, 261.

67. Edgerton, Knorr, and Callison, "Surgical Treatment," 44; see also Sir Harold Gillies and D. Ralph Millard Jr., *The Principles and Art of Plastic Surgery*, vol. 2 (Boston: Little, Brown, 1957), 376–384.

68. Hoopes, "Operative Treatment," 341.

69. Martino, *Emergence*, 163, 191, 263.

70. Richard Green, Consultation Note, November 20, 1970, Richard Green section, box 3, RSP.

71. Schaefer and Wheeler, "Harry Benjamin's First Ten Cases," 77; Benjamin, *The Transsexual Phenomenon*, 156.

72. Phoebe Smith, *Phoebe* (Atlanta: Phoebe Smith, 1979), 27; A. D. to Harry Benjamin, November 13, 1954, A. D. folder, box 4, Series IIC, HBC.

73. On Lawrence and Kinsey, see Joanne Meyerowitz, "Sex Research at the Borders of Gender: Transvestites, Transsexuals, and Alfred C. Kinsey," *Bulletin of the History of Medicine* 75:1 (Spring 2001), 72–90.

74. Schaefer and Wheeler, "Harry Benjamin's First Ten Cases," 81; Louise Lawrence to B. S., June 7, 1954, Alfred C. Kinsey folder, LLC. On Cauldwell, see Louise Lawrence to Harry Benjamin, October 28, 1953, TRNSV notebook, LLC. Lawrence appreciated recognition, but she published her article under a pseudonym because the editors of the journal thought "it would be safer"; Louise Lawrence to Alfred C. Kinsey, June 4, 1951, Alfred C. Kinsey folder, LLC.

75. Louise Lawrence to E. E., April 14, 1953, TRNSV notebook, LLC; Louise Lawrence to B. S., June 7, 1954.

76. D. M. to Harry Benjamin, November 3, 1953, D. M. folder, box 6, Series IIC, HBC; C. E. to Harry Benjamin, October 5 [1953], C. E. folder, box 4, ibid.; G. S. to Robert J. Stoller, February 1, 1970, General, Q–Z, 1969–1970 folder, box 37, RSP.

77. C. E. to Harry Benjamin, January 4, 1954, October 5 [1953], January 27 and May 9, 1954, C. E. folder, box 4, Series IIC, HBC.

78. C. S. to Harry Benjamin, November 21, 1954, C. S. folder, box 7, Series IIC, HBC.

79. Ibid.

80. Louise Lawrence to D. M., February 16, 1954; Harry Benjamin to D. M., March 14, 1954; D. M. to Benjamin, March 17, 1954; D. M. to Benjamin, December 18, 1954, all in D. M. folder, box 6, Series IIC, HBC.

81. J. S. to Harry Benjamin, May 15, 1955, J. S. folder, box 7, Series IIC, HBC; A. D. to Editor, *Journal of the American Medical Association*, June 13, 1955; A. D. to Elmer Belt [c. June 1955], both in A. D. folder, box 4, ibid.

82. Elmer Belt to Harry Benjamin, Dec. 5, 1955, C. S. folder, box 7, Series IIC, HBC; Vivien LeMans, *Take My Tool* (Los Angeles: Classic Publications, 1968), 90.

83. Smith, *Phoebe,* 48–49; Martino, *Emergence,* 170–171, 188.

84. Mark Sulcov, "Transsexualism: Its Social Reality," draft of Ph.D. diss., Indiana University, 1973, 2/15, KI Library.

85. D. M. to Harry Benjamin, April 17, 1955, D. M. folder, box 6, Series IIC, HBC.

86. Robert S. Redmount, "A Case of a Female Transvestite with Marital and Criminal Complications," *Journal of Clinical and Experimental Psychopathology* 14:2 (June 1953), 108–109; B. S. to Harry Benjamin, July 2, 1955, B. S. folder, box 7, Series IIC, HBC.

87. Robert J. Stoller, Harold Garfinkel, and Alexander C. Rosen, "Passing and the Maintenance of Sexual Identification in an Intersexed Patient," *Archives of General Psychiatry* 2 (April 1970), 379.

88. Arthur D. Schwabe, David H. Solomon, Robert J. Stoller, and John P. Burnham, "Pubertal Feminization in a Genetic Male with Testicular Atrophy and Normal Urinary Gonadotropin," *Journal of Clinical Endocrinology and Metabolism* 22 (August 1962), 844; Robert J. Stoller, "A Contribution to the Study of Gender Identity," *International Journal of Psycho-Analysis* 45 (1964), 225. See also Harold Garfinkel, *Studies in Ethnomethodology* (Englewood Cliffs, N.J.: Prentice-Hall, 1967), 134.

89. Schwabe et al., "Pubertal Feminization," 843.

90. Stoller, Garfinkel, and Rosen, "Passing," 380.

91. Elmer Belt to Willard Goodwin, June 20, 1966, Male Transsexualism section, box 9, RSP.

92. Stoller, *Sex and Gender,* 136; Richard Green to Robert J. Stoller, June 15, 1966, Richard Green folder, box 34, RSP.

93. Stoller, *Sex and Gender,* 136.

94. After the Agnes episode, Stoller seemed to place less emphasis on the "biological force," which he now regarded only "as a possibility in some extremely rare cases." See Robert J. Stoller to Saul I. Harrison, May 15, 1970, General, H–P, 1969–1970 folder, box 37, RSP.

95. Pauly, "Male Psychosexual Inversion," 175.

96. Lawrence S. Kubie and James B. Mackie, "Critical Issues Raised by Operations for Gender Transmutation," *Journal of Nervous and Mental Disease* 147:5 (November 1968), 435, 437.

97. Martino, *Emergence,* 173; Harry Benjamin to C. J., March 7, 1955, R. J. folder, box 5, Series IIC, HBC; Benjamin to D. M., December 22, 1954, D. M. folder, box 6, ibid.; Lyn Raskin, *Diary of a Transsexual* (New York: Olympia Press, 1971), 57, 84.

98. F. Hartsuiker to H. F., July 31, 1954, H. F. folder, box 4, Series IIC, HBC.

99. A. D. to Harry Benjamin, November 13 and December 23, 1954, A. D. folder, box 4, Series IIC, HBC.

100. Interview with Aleshia Brevard Crenshaw by Susan Stryker, August 2, 1997, transcript, 39, GLBTHS; Martino, *Emergence,* 213.

101. C. S. to Harry Benjamin, December 15, 1955, C. S. folder, box 7, Series IIC, HBC; Morgan, *Man-Maid Doll,* 63.

102. Martino, *Emergence,* 165.

103. Ibid., 260, 262.

104. Hoopes, "Operative Treatment," 342; Edgerton, Knorr, and Callison, "Surgical Treatment," 44.

105. Edgerton, Knorr, and Callison, "Surgical Treatment," 44; Norman Knorr, San-ford Wolf, and Eugene Meyer, "Psychiatric Evaluation of Male Transsexuals for Sur-gery," in Green and Money, *Transsexualism and Sex Reassignment,* 279.

106. Harry Benjamin to H. F., September 1, 1955, H. F. folder, box 4, Series IIC, HBC.

107. Howard J. Baker and Richard Green, "Treatment of Transsexualism," *Current Psychiatric Therapies* 10 (1970), 88; Sanford R. Wolf, Norman J. Knorr, Jogn E. Hoopes, and Eugene Meyer, "Psychiatric Aspects of Transsexual Surgery Management," *Journal of Nervous and Mental Disease* 147:5 (1968), 524.

108. Elmer Belt to Willard Goodwin, June 20, 1966; Belt to Harry Benjamin, July 26, 1965, and February 14, 1966, all in Elmer Belt, 1965–1971 folder, box 3, Series IIC, HBC.

109. Stoller, "Treatment of Transvestism and Transsexualism," 98; Robert J. Stoller to John Romano, February 28, 1968, General, Q–Z, 1967–1968 folder, box 37, RSP.

110. Harry Benjamin, "Newer Aspects of the Transsexual Phenomenon," *Journal of Sex Research* 5:2 (May 1969), 138. See also Harry Benjamin to Alfred C. Kinsey, Decem-ber 3, 1954, Correspondence file Harry Benjamin, KI.

111. Harry Benjamin to J. D., July 16, 1956, J. D. folder, box 4, Series IIC, HBC.

112. C. S. to Harry Benjamin, November 21, 1954, C. S. folder; G. S. to Harry Benjamin, April 2, 1954, J. S. folder, both in box 7, Series IIC, HBC.

113. C. E. to Harry Benjamin, January 22, 1954, C. E. folder, box 4, Series IIC, HBC.

114. Crenshaw interview, 31.

115. Elmer Belt to To Whom It May Concern, June 28, 1956, A. D. folder, box 4, Se-ries IIC, HBC.

116. A. D. to Harry Benjamin, November 13 and 22, 1954, A. D. folder, box 4, Se-ries IIC, HBC.

117. Harry Benjamin to A. D., December 3 and 22, 1954; A. D. to Harry Benjamin, December 23, 1954, all in A. D. folder, box 4, Series IIC, HBC.

118. M. H. to Elmer Belt, June 23, 1958, Elmer Belt, 1958–1959 folder, box 3, Se-ries IIC, HBC; Latina Seville, "I Want to Be Male Again," in Abby Sinclair, *"I Was Male!"* (Chicago: Novel Books, 1965), 90, 91, 94, 95.

119. Hoopes, "Operative Treatment," 346; A. D. to Harry Benjamin, February 2, 1955, A. D. folder, box 4, Series IIC, HBC; D. M. to Harry Benjamin, April 17, 1955, D. M. folder, box 6, ibid.; D. P. to Harry Benjamin, February 24, 1955, D. P. folder, box 7, ibid.

120. C. E. to Harry Benjamin, December 31, 1956, C. E. folder, box 4, Series IIC, HBC.

5. SEXUAL REVOLUTIONS

1. Vivian Le Mans, *Take My Tool: Revelations of a Sex-Switch* (Los Angeles: Classic Publications, 1968), back cover, 8.

2. Michel Foucault, *The History of Sexuality,* vol. 1: *An Introduction,* trans. Robert Hurley (New York: Vintage, 1980).

3. Christian Hamburger and Mogens Sprechler, "The Influence of Steroid Hormones on the Hormonal Activity of the Adenohypophysis in Man," *Acta Endocrinologica* 7 (1965), 170.

4. Christian Hamburger, Georg K. Stürup, and E. Dahl-Iversen, "Transvestism: Hormonal, Psychiatric, and Surgical Treatment," *Journal of the American Medical Association* 152:5 (May 1953), 391, 392, 394–395.

5. Conversation with Paul Gebhard, October 23, 1996.

6. Berdeen Frankel Meyer, "Case Summary and Closing Note," October 2, 1950, 8, S. W. folder, box 8, Series IIC, HBC; James H. Jones, *Alfred C. Kinsey: A Public/Private Life* (New York: W. W. Norton, 1997), 622.

7. Karl M. Bowman, "The Problem of the Sex Offender," 5, Menas S. Gregory Lecture, presented at New York University, January 24, 1951, Donald Lucas Collection, box 1 (unprocessed), GLBTHS.

8. Conversation with Paul Gebhard, October 23, 1996.

9. Karl M. Bowman and Bernice Engle, "Medicolegal Aspects of Transvestism," *American Journal of Psychiatry* 113:7 (January 1957), 583.

10. Daniel O. Brown, "The Development of Sex-Role Inversion and Homosexuality," *Journal of Pediatrics* 50 (1957), 618. On doctors' shifting definitions of homosexuality, see George Chauncey, *Gay New York: Gender, Urban Culture, and the Making of the Gay Male World, 1890–1940* (New York: Basic Books, 1994), 121–125.

11. Lawrence E. Newman, *Transsexualism—A Disorder of Sexual Identity* (New York: Insight Publishing, 1970), unpaginated.

12. S. W. to Alfred C. Kinsey, November 2, 1945, S. W. folder, box 8, Series IIC, HBC; T. R. to Harry Benjamin, July 14, 1957, T. R. folder, box 7, ibid. For examples of transhomosexuality, see G. S. to Robert J. Stoller, February 1, 1970, General, Q–Z, 1969–1970 folder, box 37, RSP; C. V. C. to Harry Benjamin [c. 1956], C. V. C. folder, box 8, Series IIC, HBC; J. B. to Harry Benjamin, August 4, 1967, J. B. folder, box 3, ibid.

13. Robert J. Stoller, *Sex and Gender: On the Development of Masculinity and Femininity* (New York: Science House, 1968), 147.

14. Ralph R. Greenson, "On Homosexuality and Gender Identity," *International Journal of Psycho-Analysis* 45 (1964), 218; Charles W. Socarides, "The Desire for Sexual Transformation: A Psychiatric Evaluation of Transsexualism," *American Journal of Psychiatry* 125:10 (April 1969), 1420, 1423; Charles W. Socarides, "Dr. Socarides Replies," ibid., 126:2 (August 1969), 270.

15. Ira B. Pauly, "Male Psychosexual Inversion: Transsexualism," *Archives of General Psychiatry* 13:2 (August 1965), 175.

16. Harry Benjamin, *The Transsexual Phenomenon* (New York: Julian Press, 1966), 11, 13, 26.

17. Richard Green, "Persons Seeking Sex Change: Psychiatric Management of Special Problems," *American Journal of Psychiatry* 126:11 (May 1970), 1598.

18. Pauly, "Male Psychosexual Inversion," 175; Howard J. Baker, "Transsexualism—Problems in Treatment," *American Journal of Psychiatry* 125:10 (April 1969), 1413; Harry Benjamin, "Newer Aspects of the Transsexual Phenomenon," *Journal of Sex Research* 5:2 (May 1969), 139.

19. Ira B. Pauly, "Adult Manifestations of Female Transsexualism," in *Transsexualism and Sex Reassignment,* ed. Richard Green and John Money (Baltimore: Johns Hopkins Press, 1969), 83; Robert J. Stoller to Harry Benjamin, June 13, 1966, Harry Benjamin folder, box 35, RSP; Stoller to Harry Guntrip, March 4, 1969, General, A–G, 1968–1969 folder, box 37, RSP.

20. Benjamin, *Transsexual Phenomenon,* 21, 22.

21. Harry Benjamin, "Transvestism and Transsexualism in the Male and Female," *Journal of Sex Research* 3:2 (May 1967), 109.

22. John Money, assisted by Ronald J. Gaskin, "Sex Reassignment," *International Journal of Psychiatry* 9 (1970–71), 254–255; Robert I. Simon, "A Case of Female Transsexualism," *American Journal of Psychiatry* 123:12 (June 1967), 1601; Benjamin, *Transsexual Phenomenon,* 21.

23. See, for example, Evelyn Brooks Higginbotham, *Righteous Discontent: The Women's Movement in the Black Baptist Church, 1880–1920* (Cambridge, Mass.: Harvard University Press, 1993), chap. 7.

24. P. E., letter to the editor, *ONE* 1:4 (April 1953), 20; interview with Christine Jorgensen, in *Paradise Is Not for Sale,* directed by Teit Ritzau, 1985.

25. See, for example, advertisement, ONE 2:4 (April 1954), 31; John Logan and Carl Richter, eds., *TransVestism Commentary: Notes, Comments, Discussion, and Opinion on the Subject of Transvestism* (San Francisco: Mattachine Review Reprint, Pan-Graphic Press, 1962); Karl Ericsen, "The Transsexual Experience," *The Ladder,* April/May 1970, 25–27.

26. Jeff Winters, "As for Me . . . ," *ONE* 1:2 (February 1953), 12–13.

27. P. E., letter to the editor, *ONE* 1:4 (April 1953), 20; Or Sarua, letter to the editor, *ONE* 1:5 (May 1953), 23.

28. Frankie Almitra, "Why Not Compromise?" *ONE* 7:5 (May 1959), 16.

29. Chauncey, *Gay New York;* Elizabeth Lapovsky Kennedy and Madeline Davis, *Boots of Leather, Slippers of Gold: The History of a Lesbian Community* (New York: Routledge, 1993).

30. Dana Harper, "The Truth about Homosexual Women," Part III, *Sexology* 15:3 (October 1948), 179, 181–182.

31. Letter to the editor, *ONE* 2:6 (June 1954), 27.

32. Interview with Sushi, Margo, and Inga by Verta Taylor and Leila J. Rupp, June 23, 1998, Key West, Fla.; *The Queen,* directed by Frank Simon, 1968.

33. *Transvestia: Journal of the American Society for Equality in Dress* 1:1 (1952), 4; ibid., 1:2 (1952), 2. Both issues are in Transvestite Publications—Transvestia vertical file, KI.

34. A. J. D. to Louise Lawrence, August 21, 1954, TRNSV notebook, LLC.

35. "As a person . . . ," untitled statement, typescript [n.d.], TV Letters envelope, no. 83, Diary Room, KI.

36. E. F., "Ad Appearing Currently in 'The Billboard,'" typescript [c. 1951], TRV MS, no. 103, Diary Room, KI.

37. E. F. to Dr. D. E. Alcorn, September 29, 1954, TRNSV notebook, LLC; E. F., "Transvestic Outlines," 7, 9, typescript, January 10, 1956, TRV MS, no. 103, Diary Room, KI; E. F., "Some Pertinent Observations upon the 'Christine' Jorgensen Case," typescript, TRV MS, no. 103, Diary Room, KI.

38. *Transvestia* 1:1 (January 1960), 1.

39. "The Purpose behind Transvestia," ibid., 4.

40. Virginia Prince, "A Survey of 390 Cases of Transvestism," mimeographed report, 1965, 5–6, available in KI Library.

41. Barbara Stevens, Business Manager, Chevalier Publications, to To Whom It May Concern [c. August 1962], mimeographed letter, Transvestite Publications—Transvestia vertical file, KI.

42. Virginia [Prince], "Change of Sex or Gender," *Transvestia* 9[10]:60 (December 1969), 56, 61.

43. Susanna [Valenti], "Susanna Says TS . . . sk," ibid., 80; Betty, "Hormones & Surgery: Yes or No," 67–72, ibid.; Anita, "Should I?????" 74–78, ibid.

44. [Prince], "The Life and Times of Virginia," 18.

45. M. L. [Virginia Prince] to Christine Jorgensen, May 6, 1953, Sex Change—Other than CJ folder, Letters box, CJP.

46. Richard Green, Robert J. Stoller, and Craig McAndrew, "Attitudes toward Sex Transformation Procedures," *Archives of General Psychiatry* 15 (August 1966), 178–179.

47. *Christine Jorgensen Reveals,* record album [c. 1957], available in KI Library; interview with Christine Jorgensen by Richard Lamparski, 1966, copy in author's possession; telephone interview with Jo Smith by author, January 10, 1996.

48. Christine Jorgensen, *Christine Jorgensen: A Personal Autobiography* (New York: Paul S. Erikkson, 1967), 173; Sheila Niles, "Book Reviews," *Transvestia* 8:48 (December 1967), 65.

49. Thomas M. Kando, "The Social Consequences of Sex Achievement: A Study of the Social Relations of Fifteen Transsexuals after Their Conversion Operation" (Ph.D. diss., University of Minnesota, 1969), 291; Mario Martino with harriett, *Emergence: A Transsexual Autobiography* (New York: Crown, 1977), 113; Gayle Sherman, *"I Want to Be a Woman!" The Autobiography of Female Impersonator Gayle Sherman* (Chicago: Novel Books [c. 1964]), 27.

50. See, for example, Simon, "A Case of Female Transsexualism," 1600; M. W., "Inverse Sexuality: A Hypothesis," typescript, December 1964, KI Library; James Patrick Driscoll, "The Transsexuals" (M.A. thesis, San Francisco State College, 1969), 63; Louise Lawrence, typewritten autobiography, 1947–1958, 4, large box, LLC.

51. *Gay San Francisco,* directed by Jonathan Prince and Ed Muckerman, 1970; Pauly, "Adult Manifestations of Female Transsexualism," 82. Thanks to Susan Stryker for sharing the quote from the film.

52. "Christine Jorgensen Reveals"; interview with Aleshia Brevard Crenshaw by Susan Stryker, August 2, 1997, transcript, 70–71, GLBTHS. Jorgensen remembered the letter incorrectly. In the Christine Jorgensen Papers the actual letter, with the razor blade still enclosed, says nothing about "us." The anonymous author, who signed the letter "Disgusted," invites Jorgensen to cut her throat and "do decent people a favor." Jorgensen may well have confused this letter with another one, also in the archives, in which the author wrote: "Am fed up reading all your distasteful publicity. Its only making harder for us that have to live with it . . . Every one here is laughing about it . . . Why don't you be quiet!" This letter, it turns out, came not from a gay man but from a troubled transsexual. See "Disgusted" to Christine Jorgensen [c. 1953], Sex Change—Other than CJ folder, Letters box, CJP; Anonymous to Christine Jorgensen [c. 1953] and L. H. to Christine Jorgensen, May 6, 1953, Christine folder, ibid.

53. Louise Lawrence, "Transvestites in the Bay Area," typewritten list, May 1954, TRNSV notebook, LLC. For use of the word *interesting* see, for example, Louise Lawrence to Alfred C. Kinsey, October 5, 1949, Alfred C. Kinsey folder, LLC.

54. Louise Lawrence to M. A., July 21, 1952, TV letters, no. 83, Diary Room, KI.

55. Interview with Don Lucas by Susan Stryker, June 13, 1997, transcript, 1, GLBTHS.

56. "Transvestism . . . Cont.," typewritten sheet [n.d.], Transvestism vertical file, KI; interview with Don Lucas, 3.

57. Louise Lawrence to Harry Benjamin, May 5, 1954, TRNSV notebook, LLC; for Benjamin's response, see Benjamin to C. E., May 13, 1954, C. E. folder, box 4, Series IIC, HBC.

58. John E. Hoopes, Norman J. Knorr, and Sanford R. Wolf, "Transsexualism: Considerations Regarding Sexual Reassignment," *Journal of Nervous and Mental Disease* 146:5 (1968), 514.

59. C. S. to Harry Benjamin, October 5, 1954, C. S. folder, box 7, Series IIC, HBC.

60. Lawrence, typewritten autobiography, 1947–1958, 3.

61. Michelle to Harvey Goodwin [Lee], December 19, 1964; see also same to same, March 6, 1965, both in series 1:1, Correspondence, Harvey Lee Papers, Collection A-115, Special Collections, University of Arkansas at Little Rock. Many thanks to Susan Stryker for sharing sources from this collection with me.

62. Coccinelle, "My Sex Change! My Love Affairs! My Famous Friends!" *Confidential* [c. 1962], 50, Transexualism vertical file, KI; David Shelton, "'I Was Born a Man'" [n.p., n.d.], box 1/4 Clippings, VPC.

63. Renée Richards with John Ames, *Second Serve: The Renée Richards Story* (New York: Stein and Day, 1983), 148; interview with Suzan Cooke by Susan Stryker, January 10, 1998, 2, 4, transcript available at GLBTHS.

64. Crenshaw interview, 10–11, 20; Esther Newton, *Mother Camp: Female Impersonators in America* (Chicago: University of Chicago Press, 1972), 51.

65. Crenshaw interview, 14, 59, 70. Brevard later pursued a successful career as an actress in films, television, and theater. See Aleshia Brevard, *The Woman I Was Not Born to Be: A Transsexual Journey* (Philadelphia: Temple University Press, 2001).

66. R. E. L. Masters, *Sex-Driven People: An Autobiographical Approach to the Problem of the Sex-Dominated Personality* (Los Angeles: Sherbourne, 1966), 242–243. The world of female impersonation had its own hierarchy. At the upper rungs, performers at Le Carrousel or Madame Arthur's in Paris, at Club 82 in New York, at Finocchio's in San Francisco, or in the traveling troupe of the Jewel Box Revue won national and international fame. Lower on the ladder, some professional female impersonators worked in lesser-known urban nightclubs or on the circuit of smalltown clubs. At the bottom of the ladder, on the summer carnival circuit, female impersonators worked as "real" women in the "girlie shows" or as "hermaphrodites" in the sideshow. In these venues, too, some MTFs learned about transsexuality. See Abby Sinclair, *"I Was Male!"* (Chicago: Novel Books, 1965), 23–24, 27; Minette as told to Steven Watson, *Minette: Recollections of a Part-Time Lady* (New York: Flower-Beneath-the-Foot Press, 1979), unpaginated, chapter titled "Cooching Up a Storm"; Hedy Jo Star, *"I Changed My Sex!" The Autobiography of Stripper Hedy Jo Star, formerly Carl Hammonds* (Chicago: Novel Books [c. 1964]), 36, 96.

67. Crenshaw interview, 20; interview with Major by Susan Stryker, January 29, 1998, 4, transcript available at GLBTHS; Holly Woodlawn with Jeffrey Copeland, *A Low Life in High Heels: The Holly Woodlawn Story* (New York: St. Martin's, 1991), 122–123.

68. Tamara Ching, "Stranger in Paradise," *A. Magazine* [c. late 1990s], 85–86, private collection of Susan Stryker; Woodlawn, *A Low Life,* 123.

69. On the traditions of fairies, see Chauncey, *Gay New York,* especially chap. 2.

70. Interview with Regina Elizabeth McQuade by Susan Stryker, July 17, 1997, 6–7, transcript available at GLBTHS.

71. Major interview, 6–7; Woodlawn, *A Low Life,* 102.

72. Quoted in Martin Duberman, *Stonewall* (New York: Plume, 1993), 124–125.

73. Patricia Morgan as told to Paul Hoffman, *The Man-Maid Doll* (Secaucus, N.J.: Lyle Stuart [c. 1973]), 42–43, 51.

74. Driscoll, "The Transsexuals," 41–42, 46, 53.

75. Ibid., 54, 66.

76. Cooke interview, 31; Driscoll, "The Transsexuals," 42, 52, 75, 78; Mark B. Sulcov, "Transexualism: Its Social Reality," 2/37, draft of Ph.D. diss., Department of Sociology, Indiana University, 1973, available in KI library.

77. Cooke interview, 3, 23; Angela Lynn Douglas, *Triple Jeopardy: The Autobiography of Angela Lynn Douglas* (n.p.: Angela Lynn Douglas, 1983), 21; McQuade interview, 18.

78. T. J. M. to Robert J. Stoller, November 1965, 2, 4, Female Transsexualism section, box 9, RSP; Pauly, "Adult Manifestations of Female Transsexualism," 75.

79. Sulcov, "Transexualism: Its Social Reality," 5/32, 5/60; Robert Martin, "Special Report," *C. O. G. Transsexual News* 1:2 (January 17, 1968), 2, mimeographed newsletter, COG folder, box 19, Series V: Organizations, HBC; Suzan Cooke interview, 31.

80. Robert Bogdan, ed., *Being Different: The Autobiography of Jane Fry* (New York: John Wiley and Sons, 1974), 199; Cooke interview, 2; Woodlawn, *A Low Life,* 93.

81. Norman J. Knorr, Sanford R. Wolf, and Eugene Meyer, "The Transsexual's Request for Surgery," *Journal of Nervous and Mental Disease* 147:5 (1968), 519.

82. Sanford R. Wolf, Norman J. Knorr, John E. Hoopes, and Eugene Meyer, "Psychiatric Aspects of Transsexual Surgery Management," ibid., 526.

83. Mario Costa, *Reverse Sex,* trans. Jules J. Block (London: Challenge Publications [c. 1962]).

84. See, for example, Walter H. Scott, "Boy Turned Girl Is Next Marilyn," *National Tattler,* August 30, 1964, box 3/4 Clippings, VPC; "I Know the Sex Games a Man Likes Best Because I Was Once a Man," *National Insider,* February 27, 1966, 10.

85. Star, *"I Changed My Sex!"* back cover; *Sequel to "I Changed My Sex"!* (Chicago: Novel Books, 1964), inside front cover. Later in life, Star worked as a costume designer in Las Vegas; see Harvey Lee to Juan Jose Lopez, July 20, 1981, box 1, file 12, Series 1, Subseries 1: Outgoing Correspondence, Harvey Lee Collection, University of Arkansas, Little Rock.

86. *Sequel,* 91.

87. For examples of the series and the photos, see Gayle Sherman, "I Want to Be a Woman," *National Insider,* October 27, 1963, 12; Abby Sinclair, "An MD's Knife Made Me a Woman," ibid., October 18, 1964, 10.

88. Delisa Newton, "My Lover Beat Me," *National Insider,* June 20, 1965, 4–5; idem, "Why I Could Never Marry a White Man!" ibid., July 18, 1965, 17.

89. Paula Anderson, "'I Once Had a Penis!'" *Candid Press,* March 24, 1968, 7; "Sex-Changed Son Raped by Father," *National Mirror,* April 22, 1969, 1; Carlson Wade, *Sex Perversions and Taboos* (New York: L. S. Publications, 1964); Jack Benjamin, *Transvestite 69* (North Hollywood: Barclay House, 1969).

90. "Coccinelle: France's Most Fabulous She-Male," *Female Mimics* 1:2 (August–September 1963), 3–10; "Stag Turned Doe," ibid., 1:5 (Spring 1965), 33–43; "Capucine: The Toast and Talk of Many Continents," ibid., 1:6 (August 1965), 27–37; "Abby Sinclair: Ex-G.I., Now Bride-to-Be," ibid., 54–63; "Coccinelle: World's Most Fabulous Fe-Male," *Female Impersonators,* Summer 1965, 59–65; "St. Clair Revue," ibid., Summer 1969, 38–43, quotation on 40.

91. See John D'Emilio and Estelle B. Freedman, *Intimate Matters: A History of Sexuality in America,* 2d ed. (Chicago: University of Chicago Press, 1997), 287–288.

92. "Changing Men to Women, Women to Men," *Coronet,* August 1967, 30; "Transsexual Tragedy," *Newsweek,* April 22, 1968, 64; Sinclair, *"I Was Male!"* front cover.

93. Harvey Lee to Jade East, July 7, 1966, Series 1:1, Outgoing Correspondence, box 1, file 7, Harvey Lee Papers, Collection A-115, Special Collections, University of Arkansas, Little Rock.

94. Sinclair, "An M.D.'s Knife," 11; Adam St. Cyr, "Why the Sex-Change Surgeons Would Rather Switch than Fight It," *Confidential* [c. 1966], box 3/4 Clippings, VPC. On Alegria and Starr, see also Harvey Lee to Jade East, July 7, 1966; on Alegria, see Benjamin, *Transvestite 69,* 24; on Starr, see "Vicki Starr," *Drag Queen* 1 [c. 1970], 35, 39. Both Starr and Alegria were Latinas.

95. Le Mans, *Take My Tool,* 172.

96. Lyn Raskin, *Diary of a Transsexual* (New York: Olympia Press, 1971); Morgan, *The Man-Maid Doll,* 2.

97. *An 'Intimate' and Gay Diary* 1:1 [c. 1970], front cover; *An 'Intimate' and Gay Diary* 1:2 (1970), front cover.

98. *HeShe,* 1970, front cover, 1.

99. Heidi Handman, "He Ain't Heavy, He's My Mother," *Screw,* April 5, 1971, 4.

100. Tom Buckley, "The Transsexual Operation," *Esquire,* April 1967, 111, 113; Roland H. Berg, "The Transsexuals: Male or Female?" *Look,* January 27, 1970, 29.

101. Gore Vidal, *Myra Breckinridge* (New York: Bantam, 1968), 2, 5, 17.

102. Peter Prescott, "Here Comes Gore Vidal with Charley's Aunt in Modern Drag," *Look,* March 19, 1968, T8; James MacBride, "What Did Myra Want?" *New York Times Book Review,* February 18, 1968, 45.

103. K. B. to Harry Benjamin, July 18, 1970, K. B. folder, box 3, Series IIC, HBC; Bogdan, *Being Different,* 198; radio interview with Christine Jorgensen by Doris Abramson and Haskell Coplin, 1968, audiotape in possession of author.

104. See her American Guild of Variety Artists (AGVA) nightclub contracts, filed by year, Clippings/Letters box, CJP.

105. Jack Cione to Christine Jorgensen, November 14, 1965; Jorgensen to Cione, November 17, 1965; Jorgensen to Cione [c. 1966], all in Agents folder, Clippings/Letters box, CJP.

106. Page Cole to Donald Segretti, September 15, 1981, Bantam–Don Segretti folder, Letters box, CJP; telephone interview with Paul Erikkson by author, January 22, 1996.

107. Warren Bayless to Christine Jorgensen, July 9, 1969, Autobiography Correspondence folder, Letters box, CJP; Hoke Norris to Christine Jorgensen, March 5, 1968, Autobio—Foreign folder, Clippings/Letters box, CJP.

108. Jo Smith interview; *The Christine Jorgensen Story,* directed by Irving Rapper, 1970.

109. "Rebuttal to Memorandum from Baerwitz," October 6, 1977, 1, 2, Legal box, CJP.

110. Peter Buckley, "The Christine Jorgensen Story," *Films and Filming,* December 1970, unpaginated, Christine Jorgensen folder, ONE; Howard Thompson, "'Jorgensen Story,'" *New York Times,* July 25, 1970, 12.

6. THE LIBERAL MOMENT

1. In re Anonymous, 293 N.Y.S. 2d 834, 836, 838 (1968); Bill Semple, "Boys Can Be Girls!" *National Insider* [c. September 1968], 21, box 4/4 Clippings, VPC.

2. "The Erickson Educational Foundation" [c. 1968], 1, General, A–G, 1967–1968 folder, box 37, RSP; "Studies in Time and Void," *Erickson Educational Foundation Newsletter* 3:1 (Spring 1970), 5.

3. Randy Smith, "Border Crossing," *Medical Dimensions,* May 1977, 14.

4. FBI Report, April 10, 1944, 2, in Reed Erickson, FBI file 100-287036, obtained by author under Freedom of Information Act. On the family wealth, see Smith, "Border Crossing," 14.

5. FBI Report, March 8, 1944; A. Cornelius Jr. to Director, FBI, November 21, 1950, 2; SAC, New Orleans to Director, FBI, May 19, 1954, 2; SAC, WFO to Director, FBI, December 13, 1974, 3, all in Reed Erickson, FBI file 100-287036. In 1954 Erickson refused to cooperate with FBI investigators, who had hoped to use him as an informant; see SAC, New Orleans to Director, FBI, July 9, 1954, in Reed Erickson, FBI file 100-287036.

6. Reed Erickson, "Foreword," in Richard Green and John Money, eds., *Transsexualism and Sex Reassignment* (Baltimore: Johns Hopkins Press, 1969), xiii; telephone interview with Stanley Krippner by author, March 4, 1996. On his surgery, see John Money and John G. Brennan, "Sexual Dimorphism in the Psychology of Female Transsexuals," *Journal of Nervous and Mental Disease* 147:5 (1968), 488, table 1, "E. N."

7. Helen Kruger, "Do You Feel Trapped in the Wrong Body?" *Village Voice,* August 8, 1974, 30; Krippner interview.

8. In the late 1970s Erickson divorced his wife Aileen and married another woman whom he had met in Mexico. For more on Erickson and the EEF, see Holly Devor's website at http://web.uvic.ca/~erick123; and Holly Devor, "Reed Erickson: How One Transsexed Man Supported ONE," in *Risk Takers and Trend Setters: Biographies of Pre-Stonewall Gay Activists and Supporters,* ed. Vern Bullough, Judith Saunders, and Sharon Volente (Binghamton, N.Y.: Haworth, 2002).

9. Reed Erickson to Christine Jorgensen, June 2, 1969, Sex Change—Other than CJ folder, Letters box, CJP.

10. Paul Starr, *The Social Transformation of American Medicine* (New York: Basic Books, 1982), 341, 342, 347.

11. Christian Hamburger to Christine Jorgensen, November 9, 1955, Hamburger folder, Clippings/Letters box, CJP.

12. In addition to Bowman, Belt, Kinsey, and Benjamin, the physician Walter Alvarez participated in the first national networks. Alvarez wrote a syndicated newspaper column from his home base in Chicago. His sympathetic columns about transvestites and transsexuals attracted patients seeking his advice and help.

13. Conversation with Richard Green, July 24, 1997; Robert J. Stoller to Richard Green, February 12, 1965, Richard Green folder, box 35, RSP; Stoller to William W. Bonney, November 22, 1966, General, A–G, 1965–1966 folder, box 37, RSP. For a more extended account of Stoller's ambivalence, see Robert J. Stoller, "A Biased View of 'Sex Transformation' Operations: An Editorial," *Journal of Nervous and Mental Disease* 149:1 (1969), 312–317.

14. Richard Green to Robert J. Stoller, February 24 [1965], Richard Green folder, box 35, RSP; Stoller to T. B., April 14, 1970, General, A–G, 1969–1970 folder, box 37, RSP. Richard Green told me about the surgery performed at UCLA; conversation with Green, July 24, 1997.

15. Reed Erickson to Harry Benjamin, August 31, 1964, Erickson Educational Foundation, Reed Erickson folder, box 19, Series V, HBC.

16. *Harry Benjamin Foundation: For Research in Gender Role Orientation,* pamphlet [c. 1965], Gender Role Identification—Harry Benjamin Foundation vertical file, KI; Harry Benjamin to Paul Gebhard, July 15, 1965, Correspondence file Harry Benjamin, KI.

17. Robert J. Stoller to Richard Green, December 8, 1954, and December 28, 1964, Richard Green folder, box 35, RSP; conversation with Green.

18. Robert J. Stoller to Richard Green, September 27, 1966, Richard Green folder, box 35, RSP.

19. Harry Benjamin to John Money, December 14, 1967, Organizations, Erickson, 1967 folder, box 19, Series V, HBC. On the course of the disputes, see other correspondence in the same folder.

20. Handwritten notes, "The year 1968," January 1, 1969, Erickson Educational Foundation Business folder, box 19, Series V, HBC.

21. Harry Benjamin to Stanley Krippner, April 28, 1969, personal files of Stanley Krippner, photocopy in possession of author. See also "Benjamin Gender Identity Research Foundation, Inc.," leaflet [c. early 1970]s, Harry Benjamin folder, ONE.

22. Stanley Krippner, *Song of the Siren: A Parapsychological Odyssey* (New York: Harper and Row, 1975), 30; Krippner interview. See Stanley Krippner, Geraldine M. Lenz, Warren Barksdale, and Richard J. Davidson, "Content Analysis of 30 Dreams from 10 Pre-Operative Male Transsexuals," *Journal of the American Society of Psychosomatic Dentistry and Medicine,* monograph suppl. 2 (April 1974).

23. Robert E. L. Masters to author, November 20, 1996. See also R. E. L. Masters to Harry Benjamin, May 28, 1967, R. E. L. Masters folder, box 6, Series IIC, HBC.

24. Conversation with Green. On Benjamin, see, for example, interview with Aleshia Brevard Crenshaw by Susan Stryker, August 2, 1997, 72, transcript available at GLBTHS.

25. James H. Jones, *Alfred C. Kinsey: A Public/Private Life* (New York: W. W. Norton, 1997), 481. On Ihlenfeld, see "Doctor No Longer Treats Transsexuals," *Gay Scene* (New York), January 1977, Transsexuals folder, ONE; on Doorbar, conversation with Green.

26. "Memorial for Harry Benjamin," *Archives of Sexual Behavior* 17:5 (October 1988), 10.

27. J. B. de C. M. Saunders to Norman Q. Brill, August 26, 1964; University of California, San Franciso Medical Center, press release, August 6, 1964, 7, both in Male Transsexualism section, box 9, RSP.

28. On Money, see John Heidenry, *What Wild Ecstasy: The Rise and Fall of the Sexual Revolution* (New York: Simon and Schuster, 1997), 97–98.

29. John Money and Florence Schwartz, "Public Opinion and Social Issues in Transsexualism: A Case Study in Medical Sociology," in Green and Money, *Transsexualism and Sex Reassignment,* 255; letter reproduced in Hedy Jo Star, *"I Changed My Sex!"* (Chicago: Novel Books [c. 1964]), 59.

30. Robert J. Stoller to Richard Green, June 19, 1967, Richard Green folder, box 35, RSP; John Colapinto, *As Nature Made Him: The Boy Who Was Raised as a Girl* (New York: HarperCollins, 2000), 36.

31. Harry Benjamin to Reed Erickson, May 12, 1965; Aileen Erickson to Benjamin, June 14, 1965, both in Erickson Educational Foundation, Reed Erickson folder, box 19, Series V, HBC.

32. On the origins of the Hopkins program, see Money and Schwartz, "Public Opinion"; "Statement on the Establishment of a Clinic for Transsexuals at the Johns Hopkins Medical Institutions," in Green and Money, *Transsexualism and Sex Reassignment,* 267–269; "Surgery: A Body to Match the Mind," *Time,* December 2, 1966, 52. On EEF funding of the program, see John Money to Burton H. Wolfe, March 28, 1969, Correspondence folder WH–WZ, John Money Collection, KI.

33. Money and Schwartz, "Public Opinion," 256.

34. Thomas Buckley, "A Changing of Sex by Surgery Begun at Johns Hopkins," *New York Times,* November 21, 1966, 1; "A Change of Gender," *Newsweek,* December 5, 1966, 73; "Surgery," *Time,* 52; "Sex-Change Operations at a U.S. Hospital," *U.S. News & World Report,* December 5, 1966, 13.

35. Letters to the editor, *Time,* December 16, 1966, 18; Wesley Hartzell, "City Medics Cool to Sex Surgery," *Chicago's American,* November 27, 1966, "Christine" Chicago Scrapbook; "Surgery," *Time,* 52; "Clerics Approve of Sex-Change Operation," *Baltimore Sun,* November 23, 1966, John Money Collection, unprocessed part of collection, KI.

36. Christine Jorgensen to Christian Hamburger, November 22, 1966, Christian Hamburger folder, Clippings/Letters box, CJP.

37. Interview with Suzan Cooke by Susan Stryker, January 10, 1998, 6, transcript available at GLBTHS; Milton T. Edgerton, Norman J. Knorr, and James R. Callison, "The Surgical Treatment of Transsexual Patients," *Plastic and Reconstructive Surgery* 45:1 (January 1970), 38.

38. Robert J. Stoller to Willard E. Goodwin, March 15, 1967, General, A–G, 1966–1967 folder, box 37, RSP; Stoller to Richard Green, June 19, 1967, Richard Green folder, box 35, RSP.

39. Renée Richards with John Ames, *Second Serve: The Renée Richards Story* (New York: Stein and Day, 1983), 209.

40. Donald W. Hastings, "Inauguration of a Research Project on Transsexualism in a University Medical Center," in Green and Money, *Transsexualism and Sex Reassignment,* 245; idem, "Experience at the University of Minnesota with Transsexual Patients," in *Proceedings of the Second Interdisciplinary Symposium on Gender Dysphoria Syndrome,* ed. Donald R. Lamb and Patrick Gandy (Stanford, Calif.: Division of Reconstructive and Rehabilitation Surgery, Stanford University Medical Center, [1974]), 234.

41. Jane E. Brody, "Benefits of Transsexual Surgery Disputed as Leading Hospital Halts the Procedure," *New York Times,* October 2, 1979, C1, C3. On the programs at Northwestern, Stanford, and Washington, see "Transsexualism: Current Research and Treatment in the United States," leaflet, Erickson Educational Foundation, 1969, Transsexualism 1 vertical file, KI; Alex J. Arieff, "Five-Year Studies of Transsexuals: Psychiatric, Psychological and Surgical Aspects," *Proceedings of the Second Interdisciplinary Symposium on Gender Dysphoria Syndrome,* 240; Norman Fisk, "Gender Dysphoria Syndrome (The How, What, and Why of a Disease)," ibid., 7.

42. See Richard Green to Robert J. Stoller, November 15, 1965, Richard Green folder, box 35, RSP.

43. Robert J. Stoller to Henry Lihn, August 18, 1965, Richard Green folder, box 35, RSP.

44. Richard Green and John Money, "Preface," in Green and Money, *Transsexualism and Sex Reassignment,* xv–xvi. On the symposium, see *Erickson Educational Foundation Newsletter* 2:2 (Fall 1969), 1–2.

45. Robert J. Stoller to Richard Green, December 28, 1964, Richard Green folder, box 35, RSP; statement enclosed with Gilbert Sills to Robert J. Stoller, August 17, 1967, General, H–P, 1967–1968 folder, box 37, RSP; William E. Kline to Stoller, March 3, 1970, General, H–P, 1969–1970 folder, ibid.; Stoller to Kline, March 10, 1970, ibid.

46. Richard Green, "Conclusion," in Green and Money, *Transsexualism and Sex Reassignment,* 473.

47. For criteria at Johns Hopkins, UCLA, and the University of Washington, respectively, see Edgerton, Knorr, and Callison, "The Surgical Treatment," 41–43; Howard J. Baker and Richard Green, "Treatment of Transsexualism," *Current Psychiatric Therapies* 10 (1970), 94; D. Daniel Hunt and John L. Hampson, "Follow-Up of 17 Biologic Male Transsexuals after Sex-Reassignment Surgery," *American Journal of Psychiatry* 137:4 (April 1980), 433.

48. Ira B. Pauly, "Adult Manifestations of Male Transsexualism," in Green and Money, eds., *Transsexualism and Sex Reassignment,* 56; idem, "The Current Status of the Change of Sex Operation," *Journal of Nervous and Mental Disease* 147:5 (1968), 469; Harry Benjamin, *The Transsexual Phenomenon* (New York: Julian, 1966), 110.

49. Benjamin quoted in C. Robert Jennings, "Women Who Dare to Become Men," *Cosmopolitan,* August 1975, 136–154; minutes, Harry Benjamin Research Project, May 4, 1971, 3, personal files of Stanley Krippner, photocopy in possession of author.

50. Fisk, "Gender Dysphoria Syndrome," 7, 8; D. B. to Harry Benjamin, August 18, 1972, D. B. folder, box 3, Series IIC, HBC. On transsexuals' coaching one another, see Geri Nettick with Beth Elliott, *Mirrors: Portrait of a Lesbian Transsexual* (New York: Masquerade, 1996), 163–164.

51. A. S. to Christine Jorgensen, February 26, 1953, Sex Change—Other than CJ folder; R. M. to Jorgensen, March 21, 1953, Miscellaneous Correspondence folder; W. W. to Jorgensen, February 18, 1953, Sex Change—Other than CJ folder, all in Letters box, CJP.

52. C. J. to Harry Benjamin, January 3, 1955, R. J. folder, box 5, Series IIC, HBC.

53. Mario Martino, with Harriet, *Emergence: A Transsexual Autobiography* (New York: Crown, 1977), 169.

54. Richards, *Second Serve*, 167–68; Martino, *Emergence*, 189.

55. Doug Rossinow, *The Politics of Authenticity: Liberalism, Christianity, and the New Left in America* (New York: Columbia University Press, 1998), 4.

56. Quoted in Gay and Lesbian Historical Society of Northern California [Susan Stryker], "MTF Transgender Activism in the Tenderloin and Beyond, 1966–1975: Commentary and Interview with Elliot Blackstone," *GLQ: A Journal of Lesbian and Gay Studies* 4:2 (1998), 350–351; "From the Press Release," *V* 1:2 (October 1966), 5; Cooke interview, 21. This brief discussion of the Tenderloin relies heavily on sources generously shared by Susan Stryker, who is writing a history of transgendered people in San Francisco.

57. Cooke interview, 19, 21.

58. Keith Power, "San Francisco's Transsexuals," *San Francisco Chronicle*, March 6, 1967, 12. On Blackstone's involvement, see Elliot Blackstone, "The Transsexual: The Recognition of a Problem at the Local Level and the Steps Taken to Resolve That Problem" [c. 1967], typescript, box 4, Don Lucas Papers, GLBTHS; interview with Elliot Blackstone by Susan Stryker, November 6, 1996, 3–4, transcript available at GLBTHS.

59. See Jack Leibman and J. M. Stubblebine, "Transsexuals," typewritten memo, May 16, 1967, folder 64, box 16, Series IIIB, HBC; interview with Joel Fort by Susan Stryker, July 23, 1997, transcript available at GLBTHS.

60. George L. Kirkham and Edward Sagarin, "Transsexuals in a Formal Organizational Setting," *Journal of Sex Research* 5:2 (May 1969), 90–91; "Goals for C. O. G.," typed sheet [c. 1968], folder 64, box 16, Series IIIB, HBC.

61. "C. O. G. Transsexual News," mimeographed newsletter, January 17, 1968, 1–2, COG folder, box 19, Series V, HBC. See also "C. O. G. News," mimeographed newsletter [c. 1968], Transsexual Organizations vertical file, KI; Burton H. Wolfe, "Men Who Are Women, Women Who Are Men," *Knight* 7:6 (October 1969), 17, 30–38.

62. Paul Gabriel, "Lucas Receives Award," *Our Stories: The Newsletter of the Gay and Lesbian Historical Society of Northern California* (Winter/Spring 1999), 11.

63. Kirkham and Sagarin, "Transsexuals," 101. See also James Patrick Driscoll, "The Transsexuals" (M.A. thesis, San Francisco State College, 1969), 80–81; Blackstone interview, esp. 5–7, 39; Fort interview, 13–15.

64. Interview with Don Lucas by Susan Stryker, June 13, 1997, 17, transcript available at GLBTHS; Cooke interview, 25–26; see also Wolfe, "Men Who Are Women," 32–33.

65. Wendy Kohler to Harry Benjamin, January 27, 1970, Wendy Kohler folder, box 5, Series IIC, HBC; Cooke interview, 44. On Kohler and NTCU, see "Pioneer Seminar on Transsexualism" and "Eyes Right on San Francisco!," *Erickson Educational Foundation Newsletter* 3:1 (Spring 1970), 1; Julie Smith, "The Transsexual's Plight," *San Francisco Chronicle,* January 10, 1970, TS folder, ONE.

66. Cooke interview, 36.

67. Cooke interview, 16.

68. Douglas Cruickshank, "The Cockettes: Rise and Fall of the Acid Queens," *Salon,* August 23, 2000, at www.salon.com; The Kinks, "Lola," written by Raymond Douglas Davies, published by Hill and Range Songs, Inc.–BMI, released 1970 by Reprise.

69. Cooke interview, 29; Kirkham and Sagarin, "Transsexuals," 102.

70. Cooke interview, 28, 29.

71. Cooke interview, 30.

72. "Ms. Leslie: A Transsexual Counselor," *DRAG* 3:10 (1973), 42.

73. "National," *Moonshadow* (January–February 1974), 3, in Angela Douglas, ed., "Transsexual Action Organization Publications, 1972–1975" (spiral-bound photocopies of original publications, copy in possession of author; hereafter "TAO Publications"), 14.

74. Beverly Koch, "Making Life Easier for Transsexuals," *San Francisco Chronicle,* May 4, 1971, 20; Laura Cummings to Harry Benjamin [c. January 1973], TTS Organizations, Counseling Services folder, box 19, Series V, HBC.

75. "46 Busted in Tenderloin Sweep," *Advocate,* December 8, 1971, 10; Maitland Zane, "Drag Queens Protest Tenderloin Housing Pinch," *San Francisco Chronicle,* September 7, 1973, 4.

76. Quoted in Donn Teal, *The Gay Militants* (New York: Stein and Day, 1971), 212. See also Marc Stein, *City of Sisterly and Brotherly Loves: Lesbian and Gay Philadelphia, 1945–1972* (Chicago: University of Chicago Press, 2000), 322–323.

77. "Queens Liberation Front . . . What Is It?" *DRAG* 1:10 (1972), 13. On STAR, see Teal, *The Gay Militants,* 209; on Rivera, see Sylvia Rivera, "I Never Thought I Was Going to Be a Part of Gay History," *New York Times Magazine,* June 27, 1999, 66.

78. "Sincerely Yours," *DRAG* 1:1 (1970–71), 30; "Queens Liberation Front," 13. On drag queens in New York's gay liberation movement, see Martin Duberman, *Stonewall* (New York: Plume, 1993), 235–239.

79. "Sincerely Yours," 30.

80. Mark B. Sulcov, "Transexualism: Its Social Reality," 2/37–38, draft of Ph.D. diss., Department of Sociology, Indiana University, 1973, available in KI library. On TAT, see also Teal, *The Gay Militants,* 212.

81. Sulcov, "Transsexualism," 2/15; Zelda Suplee to Reed Erickson, January 14, 1970 [1971], Eric 1971 folder, EEF box, ONE; Sulcov, "Transsexualism," 2/38. See also Zelda Suplee to Harry Benjamin, August 6, 1970, Zelda Suplee folder, box 7, Series IIC, HBC.

82. Martino, *Emergence,* 240.

83. "Los Angeles," *DRAG* 1:4 (1971), 9; "Hawaii," *DRAG* 3:10 (1973), 5.

84. On various groups, see "Organizations," *Moonshadow* (August 1975), 4, 6; "Organizations," *Mirage* 1:1 (1974), 25; "Transceiver," *Mirage* 1:2 (1974), 5, all in Douglas, "TAO Publications," 33, 35, 67, 72. On Hidden Life in Hawaii, see "News,"

Drag 3:10 (1973), 5; on the Jorgensen Society, see N. M. to Erickson Educational Foundation, September 5, 1974, Transsexual Self-Help folder, EEF box, ONE.

85. Douglas went by the names Angela Keyes Douglas, Angela Lynn Douglas, and, for a short time in the mid-1970s, Anita Douglas.

86. Teal, *The Gay Militants*, 210; Angela Lynn Douglas, *Triple Jeopardy: The Autobiography of Angela Lynn Douglas* (n.p.: Angela Lynn Douglas, 1983), 23, copy in possession of author.

87. Douglas, *Triple Jeopardy*, 24; TAO, press release [c. January 1971], Transsexuals folder, ONE.

88. *Moonshadow* (August 1973), 2; *Moonshadow* (Lunar eclipse 1975), 10, both in Douglas, "TAO Publications," 4, 20.

89. Angela Douglas to Harry Benjamin, October 9, 1970, Angela Douglas folder, box 4, Series IIC, HBC; "The Way of TAO," *Playboy*, October 1970, photocopy in Douglas, *Triple Jeopardy*, 88.

90. *Moonshadow* (Lunar eclipse 1975), 10, in Douglas, "TAO Publications," 20.

91. "Media Guidelines," *Mirage* 1:2 (1974), 26; "Miami," *Mirage* 1:4 (1975), 9, both in Douglas, "TAO Publications," 89, 135.

92. Kate More, "Never Mind the Bullocks: 2. Judith Butler on Transsexuality," in *Reclaiming Genders: Transsexual Grammars at the Fin de Siècle*, ed. Kate More and Stephen Whittle (London: Cassell, 1999), 290; *Mirage* 1:1 (1974), 6, in Douglas, "TAO Publications," 44. Douglas was ahead of her times: "transsexualism" was not even listed as a psychiatric disorder in the APA's official manual until 1980.

93. Douglas, *Triple Jeopardy*, 27, 45.

94. Canary Conn, *Canary: The Story of a Transsexual* (Los Angeles: Nash, 1974), 202; Douglas, *Triple Jeopardy*, 33; "Surgeons Want to Begin Brain Transplants Using Transexuals as Guinea Pigs—Transexuals Reject Suggestion, Charge Surgeons with Experimental Abuse," TAO press release, March 29, 1974, W. D. folder, box 4, Series IIC, HBC; Cooke interview, 53.

95. Douglas, *Triple Jeopardy*, 42.

96. *Moonshadow* (Lunar eclipse 1975), 12, in Douglas, "TAO Publications," 22.

97. "Transceiver," *Mirage* 1:2 (1974), 7, ibid., 74.

98. Jeffrey Weeks, *Sex, Politics and Society: The Regulation of Sexuality since 1800* (London: Longman, 1981), 287.

99. See Julie A. Greenberg, "Defining Male and Female: Intersexuality and the Collision between Law and Biology," *Arizona Law Review* 41:2 (1999), 265–328.

100. Harry Benjamin to Elmer Belt, March 7 and May 10, 1960, Elmer Belt, 1959–1962 folder, box 3, Series IIC, HBC.

101. Anonymous v. Weiner, 270 N.Y.S. 2d 319 (1966).

102. Army Regulations, C 15, AR 40–501, IX, 2–14s, in Department of Army, *Medical Service: Standards of Medical Fitness*, December 1960, 2/9.

103. Subcommittee on Birth Certificate, Minutes, June 14, 1965, 5–6, "Birth Certificates. Change of Sex. 1965" folder, Committee on Public Health, Public Health Archives, NYAM.

104. Subcommittee on Birth Certificate, Minutes, April 26, 1965, 4, "Birth Certificates. Change of Sex. 1965" folder, Committee on Public Health, Public Health Archives, NYAM.

105. The report noted, but did not necessarily endorse, "other ways to help" transsexuals, including "relief by court order to change name and sex, or amendment of the birth certificate by showing the new sex but still showing the original sex and the change of sex." It would not consider, however, record changes that would conceal the change of sex from the public eye. Committee on Public Health, "Change of Sex," 724.

106. Committee on Public Health, New York Academy of Medicine, "Change of Sex on Birth Certificates for Transsexuals," *Bulletin of the New York Academy of Medicine* 42 (August 1966), 724; Subcommittee on Birth Certificate, Minutes, April 26, 1965, 5.

107. Letter from Charles R. Council, Chief, Registration Methods, Division of Vital Statistics, Public Health Service, Department of Health, Education and Welfare, to Carl L. Erhardt, Director, Bureau of Records and Statistics, City of New York Department of Health, June 11, 1965, 2, "Birth Certificates, Change of Sex. 1965" folder, Committee on Public Health, Public Health Archives, NYAM.

108. Subcommittee on Birth Certificate, Minutes, June 14, 1965, 2, "Birth Certificates. Change of Sex. 1965" folder, Committee on Public Health, Public Health Archives, NYAM. The lawyer was addressing the issue of marriage between a transsexual woman and a nontranssexual man. He doubted whether such a marriage would be legal with or without a change in the birth certificate.

109. Letter from George James, Commissioner of Health, New York City Department of Health, to Harry Kruse, Executive Secretary, Committee on Public Health, New York Academy of Medicine, April 2, 1965, "Birth Certificates. Change of Sex. 1965" folder, Committee on Public Health, Public Health Archives, NYAM; Subcommittee on Birth Certificate, Minutes, April 26, 1965, 5.

110. On changes in the law, see Michael Grossberg, "How to Give the Present a Past? Family Law in the United States, 1950–2000," in *Cross Currents: Family Law and Policy in the United States and England,* ed. Sanford N. Katz, John Eekelaar, and Mavis Maclean (Oxford: Oxford University Press, 2000), 1–29.

111. Anonymous v. Weiner, 319.

112. In re Anonymous, 293 N.Y.S. 2d 834 (1968).

113. Edward S. David, "The Law and Transsexualism: A Faltering Response to a Conceptual Dilemma," *Connecticut Law Review* 7 (1975), 307.

114. In re Anonymous, 836, 837.

115. "Science vs. the Law" and "Landmark Opinion," both in *Erickson Educational Foundation Newsletter* 2:1 (Spring 1969), 2.

116. Douglas K. Smith, "Transsexualism, Sex Reassignment Surgery, and the Law," *Cornell Law Review* 56 (July 1971), 965.

117. "Transsexuals in Limbo: The Search for a Legal Definition of Sex," *Maryland Law Review* 31 (1971), 253, 254.

118. Smith, "Transsexualism," 1009.

119. Grossberg, "How to Give the Present a Past?" 17.

120. James A. Plessinger to Harry Benjamin, July 16, 1970; and Benjamin to Plessinger, July 20, 1970, both in James A. Plessinger folder, box 7, Series IIC, HBC; Benjamin to Douglas K. Smith, January 6, 1979, Douglas K. Smith folder, ibid.

121. William N. Eskridge Jr. and Nan D. Hunter, *Sexuality, Gender, and the Law* (Westbury, N.Y.: Foundation, 1997), 1139; Cooke interview, 17; "Crossdressing Ban under Fire," *Erickson Educational Foundation Newsletter* 6:2 (Fall 1973), 2.

122. On ACLU support, see *Mirage* 1:1 (1974), 6, in Douglas, "TAO Publications," 44.

123. "First Pamphlet of Advice Series Printed," *Erickson Educational Foundation Newsletter* 3:2 (Fall 1970), 1. On identification cards, see "Identification Card for Cross-Dressing," *Erickson Educational Foundation Newsletter*, ibid., 3.

124. Smith, "Transsexualism," 1001.

125. David, "The Law and Transsexualism," 334.

126. Ibid., 308. The case is Hartin v. Director of Bureau of Records, 347 N.Y.S. 2d 515 (1973).

127. In re Tenure Hearing of Grossman, 127 N.J. Super. 26 (1974).

128. Corbett v. Corbett, [1970] 2 All ER at 33, 47. The judge concluded further that sex with an artificial vagina constructed in a male "could never constitute true intercourse"; ibid., 33.

129. B. v. B., 355 N.Y.S. 2d 713, 716, 717 (1974).

130. M.T. v. J.T., 355 A. 2d 204, 206, 207 (1976).

131. Ibid., 209.

132. Ibid., 207, 208, 209, 211.

133. Richards v. United States Tennis Ass'n, 400 N.Y.S. 2d 267 (1977).

134. David, "The Law and Transsexualism," 341; Richard Levidow, "Rebuttal" [c. spring 1973], Richard Levidow folder, box 5, Series IIC, HBC; Judith Shapiro, "Transsexualism: Reflections on the Persistence of Gender and the Mutability of Sex," in *Body Guards: The Cultural Politics of Gender Ambiguity*, ed. Julia Epstein and Kristina Straub (New York: Routledge, 1991), 272.

135. "N.Y. Times Rides Again!" *Erickson Educational Foundation Newsletter* 5:4 (Winter 1972), 1; "Magazine Material," ibid., 8:2 (Winter 1975), 5; "TS on TV," ibid., 1.

136. Roland H. Berg, "The Transsexuals: Male or Female?" *Look*, January 27, 1970, 29; "Mail Response to Look Article," *Erickson Educational Foundation Newsletter* 3:1 (Spring 1970), 1.

137. "Dear Abby," *Erickson Educational Foundation Newsletter* 7:1 (Spring 1974), 3; "Now Read This," ibid., 8:1 (Spring 1975), 1.

138. John Money, "A Greeting to Harry Benjamin on His Ninetieth Birthday," January 10, 1975, typewritten comments, unpublished manuscripts folder, John Money Collection, unprocessed part of collection, KI; Fisk, "Gender Dysphoria Syndrome," 10, 14.

139. See "National Society Discussed," *Erickson Educational Foundation Newsletter* 6:1 (Spring 1973), 2; "1975 Stanford Symposium," ibid., 8:1 (Spring 1975), 2; Richard Green to Paul Gebhard, February 18, 1976, Correspondence file Richard Green, KI. On the 1977 conference and the vote to add a transsexual, see *Renaissance Newsletter* 11:2 (May 22, 1977), 1.

7. THE NEXT GENERATION

1. "Standards of Care: The Hormonal and Surgical Sex Reassignment of Gender Dysphoric Persons," *Archives of Sexual Behavior* 14:1 (1985), 80, 84. In 1981 HBIGDA rescinded its requirement that all recommendations for surgery come from licensed psy-

chologists or psychiatrists, and replaced it with required recommendations from "clinical behavioral scientists"; ibid., 82.

2. American Psychiatric Association, *Diagnostic and Statistical Manual of Mental Disorders,* 3d ed. (Washington, D.C., 1980), 261–264. The term *transsexualism* no longer appears in the *DSM.* In the latest edition, the desire "to acquire the physical appearance of the other sex through hormonal or surgical manipulation" is included under the broader diagnostic rubric of "gender identity disorder"; American Psychiatric Association, *Diagnostic and Statistical Manual of Mental Disorders,* 4th ed., text revision (Washington, D.C., 2000), 577.

3. See interview with Suzan Cooke, January 10, 1998, 54–58, and interview with Elliot Blackstone, November 6, 1996, 8–9, both by Susan Stryker, transcripts available at GLBTHS.

4. Angela Lynn Douglas, *Triple Jeopardy: The Autobiography of Angela Lynn Douglas* (n.p., 1983), 72, copy in possession of author.

5. "Janus Information Facility" and "Now in San Francisco," both in *Erickson Educational Foundation Newsletter* 10:1 (Spring 1983), 5.

6. T. E. A. von Dedenroth to Monica Erickson, August 26, 1989, 2, Erickson Legal Documents box, ONE. Von Dedenroth dated the psychotic episode to late 1977 and early 1978. Erickson's rigorous biographer, Holly Devor, says it occurred in December 1976. See Holly Devor to author, email correspondence, August 15, 2001.

7. Cooke interview, 59.

8. Quoted in Angela K. Douglas, "Interview with Barbara," *Mirage* 1:1 (1974), 30, in Angela Douglas, ed., "Transsexual Action Organization Publications, 1972–1975" (spiral-bound photocopies of original publications, copy in possession of author; hereafter "TAO Publications"), 65.

9. For the most extensive feminist critique of transsexuals, see Janice G. Raymond, *The Transsexual Empire: The Making of the She-Male* (Boston: Beacon, 1979); for a recent account, see Sheila Jeffreys, *Anticlimax: A Feminist Perspective on the Sexual Revolution* (London: Women's Press, 1990), 175–188. For a summary of the debates among 1970s feminists, see Janice M. Irvine, *Disorders of Desire: Sex and Gender in Modern American Sexology* (Philadelphia: Temple University Press, 1990), 268–270.

10. Andrea, "On Women's Lib," *Transsexual Action Organization Newsletter* [c. 1971], 3, Transsexuals folder, ONE; Thomas Kando, *Sex Change: The Achievement of Gender Identity among Feminized Transsexuals* (Springfield, Ill.: Charles C. Thomas, 1973), 145; Deborah Heller Feinbloom, *Transvestites and Transsexuals: Mixed Views* (n.p.: Delacorte Press/Seymour Lawrence, 1976), 142; Anne Bolin, *In Search of Eve: Transsexual Rites of Passage* (New York: Bergin and Garvey, 1988), 119.

11. For an early debate among MTFs, see S. W. to Harry Benjamin, February 7, 1956, S. W. folder, box 8, Series IIC, HBC; for an antifeminist FTM, see Daniel Brendan Presley, "The Playboy Forum," *Playboy,* July 1970, 44–45; for a profeminist FTM, see Brooklyn Stothard, "Transexualism and Women's Liberation," *Mirage* 1:2 (1974), 29–30, in Douglas, "TAO Publications," 87–88.

12. Angela K. Douglas, "Transexual and Transvestite Liberation," *Mirage* 1:2 (1974), 16, in Douglas, "TAO Publications," 83.

13. Robin Morgan, "Lesbianism and Feminism: Synonyms or Contradictions?" reprinted in Robin Morgan, *Going Too Far: The Personal Chronicle of a Feminist* (New

York: Random House, 1977), 181. See also Barbara McLean, "Dairy [*sic*] of a Mad Organizer," *Lesbian Tide* 2 (June 1973), 36–37; Geri Nettick with Beth Elliott, *Mirrors: Portrait of a Lesbian Transsexual* (New York: Masquerade, 1996), 169–170.

14. See, for example, Candace Margulies, "An Open Letter to Olivia Records," *Lesbian Connection*, November 1977, 3–4; and responses, mostly in support of Stone, in ibid., February 1978, 16–17.

15. Raymond, *Transsexual Empire*, xix, 104.

16. Ibid., 110.

17. Margo, "The Transsexual/Lesbian Misunderstanding, Part II," *Gay Community News*, March 15, 1975, 8–9.

18. "Festival Forum," *Lesbian Connection*, November/December 1999, 6. For a more general discussion of recent lesbian and feminist approaches to transsexualism, see Kathleen Chapman and Michael du Plessis, "'Don't Call Me *Girl*': Lesbian Theory, Feminist Theory, and Transsexual Identities," in *Cross Purposes: Lesbians, Feminists, and the Limits of Alliance*, ed. Dana Heller (Bloomington: Indiana University Press, 1997), 169–185.

19. See Riki Anne Wilchins, *Read My Lips: Sexual Subversion and the End of Gender* (Ithaca, N.Y.: Firebrand, 1997), 109–114; Nan Alamilla Boyd, "Bodies in Motion: Lesbian and Transsexual Histories," in *The Queer World: The Center for Lesbian and Gay Studies Reader*, ed. Martin Duberman (New York: New York University Press, 1997), 144–145; Joshua Gamson, "Messages of Exclusion: Gender, Movements, and Symbolic Boundaries," *Gender and Society* 11:2 (April 1997), 187–192.

20. Marcia Yudkin, "Transsexualism and Women: A Critical Perspective," *Feminist Studies* 4:3 (October 1978), 105.

21. Suzanne J. Kessler and Wendy McKenna, *Gender: An Ethnomethodological Approach* (New York: John Wiley and Sons, 1978), 13, 112, 162, 163.

22. Alice Echols, "The Taming of the Id: Feminist Sexual Politics, 1968–83," in *Pleasure and Danger: Exploring Female Sexuality*, ed. Carole Vance (Boston: Routledge, 1984), 51.

23. Raymond, *Transsexual Empire*, xvi, xxiii, 64, 66.

24. Ibid., 5.

25. Richard Green, *The "Sissy Boy Syndrome" and the Development of Homosexuality* (New Haven: Yale University Press, 1987), 261.

26. David M. Rorvik, "The Gender Enforcers," *Rolling Stone*, October 9, 1975, 53, 67.

27. Paul Starr, *The Social Transformation of American Medicine* (New York: Basic Books, 1982), 409.

28. Stephen F. Morin and Stephen J. Schultz, "The Gay Movement and the Rights of Children," *Journal of Social Issues* 34:2 (1978), 142.

29. See Irvine, *Disorders of Desire*, 275–276.

30. Joost A. M. Meerloo, "Change of Sex and Collaboration with the Psychosis," *American Journal of Psychiatry* 124:2 (August 1967), 263; Charles W. Socarides, "The Desire for Sexual Transformation: A Psychiatric Evaluation of Transsexualism," *American Journal of Psychiatry* 125:10 (April 1969), 1424.

31. Robert J. Stoller to C. Peter Rosenbaum, October 12, 1967, General, Q-Z, 1967–1968 folder, box 37, RSP; Jon K. Meyer and John E. Hoopes, "The Gender

Dysphoria Syndromes: A Position Statement on So-Called 'Transsexualism,'" *Plastic and Reconstructive Surgery* 54:4 (October 1974), 450, 451; "Long-Term Benefits Questioned in Sex Changes for Transsexuals," *Clinical Psychiatry News* 3:8 (August 1975), 3; "Doctor No Longer Treats Transsexuals," *New York Gay Scene* 7:8 (January 1977), Transsexuals folder, ONE.

32. Jon K. Meyer and Donna J. Reter, "Sex Reassignment: Follow-up," *Archives of General Psychiatry* 36 (August 1979), 1011, 1013–1015.

33. Mark Bowden, "A Squabble over Sex Operations," *Philadelphia Inquirer,* March 24, 1980, 1A; Jane E. Brody, "Benefits of Transsexual Surgery Disputed as Leading Hospital Halts the Procedure," *New York Times,* October 2, 1979, C1.

34. Brody, "Benefits of Transsexual Surgery Disputed," C3; T. E. A. von Dedenroth to Monica Erickson, August 26, 1989, 2.

35. See, for example, Michael Fleming, Carol Steinman, and Gene Bocknek, "Methodological Problems in Assessing Sex-Reassignment Surgery: A Reply to Meyer and Reter," *Archives of Sexual Behavior* 9:5 (1980), 451–456.

36. Richard M. Restak, "The Sex-Change Conspiracy," *Psychology Today,* December 1979, 20, 25.

37. Bowden, "A Squabble over Sex Operations," 2A.

38. Fleming, Steinman, and Bocknek, "Methodological Problems," 455.

39. In re Ladrach, 513 N.E. 2d 832 (Ohio Prob., 1987).

40. Richard Green, "Spelling 'Relief' for Transsexuals: Employment Discrimination and the Criteria of Sex," *Yale Law and Policy Review* 4:103 (1985), 125–140; Ulane v. Eastern Airlines, Inc., 581 F. Supp. 821 (1983); Ulane v. Eastern Airlines, Inc., 742 F.2d 1081 (1984).

41. Roger Starr, "Cutting the Ties That Bind," *Harper's* 256 (May 1978), 49. Before its decline, the Erickson Educational Foundation began to compile lists of sympathetic surgeons. A 1972 EEF list of surgeons included Drs. Stanley Biber (Trinidad, Colorado), Irving Bush (Chicago), Robert Oliver (Tucson), Ira Dushoff (Jacksonville, Florida), Benito Rish (Yonkers), and Robert Granato (Elmhurst, New York), as well as doctors affiliated with university-based clinics. See Erickson Educational Foundation, "Gender Identity Clinics and Private Surgeons," April, 26, 1972, Transsexual Organizations vertical file, Erickson Educational Foundation, KI.

42. Douglas, *Triple Jeopardy,* 57.

43. Paul Ciotti, "Organ Grinder," *San Francisco Metropolitan,* March 20, 2000, 11; "Doctor's License Revoked," *San Francisco Gay Crusader,* January 1978, 9.

44. Gail Sondegaard, "Sex Surgery Underground: An Interview with Donna Colvin," *Transsexual News Telegraph* 6 (Spring 1996), 38–39, 42; Ciotti, "Organ Grinder," 11, 13–15.

45. John Boslough, "Trinidad Is Sex-Change Surgery 'Capital,'" *Denver Post,* April 18, 1976, 1, 4; James Brooke, "Sex-Change Industry a Boon to Small City," *New York Times,* November 8, 1998, 14.

46. Nettick, *Mirrors,* 334.

47. Susan Stryker, "Portrait of a Transfag Drag Hag as a Young Man: The Activist Career of Louis G. Sullivan," in *Reclaiming Genders: Transsexual Grammars at the Fin de Siècle,* ed. Kate More and Stephen Whittle (London: Cassell, 1999), 68, 71.

48. Interview with Diana Slyter by Margaret Deirdre O'Hartigan, c. November 1995, transcript in personal files of Susan Stryker; "Vote to Let Transsexuals Adjust ID," *San Francisco Chronicle,* September 13, 1977; *Renaissance Newsletter* 3:1 (February 1978), 1.

49. "Stanford Spotlights," *Erickson Educational Newsletter* 6:1 (Spring 1973), 2.

50. "My Daughter Changed Sex," *Good Housekeeping,* May 1973, 87, 152–158; "Magazine Material," *Erickson Educational Newsletter* 8:2 (Winter 1975), 5; C. Robert Jennings, "Women Who Dare to Become Men," *Cosmopolitan,* August 1975, 136.

51. See Marcie Rasmussen, "Sex-Change Furor: Emeryville Teacher Arrested," *San Francisco Chronicle,* September 3, 1976, 1, 20; Mario Martino with harriet, *Emergence: A Transsexual Autobiography* (New York: Crown, 1977). On Dain, see also the documentary film *What Sex Am I?,* directed by Lee Grant, 1984.

52. *Renaissance Newsletter* 3:1 (February 1978), 1.

53. Quoted in Stryker, "Portrait of a Transfag Drag Hag," 65.

54. *FTM* 1 (September 1987), 1, in personal files of Susan Stryker.

55. Eli Coleman and Walter O. Bockting, "'Heterosexual' Prior to Sex Reassignment—'Homosexual' Afterwards: A Case Study of a Female-to-Male Transsexual," *Journal of Psychology and Human Sexuality* 1:2 (1988), 78. See also Stryker, "Portrait of a Transfag Drag Hag."

56. Leslie Lothstein, *Female-to-Male Transsexualism: Historical, Clinical, and Theoretical Issues* (Boston: Routledge and Kegan Paul, 1983), 310–311.

57. Renée Richards with John Ames, *Second Serve: The Renée Richards Story* (New York: Stein and Day, 1983), 324–325.

58. See Eric Schaefer, *"Bold! Daring! Shocking! True!": A History of Exploitation Films, 1919–1959* (Durham, N.C.: Duke University Press, 1999), 337–339.

59. See Tony Volponi, "I Want What I Want," *Drag* 1:6 (1972), 22; Kevin Thomas, "Transsexual Theme in 'I Want What I Want,'" *Los Angeles Times,* March 25, 1972, sec. II, 7.

60. "Thank You, MGM-TV," *Erickson Educational Foundation Newsletter* 8:2 (Winter 1975), 1. On *NBC News,* see "TS on TV," ibid.

61. See *Renaissance Newsletter* 1:3 (August 27, 1976), 1, and ibid., 2:2 (May 22, 1977), 4.

62. Blaine R. Beemer, "Gender Dysphoria Update," *AEGIS* Offprint no. 1006, 1, reprinted from *Journal of Psychosocial Nursing and Mental Health Services* 34:4 (1996), 12–19; Joshua Gamson, *Freaks Talk Back: Tabloid Talk Shows and Sexual Nonconformity* (Chicago: University of Chicago Press, 1998), 103, 104.

63. Gamson, *Freaks Talk Back,* 153, 155.

64. Zelda Suplee to Christine Jorgensen, August 5, 1985, Miscellaneous Correspondence folder, Letters box, CJP.

65. "Memorial for Harry Benjamin," *Archives of Sexual Behavior* 17:5 (October 1988), 16, 21, 22, 25. See also Tom Buckley, "Transsexuality Expert, 90, Recalls 'Maverick' Career," *New York Times,* January 11, 1975, 31; Eric Pace, "Harry Benjamin Dies at 101; Specialist in Transsexualism," ibid., August 27, 1986.

66. James Lincoln Collier, "Live Lectures," *New York Times Magazine,* March 3, 1974, 59.

67. James F. Clarity, "Notes on People," *New York Times,* September 28, 1972, 57; Elaine Markoutsas, "Christine Jorgensen Celebrates 26 Years as a Woman," *Chicago Tribune,* January 14, 1979, sec. 12, 3; "There Are No Real Men Now," [Boston?] *Globe,* August 3, 1982, Ephemera, Subject: Transsexualism, International Gay Information Center Collection, New York Public Library.

68. David Galligan, "Christine Jorgensen," *Advocate,* December 27, 1978, 52; Christine Jorgensen to Christian Hamburger, handwritten draft or copy, September 17, 1983, Denmark—Documentary folder, Clippings/Letters box, CJP.

69. Jerry Parker, "Remember Christine Jorgensen—The First?" *Courier-Journal,* October 21, 1979, G4, Christine Jorgensen vertical file, KI; "Jorgensen Speaks on Transsexual Rights," *Open Forum,* October 1982, Christine Jorgensen folder, ONE.

70. Patrick Flanigan, autobiographical letter [c. 1985], Frances Farmer/Patrick Flanigan folder, Clippings/Letters box, CJP; interview with Christine Jorgensen, in *Paradise Is Not for Sale,* directed by Teit Ritzau, 1985. See also telephone interview with Jo Smith by author, January 10, 1996.

71. See Moton Bryan Holt Jr. to Corinne [at Edward Small Productions], January 24, 1977; "Christine Jorgensen Suit vs. UA Claiming Profits from Biopic," *Variety,* September 7, 1977; Superior Court of California, County of Los Angeles, Christine Jorgensen v. Bank of America et al., Judgment in Favor of Defendants, May 5, 1981, all in Legal Documents box, CJP.

72. See "At 50, Christine Jorgensen Still Enjoys Being a Girl," *People,* May 3, 1976, 62, Christine Jorgensen folder, ONE; "Miss Jorgensen Busy, Contented 23 Years Later," *Westchester Daily Local News,* October 17, 1975, Transsexual Clippings folder, Erickson Educational Foundation box, ONE.

73. See "Jorgensen Enjoys Being Christine," *Newsweek,* March 30, 1981, 11; "Christine Jorgensen Hits 55," *Toronto Star,* June 21, 1981, Ephemera, Subject: Transsexualism, International Gay Information Center Collection, New York Public Library.

74. Christine Jorgensen to Esther [Margolis], January 19, 1984, Dress-Crossdress-Undress folder; Christine Jorgensen to Teit Ritzau, June 4, 1986, Denmark—Documentary folder; Christine Jorgensen to James Kirkwood, September 14, 1983, Christine the Musical folder, all in Clippings/Letters box, CJP.

75. Untitled clipping from San Francisco newspaper [c. May 5, 1989], Christine Jorgensen folder, ONE; "A Girl at Heart," *U.S. News & World Report,* May 15, 1989, 17; Galligan, "Christine Jorgensen," 52; "Lavish Party to Remember Jorgensen," *San Francisco Examiner,* May 6, 1989, Christine Jorgensen folder, ONE; Brenda Lana Smith, R. af. D., "To Be Discussed with Paul Sowa, Esq.," March 22, 1990, 3, copy in possession of author. On guests in attendance, see guest book with signatures of guests [c. May 1989], Photos and Books box, CJP.

76. For insights into the 1990s activism, see "Selected Chronology of the Transexual Menace and GenderPAC," in Wilchins, *Read My Lips,* 210–221.

77. Sandy Stone, "The *Empire* Strikes Back: A Posttranssexual Manifesto," in *Body Guards: The Cultural Politics of Gender Ambiguity,* ed. Julia Epstein and Kristina Straub (New York: Routledge, 1991), 286, 299.

78. Martine Rothblatt, *The Apartheid of Sex: A Manifesto on the Freedom of Gender* (New York: Crown, 1995), 1; Henry S. Rubin, "Phenomenology as Method in Trans Studies," *GLQ: A Journal of Lesbian and Gay Studies* 4:2 (1998), 263–281; Kate

Bornstein, *Gender Outlaw: On Men, Women, and the Rest of Us* (New York: Vintage, 1995), 52; Jason Cromwell, *Transmen and FTMs: Identities, Bodies, Genders, and Sexualities* (Urbana: University of Illinois Press, 1999), 127; Susan Stryker, "Transsexuality: The Postmodern Body and/as Technology," *Exposure: The Journal of the Society for Photographic Education* 30 (1995), 42.

79. Wilchins, *Read My Lips*, 48.

80. Christine Jorgensen to June Larsen and Warren Bayless, January 12, 1966, Autobiography Correspondence, Creative Management Corp. folder, Letters box, CJP.

81. Frederic G. Worden and James T. Marsh, "Psychological Factors in Men Seeking Sex Transformation: A Preliminary Report," *Journal of the American Medical Association* 157:15 (April 9, 1955), 1292.

ACKNOWLEDGMENTS

When I undertook to write this book, I expected the long hours of solitude in archives and libraries and at my desk at home. But I also found myself immersed in a surprisingly social project. Friends, colleagues, acquaintances, and even strangers responded to my work with extraordinary generosity. I hope to thank at least a few of them here.

Susan Stryker deserves first mention for showing me the benefits of collaborative endeavor. We worked together on our overlapping historical research via email, snail mail, and telephone, and in person in Cincinnati, Copenhagen, and Oakland. Thank you, Susan, for your cooperative ideals, your open research files, your smart ideas, and your comments on the draft manuscript. You will see your mark in the pages of this book.

Other friends and colleagues also took substantial time from their own work in order to improve mine. Regina Kunzel, Leila Rupp, James Reed, Pat Swope, Edward Countryman, and Stephen Whittle read the draft manuscript and offered astute suggestions on how I might improve it. Estelle Freedman, Sherry Ortner, Michael Grossberg, and Holly Devor provided crucial commentary on excerpts and chapters. At Harvard University Press, Joyce Seltzer read it all, and some of it more than once, and exercised her abundant editorial talents at key moments in the writing process.

An astonishing number of people supplied me with critical sources, information, leads, photos, clippings, and citations, including treasures from their own private collections and research-in-progress. Special thanks to Doris Abramson, Joseph T. Agnew, Rob Bienvenu, George Chauncey, Leigh Cleven, Dallas Denny, Holly Devor, Angela Lynn

Douglas, John Efron, Jim Gavin, Karla Goldman, Lynn Gorchov, Dayo Gore, Jamison Green, Preben Hertoft, Daniel Horowitz, Gerard Koskovich, Stanley Krippner, Richard Lamparski, James Loewen, R. E. L. Masters, Elliot Meyerowitz, Henry Minton, Peggy Pascoe, Marisa Richmond, Bean Robinson, Don Romesburg, Leila Rupp, Brigitte Søland, Marc Stein, Nancy Stoller, Jennifer Terry, Nancy Tomes, Beth White, and Jeannie Youngson. Thanks also to John Bancroft and Stephanie Sanders, who allowed me access to the Kinsey Institute's unsurpassed collections and introduced me to the intriguing world of contemporary sexual science. Among the many friends of Christine Jorgensen who took the time to write or talk to me, Brenda Lana Smith, R. af. D., merits special mention. She not only provided important insights and information but also managed to convince the Royal Danish Library to open the Christine Jorgensen Collection, which I had been told was closed until the year 2035.

Numerous friends and colleagues encouraged me, humored me, advised me, challenged me, and listened to me graciously as I obsessed about my work. I am especially grateful to Joanne Belknap, Anne Boylan, Edward Countryman, John D'Emilio, Estelle Freedman, Lynn Gorchov, C. Jacob Hale, Nancy Hewitt, Kathi Kern, Regina Kunzel, Deirdre McCloskey, Garay Menicucci, Yasmin Nair, Sherry Ortner, Leila Rupp, Christina Simmons, Jennifer Terry, and David Thelen. For hospitality as well, I am indebted to Preben and Nanna Hertoft, Karin Lützen, Gitte-Maria Rynning, and Kim Toevs. Beth Meyerowitz, as always, made her house my house. She took an avid interest in this project from the start, and she helped me place it, and everything else, in appropriate perspective. Faculty and staff at the University of Cincinnati, Indiana University, and the *Journal of American History* created the congenial and collegial settings that made research and writing possible. Stacy Braukman, Lori Creed, Kirsten Gardner, Sarah Heath, and Kevin Marsh provided excellent research assistance, and Kirsten Streib and Thomas Winter offered their native tongues to help me with translations.

Archivists and librarians provided crucial help with obscure sources and unprocessed manuscript collections. In the archives and library of the Kinsey Institute, Ruth Beasley, Margaret Harter, Kath Pennavaria,

Shawn Wilson, and Liana Zhou offered generous assistance. At the National Humanities Center, Jean Houston and Eliza Robertson kept me supplied with a steady stream of books and articles and delivered important clippings and videotapes I had not even requested. At the ONE Institute collections, now safely housed at the University of Southern California, John O'Brien spent hours in the temporary poolside archives, cheerfully locating records amid the boxes stacked floor to ceiling and toting them for me to read under a patio umbrella. Thanks also to Tony Gardner at Special Collections, Oviatt Library, California State University–Northridge, Michael North at the New York Academy of Medicine, Jesper Düring Jørgensen and Palle Ringsted at the Royal Danish Library, Russell A. Johnson at the University of California at Los Angeles, and Sally Moffitt at Langsam Library, University of Cincinnati.

Gratitude is also due to the various panel and committee members who voted to fund this project through the University of Cincinnati's Charles Phelps Taft Memorial Fund, the Sexuality Research Fellowship Program of the Social Science Research Council, and a National Endowment for the Humanities fellowship at the National Humanities Center. The SSRC fellowship provided the funds for a critical year in residence at the Kinsey Institute at Indiana University and for an oral history project centered in San Francisco. Susan Stryker conducted the interviews; the tapes and transcripts are now housed at the Gay, Lesbian, Bisexual, Transgender Historical Society of Northern California.

Earlier versions of parts of Chapters 1 and 2 originally appeared in "Sex Change and the Popular Press: Historical Notes on Transsexuality in the United States, 1930–1955," *GLQ: A Journal of Lesbian and Gay Studies* 4:2 (1998).

Finally, I owe my greatest debt to Pat Swope, who understands the many pleasures of shared everyday life.

ILLUSTRATION CREDITS

1. Source: Eugen Steinach, *Sex and Life* (New York: Viking, 1940); Courtesy, The Kinsey Institute for Research in Sex, Gender, and Reproduction

2. Source: Niels Hoyer, ed., *Ein Mensch Wechselt Sein Geschlecht: Eine Lebensbeichte* (Dresden: Carl Reissner, 1932); Courtesy, The Kinsey Institute for Research in Sex, Gender, and Reproduction

3. Source: *Sexology* (September 1937); Courtesy, The Kinsey Institute for Research in Sex, Gender, and Reproduction

4. Source: *Sexology* (December 1949); Courtesy, The Kinsey Institute for Research in Sex, Gender, and Reproduction

5. Photograph by William Dellenback; Courtesy, The Kinsey Institute for Research in Sex, Gender, and Reproduction

6. Source: *New York Daily News,* December 1, 1952; New York Daily News, L.P., reprinted with permission; Courtesy, The Kinsey Institute for Research in Sex, Gender, and Reproduction

7. Source: *New York Daily Mirror,* February 13, 1953; New York Daily News, L.P., reprinted with permission; Courtesy, The Kinsey Institute for Research in Sex, Gender, and Reproduction

8. Source: *People Today,* May 5, 1954; Courtesy, The Kinsey Institute for Research in Sex, Gender, and Reproduction

9. Courtesy, The Kinsey Institute for Research in Sex, Gender, and Reproduction

10. Courtesy, The Kinsey Institute for Research in Sex, Gender, and Reproduction, Harry Benjamin Collection

11. Source: Mario Costa, *Reverse Sex* (London: Challenge Publications, c. 1962); Courtesy, The Kinsey Institute for Research in Sex, Gender, and Reproduction

12. Source: Hedy Jo Star, *"I Changed My Sex!"* (Chicago: Novel Books, c. 1964); Courtesy, The Kinsey Institute for Research in Sex, Gender, and Reproduction

13. Source: *Sepia,* April 1966; Courtesy, The Kinsey Institute for Research in Sex, Gender, and Reproduction

14. Source: CHASE, Washington

15. Copyright, 1970 Edprod Pictures, Inc.; all rights reserved; Courtesy of MGM CLIP+STILL; Courtesy, The Kinsey Institute for Research in Sex, Gender, and Reproduction

16. Courtesy, Holly Devor

17. Photograph by William Dellenback; Courtesy, The Kinsey Institute for Research in Sex, Gender, and Reproduction

18 and 19. Courtesy, The Kinsey Institute for Research in Sex, Gender, and Reproduction, Harry Benjamin Collection

20. Copyright, Mariette Pathy Allen; Courtesy, GLBT Historical Society of Northern California, Lou Sullivan Papers

INDEX

INDEX

360

Richter, Dorchen, 19–20, 292n13
Rish, Benito, 236, 338n41
Rivera, Geraldo, 278
Rivera, Sylvia, 191–192, 235
Roberts, Whitey, 77
Robinson, Paul, 91
Rorvik, David M., 265
Rosello, Barbara, 240–241
Rosenberg, Julius and Ethel, 66
Rossinow, Doug, 228
Russell, Nipsey, 89, 98

St. Clair, Leslie, 234
St. Clair, Lily, 200
Salmacis Society, 237
San Francisco Gender and Sexuality Center, 234–235
Sanger, Margaret, 46
Savon, Albert (pseudonym), 94
Sawyer, Carla (pseudonym), 156, 157, 163, 187
Schizophrenia, 106, 107
Schrang, Eugene, 272–273
Schreckengost, Claire, 31, 33, 34
Science: heightened concerns about, 2, 52, 67, 69; authority of, 9; and discourse on transsexuals, 10–11; and popular culture, 32, 41, 65–66, 279; as solution, 53, 58–59, 65–66; and medicine, 212. See also Biological sex; Doctors
Screw, 202
Second Serve, 133–134, 278
Seville, Latina, 199
Sex: mutability of, 1–2, 4, 91; multiple meanings, 2, 3; reconceptualization of, 4, 127–128, 209, 246, 253, 262, 284–286; legal definitions, 8–9, 51, 207–209, 241–242, 245–247, 250–253, 270; popular cultural definitions, 32, 33, 168, 170, 199, 201, 279; doctors' and scientists' definitions, 43, 98–100, 101–103, 105, 117, 118, 127, 242, 243, 266; transsexuals' definitions, 130–131, 261, 262; feminists' definitions, 260–261, 262–263. See also Biological sex; Bisexuality; Gender; Sexuality
Sex and Character, 23–25
Sex and Gender, 116–117, 155, 161
Sex change: early experiments, 5, 15, 16–20, 29–30, 48–49; spontaneous, 33, 39, 49, 88. See also Sex-reassignment surgery

Sex-change surgery. See Sex change; Sex-reassignment surgery
Sex Gantlet to Murder, 90
Sexology: and theory of universal bisexuality, 28; and stories of sex change, 31, 32, 34, 42, 145, 316n48; letters to editor, 35–36, 37–38; and Cauldwell, 41, 42, 44, 105, 121
Sex-reassignment surgery, 6, 7–8; Christine Jorgensen's, 1, 59–60, 61–62, 76, 80, 132; and Johns Hopkins University, 7, 147, 151, 218–222, 243, 268; early experiments, 15, 17–20, 30, 33–34, 40, 47–49; doctors' reluctance to approve or perform, 38–39, 47–48, 100, 120–125, 142, 217–218; in 1950s, 82–88; advocates of, 103–104, 109–110, 111, 113, 124, 173, 225, 270; opponents of, 105–111, 180, 181–182, 256, 262, 266–269; follow-up studies, 124, 163, 216, 267–268; patients' demand for, 129, 130, 131–132, 141–153, 156–157, 158–162; costs of, 141–142, 162; and MTFs, 145–148, 166–167, 189, 192, 222, 225, 271–273; and FTMs, 149–153, 162, 163, 166, 274, 276–277; complications following, 163, 267; increasing availability of, 222, 254, 256, 273; doctors' criteria for, 224–225; privatization of, 271–274, 338n41. See also Phalloplasty; Vaginoplasty
Sexuality: distinguished from biological sex and/or gender, 3, 4, 7, 44, 127, 172, 196; of transsexuals, 10, 44, 158–159, 168–176, 256, 275; in 1950s popular accounts of sex change, 52, 63–64, 68–69, 76–78, 82–86; and definitions of sex, 168, 170, 199, 201, 207, 250–252; in 1960s popular accounts of sex change, 168, 169, 170, 197–206; medicalization of, 170; of doctors, 217. See also Homosexuality; Jorgensen, Christine
Sexual revolution, 7, 169–170, 196, 206, 251
Sex Variants, 28
Shaw, Lee. See Brevard, Aleshia
Sherman, Gayle, 184, 199
Sherman, Irene Case, 104
Sherwin, Robert Veit, 121, 213
Sinclair, Abby, 199, 200
Slyter, Diana, 274
Smith, Brenda Lana, 282–283